# Guiding Young Children

THIRD EDITION

# Guiding Young Children
## A PROBLEM-SOLVING APPROACH

*Eleanor Reynolds*

Mayfield Publishing Company
Mountain View, California
London • Toronto

*With special gratitude to my grandson, Trey, and my granddaughter, Tabitha, who are teaching me more new and amazing things about children and showing me how "kids do what kids do."*

**Library of Congress Cataloging-in-Publication Data**
Reynolds, Eleanor.
    Guiding young children : a problem-solving approach / Eleanor Reynolds.—3rd ed.
        p. cm
    Includes bibliographical references and index.
    ISBN 0-7674-1796-8
    1. Education, Preschool.   2. Problem solving in children.   3. Preschool
        teachers—In-service training.   I. Title.
    LB1140.2.R495 2000
    372.21—dc21

                                                                00-026305

Manufactured in the United States of America
10    9    8    7    6    5    4    3    2    1

Mayfield Publishing Company
1280 Villa Street
Mountain View, California 94041

Sponsoring editor, Franklin C. Graham; production, Mary Douglas; manuscript editor, Mary Roybal; art director and text designer, Jeanne M. Schreiber; cover designer, Ann Vestal; illustrators, Jean Mailander and Robin Mouat; print buyer, Danielle Javier. The text was set in 10/12 Palatino by TBH Typecast, Inc., and printed on 45# Highland Plus by R. R. Donnelley & Sons Company.

Cover and text photographs: Richard Shulman

 This book was printed on acid-free, recycled paper.

# Contents

CHAPTER
**4**   *Listening for Feelings*   **91**

CHAPTER
**5**   *Negotiation*   **135**

## 9  The Problem-Solving Approach to Curriculum    328

## 10  Training Teachers for Problem Solving    382

# *Preface*

Is it possible to care for and teach a group of young children without using rules, punishment, scolding, lecturing, or "time out"? What do you do when children fight over a toy, jump on the table, or throw sand at each other? Students preparing to work with children are looking for the most effective ways to address these problems and interact with children. They hope to apply their ideals and high standards to enrich the lives of the children in their care, for this is what brings satisfaction and a sense of achievement.

The philosophy presented in this book is a balanced, child-centered philosophy that addresses the developmental needs and abilities of young children and enables teachers to implement their high standards. The philosophy is called problem solving because it emphasizes children's ability to solve their own problems when they are trusted and encouraged to do so. Teachers who apply problem solving use techniques such as active listening, negotiation, I-messages, and other limit-setting methods to help children learn to accept responsibility and communicate with each other. These and other problem-solving techniques are described and illustrated in this book.

Basic to the problem-solving philosophy is the concept of freedom with responsibility. In a child-centered program, kids do what kids do, but they also take responsibility for their actions. Problem solving is neither permissive nor authoritarian. When children fight over a toy, they are encouraged to negotiate, a technique that requires listening to another child's feelings. Also basic are acceptance and trust. Teachers accept children as they are and trust them to be responsive and responsible. Each child is considered a unique person with feelings, preferences, and rights that must be respected.

Problem solving, as presented in this book, originated with Louise Maddox, who in 1970 founded the child care center now called the Isabel Patterson Child Development Center on the campus of California State University at Long Beach. The philosophy drew on Maddox's own experiences and the works of Carl Rogers, Jean Piaget, Haim Ginott, Rudolf Dreikurs, and others. When Thomas Gordon's *P. E. T.: Parent Effectiveness Training* was published in 1970, Maddox realized that Gordon had described the essence of the philosophy she had been using and teaching. Although Gordon's book was written for parents rather than teachers, Maddox began to use some of its terminology and to adapt it for teachers working with young children. Over the years, the problem-solving philosophy has been used with children of all ages. This book describes how to use problem solving with groups of infants, toddlers, and preschoolers. Since 1981, I have applied and refined the philosophy first at the Discovery Center in Mukilteo, Washington, then at Green Tree Child Care Center in Seattle, and currently at the Play and Learn Preschool, also in Seattle.

This book is a practical guide to understanding and using this child-centered philosophy. It contains the basic theoretical information needed to understand problem solving, yet its emphasis is on application, on working with groups of children in day care or preschool on a daily basis. The chapter titles reflect the techniques used in problem solving. The importance of the environment is stressed in the beginning chapters and throughout the book. Supervision, necessary for providing freedom and safety, is also discussed. The core of the philosophy is found in Chapters 4, 5, and 6: Listening for Feelings, Negotiation, and Setting Limits. Chapter 6, Setting Limits, is the most complex in the book. In my experience, the most difficult part of problem solving is learning to set limits effectively. The instructor may choose to divide Chapter 6 when giving reading assignments to the class. Chapter 9, The Problem-Solving Approach to Curriculum, integrates the problem-solving philosophy with an approach to curriculum that is child centered and compatible.

Discussion questions and exercises appear at the end of all the chapters. A few of the questions can be answered directly by finding the answers in the text. Most, however, are meant to help teachers evaluate themselves and their attitudes toward the problem-solving philosophy. Many of the exercises are conducive to small group work. There are also a number of suggestions for role playing. For teachers who have not used role playing in the classroom, Chapter 10 provides an extensive description.

This book is dedicated to Joan Whitley, my partner at the Discovery Center (now at Mount St. Vincent's Intergenerational Learning Center in Seattle), who has contributed her knowledge of intergenerational programs to this book. I want to thank my husband, Nick Robertson, who helped and supported my efforts with research and understanding. Thanks also go to my daughters, Michelle and Tiphanie, for inspiring my interest in children and for allowing me to make my mistakes on them, and to my grandchildren, Trey and Tabitha, who taught me how to be a grandmother. Richard Shulman, a parent of two Discovery Center daughters and photographer for the *Everett Herald*, graciously provided all the wonderful photographs of children in this book. My appreciation goes to the teachers at the Discovery Center, Green Tree, and Mount St. Vincent's for their contributions of love, knowledge, and talent.

Finally, I am grateful to all the children who have been my friends at the Discovery Center, Green Tree, and the Play and Learn Preschool. Their joy and enthusiasm are the basis for this book.

# 1

# The Program and the Philosophy: An Overview

Imagine yourself on the playground with ten preschoolers. Suddenly, two children are fighting over the red tricycle. This one is the "best" of all the tricycles, according to the children, and it is often the focal point of fights in the yard. What can you, the teacher, do about this fighting?

Your response represents your philosophy, or set of principles, for working with children. As a student, you may not have given much thought to a particular philosophy, but you are probably forming one. If you are already working with children, you may have a thoughtfully written, formal philosophy that you apply faithfully and consistently. In either case, your philosophy may or may not be completely satisfying to you. Perhaps it works sometimes and not at other times; it may often leave you feeling frustrated and bewildered. Because you are taking the time to read this book, let us assume that you are exploring alternative ways to interact with the children who are, or will be, in your care.

The philosophy in this book is based on problem solving. I have adapted, applied, and refined it over the course of twenty-four years of working with infants, toddlers, preschoolers, and school-age children in four child care centers. Problem solving emphasizes humans' innate ability to solve their problems by calling on their inner resources. Its goal is to help children learn to solve their own problems in a respectful, mutually satisfying way. If this sounds vague and idealistic, be assured that you cannot depend on vague ideals to solve the problem of which preschooler gets the red tricycle; you must be totally practical and realistic. Every example in this book is real, taken from the daily events in three different children's programs. The examples demonstrate the variety of possible problems and solutions.

Before exploring problem solving in detail, I present a few of the concepts behind this philosophy. Rather than a set of rules for children to obey or another name for discipline, problem solving is a natural part of the learning process based on trust and respect for the child. Unlike lecturing, preaching, or moralizing, problem solving builds on the innate intellect and reasoning power of every child. The process presumes a link between freedom and responsibility and assumes that power and control belong to children as well as to adults. When we think about alternatives to discipline, we may envision children who are either spoiled and demanding or who are aggressive bullies. Problem solving condones neither extreme; it enables children to use their power and control to enhance their lives and relationships.

Why is the popular term "discipline" not included in the problem-solving philosophy? According to the *Random House Dictionary of the English Language,* discipline has the following meanings: training to act in accordance with rules . . . punishment inflicted by way of correction and training . . . behavior in accord with rules of conduct . . . a set or system of rules and regulations . . . to bring to a state of order and obedience by training and control . . . to punish or penalize in order to train and control; correct; chastise.[1] These words depict an effort to transform another person. Problem solving, however, is a philosophy that allows children to be themselves, to develop their own unique personalities, including both flaws and virtues. No attempt is made to mold the child into some more perfect person.

Although many enlightened and enlightening child psychologists, such as Haim Ginott, have tried to modify the essence of discipline, in my estimation the dictionary meaning still represents the common understanding of the term. In *Teacher and Child,* Ginott said, "The essence of discipline is finding effective alternatives to punishment" and "Good discipline is a series of little victories in which a teacher, through small decencies, reaches a child's heart."[2] In *Your Child's Self-Esteem,* Dorothy Briggs reminds us that "the word discipline stems from 'disciple,' a follower of a teacher. We do not think of a disciple following his teacher out of fear of punishment," she

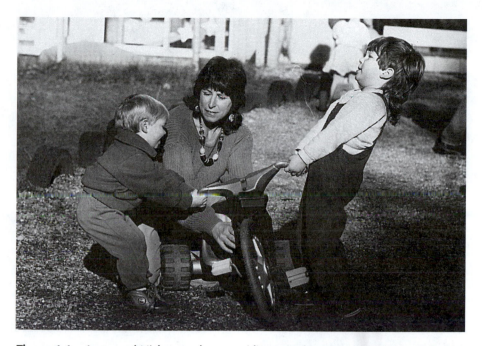

**Figure 1.1** *Jonny and Nick want the same riding toy. They scream, "It's mine! I had it first!" The teacher facilitates with active listening and negotiation techniques.*

states, "but rather from inner conviction."[3] If discipline were universally perceived in this way, I would use the term in this book. But because the dictionary definition seems more prevalent, I refrain from using the word in relation to problem solving so as to avoid confusion and misinterpretation.

The absence of the word "discipline," however, does not imply the absence of a moral aspect in this approach. Problem solving provides a moral framework by teaching children to take responsibility for their actions and to show respect for the ideas and feelings of other people. Throughout the text, I will comment briefly on morality as it applies to problem solving and its various components.

## An Example of Problem Solving

To demonstrate the effectiveness and practicality of problem solving, I return to the red tricycle and observe a teacher applying this principle. The example specifically involves negotiation, but it includes active listening as well. I define these terms in the following section.

Jonny and Nick are tugging on the red trike and trying to push each other away. They scream at each other (Figure 1.1).

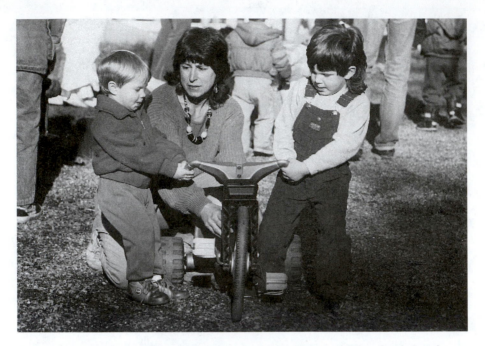

**Figure 1.2**    *The boys slow down and begin to think of solutions. They decide to take turns. The teacher reinforces their decision. The problem is solved.*

NICK:  It's mine!

JONNY:  I want it!

*Kneeling down to the eye level of the children, the teacher facilitates.*

TEACHER:  Looks like there's a problem. You both want the same trike.

NICK:  I had it first!

JONNY:  No, it's mine.

TEACHER:  I hear both of you saying you want the same trike. Nick says he wants it, and Jonny says he wants it, too. What can you do when two people want the same toy? Do you have an idea, Nick? How about you, Jonny?

*Nick and Jonny continue to push and scream.*

TEACHER:  Is it okay with both of you to get pushed? If you don't want to be pushed, you can say "Stop!"

*Both children yell "Stop!" at each other and stop pushing. But they continue to tug on the trike and scream.*

TEACHER:  Looks like you've stopped pushing each other. Are you ready to solve the problem now?

*The boys are slowing down now and starting to think (Figure 1.2).*

NICK:    Jonny could have the green trike.

JONNY:    No, I want this one! Nick can ride the green trike.

TEACHER:    You each had an idea about riding a different trike. But both of you still want this one. Any other ideas?

NICK:    I can ride the red one first; then Jonny can ride it.

TEACHER:    Nick has an idea about taking turns. He would ride the red trike, then give it to Jonny. What do you think, Jonny?

JONNY:    I want to be first.

TEACHER:    Sounds like Jonny agrees to taking turns, but he wants to be first.

NICK:    Okay. You can be first, but just for one minute.

TEACHER:    Is that okay with you, Jonny?

JONNY:    No, I want five minutes.

TEACHER:    How does a turn of five minutes sound to both of you?

NICK AND
JONNY:    It's okay.

TEACHER:    Great! You solved the problem. I'll let you know when five minutes are up.

Jonny hops on the red trike, and Nick gets on the green one. They go off riding, still friends, feeling proud of their solution. By the end of five minutes, they are in the sandbox and have forgotten about the trikes. A skilled teacher acted as a facilitator while two preschoolers negotiated to solve their problem. Chapter 5 contains many more examples of negotiation. For now, keep this example in mind as you read more about the process of problem solving.

## Terms of Problem Solving

Problem solving is a philosophy that embodies five major procedures: active listening, negotiation, setting limits, modifying the environment, and affirmations. The first and fourth terms are taken from Thomas Gordon's *Parent Effectiveness Training* and have been adapted for working with groups of young children. The term "I-message," also Gordon's, is used as a way of setting limits. This section presents a summary of these terms and their relationship to problem solving. Each term is described in detail in later chapters, beginning with Chapter 2. Following the five major procedures is a brief definition of other terms used in problem solving.

Problem solving uses specific terms in prescribed ways. The reader, however, should not feel intimidated by either the terminology or the structure it suggests. Having such a structure is helpful when teachers are first learning problem solving. The more closely the structure or guidelines are followed, the more effective will be the interactions between teacher and

**Table 1.1**    *Terms Used in Problem Solving: The Teacher's Role*

| Term | Teacher's Role |
| --- | --- |
| Active listening | Interpret and reflect feelings |
| Negotiation | Help children resolve conflicts |
| Setting limits | Keep children safe, in bounds |
| Modifying the environment | Make changes, enrich, impoverish |
| Affirmations | Help children feel important |
| Facilitating | Help children solve problems |
| Removing and sitting apart | Remove child from group; child decides when to return |

children and among the children. The use of any formula for human relationships may feel alien, contrived, and phony at first, but the longer the formula is practiced, the more natural and comfortable it feels. The primary result of "going by the book" is that it helps the teacher internalize the philosophy and incorporate it into all the knowledge and skill the teacher brings to the class. The philosophy becomes part of that teacher's classroom personality (Table 1.1).

## Active Listening

Active listening describes the first step of many problem-solving interactions. Active listening is the teacher's tool for interpreting a child's feelings and reflecting them back to the child. The child thus receives a message of acceptance and trust. A child may have feelings inside that he has brought from home to the children's center. These feelings may cause him to be cheerful and friendly or upset and aggressive. The child may also have feelings derived from his need to control his body and his world. Whatever feelings belong to the child, he can face them if he feels free to express them and knows that someone will understand and accept him, along with those feelings. When practicing active listening, the teacher listens for those feelings, interprets them, and reflects them back to the child.

## Negotiation

The term in problem solving that refers to resolving conflicts between children is "negotiation." The teacher helps the children identify their problem, encourages them to contribute their own ideas toward a mutually acceptable solution, helps them decide on their preferred solution, and oversees the implementation of their chosen solution. When the problem has been solved by the children involved, the teacher gives positive reinforcement to let them know what a good job they have done. As well as solving problems, negotiation helps build self-esteem. When children can call on their inner resources and find validation for their own ideas, they perceive themselves as capable, effective, and powerful. They consequently become more independent and self-reliant.

## Setting Limits

A program in which groups of young children are cared for requires a system for keeping children safe, protecting materials and equipment, teaching children to accept responsibility for their actions, and shielding children from discrimination. The problem-solving philosophy is based on limits rather than rules. Whereas rules are absolute, may be broken, and result in punishment, limits are boundaries that are flexible and negotiable. Limits are set with "I-messages," information, natural consequences, contingencies, and choices. The "I-message," the most desirable way to set limits, consists of a statement of the teacher's feelings, what the teacher sees happening, and the reasons for those feelings.

Limits are based on four guidelines, which are repeated in Chapter 6. These guidelines, which encompass all types of behavior, are statements of the values espoused in the problem-solving philosophy. Limits are set for these reasons:

1. To assure the safety of each child and adult
2. To prohibit the destruction of nondisposable materials and equipment
3. To assure that children accept responsibility for their own actions
4. To assure equal and respectful treatment of all people

## Modifying the Environment

Modifying the environment is a technique for responding to children's inappropriate behavior by childproofing, simplifying, restricting (limiting), enriching, and impoverishing (subduing) the child's surroundings. Teachers sometimes overlook it as a way to avoid inappropriate behavior, instead attempting to fit the children into the existing environment. In times of stress, such as transition times, modifying the environment is often the most effective technique.

## Affirmations

Affirmations are the teacher's tools for helping children feel important. They are the way to give attention to every child, whether or not he has earned it by a particular action. Every human being needs acknowledgment and validation just because he exists. Behavior that is appropriate and safe is always worthy of comment, but the child who is sitting quietly by himself also deserves to be noticed and shown that someone cares. The simple act of greeting a child with a personal remark helps him feel important. Types of affirmations will be defined in detail in Chapter 7.

## Facilitating

In the problem-solving philosophy, the term "facilitating" is used to describe the role of the teacher or caregiver and the way she helps children solve problems. The teacher's role is to make problem solving easier for children, allowing them to call on their own inner resources. The ways in which the teacher facilitates are demonstrated through the many examples in this book.

## Removing and Sitting Apart

When all else has failed, it may be necessary for a teacher to remove a child from the source of her inappropriate behavior. Because the child understands why she is being removed, explanations are not always necessary. Removal gives the child a chance to exercise her own inner controls and enables her to make herself ready to return to the activity in a safer, less disruptive frame of mind. In *Children: The Challenge,* Rudolf Dreikurs describes removing a child from a dangerous situation to protect her.[4] In problem solving, a child may also be removed to protect the rights and safety of other children.

When a child is causing harm or disruption, the teacher may have the child sit apart after she has been removed from an activity or group. This is not the same as "time out," because the child is usually kept in the same area as her group and is permitted to return to the activity as soon as *she feels ready.* Time out generally means confining a child to a chair or special isolation area for a certain amount of time determined by the teacher. The teacher, not the child, is in control of the child's return to the group. When sitting apart, however, the child retains control and is seldom isolated from her group. This is an important distinction. Because the procedure of removing and sitting apart is not punishment and does not damage the child's self-esteem, it can be used with children as young as twelve months. It is seldom needed, however, when problem solving is used.

## *Trusting the Process*

The goal of problem solving is simple yet rich with possibilities: to help children learn to solve their problems in a respectful, mutually satisfying way. In so doing, problem solving frees children to form close, bonding relationships without fear of domination. It builds self-esteem and self-reliance and allows children to express their needs and feelings. It liberates their intellects as they probe and search for ideas and answers. It enhances children's natural creativity as all things become possible.

But what about control, respect, responsibility, moral character, and good manners? These are also an outgrowth of this philosophy but in a self-directed way. Children who learn in a problem-solving environment develop empathy, self-control, and self-respect. They also develop a sense of responsibility to themselves and others, which leads to making moral choices. Manners, too, are a natural part of all these characteristics. Every chapter of this book demonstrates how problem solving helps develop these desirable human qualities.

Adopting problem solving is an act of trust—trust in the process of normal growth and development in children. "Process," for our purposes, may be defined as change, actions leading toward a desired goal. Physical growth, for example, is a process involving countless actions taking place within the body. Growth proceeds at its own pace and cannot be hurried to any great degree. Children are in their late teens before the process reaches its pinnacle; even then, bodies continue to change as long as they are alive. The same is true for intellectual, emotional, and social development. Experts such as Piaget, Erikson, Gesell, and Kohlberg, each from his own perspective, have organized their research into stages of development. Every teacher of young children will benefit from learning about these stages. Developmentalists help us understand that we cannot cause a child to become well behaved, responsible, and considerate just by admonishing him to do so, any more than we can accelerate his growth into adulthood by feeding him more vitamins.

Just as physical growth is built on a foundation of nutrition, hygiene, medical care, safety, and time, the development of the child's inner self and the self she presents to the world requires many building blocks and adequate time. The development of the social-emotional-intellectual self is based on love, acceptance, respect, encouragement, freedom to experiment and make mistakes, role models to set appropriate examples, and, again, time. As caregivers and teachers, we are generally involved in only a segment of the time in a child's life, perhaps one year or several years. There may have been different caregivers before we came along, and there may be others after us. Unfortunately, modern children seldom have the opportunity to stay with one caregiver from cradle to high school. Every teacher will know each child as the child is passing through a particular stage of development. If those teachers understand the significance of process, they will trust, nurture, and support the natural process of development, allowing the child's inner self to grow and blossom at her own pace and to her fullest potential. What a lucky child she will be!

Many parents want very much to find such teachers for their children. Without even realizing it, these parents are trusting the process of natural development, accepting their children as the children are, and enjoying the early years to the fullest. These same parents are seeking a program that will reflect and expand on their parenting style and the values they hold for their children. There are also parents who are attempting to do their best at parenting but lack the skills and knowledge they need. They, too, would welcome a program that could do for their children what they themselves are unequipped to do and that may even help them improve their parenting skills.

## Becoming Child Centered

As part of placing trust in natural processes, problem solving embraces an attitude referred to as "child centered." A program or person perceived as child centered allows children to think and act as children do. In our era, we might call these children liberated. They are free to experience childhood to the fullest, with all the emotions and behaviors involved and without fear of criticism or repression. They are also free to accept as much responsibility for their behavior as is appropriate for their age. A program that is child centered puts the needs and rights of the child before the convenience or preconceptions of the staff. Children are seen as individuals with inherent rights who are worthy of respect.

Many programs for children describe themselves as child centered yet place a heavy burden of rules and restrictions on their children. Figure 1.3 compares a child-centered program with one that is adult centered. The philosophy in the child-centered program is problem solving. Circle 1 shows a large outer circle filled with "Kids Doing What Kids Do." This area represents the natural behavior of children when there are few restrictions placed on them. The smaller, inner circle shows the proportion of limits to natural, childlike behavior. The limits are kept to a minimum and are based on creating an environment in which kids do what kids do. In this environment, children learn to respect themselves and others, accept responsibility for their own actions, think for themselves, express their feelings, empathize with others, solve problems, and communicate effectively. Beside circle 1 are terms used in the problem-solving philosophy.

Circle 2 represents the adult-centered program. The larger, outer circle is filled with rules, leaving only a small inner circle for "Kids Doing What Kids Do." When rules restrict so much of their behavior, children learn to behave differently when adults are watching them. They depend on adults for solutions to problems, rely on external rather than internal controls, repress and inhibit their feelings, conform to the group, work at evading punishment, and try to shift blame to their peers. Beside circle 2 are terms used in discipline, the more common method of relating to children.

The child-centered approach is based on an attitude of respect for and delight in children. To foster this approach, adults are needed who are authentic and open and who enjoy children as they are, rather than as mate-

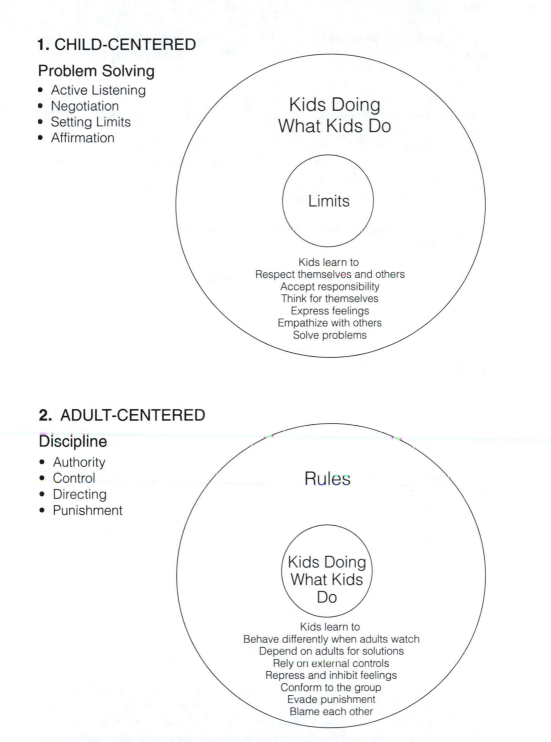

**1. CHILD-CENTERED**

## Problem Solving

- Active Listening
- Negotiation
- Setting Limits
- Affirmation

Kids Doing
What Kids Do

Limits

Kids learn to
Respect themselves and others
Accept responsibility
Think for themselves
Express feelings
Empathize with others
Solve problems

**2. ADULT-CENTERED**

## Discipline

- Authority
- Control
- Directing
- Punishment

Rules

Kids Doing
What Kids
Do

Kids learn to
Behave differently when adults watch
Depend on adults for solutions
Rely on external controls
Repress and inhibit feelings
Conform to the group
Evade punishment
Blame each other

**Figure 1.3**    *A comparison of child-centered and adult-centered programs.*

rial in need of molding and improving. Watching young children for hours at a time can be boring unless teachers realize it is an education. If the teachers' minds are open to expanding their view of human nature, they will learn more from children than they can ever hope to teach the young ones. Above all, the child-centered approach is more fun for everyone concerned, both children and adults. What greater joy can be found than the free, liberated experience of childhood?

Even after adopting a child-centered approach, teachers may not automatically come to every problem in a child-centered way. It is easy to drift off target and see things in terms of convenience and ease. Teachers should remain aware of these tendencies and continually measure their interactions with children against their true goals and beliefs. After they work within a child-centered program, however, an almost subconscious awareness compels teachers to internally evaluate their own words and actions. Once you become a child-centered person, it is doubtful that you can ever revert to being adult centered. You would miss the joy and the fun too much.

## Problem Solving and Self-Esteem

The problem-solving philosophy is more than a technique for managing children's behavior. Its most important benefit is the building and strengthening of the child's self-esteem. Although self-esteem begins with the attachment process between parent and child, many factors contribute to its development. Those significant others who interact with the infant also help him form his own feelings about himself.

Briggs calls self-esteem "the mainspring that slates every child for success or failure as a human being." In *Your Child's Self-Esteem,* she bases the child's development of high self-esteem on whether he feels lovable and worthwhile. The key word is "feels." Telling a child he is loved and valued is not enough. According to Briggs, "Children need living experiences that prove their lovability and worth," and they "value themselves to the degree that they have been valued."[5]

How does problem solving build and strengthen self-esteem? In problem solving, the child's needs and feelings are accepted nonjudgmentally. The teacher of infants in a problem-solving program responds to the baby's verbal and nonverbal cues with the "guessing game" until the infant's needs have been satisfied. The baby's attempts at communication are met with respect and reflected back warmly and affectionately by the teacher. The baby learns that her needs and feelings are important, and she interprets this as evidence that she is lovable and worthwhile.

As the infant grows toward toddlerhood and becomes more capable of meeting her own needs, the teacher respects her new abilities and trusts her to make appropriate choices. When the toddler's choices are inappropriate, the teacher shares her own concerns with an "I-message," even as she demonstrates that the toddler can exercise control over much of her body and her world. With this safety net of the teacher's trust and supervision, the toddler has the freedom to take risks and test herself at her own rate. With this freedom, the toddler learns to seek the source within herself that allows and encourages her to become her own person.

Toddlers and preschoolers not only seek love and worth from adults but begin to look to their friends for affirmation. Toddlers begin to share feelings with other children and expect others to comply with their needs. When another child fails to comply, there is a conflict. In problem solving, conflicts between children are resolved through negotiation. The equal say of each child and the freedom for each to find his own mutually satisfying resolution give children a sense of self-reliance and self-respect they may not gain from any other source.

Problem solving also involves children in taking responsibility for their own actions according to their developmental level. When children perceive themselves as competent and capable, their feelings of self-love and self-worth grow. They begin to internalize the process and reinforce their behavior positively, strengthening their self-esteem. When children choose not to accept responsibility, the teacher sets limits in such a way that children are trusted to consider the needs and feelings of others as well as themselves. With every decision they make to respond to the needs and feelings of other people, children see themselves as having a meaningful impact on other lives. In this way, problem solving continues to enhance self-esteem.

## Making the Change

When you make the change to the problem-solving philosophy, you must consider the extent of parental support. Your present situation will determine just what must be considered. A beginning child-care professional may gain parental support more easily than one who is already caring for a group of children. As a newcomer to the field, this teacher can attract those parents who are seeking a provider to implement their own similar child-rearing philosophy or to compensate for their own lack of skill. Advertising, word of mouth, and written materials are invaluable aids for communicating with the target population. Parents such as these are found everywhere. The necessary parental support is there; the provider must be accessible to being found. When parents call and ask only about charges or location, you need good telephone communication skills. Rather than give only prices or location, interject the features of the program, such as the problem-solving philosophy.

The teacher who is already caring for children may face a challenge from parents and other teachers who fear the change to a problem-solving approach. Parents may mistakenly believe that without the use of discipline (interpreted as rules and punishment) their children will become spoiled and uncontrollable. Many such parents believe that force of some sort is required to make children grow up to be law-abiding citizens. Many teachers will feel threatened because they do not understand the problem-solving philosophy and have no interest in learning how to implement it.

Before making a change publicly, think about it privately. Consider the entire program in which you work. If you own or direct the program, how will you motivate and encourage your staff to change? Every program needs at least one strong supervisor to initiate, implement, and train teachers in the philosophy. Are you that person? If you are a teacher, how does your supervisor feel about problem solving? Is she willing to have one teacher, you, use a different approach? If your supervisor is resistant, will she negotiate with you for a trial period of, perhaps, six months? Are other teachers in your center open enough to observe and learn from you, or will conflict arise?

Once you have decided to make the change, set up a meeting for parents and teachers to discuss the problem-solving philosophy. Discuss any changes you plan for the environment and allow an exchange of ideas, questions, and apprehensions. Respond as honestly as possible; when you don't know an answer, emphasize that everyone will learn by experience. Reassure the staff that they have not been doing things the "wrong" way but that this new way will provide learning and growth for both them and the children. Stress to parents that problem solving emphasizes responsibility on the part of the child and that parents may even notice a positive change in the child's behavior at home. Be prepared to offer suggestions on how parents can reinforce what children learn about putting away toys and negotiating, and discuss ways for parents to set limits.

As for any children's program, you will need a written philosophy, a statement of principles by which your program operates. It should tell parents what to expect from the program and tell teachers what is expected of them. Most important, your philosophy should realistically and accurately reflect what is happening throughout your center. Keep your written philosophy brief enough to hold the reader's interest but long enough to include whatever information you want parents to have. Figure 1.4 is an example of a brief philosophy based on problem solving. The outline may be shortened or lengthened to fit your needs.

## Considering Cultural Differences

Some of you may become teachers or directors in an area in which your enrollment includes a diversity of socioeconomic groups, ethnic cultures, and races. You may encounter attitudes that stem from generations of poverty and racial injustice. Such a situation is described below by Patricia McFarland-Kern of Milwaukee Area Technical College. She recounts her own experiences and those of her colleagues while applying the problem-solving philosophy in an urban child care center. Although the population these teachers serve is primarily African American, similar child-rearing

**Figure 1.4**    *Our Program's Philosophy*

---

Our program is based on two main concepts: child centeredness and problem solving. Our motto is "Kids Doing What Kids Do." Our teachers are warm, nurturing, knowledgeable about child development, trained, and committed to this philosophy. Here are some brief descriptions of the two main concepts.

> **Child centered** means that our program is here to meet the real needs of the children, allow them the freedom to be children, and put their physical, emotional and intellectual well-being first. We believe that children learn best through play and social interactions. Our main goals are to nurture children and to help them learn to get along with their peers.

> **Problem solving** is the way we teach children to form positive relationships, resolve conflicts, learn self-discipline, and show respect for others. We see inappropriate or destructive behavior as a problem to be solved, primarily by the children involved with the help of a teacher-facilitator. Following are the major terms used in the problem-solving philosophy:

>> **Active listening** is a way to interpret and reflect a child's feelings. Active listening lets children express and think through their problems and find their own solutions.

>> **Negotiation** teaches children to talk to each other about their problems, look for solutions, and resolve conflicts nonviolently.

>> **Setting limits** is a way to teach children how to stay within safe boundaries and learn self-control. Limits are based on safety, responsibility, and respect. We set limits with I-messages, consequences, choices, information, and contingencies. Our last resort is "removing and sitting apart."

>> **The learning environment** is built around the child's need for nurturing relationships, safety, comfort, physical activity, emotional expression, social interaction, and intellectual stimulation. Whenever possible, we modify our environment and adapt it to meet children's individual needs instead of trying to adapt children to the environment.

>> **Affirmations** are the way we make children feel important. Affirmations include positive I-messages, reinforcement, noticing, strokes, and narrating.

We are always happy to discuss our philosophy with you, along with the individual needs of your child. We avoid talking about children when they are present, but feel free to call for an appointment.

attitudes are found in many groups. In the following passage, McFarland-Kern notes some of the challenges she and her colleagues face and the responses they make.

> After teaching the problem-solving philosophy to college students for four years, I asked my college to send me back into the day-care center. I wanted to work on this approach and refine my understanding of how it applies to guiding children. I learned immediately that I had to manage the children's aggression as quickly as possible. Then children could feel safe enough to practice problem solving. The children responded quickly to problem solving. The staff observed me and began to use the same approach successfully.
>
> I want to point out that all parents are struggling, not just African-American parents. They fear for the safety of their children! Some of these parents are skeptical about a guidance technique that seems to reduce their hold on the child. Lorraine Tyler, an African-American early childhood educator and preschool teacher, adds, "Parents see spanking as easy and fast. Hitting a child doesn't require time and patience like problem solving does. You have to give so much control to the children. It's hard for some to make that transformation of letting children make decisions. We somehow feel like we have less power if we let go of that authority."
>
> "You may say 'I'm O.K. even though I was beaten as a kid,'" continues Ms. Tyler, "but you're still carrying some of that garbage around. It doesn't have to be that way. I tell parents, 'Here's another way to raise your child.' It takes a conscious effort to change and say, 'I want to make a difference.'"
>
> Ann Terrell, an African-American director of an urban child care center, reflects, "My mother never hit us. She didn't believe in physical punishment. When I'm in conversations with other people and say, 'I don't believe in physical punishment,' I feel like I am standing alone. African Americans learned about physical punishment from the master-slave relationship. I've learned from my African friends that African families traditionally don't beat, spank, or whip their children."
>
> Inner-city children face so many problems that it is more important for them to be skilled in problem solving. Having this skill will prevent violence. I have taught in the inner city for twelve years, and I know this approach of negotiating and setting limits works. I've seen children avoid confrontation by knowing how to identify their problem, contributing ideas to the list of solutions, restating ideas positively, and carrying out agreed-upon solutions. I challenge my students to try it. What amazes them is how easily the children respond to this warmth and respect and acceptance. It really works with almost all children.

## Considering Generational Differences

Along with cultural differences, it is important to consider the need for children to know people of all ages. Currently, many innovative intergenerational programs allow children and older adults to spend time together and form meaningful relationships. Joan Whitley, director of Mount St. Vincent's Intergenerational Learning Center, describes the need for such programs. In later chapters of this book, she will add relevant information and insight for those who may want to consider initiating such a program.

In today's society of working parents, we begin, often at infancy, to place children in age group settings. Even in developmentally appropriate, culturally supportive programs, there is often missing the wider connection to the full range of the human life span. Children miss the concrete information they gather from wrinkled faces, spotted hands, knuckles thickened from years of hard work, and voices low and soft from years of quieting the worried or frightened. Children miss learning firsthand about bodies that move more slowly and persons who take more time because they have additional years of caring for and observing children and humanity in its many varied forms.

Children benefit from time spent with all ages of people. The energy and life-embracing attitudes of youth and young adulthood give children an early set of aspirations, things to strive for. The middle adult years of parents, aunts and uncles, or even some grandparents stay the course for children. They guide their growth and set the values. The oldest generations, although not exclusively, give unconditional love. They accept children as truly wonderful gifts to the future. Members of the oldest generation have often given up their roles, their variety of hats—caretaker, teacher, mother, father, coach, instructor, minister, rabbi—for the original role of person: Harold, Rosa, Helen, Kermit. They meet the "gift to the future" as another person, one to one. At its best, it becomes mutually rewarding, a caring, loving acceptance of one person by another.

One solution to the narrow placement of children in group settings is intergenerational programming. Such a program benefits young and old alike. There are several ways to accomplish this: encouraging older adults to volunteer in the children's program; bringing children on regular visits to a senior center, nursing home, or family care home to participate in intergenerational activities; or locating the children's program in a retirement complex or nursing center. The last idea performs several functions. The employees of the complex are provided on-site child care, often as an employee benefit or at a reduced fee, while children experience being around healthy and active elders as well as those who need a great deal of support for daily living. The value to the child is having the experience of an older friend.

Babies, toddlers, and preschoolers can learn from such an older friend— how to mix cookies, sing old songs, bask in the joy of a story read aloud, write the letters of one's name, and spell the names of all their friends, younger and older. Children can also help an older friend by pushing a wheel chair to the door, carrying a cane left behind, giving special drawings to brighten a room, and bringing smiles and laughter to persons feeling left behind by the world. There are many ways to learn about the differently abled. Often older adults are open to helping children understand about stroke, arthritis, osteoporosis, diabetes, or other conditions. Children can feel the stiff fingers or hand. They can see the leg missing at the knee or the body bent double (Figure 1.5).

As a teacher, your first thought may be "How frightening for the child." For some children this may be true. They may at least feel shy around someone who looks very different from anyone they know. When children experience and are allowed to talk about the vast differences among people

**Figure 1.5**   *Intergenerational programming is beneficial to young and old alike.*

and are allowed to know that people come in all shapes, sizes, colors, and abilities, they can be very accepting. The teacher is the key. We need to discuss our feelings and fears as well. We, too, need the opportunity to learn about aging.

## Considering Language Differences

We live in a mobile world, and more and more children are moving from country to country. Most of us will at some time be confronted with the problem of communicating to a child in a language other than our own. Many of us know a few words of Spanish, a familiar language to Americans; fewer are likely to understand Icelandic or Chinese. Problem solving is a very verbal approach, yet it is not so much the words themselves that comfort a crying child as the sound of our voice, the expression on our face, and the reaching out of our arms. These gestures are understood and accepted in every language.

When faced with a language challenge, begin with basics. Whatever the age of the child, think in terms of communicating with a young toddler. Use the gestures mentioned above and more. When you want to show the child something, take his hand and guide him to it. Point to where toys go on the shelf, show him the bathroom, and put the apron on him when he paints. Always use the appropriate words with your actions. Children learn language rapidly, and within six months most understand enough to get along just fine. They'll miss out on some of the nuances, but they'll catch up later.

Several words are critical to the child's ability to negotiate with other children, so as soon as you have established a good relationship, teach some "getting along" words. These include "stop," "mine," "I want," "more," "wait," "come," "take turns," and "trade." Use these words in simple phrases when you help the child solve problems with peers. Keep in mind that many children decline to use another language until they feel competent enough to be in control. Remember, too, that, whatever the cultural or language differences, every child possesses an individual temperament. The child with an outgoing, friendly nature will make friends in any language; the more introverted or shy child will need more time.

## Helping Children Make the Change

Some undesirable behavior on the part of the children may occur temporarily as a result of making the change to problem solving. If present interactions are based on an authoritarian, disciplinarian approach, the children will at first be confused by the shift. They may test limits to see how far they can actually go. As with the staff and parents, communication with the children is of the utmost importance at this time. Children need to know and understand what is happening in their immediate surroundings. Open and honest discussion with children, especially those over three years of age, may bring amazing results. Without going into unnecessary detail, you can tell them about the new way of relating to each other, about helping them solve their own problems, and about expressing their feelings and being responsible for their actions. Role playing is a tangible way to demonstrate what problem solving is about. The children act out various situations that are common to their group and figure out ways to negotiate solutions. Little explanation is needed for children under three years of age. It is important to be as committed as possible when using problem solving. If you use punishment along with problem solving, children become confused and distrustful.

If you are already working with children, you need not wait until you complete this book before experimenting with problem solving. At first it may seem awkward, unnatural, and contrived, but stick with it. Positive, observable changes will occur even during the first few weeks. The major change will be in your attitude toward the children and their attitudes toward each other. Problem solving is not a magic formula for making instant transformations. Yet you may experience the thrill of seeing children solve their own problems sooner than you expect. Even when doing so is hard and takes time and effort, it is a rare child who would not prefer to find his own solution rather than have one imposed by an adult.

During the first weeks and months, you will make mistakes. At first, they will go unnoticed by you. With experience, however, you will come to recognize them. Mistakes are an important part of the learning process for adults as well as for children. By analyzing mistakes, teachers find their strengths and weaknesses and work on ways to improve their skills. Mistakes also offer an opportunity for relating to children on their own level. Children understand mistakes; they make them all the time. They often try to express feelings for which they do not yet have words. Their phrases come out sounding unintelligible and nonsensical. Teachers who can say "Oh, oh, that isn't what I really meant to say" will endear themselves to children and gain their trust. Such teachers are also setting a good example for children, who learn that it is acceptable to make a mistake and even better to use a positive approach to correct it. What a significant lesson to learn!

One of the giants in the field of education, Alfred Adler, based his educational approach on the social life of the child.[6] Early in this century, when a more popular view was that humans are the victims of biological forces beyond their control, Adler came to believe that people are capable of making decisions that control the direction of their lives. He included children in this view, believing that, from early infancy, children are striving to reach their fullest potential. He was convinced that young children have within them the power to think and imagine and attempt to be the best people they can envision.

Adler also believed that a child's style of life was determined by age five. He knew that, to achieve their full potential, children need much more than academic subjects; they need an environment that promotes learning about life and ways of living. Adler envisioned the school as a place where any deficiencies in the child's home life could be overcome by trained teachers in a democratic setting.

The problem-solving philosophy fits well into such a democratic setting, allowing and encouraging children to use their personal power to make decisions, assert themselves, and take charge of their own lives. At the same time, through social interactions, children develop empathy and learn to consider what is good for others and for the group as a whole.

How does problem solving correspond to the academic program? Jean Piaget taught that infants and toddlers learn primarily through their senses.[7] To learn in this style, young children need exposure to a variety of enriching experiences. As they grow older, children make more use of verbal and intellectual skills to process new information. The problem-solving approach to learning encourages infants and toddlers to explore their environment. Limits are kept to a minimum and are based mainly on safety considerations so that young children feel free and confident while questioning and investigating their surroundings. This philosophy also facilitates the development of skills in preschool-age children and encourages them to use verbal and intellectual ways to solve cognitive, creative, and physical problems as well as those that are social and emotional. Chapter 2 includes a discussion of the type of program in which the problem-solving philosophy will most likely flourish, and Chapter 9 discusses the problem-solving approach to curriculum.

## Summing Up the Problem-Solving Philosophy

Problem solving is a philosophy that succeeds in teaching young children the necessary skills to solve their own problems. This philosophy has nurtured and supported hundreds of children who, under its encouragement, have developed independence, individuality, self-reliance, and a sense of responsibility. I have observed these children personally over twenty-four years in four children's centers.

Although problem solving is based on a set of terms and formulas for using those terms, its intent is never to produce teachers who react like robots or who present a "united front." Problem-solving techniques, when properly implemented, enhance teachers' ability to respond with warmth, authenticity, understanding, and individuality. Teachers who work with this philosophy trust in the natural processes of growth and development and recognize time as a major ingredient in these processes. The five major terms used in problem solving are active listening, negotiation, setting limits, modifying the environment, and affirmations.

In a program that is truly child centered, children are free, within safety limits, to "do what kids do." They are also free from criticism, repression, and punishment. Authority is replaced by problem solving; rules are replaced by limits. Emphasis is also placed on accepting responsibility. Problem solving contributes to healthy self-esteem by helping children feel lovable and worthwhile.

Making the change from a conventional program that uses rules and punishment to a child-centered, problem-solving program may be difficult at first if children, parents, and staff are accustomed to a different environment. The sensitivity and strategy used by the supervisor will help determine the attitude of the staff and parents. Conferences and meetings with the parents and teachers will make a great difference in whether they support the change. Role playing and frank discussion will help the children make a smooth transition. Making the change is worth the effort. Children will love learning to solve their own problems, and teachers will love watching them learn.

## Practice and Discussion

1. In several paragraphs, describe your own philosophy for working with young children, whether or not it coincides with the philosophy in this book. Be specific about how you would manage and encourage children's behavior. Save this paper to compare with one you will write at the completion of the book.

2. Write your own version of the teacher's role when two children are fighting over the red trike. What would she say, and how would the children respond? What would be the outcome of the confrontation?

3. What does the word "discipline" mean to you? How does your meaning differ from or resemble the dictionary definition?

4. Give a brief definition of the following terms as you understand them now: "active listening," "negotiation," "setting limits," "modifying the environment," "affirmations," "facilitating," and "removing and sitting apart."

5. What does the phrase "trusting the process" mean to you as a teacher of young children? How can trust be demonstrated to children?

6. What does the term "child centered" mean to you right now? Do you presently consider yourself child centered? If you are working with children, is your program child centered? Name several ways it is child centered, adult centered, or both.

7. Examine your own sense of self-esteem. What relationships and events contributed to your self-esteem? What part did a children's program play in the development of your self-esteem as a child? As an adult? As a teacher?

8. Suggest ways to facilitate the transition from a conventional to a problem-solving program. How would you approach parents, teachers, and children with the changes you plan to make? Compose a written philosophy that you could provide for parents in your program.

9. After reading Chapter 1, evaluate your attitude toward the use of problem solving. How do you feel about adopting it as your own teaching philosophy?

10. What drawbacks and advantages do you see so far in the problem-solving philosophy? Make a list of each.

---

## Notes

1. *Random House Dictionary of the English Language* (New York: Random House, 1987), p. 562.

2. Haim Ginott, *Teacher and Child* (New York: Collier, 1993), pp. 147, 148.

3. Dorothy Briggs, *Your Child's Self-Esteem* (Garden City, NY: Dolphin Books, 1975), p. 226.

4. Rudolf Dreikurs and Vicki Stoltz, *Children: The Challenge* (New York: Penguin Group, 1992), p. 81.

5. Briggs, *Your Child's Self-Esteem*, pp. 3, 14.

6. Alfred Adler, *The Education of Children* (Chicago: Henry Regnery, 1970; originally published 1930).

7. Dorothy G. Singer and Tracey A. Revenson, *A Piaget Primer: How a Child Thinks* (New York: Dutton, 1989).

# Recommended Reading

Adler, Alfred. *The Education of Children.* Chicago: Henry Regnery, 1970.

Brazelton, T. Berry. *Touchpoints.* Reading, MA: Addison-Wesley, 1992.

Ginott, Haim. *Teacher and Child.* New York: Collier, 1993.

Gordon, Thomas. *P.E.T.: Parent Effectiveness Training.* New York: New American Library, 1975.

Gordon, Thomas. *Teaching Children Self-Discipline.* New York: Random House, 1989.

Gottman, John. *The Heart of Parenting.* New York: Simon & Schuster, 1997.

# CHAPTER 2

# *Setting Up the Problem-Solving Environment*

Although the problem-solving philosophy can be used effectively in many settings, the environment in which children spend their days does directly influence their thoughts, feelings, behavior, health, creativity, and relationships. Imagine the perfect environment in which to care for groups of young children. Everyone would have a different vision of it. When I was a college student, one of my assignments was to design the ideal children's center. My creation was a glass dome that made the outdoors seem part of the indoors. The outdoor area was green and natural with hills, trails, and farm animals. My dream site was also close to a body of water, within walking distance of a sandy beach. There was open space as well as room for privacy. Color and texture added warmth and dimension. It was a place filled with the sounds of joy and wonder, a place of discovery.

The vision that each student and future teacher carries in his or her mind is significant. It is more than simply a design for a building. This vision is an expression of personality, teaching style, ideals, values, goals, and attitudes toward children. When you picture a dream facility filled with children, you create an ideal worth working for. Whether or not the ideal is fully attainable, you will certainly incorporate at least some fragments of the dream into the real environment. Because you will spend a great deal of time in it, you will be drawing on the environment to maintain energy, enthusiasm, comfort, and tranquility.

The purpose of this chapter is not so much to provide specific ideas as to describe the general type of environment in which problem solving works best. The physical environment provides the background for the psychological, intellectual, and social environments. All are intertwined and interdependent. Because problem solving promotes freedom with safety and independence with responsibility, the physical environment should reflect these characteristics and provide many opportunities for children to experience, experiment, and explore. Even more important to the problem-solving environment are the teacher and the number of children for whom he or she is responsible. The characteristics needed for the teacher in a problem-solving program and the ratio of children to teachers will also be covered in this chapter. The last section addresses a strategy of the problem-solving philosophy known as modifying the environment.

In Chapter 9, "The Problem-Solving Approach to Curriculum," the environment is discussed in the context of curriculum—focusing on the process of maintaining an evolving, expanding environment to enhance the learning experience. The discussion in Chapter 9 builds on the foundation laid in this chapter and carries us into the realm of intellectual and creative development.

## The Child-Centered Classroom

The principles and descriptions of the total environment for problem solving found in this chapter apply equally to infants, toddlers, and preschool-age children. A day-care home may have only a small area that can be geared specifically to the needs of infants. In a children's center, a larger area will be specially licensed to meet the needs of babies who are not yet walking. When you plan or furnish any play and learning area, consider the age, mobility, and interest level of the children who will be there. The child-centered classroom is first discussed in a general way to apply to all age groups. Later sections discuss specifics of infant, toddler, and preschool environments.

How does the physical environment influence the child's ability to solve problems? Whether through interactions with people, materials, or equipment, the child's mind needs the stimulation and challenge of making choices and decisions. Every choice and decision carries its own consequences and problem-solving opportunity. To develop those emerging skills, the child needs an enriched environment filled with possibilities for exercising his decision-making skills. He also needs a facilitator who understands his needs to help him accept responsibility for his decisions.

The child-centered classroom provides such an environment. The child is free to choose the toys or materials that interest her most and to decide how to play with them. The child's own level of interest, skill, and development will lead her to play with the toy in a way that is appropriate for her and for as long as it holds her interest. Her playing is likely to change from day to day as she experiments and explores innovative ways to use the same toy. Responsibility comes through taking good care of the toy and putting it away when she has finished playing. This approach to learning is most compatible with the problem-solving philosophy.

A child-centered classroom also addresses the specific needs of both genders. Acknowledging the differences between girls and boys enables us to provide for the needs of both. Without realizing it, many programs set up their environments primarily to meet the needs of girls. For example, girls tend to huddle in small groups, verbalizing and making eye contact while they play, whether during dramatic play, block building, working on puzzles, or making art projects. Because of this, girls operate well in relatively small spaces. Boys, on the other hand, seldom huddle; they go in many directions at once. They often play without making eye contact or carrying on conversations. Boys are generally more active and aggressive and require more physical space. In *The Wonder of Boys*, Michael Gurian writes, "The boy's brain tries to recreate itself in the outside world by creating and playing games—like baseball and football, etc.—that fill large spaces and challenge the male brain to hone its skill at moving objects through space."[1] In order to meet the physical and social needs of boys, we must provide spaces for rough-and-tumble play (Figure 2.1). Throughout this book, I will highlight the particular needs of each gender whenever they differ.

The goal of the child-centered classroom is to stimulate the child's natural curiosity, provide experiences, promote experimentation and exploration, and address the child's needs and desires. All these allow learning to take place through the child's own senses and thought processes. The more independently the child can proceed, the more highly developed will be his sense of self-esteem and confidence. He can learn through taking risks, making his own mistakes, and accepting the responsibility involved. He becomes a problem solver.

## Learning Centers

A child-centered classroom is one in which movement and exploration are encouraged. Generally, learning centers are set up at various places in the

**Figure 2.1**    *A child-centered program provides space for active play.*

room. A learning center may consist of a table furnished with materials for exploring a theme, such as magnets; a section of shelves holding art materials; or a soft pile of pillows the child can sit on while he looks at books. A learning center may also consist of equipment, such as a toy stove, sink, and refrigerator for dramatic play. The idea is to make each learning center revolve around a learning category, such as manipulatives, music, or imaginative play (Figure 2.2).

For young children, the learning center should be kept as simple and as manageable as possible. The children should be able to use the materials and equipment independently and be able to put things away easily. The learning center should be arranged so that several children can use it together without being crowded or having to fight over the materials. The theme of some centers may change periodically to keep them evolving and stimulating, but others may remain the same with minor changes in materials. A trip to the library every few weeks will keep the book center fresh. The introduction of pastel chalk to the art center may renew children's interest in art. A few new puzzles from time to time will give the puzzle center a boost.

The number of learning centers in any room will depend on the size of the room and its other uses. A large table may be used for eating meals as well as working on art projects or manipulatives. A low mat or pile of pillows can be a cozy place to drink a bottle as well as to look at books. Learning centers should be scaled down to fit into the room and to leave open

**Figure 2.2**    *This learning center emphasizes art. Materials are accessible for self-directed play.*

space, too. For example, a table that might take up too much space may be omitted by simply allowing the children to work on the floor. An area rug can even serve as a place to work on puzzles or manipulatives, thus eliminating the need for a space-consuming table. Rugs should be taped down so the children do not trip on them.

Depending on the floor plan of the facility, one room may be available for a small group or several rooms for a larger group. If each room is being used as a self-contained classroom for a small group of the same age, learning centers from the various categories of learning should be included in each. These categories consist primarily of the following: music, art, and imaginative, cognitive, large and small motor, and language development. When you arrange the room, remember the significance of social interactions and create spaces for one-on-one encounters between children. In many cases, it is desirable to group active and quiet areas separately. If one room is used, you may need to combine some learning categories. A shelf of puzzles may work well next to the art materials when children are old enough to resist painting the puzzles. Both artwork and puzzle making may then be done on the same table.

If several rooms are used for a larger group, learning centers can be larger, with the learning categories spread out among the rooms. For exam-

**Figure 2.3**    *Some boys show their affection by wrestling.*

ple, a block center, an art center, a water play center, a reading center, and a music center could be in one room and centers of different categories in other rooms. The centers may be defined and bordered with area rugs, low shelves, cabinets, or other devices. Keep the boundaries low so the teacher can see all the children all the time.

What other features should generally be included in the child-centered classroom? To begin with, space. Children need open space to move about freely. An open space may be just the spot for periodically spreading out a large mat for acrobatics or wrestling, a small piece of outdoor equipment, or an area for riding on wheel toys (Figures 2.3 and 2.4). Open space also inspires dancing, "picnicking" with toy dishes on a blanket, making a "train" from chairs, or taking dolls for a walk. One precaution for open areas is to be sure there are some barriers to limit unwanted running. Avoid crowding in any area, even if something must be eliminated. Crowding can be the cause of accidents as well as conflicts between children; it is also frustrating for teachers.

As important as open spaces are private spaces. Children who are spending much of their time in a group need someplace where they can get away and be alone or be with just one friend. This may be extremely difficult to arrange in some rooms. If it is not provided, however, the children will find their own, perhaps inappropriate, private spaces. A private space must

**Figure 2.4**  *A child-centered classroom addresses the needs of both genders.*

also be one that the teacher is able to see well enough to supervise. Sometimes a large playhouse, an appliance carton, an empty cabinet, a fold-up tunnel, or simply a corner can be an acceptable private space.

Color is extremely important to any classroom. Because walls and floors cover the largest areas, their color is bound to have an effect on the inhabitants of the room. Teachers work best when surrounded with colors that make them feel energetic, creative, and harmonious. It is safe to assume that children will respond similarly to such colors. Carpeting should be warm and inviting to the children and, of course, easily cleaned. If possible, at least one floor or one area should be carpeted to add warmth, texture, and color. Windows can bring the colors and tranquility of the outdoors into a room. Large picture windows of safety glass make a room seem larger and, if there is greenery outdoors, add the colors of nature.

Other items that bring color and harmony to the classroom include pillows, cupboards, tables, chairs, resting or acrobatic mats with covers, posters and pictures on the walls, and, of course, toys. Primary colors that are clear and easily identifiable are decorative and help children learn colors. Pictures and posters are best placed at the child's eye level and covered with clear contact paper for protection. Children's artwork, proudly displayed, always contributes color to the walls and also contributes to the children's self-esteem. Photos of the children themselves make wonderful posters and allow children to admire themselves and their friends.

**Figure 2.5**   *Toddlers need a place to rest, drink bottles, look at books, and socialize.*

Often overlooked is the role of texture in the environment. Surfaces and accessories may be hard, soft, rough, smooth, shaggy, or flat or have other tactile qualities. Children love soft, smooth surfaces, such as the bindings on their blankets, which are soothing and comforting. Infants and toddlers especially need at least one soft, comfortable place to rest, drink a bottle, look at a book, or just retreat from the group (Figure 2.5). Having a variety of textures encourages making choices and provides stimulation for young children.

## Infant Environments

As more infants are enrolled in children's programs, their environmental needs as well as their psychological and intellectual needs must be understood. For infants, in fact, all needs are intertwined. The primary need for an infant is attachment to other human beings. Such bonding takes place through intimate contact with an adult—as when the caregiver holds the child, rocks her, responds to her crying, or talks to her or when caregiver and infant simply gaze into each other's eyes. Assuming that this bonding takes place, what type of environment does an infant need when she is observing her surroundings, sitting up, grasping objects, and learning to creep, crawl, walk, and feed herself?

I spend time with infants every day, and I now have grandchildren of my own. Each encounter with infants is a learning experience for me, and I am amazed by what I see. Consequently, my knowledge of what infants need is constantly evolving. More surprising to me is what infants do *not* need and what should be eliminated from infant environments.

The first thing to eliminate is the infant swing, which I see being used to pacify and hypnotize infants into a state of lethargy and apathy. Swings are convenient for caregivers, especially when they are working with unrealistic teacher-infant ratios, but they provide no beneficial experience for infants. Swings are no substitute for the holding that is critical to the infant's normal development.

Next, eliminate playpens, whose main function is to inhibit the normal mobility of babies who are learning to crawl and walk. Other than providing a temporary place to keep a nonmobile infant safe, playpens have no developmental purpose and take up space that is needed for crawling. In the playpen category, I include infant seats that keep babies strapped into one position and serve mainly to restrain and walkers that are also used to control the normal mobility of infants. In addition to providing inappropriate control, walkers have been shown to cause physical injury and even delay the beginning of walking.

The high chair is another piece of equipment that is frequently abused. I have seen babies lined up in a long row of high chairs and left there for long periods of time in centers with few caregivers. Although two or three high chairs may be necessary for feeding (and only feeding), they should not be used to keep mobile children entertained or restrained.

What, then, is an appropriate environment for infants? It is one that meets their developmental needs for nurturing and exploration. The basic requirements include open space for crawling and for pushing pushtoys around the room. A soft, comforting space allows an infant to observe the surroundings safely, drink her own bottle when she is old enough to choose (usually at least over six months of age), look at books, examine small toys, and relax with a caregiver (Figure 2.6). A rocking chair or two provide comfort to breast-feeding mothers as well as bottle-feeding caregivers. A climbing structure that is developmentally appropriate in safety, size, and challenge should always be available for older infants.

In addition to basic equipment, other useful items are an infant mirror, a bar the child can use to pull himself up and stand (Figure 2.7), and a sensory tub big enough to sit in. (I find the strongest, most pliable tubs in animal feed stores; see Figure 2.8.) Low, stable shelves and small containers for assortments of toys are also good to have. Smaller containers allow easy access by infants and keep toys sorted into loose categories. Avoid using large tubs or boxes for toy storage; toys are hard to find at the bottom of a big container, and parts of toys can be easily lost in a large storage box.

Color and texture are as important to infant environments as they are to those of older children. The environment sends a clear message: "This is

**Figure 2.6**    *A soft, comforting space allows infants to observe their surroundings safely.*

here for you; come and explore." When you are setting up an infant environment be creative and willing to try new ideas. You will learn through experience what works, and in the process you, too, will be amazed by what you learn.

## Toddler Environments

Toddler programs are also relatively new, and we have much to learn about appropriate environments for groups of toddlers. Whereas we generally understand that infants need holding and cuddling and that preschoolers need intellectual and social stimulation, many dedicated teachers are baffled and overwhelmed by the demands and needs of toddlers. As with infants, I begin with what to eliminate and progress to what is needed.

Much of what should be eliminated from infant environments should also be eliminated from toddler environments: playpens, or other restraining devices such as walkers, and high chairs that are no longer needed. Toddlers need space in which to move about so they can use their large muscles. But they need more than open spaces to support the other facets of their development.

**Figure 2.7**   *A mirror with bar for pulling themselves up gives infants a sense of self and independence.*

**Figure 2.8**   *This strong, pliable sensory tub was purchased at an animal feed store.*

**Figure 2.9**  *A toddler environment should promote independence, and a toddler teacher should provide support.*

While visiting dozens of toddler programs, I was disheartened by the lack of such support materials. I have consistently seen toddler environments in which most toys are kept on high shelves so children must ask for them and where art and imaginative materials are nonexistent. When I inquired about the lack of access to toys and the absence of materials, I was told authoritatively that toddlers eat art materials, that they use homemaking accessories such as toy dishes only to hit each other, and that puzzle pieces get lost. Also, because toddlers dump everything on the floor, teachers don't want to give them access to small toys. Toddlers frequently have access only to one-piece, molded plastic toys that have a single use, have no meaning, inspire no experimentation or exploration, and are primarily good for pounding on the floor or on someone's head!

My profound hope is that some of you who read this will take up the cause of toddlers and commit yourselves to filling the great need for teachers who really enjoy and understand this age group and who see limitless horizons for their capabilities. Toddlers are indeed difficult and complex; in this, they are similar to adolescents. They demand both total independence and your supportive presence when they need you (Figure 2.9). Working with toddlers is physically and mentally taxing, but it is also joyous and rewarding.

**Figure 2.10**    *Every category of materials should be represented in a toddler program.*

What should we find in a basic toddler environment? Every category of material and equipment that is represented in a child-centered preschool environment should be there, but scaled to a toddler level. Toys, manipulatives, puzzles, dramatic play props and accessories, books, sensory materials, large muscle equipment, and creative supplies should be on low shelves, but some in smaller quantities than for preschool-age children (Figure 2.10). For example, younger toddlers, from twelve to eighteen or twenty months, should have access to art materials such as fat crayons and washable markers in assorted colors. Throw away broken crayons that are small enough for a child to choke on, and discard the caps to the markers for the same reason. The markers will dry out (it helps if you cover them at night) and will need replacing, but if you put out only eight or ten at a time, you won't have so many to replace. Keep extras on a higher shelf for times when everyone wants them at the same time.

Keep homemade playdough on a low shelf in individual clear plastic containers, the kind you get at the deli, along with safe kitchen utensils from a thrift store. If you have a number of small containers, you will avoid unnecessary conflicts. An easel can be made on a door that is not used for traffic, such as the door of a seldom-used closet, with one or two containers of paint always available (Figure 2.11). When you first make such materials available, expect an initial rush to get at them, and be sure to offer interesting

**Figure 2.11**  *An easel can be attached to a wall or a seldom-used door.*

alternatives as well. Also expect children to sometimes put these materials in their mouth. The items just mentioned are nontoxic, and, as you will see in Chapter 6, you can set limits for art supplies as well as other materials and toys. After the items have been in the environment for a few weeks, the children will treat them much more casually and responsibly.

Toddlers over twenty-four months old should have access to the same materials but in larger quantities. In addition, they can use children's scissors, water colors, and colored pencils, all of which can be kept on low shelves. White glue should be kept on a higher shelf for teachers to dispense. The same approach works with puzzles, pegs, snap beads, Duplos, and other toys with multiple pieces. Make them accessible, but for toddlers put out an amount they can pick up and put away easily. More complex puzzles can be stored at a higher level, but four or five simple puzzles should always be within reach. As children develop, they are able to begin to put toys away, and by age three they are capable of dealing with greater numbers of pieces. Be sure, however, that all parts of toys meet safety requirements for toddlers so the pieces cannot be swallowed or cause choking. Most school suppliers sell a small, plastic, cylinder-shaped device for sizing objects so you can determine which ones are large enough to be safe.

Some teachers believe that, if many toys and materials are accessible to children, the environment will be too difficult to supervise. This depends somewhat on the teacher-child ratio, but, generally, the opposite is true. When children are in an environment that keeps them interested and stimulated, they engage in less conflict, they do not run and wander aimlessly, and they spend more time in meaningful play. The result is happier children and more fulfilled teachers.

## Preschool Environments

Practically everything mentioned for toddlers can be adapted to preschool-age children. Chronologically, preschoolers range in age from thirty to sixty months. Some programs include the entire age range in their preschool program; this mix requires teachers to incorporate the needs of older toddlers into the preschool program. Others consider preschoolers as children who are either three to five or four to five years old. In programs limited to children of these ages, you will have less need to consider, for example, whether children will put small parts of toys in their mouths or find certain puzzles too difficult.

The length of your program will also play a part in the kind of environment you provide for preschoolers. Children who attend a shorter preschool program tend to have more experiences outside of preschool: running errands with a parent, visiting friends and relatives, going to the park, playing with siblings who are older or younger than themselves. Preschool is often the high point of their week, and they return to the classroom with the eager anticipation of being reunited with familiar playmates. They play, and then they leave, unencumbered by the routines and transitions that are required in a full-day program. There are no meals or naps, two of the most difficult times in day care, and no long hours to be filled. A short preschool program with an ample indoor area for active play has less need for an elaborate outdoor playground. In preschool, the focus should be primarily on social interaction, and the classroom should reflect that focus.

Whatever the age range or the length of the program, keep in mind certain characteristics of the preschool stage of development. Three of these traits that relate to the environment are the children's developing independence, productivity, and sociability. An environment for preschoolers should provide opportunities for them to use their growing number of skills to work independently or in groups, to turn their ideas into reality, and to form meaningful peer relationships. In Chapter 9, we discuss the preschool curriculum, which is certainly important in the environment. For the present, however, our focus is on the physical surroundings.

*Independent Play*    The preschool environment encourages children to work and play independently, without need of assistance, by making everything readily available to them. Except for small pieces that may cause choking, all materials should be within reach of children this age. The room should have low shelves to hold materials, and several tables ranging in size from one large enough for the entire group to small ones with room for only one or two children so a child may work alone when he chooses. Smaller tables are conducive to more intimate interaction; larger tables provide opportunities to interact with many children during meals and group projects.

A computer might be placed on a small table to allow one child to work independently. A bin of seashells and some magnifying glasses on a small table may inspire one or two budding scientists to contemplate the secrets of the sea. A bean bag, easy chair, or crib mattress provides a reading or daydreaming space for thinkers. These same spaces may accommodate a larger group at times but are available for solitary, independent play as well.

*Productivity*    Preschool-age children are filled with ideas and are eager to turn them into recognizable products. Blocks become a fire station, an airport, or a house; such building requires open space. Paper, markers, scissors, paint, tape, and other creative supplies become drawings, paintings, hats, masks, pouches, telescopes, and countless other imaginative items. Preschoolers will change a pegboard and pegs into a birthday cake with candles and create a theatrical event with secondhand dress-up clothes. The environment must provide the raw materials for productivity. If cost is a consideration, you can find many ideas for inexpensive materials in Chapter 9.

As described in Chapter 9, the emphasis in curriculum is on process; therefore, the materials in the environment should be basic, so that children can use their own creativity. Materials should give children the choice of experimenting in a purely scientific, information-gathering manner or of shaping an idea into an end product. The process of seeing how many Legos can be joined together is as meaningful to the child as producing a Lego castle.

*Sociability*    For preschoolers, the most important benefit of a children's program is the development of peer relationships. Children want and need playmates and friends. The environment should provide spaces where large groups can play and work together, as well as private spaces where two or three can develop intimacy. A loft that has usable space both above and below may fill both needs. If space is a problem, a small loft may be constructed by a relatively competent carpenter. If you plan to construct a loft, whether large or small, consider how the space underneath will be used and supervised. Boys generally do some of their socializing by role-playing the current superheroes. Both boys and teachers are helped by having an area that can be used for that purpose.

At times a child feels unsociable and needs absolute privacy. Privacy can be difficult to provide, because space is usually at a premium. Also, complete privacy is difficult to supervise. You may find it necessary to designate an area that is relatively removed and where a child can ask others to give him or her time alone. A small table with a sheet draped over it may provide enough secluded space underneath to satisfy the child's need for privacy.

## Cubbies

To make putting away belongings as convenient as possible, each child should have a special place that is only his or hers. It may be a locker, a basket, or another container such as a five-gallon cardboard ice cream tub. For infants and toddlers, these containers are best placed out of their reach; otherwise, everyone will be removing items from everyone else's container. Preschoolers are capable of having theirs within reach. In fact, having the containers, sometimes called "cubbies," available at all times fosters preschoolers' independence and teaches them about the right to privacy. A cubby is to be used by others only with the permission of its owner.

A toddler may have a special blanket, stuffed animal, or other toy she has brought to give her comfort or to show other children. Because it is her responsibility to take care of the item and she will tire of carrying it around, she may ask a teacher to put it in her cubby, where it is safe. Sometimes children think they want to share a toy; then when others have it they change their minds. The cubby is a safe place for such a toy. The teacher will probably want to limit the number of times she is willing to put in or take out any item from a toddler's cubby.

The cubby serves the same function for the preschooler, but because it is accessible it is also a place for him to put away his shoes or clothes when necessary. Children may remove some of their clothing to put on dress-up clothes, to be more comfortable, or to take naps; also, they may prefer to have their shoes and socks off while they are indoors. They may also remove their shoes to put on boots in rainy or snowy weather. They easily learn that all personal items are kept in their cubbies. Note: If there is a possibility of an unannounced fire drill in a frigid climate, teachers should provide a container near the fire exit for children's shoes instead of keeping them in cubbies.

## *The Outdoor Environment*

If a playground is part of the facility, it should be arranged with safety as a primary goal. Only when children are safe to take risks, explore, and experiment with their bodies can they feel free. The playground should be as child centered as the rest of the facility. It should require the smallest number of limits and allow for the greatest number of choices. The playground should be as easy as possible for teachers to supervise so that when conflicts arise teachers can facilitate while watching the other children.

As a student and future teacher, you may be called on to help create or improve a playground. If you own your own center, you may have full control over such a project. This section stresses the use of natural materials in creating a natural environment. In my opinion, such an environment, with the softness of grass and the blues and greens of sky and trees, is soothing, comforting, and stress reducing. This does not mean that problem solving is

**Figure 2.12**   *Even a downtown playground can provide a natural and varied environment.*

less effective in a less natural setting, but children seem to be more relaxed in natural surroundings (Figure 2.12).

A variety of inexpensive materials that are functional as well as attractive and can help create a natural-looking environment is available. Grass is always desirable; children can run, roll, and lie on it, look for worms under a wooden board, and smell and feel the earth. Sand may be carted in to fill sandboxes and to spread under swings or climbing structures. There may even be a source of free sand close by. Some sand suppliers will give away a pickup truck full of sand for a worthy cause such as a children's center. Gravel is relatively cheap, and a gravel area supplies materials for toy trucks to load and unload. Another, more unusual ground cover is shredded tires. You may have to search for them, but shredded tires make a safe, durable, resilient ground cover under swings and climbers. They are not an appropriate material to play with, as are sand and gravel, but, if deep enough, shredded tires protect children against being hurt in a fall. Maximize your playground's safety by checking your state's recommendations for ground covers and their depth.

To divide play areas, materials such as railroad ties, half-buried tires, large rocks, and tree logs are recommended. The rocks may even be found in the yard or dug up in the area and laid out in a row, side by side. If rocks are

**Figure 2.13**    *Bark is used under the climbing structure, but other ground covers are also used on this playground.*

used, choose them carefully, rejecting any with jagged edges. Logs or ties may be laid out horizontally to form a low barrier that separates sand from gravel or grass from shredded tires. Bark, although a natural product, has tiny splinters that prohibit children from walking barefoot, one of summer's delights. Although bark may work in some areas, it should not be used as the only ground cover on a playground (Figure 2.13).

A more natural environment has some inconveniences, but they are minor compared to the enrichment it brings. Sand and gravel must be replenished, requiring several hours of work by a strong person with a pickup truck and wheelbarrow several times a year. Shredded rubber need not be replaced if children are not permitted to play with it. On rainy or snowy days, a few extra minutes may be needed to put boots on the children so they can go outdoors, but even cement gets wet, so there is not a great difference between it and grass in that respect.

It is certainly an advantage to have a covered indoor-outdoor area where children can use their muscles and make noise even in rainy or snowy weather (Figure 2.14). This space could be a garage with a removable fence built across the wide open doors, or the area under a roof that extends out from the main building. In this area, a blacktop or cement floor may be desirable so children can ride trikes or other riding toys under the roof. Without a

**Figure 2.14** *A covered area for indoor-outdoor play provides a place for physical activity on rainy days.*

place to exercise, children confined to the indoors on rainy days may use their pent-up energy to create conflicts.

Children love gardening. A separate, fenced garden area will provide rich learning experiences. Planting seeds, watering, and watching plants grow are exciting activities that children will think are wonderful. With luck, your young gardeners may even eat vegetables they have grown themselves.

If there is room for a few farm animals in a yard of their own or in a yard with older preschoolers, they too will provide rich experiences for the children. Animals also teach children a sense of responsibility toward less powerful creatures. Goats are especially good pets. Pygmy goats are more expensive than regular-size goats but remain small, do not bite, have no claws with which to scratch, and are generally friendly toward children (Figure 2.15). They should be dehorned, and males should be neutered. Goat droppings are more easily managed than wastes of most animals, being similar to those of rabbits, guinea pigs, and pet rats. Rabbits also make wonderful pets. If at all possible, have an outdoor pen where rabbits can run around; this is much better than an indoor cage. Rabbits do need an easy-to-clean house or hutch filled with warm straw inside their pen. Rabbits are gentle and easily trained to allow children to pet them. Chickens can also be delightful, especially hens, because children love to find eggs they've laid.

**Figure 2.15**    *When animals are part of the environment, children lose their fear of them. Pygmy goats remain small; these goats are only part pygmy.*

Their droppings, however, are not as neat as those of goats and rabbits. Roosters, by the way, can be quite unfriendly.

Many children are frightened by animals, but exposure to them in the environment day after day helps children learn to accept them. The teacher's attitude influences how children feel about animals (Figure 2.16). If the teacher is positive and shows affection for the animals, the children will follow her lead. A child who is terrified of an animal should not be forced to come in contact with it, but the teacher can casually communicate that she expects the child to enjoy the animal someday. Gradually, the child will lose his fear and venture closer. Children gain an enormous feeling of self-confidence and pride in overcoming their fears. Animals also teach children about death. Small animals and birds kept indoors in cages have a short life span and provide many occasions for funerals and burials.

A word of caution about animals: Before investing in any animal, investigate the care and maintenance it requires. Farm animals need daily feeding and watering, even on weekends and holidays. All animals consume extra time, money, and energy. There may also be zoning or licensing regulations that apply to large animals. Some children and teachers are allergic to certain animals, especially those that are fur bearing. Another consideration is the birth of baby animals. Although this can be a wonderful

**Figure 2.16**  *Infants may approach an animal cautiously but soon overcome their fears.*

experience for children, the babies are usually hard to give away and may end up at the pet store.

The outdoor environment should be vibrant with life. Children are entitled to the riches of the great outdoors. They need to experience the blue sky with its birds, jet planes, and cloud formations; shades of green in trees, grass, and plants; and rich, brown dirt teeming with worms and insects. Even if the area is already covered with cement, you may be able to plant flowers, bushes, and trees in half-barrels or redwood boxes. A sand area can be created within a wooden frame. An animal pen can be built on cement if it is carefully designed to provide drainage. A flower or vegetable garden can be built with railroad ties.

Safe and age-appropriate equipment is very important. Much of the climbing, sliding, and swinging equipment available is made of metal or plastic, but wooden structures can be found. It is relatively easy to buy well-built, durable, and safe climbing structures for children of preschool age and older. A safe climber for infants or toddlers that is ready to assemble may be harder to find. If one or more exist within driving distance, your time would be well spent to look at it. In fact, looking at many varieties of climbers on playgrounds as well as in books will provide you with ideas for the best possible structure. One resource may be the architecture department at a local college or university. There may be a student who would love to design and

**Figure 2.17**    *This low, toddler-size climber was designed and constructed on-site by an architecture student.*

even build the perfect toddler climber right on your site! He or she may even be graded and receive credit for it. A toddler-size climber may be a major expense, but it is worth the investment (Figure 2.17).

Along with the climbing structure, a whole world of playground equipment can be found in various manufacturers' catalogues. A great deal of it is gimmicky or impractical, but much of it is interesting. Safety and versatility are important characteristics of any equipment for a children's center. To be safe, playground equipment should be the appropriate size and height for the children who will use it. It should be well balanced and solidly grounded. Again, for children to have the greatest amount of freedom, their environment must be as safe as possible. Consider, too, whether equipment can be used in many ways and whether it is basic enough to allow children to employ their imaginations to transform it into their own creation.

An important characteristic of playground equipment is how independently and cooperatively it can be used. You can avoid many conflicts by providing ample space on the equipment. Rather than a conventional swing that must be pushed by someone bigger, why not have a glider swing with bench seats for younger children? It may hold up to six children on the benches and allow several to stand and use their bodies to make the swing move (Figure 2.18). Infants may be held by their caregiver while riding the glider. For older preschoolers, a horizontal tire swing seats or stands three

**Figure 2.18**    *A glider swing encourages cooperation and socialization. It is safe for toddlers.*

children at a time and is pushed by their feet. Only children who are able to climb on the swing by themselves and use it without adult help should use a tire swing. This type of swing is heavy and not safe for most toddlers.

The use of old rubber tires from automobiles, trucks, and motorcycles will help the budget. Some tire sellers are thrilled to get rid of surplus tires for a good cause, as storing or disposing of them may be expensive. Many books offer ideas for using tires on the playground. Even a simple pile of tires within some sort of framework is a great place for children to sit and talk or play. Tires also make obstacle courses and boundaries between areas.

When you are looking for playground equipment, keep an open mind. Many items, although unorthodox, make wonderful play spaces. They may be donated if you ask for them in a diplomatic way. An old boat, concrete sewer pipes, and other discarded items may be cleaned up, made safe, and revitalized for playground use.

Providing an outdoor environment where children have open space for running, jumping, climbing, making noise, and generally using their bodies in physically active ways solves many problems. Infants, toddlers, and preschoolers who are confined to inadequate spaces and inhibited physically are certain to become frustrated more easily and create more conflict. A play area that offers options and choices also enhances problem solving by making many solutions possible. Children can find their own little corner or niche in which to think, reflect, and find comfort and tranquility away from the crowd. All people, both adults and children, need this.

## The Teacher's Role in the Environment

The building and playground make up only a small portion of the total environment for problem solving. They are the visible, tangible parts and are important, to be sure. Parents and children alike respond initially to what they see and are either pleased or displeased by the physical plant. But the true heart of any child care facility is the teacher, the human being with whom the child will form a significant relationship. The teacher is the person who brings the problem-solving philosophy to each child in an individual, meaningful way. Her insight, skill, sensitivity, and versatility make problem solving come alive and become real to the children in her care. She is a facilitator, substitute parent, teacher, and loving friend. A good teacher is a treasure. She can be effective in a tent in the desert, on an ocean beach, or under a tree on a mountaintop. No building, however beautiful or impressive, can take her place.

Those of you who are students may be working toward a variety of certificates or degrees that will qualify you to be teachers of young children. Some of you will become head teachers or administrators. Professionals in child care are becoming more and more important to our society. As more educated teachers enter the field, conditions and benefits will certainly be upgraded. With so much challenge ahead and so much to learn, you may ask yourself whether the extra effort required to learn a philosophy such as problem solving is worthwhile.

I think the answer is yes. Many contemporary parents are interested in alternatives to the type of discipline they perceive as rules and punishment. They are trying to rear their children to be independent thinkers who are articulate in expressing their feelings and to behave according to the parents' standards as well. Because so many families include two parents who are employed outside the home and because of the growing number of single parents, these parents are beginning to realize the degree of influence the child care center has on the formation of their child's personality, intellect, and self-esteem. They are, therefore, seeking more from a children's center than simply custodial care. They hope to find a program in which their values and goals for their children will be carried out. The problem-solving philosophy fills this need, and the teacher who is skilled in this philosophy will be an asset to any center that hopes to attract such parents.

In addition to being an asset for the center, teachers who practice problem solving are enriching their own teaching experience. Working with children has the potential for being physically taxing, emotionally draining, and intellectually unstimulating. Workers who are untrained and unskilled or who see child care as the only thing they can do are likely to feel physically and psychologically tired much of the time. This condition can result from a limited knowledge of child development and early childhood education and a lack of commitment to a philosophy in which they can wholeheartedly believe. Students who are choosing to be educated professionals in child development and early childhood education and who find the growth and development of children fascinating and enlightening have higher expectations of their teaching career. Embracing a system that applies their highest ideals can help them meet those expectations.

In my experience, most of what a student learns in child development and early childhood courses can be classified as research and theory. It is extremely important and valuable for teachers to continue to learn and have a solid foundation in research and theory to fall back on, but those who intend to apply their knowledge to working with children also need a strong foundation of application. Many students are fortunate enough to spend time in a college child development lab doing a practicum, but others' first contact with a group of children is on their first job. Without their own working philosophy, they are subject to indecision, apprehension, and confusion. The problem-solving philosophy, which is based on a variety of theoretical approaches, equips the new teacher with the skill and self-confidence she needs.

A teacher of problem solving needs the qualities of any good teacher, including knowledge of child development and early childhood education, sensitivity, creativity, good judgment, a sense of humor, a willingness to learn, and a love of and commitment to children. In addition to these, the teacher needs special qualities for problem solving, including authenticity; respect for the child's individual rights; acceptance of all feelings; trust in children to deal with their own feelings; interest in children's ideas, opinions, and complaints; and a willingness to communicate her own feelings openly as well as to take the time to listen to those of children.[2] She should also be willing to unlearn many of the negative lessons she learned in childhood. Of course, she must be willing to allow and help children to solve their own problems.

Once you have begun to actually use problem solving as a teacher, you will often find yourself in awe of the capabilities you observe in even the youngest children. When you emphasize children being children and trust their inner resources, your children will amaze and excite you. You will sometimes feel like a scientist observing life at its beginnings. In the process, you will learn a great deal about yourself and draw energy from the self-realization you gain. Young children who are blessed with the freedom to be themselves are witty, charming, and funny as well as assertive, opinionated, and feisty. Most of all, for a problem-solving teacher, they are fun.

## The Teacher:Child Ratio

One of the most significant contributors to the total environment for problem solving and quality child care in general is the number of children each teacher supervises. Even the best teacher becomes inadequate when faced with an overwhelming number of children. Unfortunately, this happens too often. In some states, licensing requirements, if they exist, allow too many children per teacher, creating an unhealthy and artificial situation. To be safely supervised, to have time for affection, to be challenged and stimulated, and to learn problem-solving skills, a child needs individual attention.

What is the ideal teacher:child ratio in a problem-solving program? There is probably no perfect number to fit all circumstances, but generally speaking a ratio of three infants under twelve months for each teacher works well. If the babies are all very young, perhaps under six months, even this ratio may sometimes seem inadequate. But to have more than a three-to-one ratio may be financially prohibitive. Licensing requirements usually limit the number of infants in an infant program. With a ratio of three to one, a limit of nine infants seems optimal in one area. This allows three teachers to be on duty at all times and provides them with backup and support. While one is diapering or giving a bottle, the other two are there to watch the group. Three sets of arms and three laps are available for holding, cuddling, and comforting.

For toddlers, age twelve months to three years, an effective, affordable ratio is five children per teacher. This ratio works especially well if one teacher functions as the coordinator. With a group of twenty toddlers, for example, there would be four teachers. If the twenty toddlers were divided into three groups of six or seven, the remaining teacher would be designated as coordinator. The coordinator's jobs may include changing diapers, making bottles, answering telephone inquiries, getting rooms ready for meals and naps, interacting with parents, and performing other tasks. This system allows the classroom teachers to attend directly and constantly to the six or seven children in their care. Teachers may enjoy taking turns as the coordinator, or it may be the job of the director or supervisor.

Because problem solving casts the teacher in the role of facilitator, she needs to be physically close to the children when there is a problem. If the teacher is distracted by diapering or other tasks in one part of the room and two toddlers are struggling over a toy in another part of the room, she is unable to respond immediately. She is also unable to leave a child on the changing table to attend to a biting child or to a child who is dumping several baskets of toys on the floor. When there is a coordinator who is free to change the diaper or bring the bottle, the classroom teacher can respond quickly to situations that need immediate attention. While diapering, the coordinator also has the opportunity to form a nurturing relationship with the child on an individual basis.

In an area where there is a larger group of no more than ten toddlers with two teachers, one teacher can be watching the group while the other is diapering. Depending on the floor plan of the area, the ages of the toddlers, and the efficiency of the teachers, this sort of arrangement may work well. To accommodate problem solving, the important factor is that a teacher be available to be nearby and watching at all times.

When children become preschool age, four and five, the ratio may change dramatically. Ten preschoolers with one teacher in an area where all can be seen at the same time can be an effective group. Without diapers to change or bottles to make, the teacher can supervise more easily. A group of ten children with one teacher or twenty with two teachers is appropriate for this age because the children are extremely social and need many choices for making friends. If the group is too small, the choice of friends is limited and some children may not find special playmates. If the children have been part of a problem-solving program most of their lives, supervising them is even easier for the teacher. Such children are competent and capable of solving many of their problems without any teacher intervention at all.

## The Intergenerational Environment

The enriched, diverse environment described above is needed for problem solving. Joan Whitley adds the following information concerning an appropriate environment for the intergenerational program.

> The intergenerational environment must have in it families of dolls that represent family members of all ages, including grandparents. It is important to have books with stories of children and grandparents. They should depict older adults as they might really look, with the full range of human sizes, temperaments, and appearances. The older adult may be the hero of the story, or the story may explain the condition of a failing grandparent who no longer remembers the names of people in the family. All views are important. If you are fortunate, your program may be able to locate a real wheelchair. A small adult size will allow children to learn about all the parts—brakes, wheels, foot rests—and they can become proficient at rolling themselves (Figure 2.19). Often you can find pretend wheelchairs, walkers, or canes as well. Include photos with the children and elders in the programs. You can easily and economically turn a photo into a poster. Such a poster will provide affirmation for the children.
>
> Adult furniture should be incorporated into the environment. Adult chairs that are fairly firm to sit in, and nonskid and have arms for pushing off from while getting up make it easier for older adults to visit the children's rooms. You will also need an adult-height table that easily allows a wheelchair to roll up close enough for an older adult to take part in a table game or a cooking activity. Whenever possible, allow space in a children's room for a person in a wheelchair to visit. Wheelchairs do take up more space, and the older adult will not want to feel like he or she is in the way. Be flexible, because older adults, like all of us, sometimes change their minds. Some prefer to watch from a distance and not feel like they are intruding. Others will want to get close so they can hear what the children are saying.
>
> The teaching staff is the part of the environment that helps elders feel comfortable in the children's areas. The teacher should be inviting and openly friendly whenever someone comes to visit. Teachers make the introductions between children and elders, tell the elders what the children are doing, invite

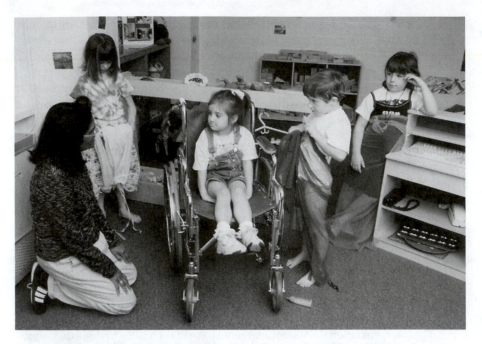

**Figure 2.19**    *A wheelchair helps children identify with their older adult friends.*

the elders to join in, and remember to include them in conversation, reminding them of a child's name or interpreting a child's intentions. When the children visit the elder's area, they should also find an environment that is child-safe. A nursing center that is worth visiting will be safe for elders as well as children. It is always wise, however, to make a quick, visual check of any environment you will bring young children into.

## Modifying the Environment

It is a rainy day. It has been raining, in fact, for several days. Ms. Smith has been confined to her room with her ten preschoolers, ages four and five, during the rainy spell. She feels she has used up all her ideas for activities, and her group really needs a greater level of physical activity. Until the rain stops, she sees little chance for that kind of active play to take place. She is at her wit's end. What can she do? A technique called "modifying the environment" may help.[3]

Modifying the environment is a simple yet often overlooked technique for responding to children's inappropriate behavior. Every teacher knows what it is like to spend a rainy day indoors with a group of active, boisterous, and perhaps irritable youngsters. In some parts of the country, the weather keeps children indoors much more than they and their teachers tolerate comfortably. Other complications may also curtail or disrupt daily activity in a children's center. Transition times, such as the time just before lunch, for example, may be especially stressful when hungry children are waiting expectantly for their meals. The time before and after naps may be difficult for some children, as are their times to be dropped off at and picked up from the center. Moving from one area to another may also prove stressful, especially for young toddlers.

The idea of modifying the environment may be new to some teachers. Rather than change the environment to meet the children's needs in a certain situation, the tendency may be to fit the children into the existing environment. By modifying the environment, however, teachers can forestall a great deal of inappropriate behavior by the children. Changing the surroundings requires some work from the teacher; sometimes planning ahead is necessary, but it is well worth the effort.

## How to Modify the Environment

There are many ways to modify an environment. Some that are mentioned in *Parent Effectiveness Training* include childproofing, simplifying, restricting, enriching, and impoverishing. The first three should already be incorporated into any environment that is child-centered. Because they have been mentioned previously, I review them only briefly here to lay a foundation for the last two modifications, which I discuss in greater detail in the remainder of this chapter.

*Childproofing*   An environment that has been made childproof has been modified by providing equipment that is safe and furniture that is child-sized and by eliminating items that are toxic or breakable, have small pieces, or are likely to be damaged. Unlike the child's home, the children's center should be a place where there is no reason to say, "No, don't touch that." Childproofing includes covering electrical outlets and meeting other requirements imposed by licensing agencies.

*Simplifying*   Children in programs should be able to function as independently as possible. Toys should be in good condition and work as intended; puzzles should have all their pieces; spindle toys, all their parts; and the pegboard, all its pegs. Materials are best kept on low shelves, easily accessible, so children can reach them without having to depend on the teacher for everything. A trash basket, paper towels, soap, toilets, and sinks should also be easy to reach and use with a minimum of help. Anything that is unnecessary or unusable, causes crowding, provokes pushing or fighting, or inhibits normal play should be eliminated from the environment.

*Restricting Play Areas*   The environment should have a variety of play areas, including places for noisy, active play and spaces for quiet, more passive play. Some areas may accommodate the entire group all at once; others may be limited to the number of children they can hold. Some areas may require more supervision by the teacher than others. The children should be made aware of their choices from among the different play areas and feel free to pick the one they prefer whenever possible.

## Enriching the Environment

Picture a teacher and seven toddlers in a room. It is fifteen minutes before lunchtime, and many of the children are hungry. They are not verbal enough to express their hunger, but they can cry, whine, or demand to be held. Some children are easily provoked by others and may start a fight. Their attention spans are also shorter than usual. What can the teacher do to alleviate this situation? If the children become restless and unhappy almost every day shortly before lunch, perhaps the teacher should serve lunch earlier. For those times when the toddlers are just restless or bored, she might try to redirect their attention by enriching the environment.

Enriching the environment is a simple, effective technique that experienced teachers use intuitively. The teacher observes what is happening in her classroom, evaluates the options, and adds something that was not previously there. In this case, the teacher realizes that because it is almost lunchtime some children are especially hungry, as they demonstrate by their behavior. She evaluates certain factors, such as the short amount of time before lunch and the children's short attention span, and decides to add singing to the environment.

Singing is her choice for several reasons. It is a cohesive activity, drawing the attention of all the children; children generally love to sing songs. Singing requires them to use their voices, so it takes the place of crying or whining. And because children's songs are short, singing can accommodate their shortened attention spans. Singing is also such a happy activity that few children can remain sad or frustrated while doing it. It fits into the time frame; fifteen minutes is a good length of time for toddlers to sing. Last, singing is extremely versatile; it can include dancing, clapping, marching, and even playing rhythm instruments (Figure 2.20).

What other enrichment of the environment would be appropriate for a room full of hungry toddlers? The teacher could put paper and crayons or markers on the table and invite the children to express their feelings on paper. Drawing can be almost therapeutic for some children and will distract them from their hunger. Materials for drawing activities can also be cleared away quickly. Remember, however, to give the children some warning when it is time to finish, so they will have a chance to complete their drawings. A physical activity, such as rolling, jumping, or playing leapfrog on a gymnastic mat (or an old mattress), will also distract, keep the group together, and allow for the safe expression of frustration. It requires no preparation or cleanup and can be accomplished in a small amount of time. Puzzles are also good for gathering a group together and holding the children's interest. The

**Figure 2.20**    *Music in all of its forms enriches the environment.*

teacher can set aside certain puzzles and not use them daily so they will remain new and interesting. They should be very easy ones unless the teacher is willing to finish them when lunch arrives.

How would enriching the environment help Ms. Smith with her ten preschoolers who are trapped by the rain? She knows that they need some physical outlets but feels that she has exhausted all the options. Here are a few ideas she may not have considered. First, she could simply take her group out in the rain. It is a good idea for any children's center to keep rubber boots on hand for wet weather. They will cost a few dollars but are reusable, and a walk in the rain is well worth the cost. If there are no rubber boots, however, plastic garbage bags may be used for improvising both boots and raincoats. For a raincoat, use a large garbage bag; cut a hole for the head and two for arms. A smaller plastic bag can be tied or taped over each shoe to make boots. Just remember that plastic bags should never be left within the children's reach when the bags are not in use.

As an alternative to going outdoors, Ms. Smith can enrich her environment in other ways. Does she have available a gymnastics mat? The mat alone (or an old mattress) will inspire active play among preschoolers. Is there a parachute for playing parachute games? If the room is large enough, parachute games may be played indoors. The parachute can also become a tent; you can either hang it from the ceiling or spread it over chairs or other

**Figure 2.21**   *A tunnel provides active play on a rainy day, then folds up flat.*

furniture. Preschoolers love such improvised tents and will play in them for long periods of time. If there is any other large muscle equipment to be found in the center, perhaps it could be borrowed for the preschoolers to use for an hour or two. You may be able to trade one piece of equipment for another among the classrooms (Figure 2.21).

As with the toddlers, music works wonders. Dancing with or without scarves, a marching band with rhythm instruments, moving to a children's exercise record, and singing songs all provide physical outlets that are fun. Imaginative props such as a box of dress-up clothes with low high-heel shoes, cowboy or cowgirl boots, uniforms from fast-food restaurants, short nightgowns, hats, and wigs will inspire animated, creative play. Leftover Halloween masks or paper bag masks stir even more inspiration. All these items are found at thrift stores and garage sales at minimal cost.

Another imaginative activity appropriate for a rainy day, or any other day, is using real tools. This activity requires an area that is easily swept. The floor should be covered with newspaper or a plastic tarp and should be relatively indestructible. The tools should be genuine but in the smaller sizes that are available. Small hammers and saws are relatively easy to find. Other tools, such as pliers, sandpaper holders, files, and small wrenches, fit well in a preschooler's hand. Screwdrivers or any tools with pointed ends are not recommended, although a screwdriver with a very short shaft is relatively

**Figure 2.22**   *Round up the "babies" to bathe on a rainy day.*

safe. Some thick boards are needed, along with nails with wide heads for nailing. If the center can accommodate sawing indoors, a four-by-four piece of lumber is needed or, even better, a section of log from a tree. Pliers and wrenches may be used to "repair" tricycles or other items in the room. Strict supervision is needed with hammers and saws. Children must learn to hold the saw handle with both hands at all times to avoid having accidents.

For bad weather days, a small wading pool filled with either sand or water may be set up indoors in an easily cleaned part of the room. Children of preschool age are capable of using both substances responsibly and cleaning up after their use. Many toys found elsewhere in the room or building can be played with in sand or water. One of the all-time water play favorites is giving the dolls a bath (Figure 2.22). All the washable dolls are rounded up, and each child is given a piece of cloth or sponge, a piece of soap from a bar that has been cut up, and a towel. Preschoolers can spend a long time washing their dolls.

Another idea Ms. Smith may have overlooked for enriching the environment is to clear out a big space in the room and bring in some of the riding toys that are normally kept outdoors. Children may have to take turns (they can decide how long), but they will certainly welcome this type of physical activity. Balls are also usually kept outside, but on a rainy day why not bring one or two indoors? They can be rolled for games played in a circle on the floor or tossed short distances. Limits should be set so the balls do not knock down objects.

A last suggestion for Ms. Smith is that she organize games that are usually played outdoors. Most can be adapted for a reasonably large room. Such games include "Duck, Duck, Goose," "Doggie, Doggie, Where's Your Bone," "London Bridge," "Red Rover," "The Farmer in the Dell," "Here We Go Round the Mulberry Bush," and "Mother, May I?" Newer books feature games in which children cooperate so that everyone wins and no one loses. *Everybody Wins* includes a cooperative version of "Musical Chairs."

Many of these activities may also be adapted for toddlers on rainy days. Plastic tools, rather than real ones, are more appropriate, but the other activities mentioned work equally well with toddlers and preschoolers.

How do infants react to long periods of rain, snow, or other reasons for confinement? If they are accustomed to going outdoors every day, and they should be, they will soon miss the stimulation of the changes in light and temperature, the smell of the outdoors, the feel of grass or dirt, and the outdoor activities. Like older children, infants respond well to an enriched environment. In fact, some of the rainy-day activities for older children can be easily adapted for infants. Many of the rhythm instruments will fit in an infant's hand, and the sound will fascinate him. Music of any kind appeals to infants. Plastic tools that provide a banging sound will also appeal. Sand and water may be brought indoors for infants, as may infant-sized riding toys. Foam rubber balls will challenge and intrigue older infants. Every infant program should already have indoor large muscle equipment for motivating infants to crawl, climb, roll, and walk. This is especially important on days when infants cannot go outside.

Many excellent books that describe activities for infants, toddlers, and preschoolers are available. A number of these activities will enrich the environment. The wise teacher will keep a file of ideas for rainy days, hungry times, boring times, and other stressful periods when the environment needs enrichment.

## Impoverishing the Environment

At times, such as before and after naps, children may need help feeling relaxed, secure, and comforted. When they are tired or sleepy, they lose control and feel vulnerable. They are reminded of home and feel their parents' absence more acutely. At nap time, you want children to rest well and, if possible, fall asleep, so stimulation is to be avoided in favor of quiet play or more soothing activities. As they awaken, their transition from sleep to play should be gradual and calm. Few people enjoy being hurried on awakening.

Although young children would probably choose to be held and cuddled when they are sleepy, this is usually not feasible when you are working with a group. In the infant section, perhaps, where there are fewer babies for

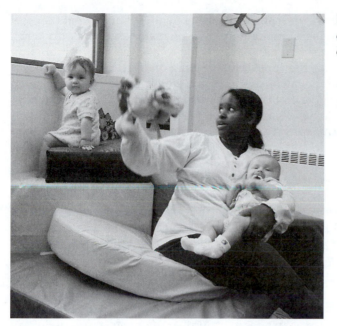

**Figure 2.23** *This environment allows for climbing and being held.*

each teacher, this might be possible. Infants demand and deserve to be held whenever this can be done (Figure 2.23). The ideal is the same for young toddlers, but the teacher:child ratio seldom allows for every child to be held at nap time. You can use other ways, however, to assure that each child feels secure and cared for at nap time. Although Gordon refers to the process as impoverishing the environment,[4] what you actually do is reduce or eliminate noise, active play, or anything that would excite or stimulate sleepy children. Richness still remains in the intimate and comforting relationship between teacher and child.

The hungry child needs temporary distraction from hunger until the food arrives, but the sleepy child needs to surrender to his sleepiness. The teacher who is caring for six or seven toddlers or ten preschoolers in a classroom just before nap time needs strategies for inducing rest but not sleep until the child is on his sleeping mat or cot. If the children must wait for someone to bring their mats or cots and change their diapers, there may be a short period of time when they should remain awake but ready for sleep. Some transitional activities, such as the following, may help.

Music seems a good place to begin. As well as providing stimulation, music comforts and soothes. Classical music has an especially calming effect on children, and it is never too soon to introduce them to Mozart, Beethoven, Brahms, and the other masters. With classical music playing in the background, the teacher might improvise a bedtime story or read a book with a restful theme. Children of preschool age may enjoy describing what they feel when the music is playing or making up their own stories, using only whispering voices. The teacher may instead decide to ask the children to sway gently to the music while they are sitting or lying on the floor.

Story time itself is a way of subduing the environment while enriching it. Focusing on a story, the child forgets about the stimulation surrounding her and withdraws into her own imagination. As she indulges her fantasies, the world around her melts away. She relaxes and becomes ready for sleep to envelop her. Stories that are read at nap time should be carefully chosen so they do not invoke anxiety or fear or provide too much stimulation.

Quiet conversation with children who are verbal may be comforting to them at nap time. Because they feel vulnerable and miss their own home and bed, some children are eager to talk about things they do at home and about parents, siblings, and pets. If the noise level is kept low, this is a wonderful way for children to share their feelings, learn about each other, and provide their own comfort.

When it is actually time for sleeping, it is important that teachers are available to pat, rock, stroke, rub backs, and otherwise help children, especially toddlers and infants, fall asleep. Because it is the children's most vulnerable time, the presence of an adequate number of caring staff is necessary for the children to feel secure. Although adults need a break from watching children and money can be saved by decreasing staff during nap time, the first concern should always be the children's comfort and feelings. Almost all infants and toddlers and most preschoolers need rest and sleep in the afternoon, and the human touch makes the difference in whether they get it.

Impoverishing, or subduing, the environment is useful at other times, also. Many children are affected by an environment filled with too many things—too many toys to choose from on overcrowded shelves, too many pictures to look at on the walls, too much noise, color, or motion. When a group is behaving in an unusually boisterous way, and the behavior is inappropriate or disruptive, the teacher will benefit from a quick evaluation of the environment. Removing the possible causes may bring an instant change in children's behavior. However, the group may need a cooling-off period or a dramatic change, such as moving outdoors, before the modification takes effect.

At certain times of the year, the environment may benefit from reduction simply by avoiding the stimulation in the outside world. The Christmas season is one such time, perhaps even the main one. No matter what the religions of the families of children in the center, children appear to endure the whole ordeal surrounding Christmas much better if their daily routine is maintained and their environment remains calm and neutral.

Christmas puts enormous pressure on young children and causes them much stress. There is all the extra shopping, being dragged from mall to mall, and being expected to sit on some huge, frightening, red-clad man's lap and act as if he were a dear friend. Then there are the threats and promises, depending on good behavior; visits to and from relatives; parents fighting over those visits and possibly over money; and television at its worst, instilling greed and frustration with every commercial. Children are bombarded at Christmas time, and it shows in their actions. They tend to react to overstimulation with frustration, agitation, aggression, and other undesirable behavior.

Signs of Christmas are practically unavoidable in the outside world, even if a family does not celebrate the holiday at all. Why subject children to more overstimulation and anxiety at the children's center? A policy of either low-level participation or nonparticipation in the frenzy will alleviate much stress for children. When the reasons for deemphasizing Christmas in the children's center are explained rationally to them, parents see the benefit to their child and are generally supportive. Other holidays that are not so blatantly commercial and stressful for children offer more low-key and, therefore, appropriate times to celebrate with activities, music, and perhaps decorations.

As with daily routines, children often require transition time when the environment is enriched or subdued. The more verbal the child is, the more information she can understand and use effectively. When foreseeable changes are made, such as taking a field trip, having a visitor, celebrating a birthday or holiday, or making other significant modifications to the environment, children respond more positively and appropriately if they are included in the planning and, if possible, the execution of the upcoming event.

## Summing Up the Problem-Solving Environment

The kind of environment provided by the children's center will determine the quality of the program. Included in the total environment are the physical site, both indoors and outdoors, the teacher staff, and the ratio of children to teachers. One feature that facilitates and supports problem solving is the child-centered classroom, with its learning centers and open and private spaces. The classroom should provide enriching experiences, numerous choices, and the possibility for solving problems; the particular needs of both genders should be considered. The outdoor area should be equally stimulating and rich with possibilities. A variety of natural materials and safe, challenging equipment encourages children to develop their problem-solving skills.

The teacher is the most important element of any environment. A teacher well versed in child development and early childhood education who has embraced the problem-solving philosophy is an asset to any program and has also enriched the teaching experience. Even the best teacher, however, is impaired if he or she is responsible for the care, nurturing, and education of too many children. Not only is a low ratio of children to teachers good for the teacher, but for children it means the difference between mere custodial care and intellectual, social, and emotional development. The problem-solving philosophy is most effectively supported when there are enough teachers to respond quickly and give time and attention to children's problem-solving situations.

In a facility that has been created especially for young children, the environment should already have been childproofed and simplified and play areas appropriately limited. Once this has been achieved, the environment can be modified in two major ways to encourage appropriate behavior: enriching and impoverishing. The teacher begins by evaluating behavior or circumstances and decides whether a change would improve the situation for the children.

When children need more stimulation than they are receiving, the teacher may enrich the environment by adding a new and stimulating activity. This need may result from bad weather, transition times, boredom, or other reasons. When the environment is too stimulating to encourage appropriate behavior (e.g., at times of sleepiness, fussiness, or approaching holidays), the teacher may impoverish the environment by toning down the amount and intensity of stimulation. In either procedure, the goal is to promote appropriate behavior through solving a problem that originates in the environment itself, a far more effective solution than attempting to fit the children into the existing environment.

## *Practice and Discussion*

1. Envision the perfect center or preschool for you. Describe it in several paragraphs, or draw up a design. Include any fantasies you have as if money were no object.

2. Visit an existing center in your area. Compare its environment with the one you have created. Do you find any similar features in your center and the center you visited?

3. Pretend that you are a child under five years of age. You have been enrolled in a new center. What needs should the center's physical environment fill for you? How does it fill your needs as a boy? As a girl?

4. Describe in detail a learning center for infants, toddlers, or preschoolers. How does it encourage making choices? What is the goal of the learning center you have chosen to describe?

5. How does the outdoor environment promote or inhibit problem solving? What elements make up an outdoor environment that supports problem solving?

6. Which qualities that a teacher needs for problem solving do you already possess? How would you improve or change yourself in order to acquire more desirable qualities?

7. Imagine yourself working with infants, toddlers, and preschoolers within your state's ratio requirements. How many of each age group would you have in your group? How would the numbers affect your capacity to care for the children?

8. What can you, as a teacher, do to improve the child care profession in general? Name at least one specific thing you can do to improve your own work situation.

9. Put yourself in Ms. Smith's place. If you are already teaching, search your center for rainy-day ideas. Make a list or card file to keep handy. If you are not already teaching, use your imagination and resources such as books to make your list or card file.

10. Evaluate your center, or look around your own home. How could either one be made more childproof, simplified, or limited to create an appropriate environment for young children?

11. Choose a situation such as the time before a meal or a transition time. List five ways to enrich the environment.

12. Choose a situation, such as nap time, that calls for impoverishing the environment. List five ways to accomplish that goal.

---

## Notes

1. Michael Gurian, *The Wonder of Boys* (New York: Tarcher/Putnam, 1997), p. 16.

2. Many of these qualities are described in Thomas Gordon, *P.E.T.: Parent Effectiveness Training* (New York: New America Library, 1975).

3. This idea comes from Gordon, *P.E.T.: Parent Effectiveness Training*. Additional terms from *P.E.T.* include childproofing, simplifying, restricting, enriching, and impoverishing the environment.

4. Gordon, *P.E.T.,* Chapter 8.

## Recommended Reading

Frost, Joe L. *Play and Playscapes.* Albany, NY: Delmar, 1992.

Gurian, Michael. *The Wonder of Boys.* New York: Tarcher/Putnam, 1997.

King, Margaret A., Anne Oberlin, and Terry Swank. *Creating a Child-Centered Day Care Environment for Two-Year-Olds.* Springfield, IL: Charles C. Thomas, 1993.

Pollack, William. *Real Boys.* New York: Henry Holt and Company, Inc., 1998.

Excellent sources for setting up environments can be requested from the following organizations:

National Association for the Education of Young Children
1834 Connecticut Ave., N.W.
Washington, DC 20009

Pacific Oaks College and Children's School
714 W. California Blvd.
Pasadena, CA 99105

# 3

# *Supervising Young Children*

When I first began working with the problem-solving philosophy, I was advised never to "turn my back on a child." Being new to this approach, I did not want to ask the obvious question, "Why not?" Instead, I imagined that, if I did, one of the children would attack me from behind! Only after working with problem solving for a while did I understand the wisdom of that advice. When children are given freedom with responsibility, the teacher must be vigilant and ready to respond immediately as a problem-solving facilitator. The foundation for a problem-solving program for young children is effective supervision. Although the goal of such a program is to teach children the skills they need for independence, freedom of expression, and acceptance of responsibility, one issue in children's programs must take precedence over all others. That issue is safety.

The teacher is, above all, mandated to create a safe and healthy environment in which children will grow and develop normally. At the end of every day, all parents expect to find their children in exactly the same condition in which they left them that morning. Of course, children can be kept safe; that is not the issue. The challenge is, rather, to keep children safe and free at the same time. Children cannot develop normally in a totally risk-free environment. They must exercise their curiosity, experience their senses, test their bodies, and approach their world in countless ways. For this, they need an enriched environment filled with possibilities for experimenting and learning. In this environment there is also need for an adult who is alert, caring, and committed to helping children stay safe. This atmosphere of freedom and safety is accomplished through effective supervision.

What is supervision? The dictionary definition uses the word "oversee," which fits the description of what problem-solving teachers do with a group of children. Their role is to watch rather than direct. There is an art to watching a group of children, responding when needed, yet allowing them to feel free and unfettered. The teacher should be perceived as a helper rather than an intruder. To the casual observer, she may not always look as if she is doing very much, but she is. This chapter describes the framework and skills teachers need for effective supervision.

## Structuring the Program

Early in the ten years that my partner and I owned and operated our center, we experimented with various structures for organizing our program. By the end of the first year, we had established a system that worked extremely well, and after that we simply took the system for granted. It was only when I began training and observing in other centers, and finally when I became the program supervisor at another center, that I became acutely aware of the importance of the program's structure and its subsequent impact on supervision.

By structure, or system, I mean the way the program is set up and organized and the way it works for both teachers and children. The quality of supervision depends not only on the skill of the teacher but also on the framework within which he or she works. Structure and organization are probably not the most inspiring part of the problem-solving philosophy, but they are essential to what is discussed in the following chapters.

In the previous chapter, in the section titled "The Teacher:Child Ratio," I touched briefly on the idea of the coordinator. I have come to believe that this concept is the key to effective supervision; therefore, I expand on the idea and discuss it more extensively in this section. In conjunction with explaining the coordinator's role, I also discuss ways to organize children into groups.

## The Coordinator

Imagine the following scene: Ms. Jones, a teacher working in a self-contained classroom with a door that closes, is responsible for seven toddlers. Seven children are within her state's legal teacher:child ratio, and some of the time she can handle them fairly well—outside on the playground, for example, or when the children are indoors and all are playing cooperatively and appropriately. What happens, however, when children need their diaper changed or need a bottle? How does she manage when tables must be cleaned off for mealtimes and children must wash their hands, eat, and brush their teeth? How does Ms. Jones deal with conflicts between some children and still supervise the others? How does she get everyone to lie down and nap at the same time?

A teacher working in these conditions cannot supervise effectively, keep children safe and free, and concurrently change diapers and meet even the physical needs of children. At those times in particular, she needs help. Many programs cannot afford to hire a second teacher for every classroom, having, for example, three classrooms, each with two teachers and seven toddlers. This arrangement would require a total of six teachers for twenty-one children. As desirable as this teacher:child ratio would be, it is too expensive for most programs. Another system that is much less costly, yet equally efficient, is to have three teachers and a coordinator.

I use the example of toddlers because their physical needs are great. They require diapers, bottles, frequent carrying, and, in general, more supervision than older children. Toddlers need a ratio of at least one adult for every five children. By adding only one teacher, the coordinator, to those three groups of toddlers, the ratio becomes roughly one to five. This system works as well with preschool-age children, especially if some are in diapers and if meals and naps are included in the program.

To explain how the coordinator system works, we continue with the example of three groups of toddlers. Whenever possible, the environment should allow for mobility among the groups so the coordinator can move from area to area. If there is one large room divided into areas by low shelves, it will need only one diaper-changing table. If the area consists of three separate rooms, some walls can be partially removed, a renovation that would be well worth the expense. Perhaps there are three separate rooms with three separate changing tables and no adjoining doors. Supervision in this case is more difficult, but still possible.

The four teachers in these three rooms or areas should rotate the coordinator's job. I have found that teachers actually enjoy having a day every week when they have a different set of duties to perform and are not actually supervising children. This provides a break in their daily routine and makes

**Figure 3.1**    *The coordinator (left) can take time to comfort a child.*

their job more challenging. The total of twenty-one toddlers is always supervised by the remaining three teachers. Their job is to be with the children: to
supervise, interact, and facilitate problem solving. They are not distracted by
diaper changing or other routine duties. They can be the teachers they want
to be.

The coordinator, meanwhile, is working hard and moving quickly, taking care of all the routine tasks. Throughout the day, she changes diapers,
gets tables ready for meals, and helps direct the flow of traffic as children
move between areas. She fills bottles and stores them in coolers with blue ice
packs, puts out the mats or cots for naps, and helps solve any problems that
arise. She comforts children, takes a sick child's temperature and calls the
parents, puts ice on a child's bite, and writes up an accident report. At the
end of the day, she is tired, but she knows that tomorrow her only job is to
supervise children as they play and learn (Figure 3.1).

To make this system work logistically and financially, it may be necessary to group children in a family-style arrangement, integrating children
from twelve months to about age three. This type of grouping makes supervision easier because a teacher has a mixture of older toddlers (easier to
supervise) and younger toddlers (more difficult to supervise), rather than
seven toddlers from twelve to eighteen months old. Toddlers in family-style
groups tend to learn from each other how to put away toys, put on their
shoes, and even use the toilet.

The coordinator system can work well with infants, with toddlers, and with preschool-age children. The concept can be adapted to fit almost any program. Initially, it might be met with some resistance from teachers, but only until they try it for several weeks and work out any problems. An important first step is developing a flexible schedule and list of duties for the coordinator, at least until everyone is familiar with the jobs to be done (Figure 3.2).

## Supervising Infants

A rapid succession of changes occurs in children during infancy. Infants under about six months need little supervision; they have little mobility. They do need holding, human contact, verbalization, and other relationship-building experiences, primarily with adults. They also need the stimulation of familiar faces, toys, and other enriching objects in their surroundings. When they are in the company of older, more mobile infants, they also need a place from which to observe the world without being fallen on, poked, pulled, or bitten.

Playpens are usually chosen with the intention of protecting younger babies from older ones. Some teachers are then tempted to stick a normal, crawling baby in the playpen to keep him from being in the path of traffic. A playpen takes up a great deal of space and is frequently overused. Any baby who is crawling or otherwise moving herself about needs as much space and freedom as possible and someone with a trained eye to watch her movements. For these reasons, I recommended in Chapter 2 that we eliminate playpens from infant programs.

Instead of a playpen, I suggest a small mattress on the floor as a safe haven for immobile babies. A cot-size mattress, three or four inches thick, may be purchased secondhand or might be donated by one of the center's families. Enclose the mattress in a zippered plastic cover and spread a colorful sheet or bedspread on top. This is a perfect place to prop an infant on a pillow or bolster. The baby is safe from older infants with riding toys and push toys and can also look around the room.

Another suggestion is a climber for older infants; the top can become a loft for immobile infants. The structure pictured in Figure 3.3 is a basic wooden climber with a platform for a roof and side enclosures of clear acrylic panels. Only babies who are not yet crawling should be confined to this loft. A playpen pad or thick quilt makes the platform warm and comfortable, and a mobile hung from the ceiling or clipped to a side rail provides an interesting focus. Teachers, who are at the child's eye level, cannot resist stopping to talk to the baby, and the baby can watch adult activity through the clear panels.

Even the youngest infant needs time outdoors every day. Cold weather requires bundling, but that should not be a deterrent to taking children outside. Infants become bored with the same four walls and are stimulated by a

**Figure 3.2** *Checklist: A Toddler Coordinator's Day\**

---

☐ Fill nursing bottles and/or cups with milk and place in cooler with blue ice.

☐ Touch base with every teacher and see if there are any pressing needs.

☐ Check to see if, when, and to whom any medications are to be given.

☐ Check and change diapers in all areas.

☐ Help teachers move their kids from indoors to outdoors as needed.

☐ Help kids trade rooms or areas as needed.

☐ Help teachers switch rooms or areas as needed.

☐ When there is a conflict, watch the other kids while the teacher facilitates negotiation.

☐ When a child is upset, watch the other kids so the teacher can comfort the upset child.

☐ Help individual kids put away their toys, go potty, get a binky or blanket, find their shoes, put on their coats, etc.

☐ Check and change diapers in all areas.

☐ Prepare for lunch or snack; arrange tables and chairs, get trays, etc.

☐ Help with group hand washing when needed.

☐ Clean up the area after the meal (especially if the area is needed for napping).

☐ Lay out the sleeping mats and blankets; cluster the older toddlers' mats for story time. Fill the nursing bottles with water.

☐ Bring in the older toddlers with a teacher to help them get ready for their nap; change their diapers if needed.

☐ Bring in younger toddlers, two at a time until you can bring in another teacher.

☐ Change younger toddlers' diapers, and put them on their mats with a teacher in between to rub backs, pat, and rock.

☐ When all of the kids are on their mats with their teachers, help pat and rub backs and rock.

☐ When all is quiet and under control, take your lunch break—you really need it!

☐ As kids wake up, change their diapers, help them dress, and take them to a waiting teacher.

☐ Put away sleeping mats.

☐ Fill bottles and cups with milk and place in cooler.

☐ Prepare for afternoon snack; arrange tables and chairs, get trays, etc.

☐ Help with group hand washing when needed.

☐ It may be time to go home, or repeat the morning routine until quitting time.

---

\* This checklist, adapted to your program, may be posted in a convenient place.

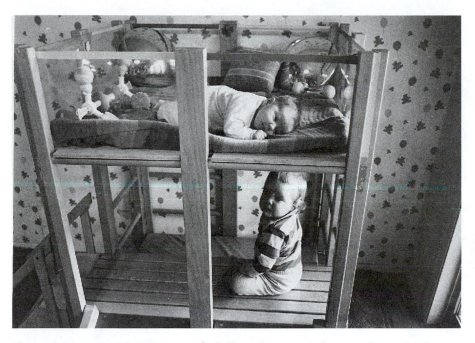

**Figure 3.3**    *A special structure can be built to give young infants a safe yet stimulating place of their own.*

change in scenery, clothing, colors, textures, and everything they sense. Crawling in the grass is a delight for children at any age, as is digging fingers and toes in the sand.

A necessary part of supervising infants is making the area safe. Even the slowest infant will quickly find any small piece of anything. Plastic tubs are excellent for keeping various categories of toys grouped on low shelves. A stable chest of drawers with easily opened lower drawers makes a practical place to keep small toys. Infants can be both entertained and challenged by learning how to open and close the drawers, although there is the possibility of an occasional pinched finger while they learn. All toys should be checked for safety features and cleanability (Figure 3.4). Anything that is unsafe for an infant should be kept on a high shelf, out of reach.

Once the area has been made safe, supervision of infants falls into two main categories. The first involves conflicts arising between two or more of the children. Chapter 5 provides information on negotiating between preverbal children. The teacher, of course, does the talking for infants and, through her actions, helps them solve their problems. The other category of supervision has to do with teaching responsibility and limits. For toddlers, responsibility consists mainly of putting away toys. Because young infants are unable to do their own picking up, the teacher models this for them and

**Figure 3.4**    *Infant toys should be safe and easy to supervise.*

enlists their aid (Figures 3.5 and 3.6). When an infant has the opportunity to imitate the teacher's actions, both physically and verbally, for a period of time, she may be able to put her toys away by the time she is one year old. I discuss this further in Chapter 6.

## Supervising Toddlers

Toddlers are generally children from over twelve months of age, who are walking, up to age two and one-half or three. During these formative years, children learn to become the people they will probably be for the rest of their lives. This thought may be somewhat dismaying until we remember that we can play a positive role in guiding them toward becoming their best selves.

Because I am talking about the safety and freedom of those in child care, this section may, at times, sound like a list of "shoulds" and "should nots." This is unintentional but hard to avoid. Supervision requires a great deal of subjective judgment on the part of the teacher, but there are also some practices that are objectively considered safe or unsafe. Most of this material applies equally to preschool-age children and toddlers. This section therefore focuses on modifications or changes in supervision techniques required by the differences in age of the children in the center.

**Figure 3.5** *When teaching an older infant or a young toddler to put away toys, the teacher begins by going through the motions. Here the teacher's hand guides the young child's hand as the child grasps and releases the toys.*

**Figure 3.6** *The teacher reinforces "putting on the shelf" with "Good work; now the pegs are put away."*

With toddlers, as well as with infants, we must begin with the environment. To allow toddlers as much freedom as they need, we must concurrently offer them the greatest degree of safety. I mentioned safety often throughout Chapter 2, and because it is so important I suggest that you take another look at your facility with safety in mind. Think about the teacher's need to supervise effectively within each area. Balance it against the child's need to explore freely and experience her environment. Correct any situation that could be unsafe. If correction is not possible, make teachers aware of a potential safety hazard and set appropriate limits with the children. Once the environment has been modified for safety, you can turn your attention to other factors related to effective supervision.

## Staying with Toddlers

It is extremely important that the teacher of toddlers stay with the group at all times, not only for safety, but also because the teacher's presence is needed for facilitating when conflicts arise between the children. Toddlers are lightning fast and can hit with a toy or bite other children swiftly and painfully. Probably more than any other age group, toddlers require constant supervision. It is also important that the teacher be aware of which children are responsible for putting away which toy; toddlers are prone to dumping toys indiscriminately while the teacher is distracted. Toddlers should never be left alone.

## Positioning of the Teacher

The position from which the teacher watches children is extremely important. The teacher stands, sits, kneels, or squats most of the time while watching toddlers, and where she places herself determines whether she can see every child in her area at once. The shape and size of the room, the types of activities in it, and the toddlers' ages determine where the teacher should be. If the room is square, for example, and contains a puzzle corner with many puzzle pieces, the teacher may feel more effective kneeling or sitting near the puzzles. This position makes it easier for her to notice which child has which puzzle and to give help and encouragement when they are needed. The teacher will still be able to see children doing other things in other parts of the room. If the room is square, everything is easy to see. If there are painting easels in one area, the greatest need may be to stay near the very young toddler painters. If, however, the painters are older toddlers who know about putting on aprons and painting only on the paper, the teacher may feel that another area needs closer watching.

Positioning is especially important when there is only one teacher in the area. Her attention may be drawn away from the group as a whole when she attends to a problem. The problem may be as simple as tying a child's shoelaces or checking a diaper. In those situations, the teacher bends or

**Figure 3.7** *The teacher positions herself at the child's eye level to see all the children at once.*

squats to the child's eye level, uses her hands, and still watches the other children (Figure 3.7). In a more demanding, complex situation, such as attending to a fight between children, she maneuvers both herself and the fighting children into a position from which she can attend to the fight and watch the others in the group at the same time. If there are two teachers in an area, the one who is attending to the fight signals to the other to watch the whole group while the first teacher helps solve the problem. The second teacher circulates, observing the group. With time and training, any good teacher can develop these skills.

## Circulating in the Play Area

In conjunction with positioning, circulating is an important supervision technique. When the teacher is not needed close to the puzzles or the easels, she moves around the room or playground, watching all the children and touching base with them. Without interfering in their play, she reinforces appropriate behavior, notices problems, remembers who is playing with what, and gives a word of encouragement. This technique is especially effective if there is only one teacher in the area or if the other teacher is facilitating a problem. While circulating, the teacher makes sure she is able to see all the children at once. None of the children are behind her as she moves. In time, this becomes second nature.

## Affirmations

Noticing the positive things children do and sending positive "I-messages," making contact in a warm and affectionate way, reinforcing appropriate behavior, and narrating what is happening are different ways of saying the same thing. All are means of communicating attention, acceptance, and approval of the child. This may not seem like a supervision technique, but it is one of the most effective. Children inherently and naturally want to please their parents and teachers. They also want to be included in whatever other children are getting. One of the most powerful tools for eliciting appropriate behavior from anyone is to comment on how well he or she is doing. It is also a powerful tool for eliciting appropriate behavior from a group. If you casually mention to one of the children that you like the way she is sitting quietly, waiting for a story, everyone else will say, "I'm sitting quietly, too" and will at least try. Chapter 7 contains greater detail about giving affirmations.

## Concentrating and Staying Alert with Toddlers

Toddlers are extremely curious, fast, and oral people. The younger ones investigate everything with their mouths. Some express anger with their mouths by biting other children. Watching such a group requires concentration above all. It is very similar to driving a car; you must keep your eyes on the road while doing other things. While you are concentrating on the children, you must stay alert. Have toys been left where children may trip over them? Is anyone eating the playdough? Is a conflict building between children? Concentration may also take the form of observation. This is one way teachers become better acquainted with and more knowledgeable about their children.

Conversations of a personal nature between teachers will most certainly distract them from supervising children, as will long conversations with parents who are picking up their children. Teachers must learn how to retreat gracefully from these types of distractions. Usually a lighthearted "Oh, oh, I'd better watch the kids" will do the trick. If a parent needs information or is looking for a child's shoes or jacket, the teacher can say, "The coordinator will help you with that in just a minute," and then move away from the parent toward the child who needs some attention. Parents appreciate teachers who are involved with watching the children in their care. They know that their child will be watched just as carefully.

## Supervising Risk Taking by Toddlers

Children are forever growing and testing their minds and bodies. They challenge themselves to try the next level of any given activity. Only the child

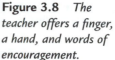

**Figure 3.8** *The teacher offers a finger, a hand, and words of encouragement.*

himself knows when he is ready for that next level. Taking periodic risks is necessary for normal development. We know from experience that a child rarely takes risks unless he feels confident about the outcome. Some built-in intuition alerts him to when his body is coordinated enough to try climbing to the top of the ladder and going down the slide. It may take a while. The child may cry, whine, and complain while climbing yet insist that he can do it by himself. Arriving at the top of the ladder, he gains a wonderful sense of achievement. He did it himself! He may repeat the same struggle going down the slide or even decide he is not ready for that. Either way, he must make the decision (Figure 3.8).

Effective supervision requires learning to know each child as an individual. This enables the teacher to react appropriately to the child as he challenges his body. Balancing the child's need to take a risk against the safety of taking that risk requires a judgment by the teacher. In a safe environment, the teacher's primary reaction may simply be to stay close to the child as he tries to climb the ladder and to give him verbal encouragement when needed. The teacher should provide a minimum of physical help when a child is challenging his body. The victory then belongs to the child alone; if he decides it is too risky, that decision is his, too. He will try again when he feels ready.

Here are some examples of supervising risk taking in toddlers.

***The First Jump***   Juanita is thirty months old. For several months, she has been jumping from a low table to a mat on the floor. She has become quite good at making that jump. But Juanita also watches toddlers her age who are ready to take greater risks. They climb to the top of the indoor climbing structure and, after sitting perched on the top rung, jump to the mat. Juanita admires them. She also climbs to the top frequently, but so far she has not been ready to jump.

Today Juanita announces that she is going to jump off the climber. The teacher watches her and moves close as Juanita climbs. The teacher makes sure there are no other children on the mat. She also makes sure that Juanita is not carrying a toy but has both hands available for climbing.

When Juanita reaches the top rung of the climber, she balances herself and looks uncertain. The teacher remains close, ready to help if needed, encouraging Juanita verbally. Only if the situation becomes unsafe will the teacher intervene. It is Juanita's decision to challenge herself, and the teacher respects that decision.

Juanita seems a bit unsteady. The teacher places a hand behind her without touching her. Finally, Juanita lets go and jumps. She lands safely on the mat. How proud she is that she jumped all by herself!

***Stuck at the Top***   Antoine, age two, is also ready to climb, but to the top of the outdoor dome. For Antoine, simply getting to the top is risk enough. When he looks down, he realizes how high up he has climbed and cannot figure out how to get down.

ANTOINE:  I stuck. I stuck.

TEACHER:  You really are stuck at the top. Can you think of how to get down?

ANTOINE:  I stuck. I stuck.

TEACHER:  Try to remember where your foot was when you climbed to the top. Can you see where you put your foot?

*Antoine looks down at the bar below him. Going down is usually harder than climbing up. When he tries to put his foot on the lower bar, he begins to lose his balance. The teacher continues to encourage him verbally, but Antoine begins to cry.*

TEACHER:  Here's my finger. Will that help?

*Antoine reaches for the finger but finds it inadequate for maintaining his balance.*

TEACHER:  How about a hand?

*Antoine grasps the teacher's hand and finally feels secure enough to come down. As soon as he no longer needs the hand, the teacher withdraws it and gives him positive reinforcement.*

## Supervising Toddlers Putting Things Away

There are several reasons for expecting children to put away their clothing and toys when they have finished with these items. Having to put things away is one of the earliest ways for children to learn responsibility through cause and effect. There is an association between making a mess and cleaning it up that children cannot learn in any way other than putting away their own clothes and toys. Toddlers can understand this association by the time they are twelve or fourteen months of age. Putting things away also accomplishes goals such as keeping the area safe and orderly, making the area a more inviting place to play, and eliminating clutter that may cause overstimulation. As a side effect of putting things away, children learn that objects have categories. Beads go in the container with other beads; pegs go in the peg container; spindle toys have pieces that fit on the spindle in a certain way. Some things belong in one place; some belong in another. This type of learning through experience is a forerunner of learning to read and mastering mathematics.

While you are supervising a group of toddlers, remember which child took out each toy. When they have finished with toys, children may need a reminder about putting away their playthings. Several ways to remind children are given in Chapter 6.

## Facilitating Routines and Transitions

Every day includes certain times when change must take place and children are required to respond as a group. Generally these are the same every day and are known as "routines" and "transitions." A routine is a set of procedures we follow to perform a task. A familiar routine for children is washing their hands before a meal. Brushing their teeth is another routine, as is getting on a sleeping mat to take a nap (Figure 3.9).

A transition is the change from play to routine and routine to play. Moving from indoor to outdoor play is also a transition, as is moving from play to circle time. The younger and newer a child is in the program, the more difficult it may be for him to make a smooth transition. Infant transitions usually occur on an individual basis; seldom do we move infants as a group. One function of effective supervision is helping each child make a transition with the least amount of distress. Teachers should always plan routines and transitions ahead of time so that the children will react predictably and consistently.

**Figure 3.9**  *Scraping the plate after the meal is part of the mealtime routine.*

Children should be allowed adequate time to prepare for a change. Begin about ten minutes before the actual transition by saying "You have five minutes until clean-up time." After the five minutes, say "It's time to put away toys for lunch." Children do not react instantly, so their response is much more cooperative if they are adequately warned.

Meal and nap times remind children of their home and parents. Often during these times, toddlers cry or have tantrums. Some of this behavior is avoidable, and some is not. The best way to avoid upsets is to be well organized. Children feel more secure when transitions are predictable and consistent. Familiarity gives them a degree of control over the situation. The coordinator and teachers can help children through these times by being especially alert and aware of what should come next in the routine and reacting quickly and appropriately.

Routines and transitions are generally not negotiable, so it is important to explain to children what is happening and what will happen next. You may have to set some limits with a routine. For example, all children wash their hands before eating; some children may resist, but they have no choice. When you narrate and describe the process beforehand, you can usually elicit their cooperation during transitions: "We're using soap to take off the germs; now we're rinsing off the soap; here's the paper towel; it's time to sit at the table." Chapter 6 presents ideas for setting limits during routines and transitions.

## Supervising Preschool Children

By the time most children reach four years of age, especially if they have been in a program for some time, they are very independent, self-reliant, and verbally articulate. They have better control over their emotions than do toddlers. Preschoolers are full of ideas, most of which their bodies are capable of carrying out. Some of their qualities make supervision easier; some make it more difficult.

Many of the procedures for supervising preschool children are the same as those for supervising toddlers, although modified to coincide with the preschooler's growing maturity. As with toddlers, safety is of the utmost importance. Evaluate the safety of your preschool area by remembering that many preschoolers will rise to any challenge and try anything that looks feasible. There is a daredevil in almost any group. Keep him or her in mind.

The teacher of preschool-age children will probably have a larger group to supervise than does a toddler teacher. Most licensing regulations require a higher ratio of teachers to toddlers than to preschool-age children. Some programs that last only a few hours a day are not restricted by any licensing regulations and may have any number of children per teacher. The problem-solving philosophy works best, however, with a maximum of ten preschoolers to each adult. Keeping ten children safe and free is, at best, demanding work. It is unfair to both teacher and children to place a greater burden of responsibility on the teacher.

### Staying with Preschoolers

Preschool children need the constant presence of a facilitator in the classroom or playground. The preschool teacher, however, is usually able to give attention to several children out of the group without having chaos erupt among the others. If the teacher is positioned carefully with the few children who need immediate attention, she will be able to keep an eye on everyone. Because there are no diapers or bottles to contend with, the coordinator may be needed less in the preschool area than in the rooms for younger children. Because the area for the preschoolers will probably function as a relatively self-contained unit, the teachers would be wise to arrange some method of communication when necessary, such as an intercom system, so no teacher will have to leave any group. Preschoolers are great deliverers of notes and runners of errands and take pride in being chosen for such responsible tasks.

### Giving Affirmations, Positioning, and Circulating

The positioning of the preschool teacher makes a difference in the teacher's readiness to act as a facilitator. Whether in the classroom or on the playground, a teacher of problem solving places herself where she can observe all the children at once and circulates among them like a host or hostess at a

**Figure 3.10**    *It is important that the teacher know when to watch and when to intervene.*

cocktail party. She communicates periodically in some unintrusive way with each child in her group. During these brief encounters, she can let the children know with a phrase or two that she notices their activities. These moments may be used for positive reinforcement, enhancing a learning experience, or engaging in casual conversation.

## Concentrating and Staying Alert with Preschoolers

Although preschoolers are not as likely as toddlers to put objects in their mouth, there are other reasons for the teacher to concentrate and remain alert. Preschoolers are physically stronger and have learned more ways to be aggressive; some have even learned how to be devious. When these characteristics are channeled appropriately and tempered with maturity, they become valuable attributes. In some four-year-olds, however, these characteristics can manifest themselves in a certain amount of pushing, hitting, excluding, teasing, name-calling, and tattling. The problem-solving philosophy addresses all these behaviors but depends a great deal on the teacher's presence on the scene as facilitator. The teacher's role is to be aware of problems and be readily available when needed (Figure 3.10).

## Supervising Risk Taking by Preschoolers

Preschoolers are generally in good control of their bodies and will risk only what they feel sure of accomplishing. Neither adults nor children hurt themselves intentionally. If equipment is as safe as possible and the teacher is close by, preschoolers need very few restrictions on their physical experimentation. Some basic limits such as using both hands for climbing, holding onto handles, and keeping hard objects out from under climbing structures are probably adequate. Remember to notice children's risk taking and give them lots of encouragement.

Here are some examples of supervising risk taking by preschoolers.

*Headfirst Down the Slide*    Three-year-old Damion has been watching the bigger preschoolers go down the slide. Some of them are going down headfirst, landing on their hands at the bottom. Damion laughs as they land and jumps with excitement. After the bigger kids run off to play elsewhere, Damion climbs the stairs to the top of the slide. He stays at the top for a long time, changing his position frequently. He is trying to find the best position from which to go down the slide headfirst. Finally, he's in the right position and starts sliding before he is ready. Halfway down the slide, Damion panics. He grabs the sides and begins to scream.

The teacher, who has been watching Damion along with the other preschoolers, responds to his cries, positioning herself so she can see the other children at the same time. As they interact, Damion continues to cry.

TEACHER:  Looks like there's a problem. This must be pretty scary.

DAMION:  I want to get down!

TEACHER:  Are you stuck?

DAMION:  Yeah. I want to get down!

TEACHER:  How can you do it?

DAMION:  I can't. You help me.

TEACHER:  What will happen if you let go?

DAMION:  I can't.

TEACHER:  I'm sure you can do this by yourself, but I can give you a finger. Will that help?

The teacher offers her finger to Damion, but he refuses it and starts inching down the slide. Because he slides down so slowly, he comes to the end and dangles there with his head hanging over. He's still crying. The teacher compliments Damion on going down the slide without her help. When Damion realizes he's at the bottom, he stops crying, reaches out his hands, eases himself to the ground, gets up, and runs off, proudly telling his friends about his great experience.

*Standing on the Swing*    Three preschool girls, Alicia, Lena, and Winnie, are on the tire swing. They know how to make the swing go fast and are swinging faster and faster. They are all holding tightly to the chains that connect the swing to the frame. As they swing, Alicia becomes very brave and stands up. She is still holding the chain very tightly, but now she looks frightened. The teacher notices the look on Alicia's face and calmly asks, "Are you okay, Alicia?" There is no answer as Alicia hangs on tightly. The other two girls continue to swing and look up at Alicia expectantly. The teacher moves closer to the swing. She is worried that Alicia will panic but only asks again, "Alicia, are you okay?" Alicia finally nods yes and suddenly breaks out in a grin. She is extremely pleased with herself. "Look at me," she calls out. "I'm standing up!" "You did it!" responds the teacher. "You're standing up on the swing."

Although Alicia had looked frightened and the teacher had been a bit apprehensive, she gave Alicia the chance to challenge herself and take a risk. The teacher provided Alicia the opportunity to say she wanted to come down but did not intervene. If Alicia had shown greater fear and had wanted to get off the swing, the teacher was close enough to react swiftly.

*Walking the Log*    On the playground is a fallen log that the preschool children love to climb. Calvin, age five, has been climbing on it for years. So far he has not tried to walk along the log. A few of his friends have been able to balance themselves well enough to walk the length of the log, but Calvin has only made some minor attempts.

Calvin's teacher notices that Calvin has spent a long time on the log this morning. He has stood up a number of times and looked around to see whether anyone was watching. The teacher is curious, and because the other children are playing appropriately she approaches Calvin and talks to him.

TEACHER:  It looks like you're enjoying the log today.

CALVIN:  I've been trying to walk on it.

TEACHER:  You're ready to give it a try?

CALVIN:  Yeah, I want to.

TEACHER:  Is it better if I stand here or closer?

CALVIN:  You stay there. I can do it myself.

Calvin takes a few wobbly steps. He looks unsure of himself. The teacher walks along with him yet keeps her distance. Calvin stops several times and starts again. The teacher quietly encourages him.

Will Calvin walk the entire length of the log? If he doesn't do it today, he will walk down the whole log another day soon. He can feel his teacher's unintrusive encouragement and knows that, if he falls off the log, he can get help. If he does make it to the end, he will have done it by himself and will feel a great sense of achievement.

**Figure 3.11** *Rough-and-tumble play takes many forms.*

## Supervising "Rough-and-Tumble" Play

An important part of socializing, especially for boys, is what is called "rough-and-tumble" play. Actually, it defies description, but it generally consists of wrestling; falling on top of each other; bumping into other children; noisily grunting, growling, and yelling; making karate-type movements; and running around. Sometimes this kind of play is connected with imitating and role-playing superheroes or other popular television characters of the day. In that case, the boys may pretend to shoot or "kill" in other ways. This kind of play is commonly restricted and even forbidden by many programs, perhaps because most teachers are women and are uncomfortable with any semblance of violence. Consequently, the environment is not arranged to accommodate such activity, and the activity becomes disruptive and problematic.

Boys express affection for one another and challenge themselves through rough-and-tumble play. They compete, compare their strength and courage to those of their friends, work off their aggressive energy, and establish a group framework that rewards leadership. They are trying on various roles to see which fit them comfortably. Because preschool-age boys are typically more physical than verbal, they act out their fantasies in physical ways. Boys are rehearsing and practicing to be the men they hope to become (Figure 3.11).

Girls also rehearse and practice for adult roles, but generally speaking their role playing does not disrupt the class or annoy the teacher to any degree. Most complaints I hear about children are definitely slanted toward boys. Boys are scolded, restrained, and punished for what should be considered normal boy behavior; we do not yet fully understand the long-term ramifications of robbing boys of their natural social and emotional outlets, but much research is being carried out on this topic.

Here is an example of supervising rough-and-tumble play. Marqus and Ye-Jun have just arrived at preschool and are standing by the door, waiting for Carson. As soon as Carson arrives, the boys erupt in frenzied motion. The three boys fall on top of one another in a pile, grabbing one another by parts of their bodies.

TEACHER:   It looks like you boys want to play rough, but you're blocking the doorway. I'll put down the tumbling mat and you can play rough on that.

*The boys wrestle and roll around on the mat but soon branch off into playing Superman. They put on capes and start to run around the room.*

TEACHER:   I see that you want to fly, but it worries me when I see you flying indoors, where you might bump into furniture. You can choose to either fly off the indoor climber onto the mat or go outside and do your flying. Which do you prefer?

*The boys choose to stay indoors and start jumping off the climber, but soon the plan changes to make-believe shooting. They point their fingers at other kids and make shooting sounds.*

TEACHER:   If you're going to pretend to shoot, remember to point at the floor, walls, or things but not at people.

*Then the boys start "shooting" at invisible aliens.*

### Supervising Preschoolers Putting Things Away

Preschoolers in a problem-solving setting are very responsive about putting away their toys and clothes. A brief, informative reminder is usually enough. Some preschoolers even enjoy helping other children put away their belongings. Parents are often amazed at how cooperative their children can be at school. Ways to elicit cooperation are explored in Chapter 6.

## *Teacher-Child Interactions*

Effective supervision is the foundation for problem solving, but it also provides a framework within which teachers can be responsive and spontaneous with the children in their care. The teacher for whom positioning, circulating, and concentrating become second nature can feel at ease and comfortable about joining in a conversation with the children, pointing out an elegant spider web, or listening to the story of a TV program a child saw the night before. This is where the endless delight of working with young children enters in. The serious and intense yet whimsical perceptions and observations children make in their daily lives of their surrounding world keep us smiling inwardly and make our days bright. No philosophy or set of guidelines can have value unless it allows for and encourages warm, personal interaction between teacher and child.

## Intergenerational Supervision

On the subject of supervision in intergenerational programs, Joan Whitley of Mount St. Vincent's Intergenerational Learning Center in Seattle writes:

> When a child care teacher is working in an intergenerational setting, there are some differences to keep in mind. If children and elders are working together on an activity that is planned for both groups, the children's teacher and the elders' staff (probably the recreation therapist) must be comfortable with clients from both areas—children and elders. Cross training both staffs (see Chapter 10) will aid each in understanding the best ways to interact with the other's clientele.
>
> The children's teachers are the key to a successful program. They are responsible for reaching out to the elders and including them in the children's daily activities. Small groups of two to four children can also go for visits to the nursing center. When the two groups come together to make a fruit salad, for example, the children and the elders are typically seated as partners working together. It is vital that there be enough staff to help with any problems that arise. An elder or a child may need to leave the area to use the bathroom, or an elder may become too tired to remain with the group. The nursing staff will help the elder, and the children's teacher will help the child. When you plan activities in a nursing home, check ahead of time to locate where to go for help. Is the nursing staff always within view, or would someone need to go a few steps down the hall for help? Is there a phone in the area? Plan the best procedure for any unusual situation that may arise.
>
> Teachers must know how to handle situations that may stem from an elder's dementia. Sometimes an elderly person living in a nursing home acts in ways in which children and teachers do not expect an adult to act. They may call a child by the name of their own family member, reach over and pinch a child (rare, but it can happen), or attempt to eat a Lego or a piece of playdough. Children might also hear someone calling out for help. The teacher cannot always foresee specific situations, but children need some general preparation for the nursing-home setting as well as the aging process. During the visit, if an elderly person did pinch a child, for example, the teacher could respond by saying "It's not okay to pinch Ian" and then comfort the child and find another place for him to sit.

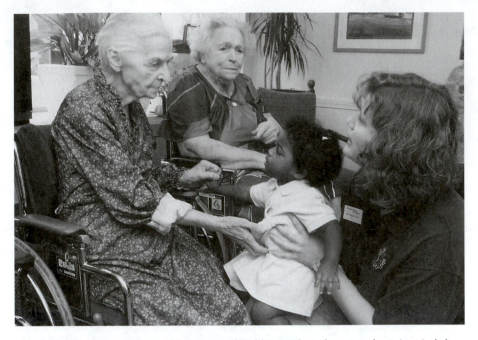

**Figure 3.12**    *The teacher reaches out to the elder residents but must keep in mind the differences in supervision.*

Baby rooms are especially popular with elderly residents, and some enjoy feeding a baby who is sitting in a high chair. However, the children's teacher should not initially expect an elderly resident to be able to hold a baby and give him or her a bottle. If the resident asks to hold a baby, the teacher can help by choosing a baby who isn't too heavy or wiggly and is in a calm state. The elder must first sit down; then the teacher places the baby in the resident's arms in a safe, secure way (Figure 3.12). The teacher should stay close, kneeling near the resident and the baby with arms outstretched to give assistance. Many residents believe they are no longer strong enough to hold a baby, but if the teacher takes the time to help make it possible, maybe for the last time, it can be very meaningful. The teacher can say, "I'll be right here to help so baby Rachel won't fall."

After a visit, the teacher should spend some time talking with the children and helping them understand what took place and why. Children may worry that the elders have an illness that they can catch. If the teacher is accepting of the elders' condition and reassures the children, most children will follow the teacher's lead. A teacher may briefly explain, "Mrs. Pello did not understand what she was doing, she is confused and her brain doesn't let her think the way it used to." There are also some excellent books, such as *Sachiko Means Happiness,* about grandparents with dementia. If a problem such as pinching arises, the children can help compose a letter to bring the event to the attention of the recreation therapist, who can then decide whether Mrs. Pello should take part in future activities. This process gives the children a feeling of control over the situation.

## Summing Up Supervision

Whether teachers are supervising infants, toddlers, or preschoolers, their primary goal is freedom with safety. Young children in the program should feel safe and free to exercise their curiosity, test their bodies, and take calculated risks. Once the environment has been made as safe and challenging as possible, the teacher's role is to oversee, watching children as they play and interfering as little as possible.

The structure of the program directly affects the teacher's ability to supervise effectively. Programs that have a coordinator enable teachers to supervise without the distraction of various other tasks. When the coordinator's job is rotated, all teachers get a break from routine, which helps them enjoy even more their time with the children.

The teacher supervises by using many strategies all at once. She stays with her group, positions herself so she can observe all her children, circulates in the play area giving affirmations, and keeps her full attention on what is happening with each child. This way of making contact with each child without inhibiting play is extremely important and keeps the teacher alert to any conflicts that may require facilitation.

The teacher's role as supervisor also includes overseeing children as they learn to be responsible for putting away their toys and clothing and negotiating with other children. The phrase "freedom with responsibility" describes the basis for effective supervision. Children must be kept free and safe but also must learn to be responsible for their behavior.

Routines and transitions require attentive supervision because changes are occurring rapidly. These changes may bring out anxieties and vulnerabilities in young children and cause erratic behavior if the shifts are not introduced carefully and consistently. Effective supervision also provides a framework for personal and social interactions between teachers and children and helps build teacher-child relationships.

## Practice and Discussion ————————————

1. Why is effective supervision so necessary in a problem-solving program? What does the phrase "freedom with responsibility" mean to you?

2. What is the main issue in children's programs, and how does it relate to supervision?

3. Describe the role of the teacher while supervising a group of young children.

4. Describe the role of the coordinator and what this role contributes to the program.

5. Name some alternative ways to organize the teaching staff so the children receive the best possible supervision.

6. Using pencil and paper, sketch several classrooms of various sizes and shapes. Make an X to indicate the best place for the teacher in each room. Supervision should be most effective from that position.

7. In your college classroom, role-play the way in which a teacher would circulate among a group, giving affirmations. Several students can demonstrate their own styles of supervising.

8. Imagine that you and another teacher are watching children on the playground. Suddenly, two children are fighting over a toy. What procedures would you follow in order to alert the other teacher? How would you position yourself?

9. What are some indications that a child is ready to take a risk? How can the teacher tell, and how can risk taking be facilitated?

10. Examine your own feelings about rough-and-tumble play. How would you react to a group of boys playing roughly? What supervising strategies would you use?

11. Do you think it is important for young children to put away their toys as they finish using them? What, in your opinion, are the pros and cons?

## Recommended Reading

Gurian, Michael. *The Wonder of Boys.* New York: Tarcher/Putnam, 1997.

Pollack, William. *Real Boys.* New York: Henry Holt and Company, Inc., 1998.

# 4

# *Listening for Feelings*

Pretend that it's your birthday. Your spouse or another special person has invited you out for a wonderful celebration. It could be dining and dancing, a picnic on the beach, bowling with friends, or reading poetry beside a stream—whatever you choose to do.

You get dressed especially for the occasion; you are happy and excited, waiting impatiently for your loved one to come pick you up. You wait and wait; an hour passes and you begin to worry. Finally, you make some phone calls, trying to find out what has happened. Someone on the phone tells you that your special person has already left with some friends to watch a company baseball game.

Stop a minute and think about how you feel. Are you hurt, rejected, disappointed, angry, or all of these and more?

Now pretend that a neighbor drops by while you're feeling this way. Your neighbor advises, "You shouldn't feel that way; it isn't nice to be angry. You're okay; stop crying. Only babies cry. And stop your screaming; it hurts my ears. There's no reason to be so mad!"

How does your neighbor make you feel?

The phone rings. You hope it's your significant other, but it's your best friend. What is your friend's comment? "Oh, never mind; don't even think about it. I'll come get you and we'll go shopping at the mall. That will make you feel better."

Do you feel better yet?

## *Acknowledging Feelings*

In the scenario presented above, you were on the receiving end of two methods frequently used for dealing with people's emotions: discounting and distracting. These ways communicate to the listener that feeling hurt, disappointed, rejected, or angry is somehow "wrong." They are methods that are constantly and especially used with children.

The term "discounting," referring to feelings, means to diminish and disregard the amount and intensity of feelings, making them seem less important than they are. When an item goes on sale at a store, it is discounted; a portion of its value is removed. When someone pats us on the head (figuratively) and says "There, there, it's really not so bad" or judges our emotions for us, saying "That's not nice," that person is robbing us of our right to feel the way we feel.

One way to discount feelings is to use criticism. Criticism can include shaming, humiliating, mocking, name-calling, and sarcasm, all of which are devastating to a young child. In *The Heart of Parenting*, John Gottman describes research showing that children who are negatively criticized by their parents experience more trouble in school, higher levels of stress, more behavior problems, and more illness.[1] Shaming is a particularly destructive way to discount feelings, especially for young boys. In *Real Boys*, William Pollack notes that, while girls are sensitive to shame at an older age, boys begin at a much younger age to fear shame and will avoid shame at any cost. Boys will display bravado and even violent behavior to avoid shame.[2]

Distracting people from their feelings also demonstrates how little those feelings are valued. The statement "This will take your mind off your trouble" rarely achieves its promise. Those words are more likely to make us resent the person who is distracting us, and we may wish that he or she would leave us alone. We sense what our friend is trying to do. Perhaps at a later time we will be ready for distractions, but not when we are dealing with strong emotions. We must be able to decide when we are ready.

What do we really need when we are feeling upset? Many people tell me they need a hug or someone to hold them while they cry. Others need a chance to express their feelings without being judged; they want acceptance of their feelings, validation, and trust that they can deal with their emotions. Although they cannot articulate this, children need the same thing. Acknowledging emotions is an essential part of the problem-solving philosophy.

## Understanding Temperament

Another important element in applying problem solving is understanding a child's innate temperament. A person's temperament, or basic nature, is directly related to that person's emotions and how they are expressed. In her book *Raising Your Spirited Child,* Mary Sheedy Kurcinka describes in depth the complexities of temperament and how human beings differ from one another from birth. Although her book focuses on children whom Kurcinka calls "spirited" (others might say "difficult," "overactive," "hypersensitive," "stubborn," or "distractible"), the characteristics she portrays are found in varying degrees in all children. I consider this a valuable and relevant book for all of us who work with children.[3]

Important in applying the problem-solving philosophy is the way temperament influences childrens' ability to express their feelings, relate to their peers, and function in groups, as well as their style of doing these things. A fundamental difference is apparent between the extroverted child and the introverted child. Most children are extroverts: They are outgoing, friendly, and expressive, and they draw their energy from being with people. These are the children most of us find easy to work with. Classrooms and activities are designed with these children in mind. Generally, extroverts adapt readily to problem solving and find that it enables them to get their needs met.

Introverts, on the other hand, are in the minority. They are introspective, slow to make transitions, and reflective before talking or acting. They make fewer but deeper friendships and draw their energy from time spent alone. Introverts are sometimes mistakenly labeled shy, withdrawn, unfriendly, and uncooperative, usually because we fail to understand their needs. Introverts need more time, space, and privacy, and they need permission to stand back and observe before joining the group. They also need the opportunity to bond closely with their favorite teacher. Toward the end of the day spent with a group, the introvert may be drained of energy and may fall apart. This child will require some respite in a quiet area before being able to successfully engage in verbal interactions with playmates.

A teacher who understands that children have different temperaments that affect their emotions and how these temperaments are expressed will have excellent information for helping children grow and develop. Understanding children's temperaments is another essential element in applying the problem-solving philosophy.

## Gender Differences in Expressing Emotions

Studies cited by William Pollack in *Real Boys* indicate that, although both boys and girls express the same feelings, mothers and fathers (and presumably teachers and caregivers) do not recognize or validate them in the same way. With the best of intentions, "mothers tend unwittingly to mimic and overly reinforce smiling in boys while discouraging more unhappy emotions" and "when mothers were interacting with infant boys, the mothers were particularly resistant to recognizing their sons' negative emotional states." Fathers similarly limited their reactions to their sons' negative feelings.[4]

These studies indicate that, even in infancy, we discourage boys from expressing a full range of emotions; we want boys to smile. This is far different from the way we interact with baby girls. Girls are accepted and validated for expressing a full range of both positive and negative emotions. We support little girls in being emotionally expressive; we discourage boys.

As they reach preschool age, Pollack notes, "mothers talk more about sadness or distress with daughters, and about anger with sons." For example, the response to a girl who is crying about a bad experience might be "Oh, you must feel awful" and to a boy "How unfair—that's ridiculous." This discrepancy applies not only to mothers. Studies show that both parents speak more about sadness with daughters but speak with sons about anger. These subtle, shame-based messages we unintentionally send both boys and girls teach them to limit their emotions to fit accepted sexual stereotypes.[5]

Gurian, in *The Wonder of Boys*, stresses biology:

> The male brain and hormones give a boy a natural tendency toward processing feeling and emotion in a very "male" way. . . . Boys are in their way "sensitive" and "compassionate." . . . And boys can always be trained to become more sensitive and empathic toward others than they are. . . . But still, their testosterone and brain wire them naturally to process their feelings and react emotionally in some boy-specific ways, and it is traumatic to make a boy change the very way he processes his own feelings.

Gurian continues by describing eight methods used by males to process emotions; among them is the method of "problem solving."[6]

Both sexes suffer from societal expectations that girls can express sadness and fear but not anger and that boys can express anger but not sadness and fear (Figure 4.1). As a result, society suffers as well. Girls who cannot express anger may become easy victims, and boys who express their negative feelings as anger may be dangerous to themselves and others. As teachers and caregivers, we should be aware of the ways in which we interact with both sexes.

This chapter introduces the first step in problem solving. In *P.E.T.: Parent Effectiveness Training*, Thomas Gordon calls this step "active listening,"[7] a process by which the teacher merges with the child in a partnership of lis-

**Figure 4.1** *Active listening allows boys to express a full range of emotions.*

tening and communicating. It enables both teacher and child to express their feelings effectively, understand the feelings of the other, and incorporate those feelings into the problem-solving process. Active listening teaches us to validate feelings instead of discounting or distracting them; it lets us see children as real people with their own range of emotions. Active listening is a gender-neutral way to allow both sexes to express their emotions. If we are to use active listening well with young children, we must learn to apply it on two levels: nonverbal and verbal.

## Nonverbal Active Listening

Busily splashing in the water table, Jimmy, age fourteen months, suddenly senses the teacher watching him. Last night at home he had been scolded for splashing in the toilet. His feeling of pleasure at the water table reminds him of his toilet experience, and he looks up at the teacher questioningly. The teacher smiles; Jimmy relaxes, smiles back, and returns to his splashing. Without a spoken word, he has learned a lesson in acceptance and trust.

It sounds so simple. Are a smile, a hug, and a loving pat all it takes to communicate acceptance and trust? Sometimes they are. Jimmy had a problem to solve: If the water in the toilet is not to play with, is all water off limits? Jimmy had feelings but no words with which to pose this problem. Yet with the appropriate expression, he did present the problem. A teacher who knew how to communicate acceptance and trust allowed him to accept and trust his own feelings about the water. The teacher did not solve his problem for him but rather demonstrated faith in his own problem-solving ability.

Nonverbal active listening is what Jimmy's teacher did with him. The teacher who can supervise children without interfering in their play, allowing them to "do what kids do," is sending a clear message that he or she recognizes, accepts, and trusts their feelings. This aspect of teaching is often underrated because we tend to feel that teachers must "do things" to and for children so the children will learn. The problem-solving philosophy, however, compels us to respect the process of learning as it is found in every child and allow it to develop at an individual rate.

The power of nonverbal active listening is enormous. We convey acceptance and trust to children when we show them by our nonverbal responses that they are capable of making choices, judging situations, processing information, and drawing conclusions. We say to them nonverbally that we understand, have the same feelings, and approve of the children as people. Five examples of nonverbal active listening follow. Experienced teachers will immediately recognize that they have had many such nonverbal interactions with the children in their care.

## I Lost My Thumb

Maurice, at three months, has recently discovered his thumb. He quickly learned to use it for comfort and to help him get to sleep. After sleeping for only twenty minutes, Maurice begins to cry. His caregiver goes to his crib and tries to figure out what Maurice might need. She notices that he has turned his body in such a way that he cannot get his thumb to his mouth. Gently, the caregiver turns Maurice and guides his thumb to his mouth. He sucks noisily and falls back to sleep.

## I Want to Get Out

Seven-month-old Susan is going for a ride in the double stroller with nine-month-old Louie. The teacher pushes them around the playground, visiting with other children who are playing outdoors. When they approach the sandbox, filled with toddlers, Susan leans over the front of the stroller and reaches out, wriggling her entire body. Observing her, the teacher interprets her movements as an expression of feelings. The teacher lifts Susan out of the stroller and puts her into the sandbox with the toddlers. Susan looks delighted, wiggles her fingers in the sand, and watches the other children. The teacher anticipated Susan's need and, through nonverbal active listening, filled it.

### I'm Getting Very Sleepy

Victor, age fifteen months, is playing in the rocking boat with other toddlers. It is late morning. Victor's eyes blink intermittently, and he reaches over and slaps at another child. When the other child slaps back, Victor cries easily and rubs his eyes. Victor's teacher remembers that he often needs a nap in the late morning. She picks him up out of the rocking boat, lays him down on the resting mat, and sits down next to him. As she watches the other children, the teacher pats Victor's back. In seconds, he is asleep.

### How Embarrassing

Three-year-old Cindy is waking up from her nap. Instead of jumping up from her mat as she usually does, she stays under the covers. When other kids call her to get up and play, she covers her head with her blanket. Seconds later, the teacher hears Cindy sobbing quietly. The teacher then understands why Cindy is staying on her mat. She goes to the cupboard and takes out a change of clothing for Cindy, who has wet her bed. Discreetly, the teacher gives Cindy some dry clothes to put on. Cindy smiles with relief.

### Feeling Left Out

Several preschool-age children are playing with a game at the table. Nolan arrives at the preschool and approaches the table. He stands watching for a few minutes and then sits down next to the players. One of the other boys tells Nolan that there is no room for more players at the game. Nolan looks disappointed and gets up, wandering around the room. He finally sits down on a big, soft chair. The teacher, sensing his disappointment, sits down next to him, and without mentioning that he has been left out she puts her hand on his shoulder. Nolan sighs and relaxes. In a few minutes, he goes to join a different group of children, this time successfully.

Although the remainder of this chapter focuses on verbal active listening, nonverbal active listening should not be overlooked or underestimated. Children need to receive the message of acceptance and trust in any way it can be sent.

## Active Listening
## and the Non–English-Speaking Child

When preschool-age children are frustrated or upset but cannot express such feelings in English, they may either revert to their language of origin or decide to remain silent. This is difficult not only for the child but also for the teacher. The situation is similar to that of an infant or toddler who cannot yet speak any language. Nonverbal active listening is especially geared to non–English-speaking children of any age. The caregiver should use words so that the child will eventually learn the words for various emotions; however, while he or she is in the process of learning, you may have to rely heavily on your tone of voice, facial expressions, and body language in responding to the child's emotions. A smile, a gentle hug, or a pat will help the child even if the words are not fully understood. Fortunately, children are fast learners, and the teacher's support will get them through their initial difficulties.

## The Morality of Active Listening

Active listening asks us to put aside value judgments and listen to the feelings behind a child's words. Any thoughts or feelings are considered acceptable; only behavior counts. Some people consider it immoral to teach a child to call on inner resources for solutions without looking to an outside authority. While it is true that the problem-solving approach in general does not rely on absolutes of right and wrong, it definitely places a high value on moral behavior.

Active listening is based on empathy, the ability to put yourself in someone else's place, to see the world as they see it and feel their feelings. In *Emotional Intelligence*, Daniel Goleman cites research on empathy by Martin Hoffman, who suggests that "the roots of morality are to be found in empathy." Hoffman's research traces the development of empathy from infancy to late childhood, and he proposes that empathy "leads people to follow certain moral principles."[8]

Through active listening, the teacher models empathy to the child while the child learns to look inward and discover the seeds of his or her own empathy. What begins as an expression of feelings by the child and a validation of feelings by the teacher hopefully will become a lifelong process of caring for the needs and rights of other people. This is the essence of morality.

## Giving Names to Feelings

The problems, needs, and feelings of most young children in programs seem to fall into three major categories: those originating from within the child, those resulting from interactions with other children, and those relating to limits. Active listening addresses primarily the first category but is also used with interactions between children when their feelings are involved. Preschoolers especially need active listening in their relationships with each other. Active listening is also used in negotiation.

Problems originating from within the child may have been brought from home that day. She may have been awakened earlier than usual and hurried to get ready. There may have been a conflict between her parents or siblings, or one involving her. Distressing changes, such as divorce, the birth of a sibling, the death of a relative, someone moving into or out of the household, or a visit from grandparents, may contribute to the child's mood. Problems from home may cause a child to cling to her parents, cry easily, throw tantrums, and initiate conflicts with other children.

Other problems involve children's need to control and master their bodies and world. Many control issues stem from physical functions such as eating, sleeping, toileting, and injuries. Frustration can also arise from the lack of physical skills, such as those a child needs to dress or undress, and from activities such as riding a tricycle, catching a ball, or completing a puzzle. One physical need that is easily overlooked is the need for closeness to another person. Holding, patting, stroking, and hugging are very real physical needs of the young child. Adults sometimes discount these needs by labeling such behavior as "looking for attention."

The need for attention is a basic human need. Through the socialization process, adults learn socially acceptable ways to gain the attention they need from other people. Children have only begun to learn that some attention-getting devices are unacceptable and may, indeed, bring negative, even painful results. When adults recognize the child's need for attention as valid, understand that both physical and emotional attention are essential to normal development, and give that attention freely and willingly, the child no longer resorts to contrived attention-getting devices.

Active listening encompasses all these problems, needs, and feelings. It is a tool that enables teachers to identify with the children's feelings, interpret them, and convey acceptance and trust to the children (Figure 4.2). Acceptance by those surrounding them helps children accept themselves. This, in turn, leads them to accept other people. Children who feel trusted by their caregivers trust themselves and, consequently, trust people in general. Self-acceptance and trust are significant building blocks for healthy and meaningful relationships. They also provide children with a solid foundation for high self-esteem.

Should any limits be placed on a child's feelings and the words used to express them? A fundamental tenet of active listening is that all feelings are normal. Feelings and words are not judged, restricted, or criticized. Guilt and shame do not contribute to self-acceptance or trust and are not part of the problem-solving process. Children, like adults, experience many of their feelings intensely and are entitled to the highs and lows of the emotional

**Figure 4.2**    *Active listening enables teachers to identify with their children's feelings and convey acceptance and trust.*

range. Children also lack a realistic perspective of time. To children, feelings of misery or joy will last forever. They cannot yet project that within minutes their feelings will have changed drastically.

The words children use to express their feelings are generally a reflection of what they hear their parents saying, what they hear on television, and what they learn from their friends. If children use a word that is offensive to the teacher, it is wise to pointedly ignore that word. To forbid or moralize about certain words will only make them more attractive to everyone, and soon those words will be used even more frequently. Because the teacher is not responsible for the words the children use, there is no need for teachers to feel guilty about offensive language. Sometimes, however, a tactfully written note to the parents will remind them that children repeat what they hear at home, on television, and from friends. Later in this chapter and in Chapter 5, I discuss ways to help the victim deal with name-calling.

The teacher's role in active listening is to interpret the child's feelings, give a name to those feelings, and reflect the feelings and the name back to the child (Figure 4.3). The teacher's ability to interpret the child's feelings accurately will grow as the relationship with the child is formed. That teacher-child relationship is fundamental to active listening. Just as the parent learns the meaning of an infant's cry or a toddler's fussiness, the teacher who is sensitive and in tune with the child will come to know why he is behaving as he is. Experienced teachers do this intuitively, but there is an element to understanding and interpreting a child's feelings that is often

**Figure 4.3** *Waiting is frustrating for toddlers. The teacher gives a name to those feelings.*

overlooked: the teacher's understanding and her inner, personal emotions. Active listening trains teachers to look within, to develop empathy, so they can identify with the child and put themselves in his place. This aspect is covered in Chapter 10.

Why is it important to give names to feelings and to teach and model this to young children? The benefits are numerous and varied. First, doing so enables children to express their needs directly and accurately to others. When children can use words that accurately describe how they feel, they are more likely to have their needs met appropriately. Children who have their needs met become more independent and self-sufficient. Second, when the teacher gives a name to children's feelings, the children begin to realize that other people share those feelings. They begin to see themselves as members of a community, with a role to play and contributions to make. Third, giving a name to feelings helps build children's vocabulary, enriching and enhancing their thought processes and communication skills. Every new word is a gift, a tool to use in life. Hearing, understanding, and using each new word adds power to a child's life and control over his or her world.

Finding the precise word to fit the child's feelings requires practice and skill. Many "feeling" words in our language are overused; others are consistently overlooked. An example of an overused word is "anger." Many feelings resemble anger but are really something else. Figure 4.4 depicts anger as

**Figure 4.4** *The anger umbrella.*

an umbrella, a visible emotion covering many invisible emotions. Because anger is usually displayed in a visible way, we sometimes forget to look beneath the overt behavior to uncover hidden feelings. As adults, we tend to use anger to hide feelings that leave us vulnerable. By doing so, we send mixed and inaccurate messages to others, perhaps even to those we love. How can we hope to understand one another if we spend so much energy trying to camouflage our true emotions? When we use active listening with children, we must look beneath the umbrella of anger and find the hidden feelings that preceded the anger and that the anger is covering and protecting. When those hidden feelings are revealed and communicated, they lose much of their power to hurt us.

"Happiness" also has many variations, and in active listening those words add dimension to feelings as well. Keep in mind words such as "joy," "satisfaction," "excitement," "pleasure," "loving," "lovable," "surprised," "peaceful," "proud," "bubbly," "giggly," "elated," and "enthusiastic."

## Steps in Active Listening

Although there is no precise formula for active listening, there are some basic steps and specific ideas to consider (Figure 4.5):

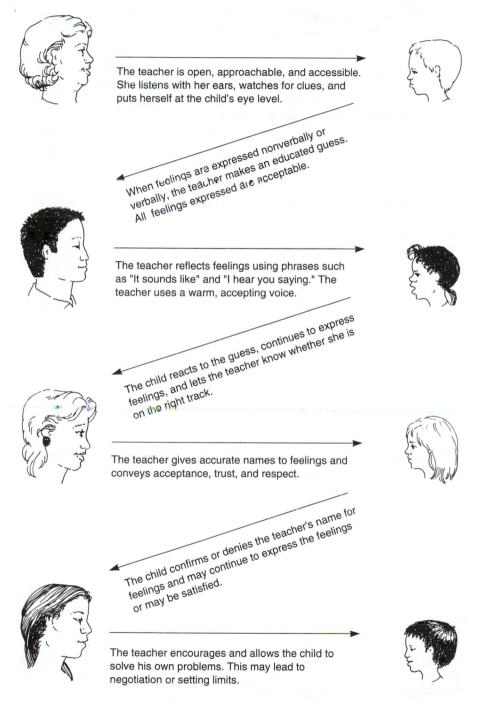

The teacher is open, approachable, and accessible. She listens with her ears, watches for clues, and puts herself at the child's eye level.

When feelings are expressed nonverbally or verbally, the teacher makes an educated guess. All feelings expressed are acceptable.

The teacher reflects feelings using phrases such as "It sounds like" and "I hear you saying." The teacher uses a warm, accepting voice.

The child reacts to the guess, continues to express feelings, and lets the teacher know whether she is on the right track.

The teacher gives accurate names to feelings and conveys acceptance, trust, and respect.

The child confirms or denies the teacher's name for feelings and may continue to express the feelings or may be satisfied.

The teacher encourages and allows the child to solve his own problems. This may lead to negotiation or setting limits.

**Figure 4.5**  *Teacher-child interactions based on active listening. Communication flows back and forth between teacher and child during active listening.*

1. The teacher is open, approachable, and accessible to the children. The feelings, opinions, and complaints of children are invited, welcomed, and treated with the same respect as those of adults. The teacher also shares in their joys, even when these are wild and silly.

2. When infants and toddlers express their feelings nonverbally, such as by crying, screaming, or whining, the teacher calls on her knowledge of the child and makes an educated guess. Is he hungry, sleepy, bored, needing a diaper change, or wanting to be held or hugged? It may take several guesses before the teacher responds appropriately.

3. All feelings are accepted as valid. Feelings are never discounted; rather, they are respected as the possessions of the child. No attempt is made to distract children from their feelings or make light of them. The teacher remembers that feelings are transitory and may change quickly.

4. The teacher reflects back to the child what he thinks the child is feeling. He restates the child's feelings using a phrase such as "It sounds like," "I hear you saying," or "It seems to me that." This leaves an opening for the child to say "No, that's not the problem" if the teacher's guess is inaccurate.

5. Names are given to feelings. Every teacher should become familiar with many words that describe feelings. A helpful practice is keeping a list of feeling words posted on the classroom wall. Feelings should be described as accurately as possible.

6. The teacher's tone of voice is extremely important. It should be warm, accepting, and empathetic. Children should not sense that their teacher disapproves of the way they feel.

7. Once children have acquired the ability and skill to take care of their own body functions, the teacher allows and encourages them to solve their own problems. The teacher's role is to demonstrate confidence and trust in the child.

There is another side to the free expression of feelings. In a group setting, a teacher must consider many children. One child who is screaming loudly and incessantly in a room of six or more children can cause other children to become anxious, fearful, and listless and will also wear down the patience of even the best teacher. We must all live together, sometimes in very close proximity. This sometimes necessitates asking the child to express herself in another room or outdoors. This should not be done in a judgmental or critical way but rather should stress that the feelings are okay but the noise level is uncomfortable.

The remainder of this chapter provides a variety of examples of active listening. Although active listening plays a distinct role in negotiation and setting limits, the focus here is on individual feelings. The examples are divided according to the needs of infants, toddlers, and preschoolers. There may, however, be some overlapping and some repetition.

## Active Listening with Infants

According to Erikson, infancy is a critical period when the infant must build trust if he or she is to develop a healthy personality.[9] For trust to develop, the infant's needs must be met in a loving, consistent way. Active listening is a way to meet the infant's emotional needs immediately and compassionately. We are rapidly learning more and more about infants. We used to think of them only as a bundle of needs waiting to be met. Now we know that they are also a bundle of preferences. If we continue to think of infants only in terms of needing food, holding, sleeping, and diapering, we are not seeing the whole child. Infants also require stimulation and have definite preferences as to what they find interesting. We know, for example, that they understand a great deal of what they hear, much more, of course, than they can verbalize. They prefer some voices, sounds, faces, and other visual stimuli to others.

In his comprehensive book *The Infant Mind*, Restak summarizes numerous studies on the emotions of infants. "Since all of this occurs in early infancy, an exciting possibility presents itself: appreciation of the emotional expression of other people may start to develop during early babyhood. The roots of compassion, love, . . . these underlying feelings start when we're still in diapers, perhaps haven't even made it out of the hospital nursery as yet."[10]

If infants can and do appreciate the emotional expression of other people practically at birth (and some observers believe this happens even before birth) and if the roots of compassion and love are already planted, perhaps in the hospital nursery, how can we fail to validate those feelings in every possible way? Infants obviously deserve the same acceptance and trust we give to older children. Empathy must be nurtured.

Restak also refers to research conducted by Peter Wolff, which "separated infants' cries into three groups: the angry cry (loud and prolonged); the hungry cry (rhythmic and repetitive); and the pain cry (sudden onset, an initial long cry and extended breath holding)."[11] If anger is indeed an umbrella for many feelings, we can speculate that infants experience a wide range of emotions. If so, active listening is the appropriate response to an infant's cry.

Parents quickly learn to distinguish the various cries of their child; to provide responsive care, caregivers who are not the parents must learn to do the same thing. When an infant's crying is in the "angry" category, active listening by the teacher helps the baby begin to learn how to get her emotional needs met.

We may think that infant emotions should be extremely simple and that adults should always be able to stop a baby's crying. This is not so. Like older people, some infants seem to need longer periods of time for expressing their feelings before they can feel ready to go on to the next emotion or activity.

Crying is only one way infants communicate their needs and preferences. They also use other body language such as squirming, clenching their fists, arching their back, vocalizing, grimacing, smiling, and much more. With so much going on, how can the teacher learn to respond appropriately to every infant as an individual? Active listening with infants is like a guessing game. The better a teacher's relationship is with the infant, the easier it becomes for her to guess what the baby needs or prefers. Active listening helps build that relationship and solve problems.

Any conversation about the well-being of infants must include a discussion of the appropriateness of placing infants in full-time day care. The best infant care professional caregivers can offer will not replace the bonding process that must take place between mother and infant. An infant under six months who spends most of his day with unrelated caregivers and sees his mother for only a short time is certainly at risk for faulty attachment. We can only hope that the infant will form an attachment to one caregiver and thus bond with another human being. Ethically, I believe that professionals are obligated to educate new parents about the probability of their child's perceiving someone else as "mother." If a parent has no choice but to work full time, caregivers must be as supportive as possible. On the other hand, if there are two working parents and any possibility exists that a change in lifestyle could give the child more time with the parent, I believe we must go to bat for the child. If a parent is offended or takes the infant elsewhere, at least we did our best!

Following are examples of active listening used with infants under twelve months of age.

## The Guessing Game

Bonnie, age fourteen weeks, is lying on her back on a pillow on the floor. Suddenly she begins to squirm and whimper. The teacher notices her distress and kneels beside her. She checks Bonnie's diaper. It is dry. She checks Bonnie's chart to see how recently she has eaten. Bonnie is probably not hungry. As she checks everything, the teacher carries on a conversation with Bonnie. She then tries turning Bonnie over on her tummy. Bonnie begins to cry loudly. Still talking to Bonnie, the teacher turns her on her back again. She notices that Bonnie keeps looking up intently. Finally, the teacher remembers. Bonnie was watching and listening to a musical mobile hanging above her. The mobile had stopped moving and playing. The teacher rewinds the mobile; Bonnie relaxes, sighs, and follows the mobile with her eyes again. She is satisfied.

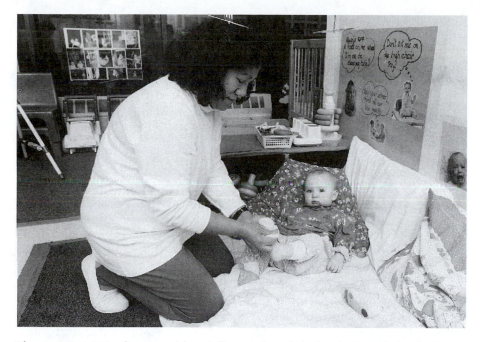

**Figure 4.6**    *Active listening with an infant consists of playing the "guessing game."*

If the mobile had not solved the problem, Bonnie's teacher could also have tried holding her, rocking her, or taking her outdoors (Figure 4.6). Hearing her teacher's voice giving her choices and feeling her teacher's responsiveness help Bonnie learn that her preferences are respected and her communication is effective.

## Chronic Crying

Timmy is now a preschooler, healthy, happy, and perfectly normal. But when Timmy started coming to the children's center at nine months of age, he was determined that his parents would not leave him and that he would hate every minute away from them. Timmy was breast-fed, and, because his mother was too far away to come to the center to nurse him on her lunch hour, she pumped her breasts and brought breast milk in bottles. Timmy, however, decided he did not like bottles and chose to cry for hours rather than take one. In fact, for his first three months in the program, Timmy's main activity was crying. In spite of this, Timmy's parents were determined to keep him at the center.

How can a teacher help the child who cries chronically? How does the teacher cope with chronic crying that continues day after day? In a well-staffed, nurturing, stimulating center, chronic crying is rare, but each child is an individual, and a few make the choice to protest and stick with it. That a child chooses to cry is neither the fault nor the responsibility of the teacher, although she may eventually feel that it is. The key to helping the child make another choice and to relieving some of the teacher's stress is active listening. Here are some of the active listening statements made to Timmy:

"Timmy, you really hate to see your mom and dad leave. It's so upsetting."

"Sounds like you're sad today—as if you wish you weren't here."

"You must really be missing mom and dad today."

"I'll bet you're hoping they'll come to pick you up soon. It must be frustrating to wait so long."

"I'll bet you'd like to go to work with your mom and dad. It's disappointing to have them leave."

"It sure makes you angry to be left here."

Along with active listening, the teachers gave Timmy physical comfort such as holding and rocking. They also tried to get him involved with toys and activities. Sometimes he would even show interest in the other babies. When he was responsive, the teachers always took note and mentioned his positive behavior. Active listening also interprets and reflects feelings of joy and happiness. Here are a few such reflections:

"Timmy, it's great to see your happy smile."

"You seem to be in a lovable mood today."

"Seeing you so enthusiastic makes me feel great."

"What a pleasure to hear you giggling."

"What a peaceful look."

Gradually, Timmy chose to smile more than cry. Because he had received so much acceptance and understanding and because his feelings had been respected, his self-esteem had not suffered. He was not made to feel like a burden or an unwelcome visitor, although his teachers probably thought of him in that way quite often. To reduce their stress, the teachers practiced stress-reduction techniques, which are discussed in Chapter 10.

Timmy did become a toddler, then a preschooler. He is still a strong-willed boy with a flair for the dramatic, but he hardly ever cries.

## I Want Attention

As the youngest of three children, ten-month-old Jessie has been the object of much attention at home. Her mother and sisters, who are much older, pick

Jessie up and play with her constantly. She is used to being entertained, cuddled, rocked, and indulged. Jessie's family is comfortable with this arrangement, and Jessie certainly enjoys it. The problem is that Jessie expects the same level of attention when she comes to the center. Consequently, she spends a great deal of time following her teachers around, on all fours or clinging to their legs. Like Timmy's parents, Jessie's mother has chosen to keep her child in full-time child care. The teachers are sensitive to Jessie's demand for attention, but they have other infants to care for. Jessie is learning that the world is a place where attention is shared with others. Active listening helps her know that her feelings are heard and understood, even when they cannot be fulfilled. In the process, Jessie is gaining confidence in herself, learning to use her own resources, and becoming an independent person. No matter how perfect life is at home, everyone must also learn to deal realistically with the rest of the world. Here are examples of active listening with Jessie:

> "You're really wanting to be held, Jessie; are you feeling neglected? Sure wish I could sit and hold you, but Jonny needs his diaper changed."
>
> "Are you feeling left out? It would be great if I could hold you all the time. Let's go for a walk instead; here's my hand."
>
> "You seem upset about sharing my lap with Sally, but that's the only way I can hold you right now."
>
> "Sounds like you're asking for attention. Jonny wants attention, too. I wonder if you two would enjoy giving each other hugs."

When Jessie does choose an independent activity, her teachers notice that, too.

> "Jessie, looks like you're enjoying that spindle toy."
>
> "I see that it's fun for you to play in the sandbox."
>
> "You did a good job with the peg game. You must be proud of yourself."
>
> "It's great to see you so enthusiastic about playing with kids."

Other situations appropriate to active listening include the following:

*Diapering:* "Sounds like it's irritating to you to be interrupted for a diaper change" (Figure 4.7).

*Mealtime:* "I see that you're spitting out your green beans. They must taste bad to you."

**Figure 4.7**  *Diapering is an ideal time for active listening.*

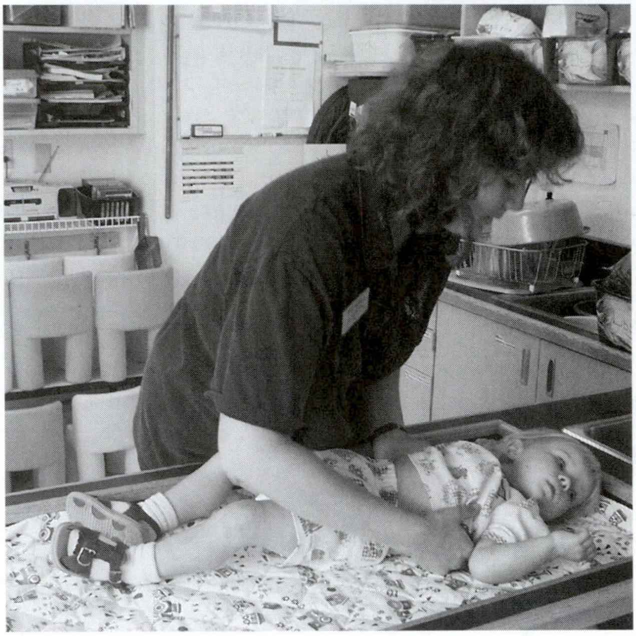

*Bottles:* "When you throw down your bottle, are you saying that it's empty? Is the nipple clogged? That must be upsetting."

*Boredom:* "Looks like you're bored with these toys. Let's bring out the water table."

*Sleepiness:* "You're trying so hard to stay awake, but I can see that you're sleepy. It must be frustrating enough to make you cry."

Sometimes when you use active listening with a very young infant, you may think you are just talking to yourself. Rest assured that your words are not lost on that tiny being. Watch his eyes and his body movements, and you will see how he responds to your voice and your words. He is constantly learning about his world, and you are providing a safe, loving conduit for his learning. Even if he is aware only of the sound of your voice, your inflections, and the feelings you communicate, he will sense your respect and learn to trust.

## Active Listening with Toddlers

Once children begin to walk, try to make wordlike sounds, and become more independent, we call them toddlers. This stage may begin much earlier than twelve months for some children, but generally it occurs when they are between twelve and sixteen months. This is usually the time when some parents and caregivers become more authoritarian in their approach to children. With babies who are helpless and controllable, it is easier for caregivers to be unconditionally loving and accepting. Toddlers, however, are mobile and fast. They get into things, dump them, chew on them, and tear them up. They do not necessarily follow orders. They wander away, are easily distracted, and think everything is a game. They also begin to demand more control over themselves.

This is a time when a child's self-esteem may be at stake. If a toddler's behavior is perceived to be willful, naughty, or selfish, he may receive the message that he is a "bad boy." Without training, many parents and caregivers resort to threatening, slapping hands, or saying "no" and "don't" continuously. These negative reactions to a toddler's bid for independence are destructive to his self-esteem and are generally ineffective. Active listening at this time is especially helpful for putting things into perspective. By putting ourselves in the toddler's place, we can see that his experimental approach to the world and his curiosity at how things work and react are not only normal and appropriate but also essential to the process of learning. Following are examples of active listening with toddlers.

## Puzzles Can Be Frustrating

Two-year-old Jenny is working on puzzles. She takes each one of the easier puzzles off the shelf and puts it together quickly. After working on five or six, she reaches over and grabs pieces of her friend's puzzle. Knowing that Jenny enjoys a challenge, the teacher takes from a higher shelf two of the more complex puzzles she thinks Jenny could put together.

TEACHER: Jenny, it looks like you're getting bored with the easy puzzles. Would you like to try one of these? When you've finished, you can ask for another one.

*Jenny eagerly chooses a puzzle and works on it. Soon she finds a piece she cannot place and, after trying hard, becomes frustrated. She whines, then pounds on the puzzle piece, trying to put it in its place.*

TEACHER: Looks like there's a problem. I hear you getting frustrated.

*Jenny continues to work on the puzzle. Periodically, she begins to whine again.*

TEACHER: Hard puzzles can sure be frustrating.

*The teacher lets Jenny know she can ask for help if she really gets stuck.*

TEACHER: You can ask for help when you're stuck. I'm willing to help kids when I see them trying.

*If Jenny does ask for help, the teacher first gives verbal clues.*

TEACHER:   What would happen if you turned that piece around? Do you think the head would fit here?

*If the teacher sees that Jenny is becoming too frustrated to work productively, she may place the puzzle piece next to its place as a hint or put her hand over Jenny's and guide the piece to the proper place. Jenny finally completes the puzzle.*

TEACHER:   Jenny, you've finished the puzzle. You must feel so proud of yourself!


## Throwing a Tantrum

Tantrums seem to intimidate adults; grown-ups don't understand them and often panic at the sight of a formerly compliant infant turning into an outraged toddler. Tantrums usually relate to power struggles emanating from the toddler's need to control his own body and, when possible, his own world. Active listening eliminates some children's need for tantrums. It helps others get through the rage that is frightening to themselves as well as to their parents.

Beckie is one toddler who uses tantrums to gain control. This morning she is asking to play in another area, but the art area already contains the maximum number of children allowed. Beckie asks for someone to trade with her, but at the moment no one wants to trade. She could go outdoors, but she wants only the art room. When no one will trade, Beckie begins to cry loudly. Her cries become a piercing scream as she flings her head back onto the carpet. Everyone in the room stops to watch her.

BECKIE:   (repeating over and over) I want to go to the art room!

*The teacher sits down on the floor next to Beckie.*

TEACHER:   Looks like you have a problem. No one wants to trade, and it's disappointing. You sound very frustrated.

BECKIE:   (screaming more loudly) I want to go to the art room!

TEACHER:   Do you want to talk about it?

*Beckie responds only with screaming.*

TEACHER:   (between screams) Sounds like you're so frustrated you just want to scream. It's up to you if you want to scream. When you've finished screaming, we could work on solving the problem.

*Beckie keeps screaming.*

TEACHER:   Because you're deciding to scream, I'm going to watch the other kids. Let me know when you're ready to talk.

*What happens if Beckie's screaming is disturbing other kids?*

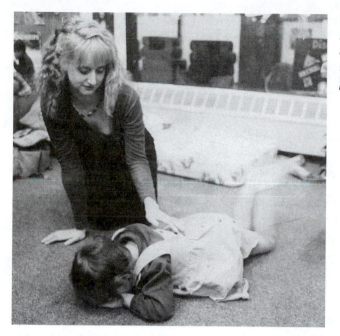

**Figure 4.8** *Active listening helps some children get through the rage that is so frightening.*

TEACHER:  Beckie, your screaming is upsetting other kids, so I'm moving you away from them. You're welcome to finish screaming in another room.

As with all active listening, the teacher's voice is warm, accepting, and nonjudgmental. This allows Beckie to confront her own feelings on her own terms. Tantrums are common with some children, nonexistent with others. As children gain greater control over their bodies and their world, they have less need for tantrums. More important than the tantrum is our response to it. Respect for the child is the key (Figure 4.8).

## I Can't

Helplessness is another way children handle a power issue. The child is expected to perform a certain task; to avoid doing it, he becomes "helpless" and asks the teacher to do it. Mark is a good example. He is a three-year-old boy who for months has had the skill to put on his own clothes and shoes. However, he does not want to do it himself. Every day, after nap time, when other kids are dressing to go outdoors, Mark sits with his clothing and shoes in front of him, staring at them. When everyone else is dressed and out, Mark is still there. He becomes distracted and takes out toys or lies on the rug, talking to himself.

TEACHER:  Mark, it's time to get dressed and go outside. The others have gone out already.

MARK:  I can't.

*He makes a half-hearted attempt.*

MARK:  See, I can't.

TEACHER:  It's hard for you to put on your clothes. It must be discouraging to see all your friends going outside without you.

MARK:  You do it.

TEACHER:  I'm willing to help kids only when I see them trying.

MARK:  I can't do it.

*He makes another feeble attempt.*

TEACHER:  Looks to me like you're not ready to work on it yet. I'm going to watch other kids now. When you're dressed, feel free to join them.

The teacher will then ignore Mark as much as possible. If she sees him making a genuine effort, she will give verbal reinforcement and help. Because she knows that Mark is capable, she treats him as a capable person who is simply not ready to do his task. She allows him to take his time. Some children are capable of procrastinating for hours, but usually as soon as they are motivated they can get dressed in seconds. The decision should be their own. There is no harm in allowing a child to sit with his clothing until he is ready to put it on.

If there is not a teacher who can stay with this one child, perhaps a cook, coordinator, or other staff member can keep an eye on him. Or he could be moved to the area where the children are playing. The adult should convey acceptance and trust that Mark can and will succeed but remember that his job is to get dressed, not to play. It is best to have him in a place where there are no toys within his reach and keep other children away until he is dressed. It is sometimes difficult for the teacher to resist the temptation to do simple tasks for children, but in the long run, it is more beneficial to the child that he do his own jobs (Figure 4.9).

## Not My Diaper

When toddlers become old enough to be involved in play, they often begin to protest diaper changing. They simply do not want to be disturbed. Changing a wet or "poopy" diaper is not a negotiable issue; it must be done. It is possible, however, to soften some of the protest through active listening. It is important to have a shoe holder or shoe bag stocked with small books and soft, washable toys to give the child a choice of diversions during the diaper change. It is also important to make diaper changing a pleasant activ-

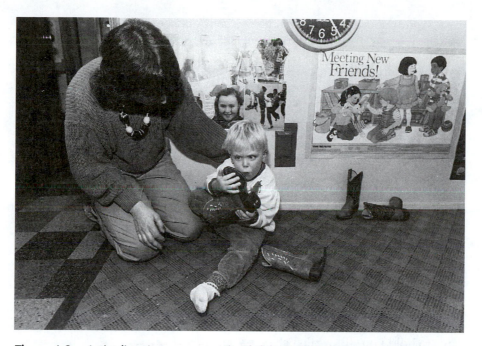

**Figure 4.9**  *Active listening encourages the "helpless" child to try.*

ity through the interactions of teacher and child. It can be a time for learning correct names of body parts such as penis and vulva. Children in diapers have few opportunities to explore their genitals or talk about them. Here is a scene between Wendy and her teacher, who is checking diapers. Wendy is two years old.

TEACHER: Wendy, I see that you have a poopy diaper. Time to go indoors and change it.

WENDY: No, not my diaper.

TEACHER: I know how you hate to be disturbed. I wish I didn't have to disturb you, but poopy diapers get changed.

*The teacher walks beside Wendy, gently guiding her toward the bathroom. Wendy, however, decides to sit down and won't budge.*

TEACHER: I understand that you don't want to have your diaper changed. You were having so much fun riding the trike.

WENDY: I want my trike!

TEACHER: Are you worried that someone else will take your trike?

WENDY: MY trike!

TEACHER: What if I ask another teacher to save the trike for you? Would that help?

Wendy looks relieved, so the teacher asks another teacher to save the trike for Wendy. If Wendy's toy were smaller, she could bring it with her. It isn't always this easy, but it is always worth trying to help the child feel comfortable about getting a diaper changed. If the child refuses, it may come down to providing the choice of walking or being carried to the changing room. Once there, the toy and book selection, along with pleasant conversation, should make things easier. There are, of course, a few children who will kick and thrash around on the changing table. Again, active listening will help.

TEACHER:  I can see that you're upset. Wouldn't it be great if you didn't have to have your diaper changed forever and ever? But a poopy diaper would make your bottom very sore, so I have to change it. I can't change you while you're moving so much, so I'll have to wait until you've finished kicking.

The teacher moves back from the changing table to avoid being kicked and waits for the kicking to stop. Most toddlers will get bored with kicking rather quickly. If not, and if time is important, the teacher may have to say, "I wish I could wait for you to stop kicking, but I have other kids to change. I'll have to hold you still while I change you."

## Toilet Training

Toilet training is usually the first control issue between parent and child and often lays the foundation for future confrontations. At the very time the child is striving for autonomy, the parents feel the need to control her. Because the power struggle revolves around when the child will deposit her bowel movement in the toilet, the child naturally has the upper hand. If a child feels pressured to use the toilet before she is ready, she may simply learn to be sneaky or defiant, depending on her parents' reaction.

Much toilet training pressure is the result of unrealistic expectation, competition with other parents, or concern about the criticism of friends and relatives. Parents may not understand at what age their child is physically capable of toilet training and may expect a toddler to do what he cannot yet do. Or the child of a friend may have been trained at a very early age (probably his parents were trained), and the parents want their child to be as good or better. Perhaps relatives and friends keep asking, accusingly, "Isn't Jonny toilet trained yet?" None of these are good reasons for pressuring a child to use the toilet.

Another, equally inappropriate reason has surfaced. Children's programs are requiring that a child be toilet trained for various reasons. It may be a requirement for enrollment, for paying a lower rate, or for allowing children to be with their age group. That those who work with children should make such arbitrary rules is most distressing and unworthy of the profession.

Until a child reaches age three, toilet training should be left entirely up to the child, with no pressure or recrimination. Some children, especially in group situations, want to use the toilet earlier than others. They virtually train themselves. Others show no interest or resist efforts to get them interested. After about three years of age, children may be gently encouraged. They may be taken to the bathroom with a group of already trained children to observe and to sit on the toilet without any expectations. Being allowed to wear special underwear or play with a certain toy on the toilet may be an incentive. For some children, the use of a low potty chair is appealing. After age three, the attitude should be that Jonny is learning about the toilet and will use it when ready. Normal children will be toilet trained when they start kindergarten. Pressure will prolong their need to show they are in control and cause unnecessary resentment. Here are some examples of active listening with toilet training.

Steven, age two and one-half, is in training pants. He has been using the toilet frequently at home, but at the center he is too busy and distracted to stop playing in time to go to the toilet. Just as he reaches the toilet, he wets himself. Steven cries.

TEACHER:    How disappointing! It looks like the pee came out before you got to the toilet. And you were trying so hard to get there. I'll get you some dry clothes while you're taking off your wet ones.

*Before nap time, all toilet trained children are taken to the bathroom. Today Steven resists going.*

TEACHER:    Sometimes it's just too much trouble to go potty. But I'm concerned that the pee will come out while you're sleeping and make you and your mat get all wet. Would you rather have a diaper on this time?

*After his nap, although Steven did go to the toilet, he still wet the bed.*

TEACHER:    It must be awfully uncomfortable to wake up all wet. Here are some dry clothes.

The child who is recently toilet trained but still wetting herself frequently may not be ready or may just be bored with the whole process. In that case, the teacher may say, "It looks like today is a good day to wear a diaper. What do you think?" If she prefers a diaper that day, there should be no guilt involved. As in everything, the child's feelings are more important than her performance.

## No More Bottles

Weaning also can become a control issue, except that parents do have the control over the breast or bottle. Again, there is often outside pressure to "get this child weaned," for the same reasons that are used to hurry toilet training. A tactful and sensitive teacher can reassure parents that it is normal and acceptable to allow children to wean and toilet train themselves.

In scores of countries and cultures, breast-feeding is the norm until a child is three years of age. Whether this practice is due to economics, health, survival, or allowing toddlers to be toddlers, there is no indication of harm to the child in the societies where breast-feeding is extended. Emotional harm is more likely when the breast or bottle is taken away prematurely. Children's centers are also responsible for much premature weaning; in many centers there are rules about bottles, as there are about diapers. These rules are not based on any developmental guidelines; they are made strictly for the convenience of the staff.

By age three, most American children are no longer drinking from bottles. They are too busy doing other things and want to be like the older kids. For a child who still has a bottle, however, age three seems to be an appropriate time to withdraw it. This decision is based primarily on concern expressed by dentists; they believe that children who continue drinking from bottles after the age of three may develop misaligned or crooked teeth.

The teacher can start the weaning process by gradually diluting milk in the bottle with more and more water, explaining her action to the child and telling him that on his third birthday he will be through with bottles.

For some children, the transition is made easier by being given a special cup to use when they would have had a bottle. Other children hardly notice. Rarely will three-year-olds really care about keeping the bottle. If, however, children have a problem with weaning, here is an active listening example that may help (see Chapter 9 for more on bottles).

Kim recently turned three. She arrives early in the morning and asks for a bottle. She is looking tearful and vulnerable.

TEACHER: Kim, sounds like you're feeling sad and missing your bottle.

KIM: Yes, and I want it now.

TEACHER: Are you thirsty? I can give you a cup of milk.

KIM: No, I don't want a cup; I want my bottle.

TEACHER: Maybe the problem is not that you're thirsty. I wonder if you want something to cuddle with.

KIM: I want to cuddle up with my bottle.

TEACHER: That would be comforting, but I don't have a bottle for you any more. What else is good for cuddling?

*Kim looks around the room and spots a soft teddy bear. She picks it up and carries it to the resting mat.*

KIM:  We'll get under my blanket together.

*The teacher sits next to Kim and holds or hugs her. As Kim finds comforting replacements for her bottle, her need for it will diminish, and it will become less and less important.*

## I Won't Eat That Yukky Food

Eating may be the most common control issue that exists between parents and children. Parents seem to worry more about their children's eating habits than anything else. Ironically, in an overweight society, parents worry about whether the child is eating enough. Children, however, are born with individual body types, generally inherited from their parents. They periodically go through "growth spurts" when they eat voraciously. When their growth is slow, they naturally eat less. Normally, children eat only when they are hungry.

If mealtime in the classroom is made as pleasant as possible, if a variety of wholesome, nutritious, tasty food is offered, and if children are allowed to choose freely what to eat, they will eat well. But at home many children are taught to be defensive about food. They may be forced, cajoled, or bribed into eating. They bring their defenses to the children's center and when served something they don't like blurt out, "I don't like that" or "I won't eat that yukky food." Whatever the child's food problems may be at home, the center or preschool can provide mealtimes that allow children to make their own choices and eat only what they like and want, scraping unwanted food into the trash without comment by the teacher. This routine guarantees children control over their eating.

Although it is best to say little about a child's eating habits, the teacher can use active listening to convey acceptance of children's mealtime needs and alleviate some of the children's anxieties. Brandon, age two and one-half, provides an example.

*At lunch, Brandon is picking the olives off his pizza.*

BRANDON:  I hate these black things. They're yukky.

TEACHER:  You prefer your pizza without olives?

BRANDON:  Yeah. I don't want these olives.

TEACHER:  What can you do with food you don't want?

BRANDON:  Throw it in the trash. It's yukky.

TEACHER:  I'm glad you remembered what to do.

*At snack time, Brandon adores what is served. He helps himself to a huge pile of fruit.*

TEACHER:  Brandon, you must really like bananas and oranges. I'll bet you could eat all of them. But it looks like some other kids like them, too, and they're waiting for you to pass them.

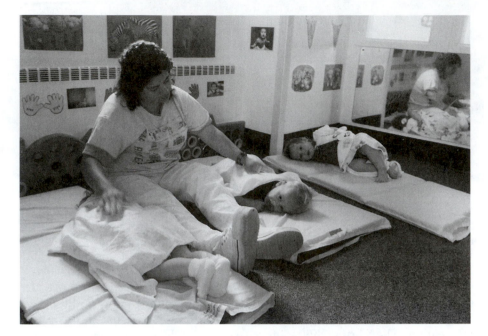

**Figure 4.10**   *Active listening can help a restless child relax and fall asleep.*

It is worth the effort to keep mealtimes neutral and pleasant for both children and teachers.

## I'm Not Sleepy

Toddlers in a stimulating program should welcome their naps and sleep soundly. After a morning of activity with plenty of outdoor play, most children are tired and need very little encouragement to fall asleep. Because nap time is usually used for teachers' breaks and various tasks, it is necessary that the children either sleep or at least rest during a certain amount of the day. With a consistent routine of diaper changing, washing up, and listening to stories or soft music, children usually need only a dark, quiet room and a gentle back rub to fall asleep (Figure 4.10).

However, every group includes one or two toddlers who are extremely restless, wide awake, or afraid to fall asleep. Here are three different napping scenes to serve as examples.

Melissa is about eighteen months old and is new to the center. Nap time is stressful for her. She is upset and crying for her mother.

TEACHER:   You must be feeling very upset and missing your mom.

*Melissa continues to sob.*

TEACHER:  It must be a little scary to sleep in a new place.

*Melissa cries more.*

TEACHER:  Will it help if I pat your back?

*The teacher pats Melissa's back gently and rhythmically. Soon the sobbing subsides, and Melissa falls asleep.*

Some days Danny's parents begin work later and allow him to sleep late in the morning. On those days, he is wide awake at nap time. Today is one of those days. Danny is two and one-half years old.

TEACHER:  Feeling wide awake, Danny? It must be annoying to have to lie down when you're not tired. Boring, too, I'll bet.

DANNY:  I not sleepy.

TEACHER:  I'm sure you'd rather be up playing.

DANNY:  Yeah. No nap.

TEACHER:  I wish I could let you get up, but the other teacher is on her break. There's no teacher to watch you while you play. When she returns, you may get up.

DANNY:  Get up?

TEACHER:  Yes, at two o'clock. Meanwhile, would you like to look at some books while you're lying on your mat?

*The teacher allows Danny, who is obviously not sleepy, to look quietly at books.*

The teacher has finished reading stories to Sarah and her group. She puts on a restful Beethoven record, tucks the nappers in on their sleeping mats, and sits next to them, catching up on her paperwork. Sarah, an energetic three-year-old, thrashes around on her mat, rearranges her blanket, does a half headstand on her mat, and hums to herself. Everyone around her finds her antics interesting. The teacher moves closer to Sarah.

TEACHER:  Restless today? Looks like you're having a hard time getting settled on your mat.

SARAH:  I want to get up.

TEACHER:  Ready to get up already? It's time to rest now.

SARAH:  I'm not sleepy.

TEACHER:  You're not sleepy yet, but I remember that every day you fall asleep at nap time. What would help you fall asleep?

SARAH:  Rub my back.

TEACHER:  Sounds like a good idea. I'll rub with one hand and write with the other.

*Minutes later Sarah is asleep.*

## My Owie Hurts

Sometimes adults think the best way to help injured children feel better is to tell them not to worry, that it's nothing. Another approach is telling them not to cry, to be brave. This is an example of discounting. Children are too smart to believe that something that hurts, makes a mark, or has blood coming out of it is "nothing to worry about." When adults encourage them to deny their fears and discount their feelings, children may lose their trust either in the adult or in their own judgment. Like adults, children prefer the truth and can deal with it much better than with denials and distractions. On the assumption that most injuries occurring in children's centers are minor (bumps, scratches, scrapes, and bites), here are some active listening responses to injuries.

Zack, age two, trips over a toy truck in the playground and bumps his face against the climbing structure. His nose begins to bleed profusely, and some blood drips on his hand. Seeing the blood, Zack panics and cries loudly.

TEACHER:  Are you hurt, Zack? Let me see your nose.

*Zack continues to cry.*

TEACHER:  How upsetting. It must hurt a lot.

   ZACK:  Owie hurts.

TEACHER:  Let's go to the bathroom and clean it off.

*In the bathroom, the teacher sits Zack down on the changing table. He is still crying.*

TEACHER:  There's some blood coming out of your nose where you bumped it. It must be scary to see your blood come out.

*Zack looks at the blood on his hands and continues to cry.*

TEACHER:  I'm washing off the blood, and now I have to pinch your nose for a minute to make the blood stop. After that, I'll wash off your hands.

*Zack begins to calm down and repeats, "Owie hurts."*

TEACHER:  I'm sure it does hurt. It will probably hurt for a while, but it will get better soon.

*The teacher gives Zack a comforting hug and takes him back outside. Soon Zack is playing with his friends again.*

Discounting a child's feelings by implying they are not real only makes the child more fearful and confused. By acknowledging Zack's fears and pain, the teacher conveys to him her acceptance of his feelings about the injury and also helps him feel reassured that his injury will heal.

## Active Listening with Preschoolers

By the time most children have reached four years of age, they have left behind many of the problems that required active listening. They have outgrown control issues involving diapering, toileting, weaning, and tantrums. Eating may still be an issue, as may napping, because some older children do not need to sleep during the day. But these issues are no longer significant. Many, if not most, preschool problems stem from the four- and five-year-old's need to be more grown up. This is a very wise, independent, and self-righteous time of life. Children's imagination is in full gear. Preschoolers absorb all they hear, whether at home, at the center, or on television, and they have no qualms about repeating everything. All is, of course, open to interpretation. Their liberal mixing of fact and fantasy brings countless smiles every day to those who are with them.

Because preschoolers are striving for personal power and control over their world, they try all the tactics they think might work. Teachers hear "MY mommy says I can SO bang on the window" or "MY daddy always lets me climb on MY fence." Conversely, parents hear "MY teacher NEVER makes me take a nap." These are not conscious lies, but rather the embellishments of wishful thinking. To their peers, children make such threats as "I won't let you come to my birthday party" or "You can NEVER come to my house." As adults, we cannot begin to understand the power these words have over a young child.

Because children's urge to control their peers is so strong during the preschool years, I offer a number of examples of ways to apply active listening to the victims of such control. The teacher's role is not to interfere with these control attempts, but to be a listener for the victims and help them call on their own inner resources to cope with the situation. This type of active listening is combined with negotiation in Chapter 5.

### Do It My Way

Alison and Kelly play together every day. Alison is bigger and more domineering than Kelly and loves to exercise her personal power. Kelly is shy and sensitive, and when Alison tries to control her Kelly becomes very upset. Seldom, however, does she stand up for herself. Today the girls are playing house.

ALISON:  We're only using the blue dishes on the table. I only like blue dishes.

KELLY:  I like yellow dishes, too.

ALISON:  My mommy says we can only play with blue dishes.

*Alison sets the table with blue dishes while Kelly watches silently.*

ALISON:  See, the blue dishes are prettier.

*Silently, Kelly places a yellow cup on the table. Alison immediately removes it.*

ALISON:  No! Just blue dishes, I said.

*Kelly's lower lip begins to quiver. Finding herself overruled, she approaches the teacher.*

KELLY:  Alison won't let me play with the yellow dishes.
TEACHER:  How annoying. Did you talk to her about it?

*Kelly puts her thumb in her mouth and shakes her head no.*

TEACHER:  Looks like that's pretty upsetting to you.

*Kelly nods her head yes.*

TEACHER:  You want to play with the yellow dishes, but Alison says no. Do you have to do what Alison tells you to do?
KELLY:  She won't let me.
TEACHER:  It seems to me that it's up to you to make that choice. What do you think?

*Kelly sucks on her thumb and thinks about it. Soon she returns to play with Alison. She picks up a yellow dish and puts it on the table.*

ALISON:  I told you we're only using blue dishes.

*Kelly responds in a stronger voice than before.*

KELLY:  I want the yellow dishes, too.

*Alison shrugs and continues setting the table, accepting Kelly's yellow dishes on the table.*

When one child asserts herself, very often the other will back off (Figure 4.11). It is surprising how a young child can sense strength or weakness in a peer and will respect assertiveness. But it may take more than one try for the less assertive child to approach the dominant child as an equal. She may fare better with children who are younger or on her own level socially, working her way up to the dominant child in the future. It is also sometimes helpful for the teacher to go with the less assertive child to help her approach the more dominant child. I discuss shyness more broadly in Chapter 8.

## Your Picture Is Ugly

Eric and James are painting at the easel, one on each side. From time to time, they stop and look at each other's pictures. They are a competitive twosome and usually try to get the better of each other.

ERIC:  Do you like my picture? It's a monster.

**Figure 4.11**    *Active listening encourages a less powerful child to be assertive.*

JAMES:  Your picture is ugly. Look at my monster. It's really scary.

ERIC:  My picture's not ugly. It's a scary one, too.

JAMES:  It is so ugly.

*James turns to another child.*

JAMES:  His picture's ugly, isn't it?

*Eric comes to the teacher.*

ERIC:  James says my picture's ugly.

TEACHER:  That must hurt your feelings. What do YOU think about your picture?

ERIC:  I like it. It's a scary monster.

JAMES:  No, it isn't; it's ugly. Mine is better.

*The teacher comments without judging the pictures.*

TEACHER:  Eric's picture is black and gray. It has lots of swirls, and here are some drips. He says it's a scary monster. James made his green with zigzags and a triangle shape on one side. He says his is a scary monster, too.

*The boys smile, a bit smugly, content that the teacher noticed both pictures.*

This scene will occur over and over, but the teacher always uses active listening and remains neutral. She can certainly tell a child that she likes his painting when there is no conflict going on. During a conflict, however, the goal of active listening is to help the child call on his own inner resources and decide for himself that his picture is fine. In this example, the teacher comments positively about both boys' pictures without encouraging rivalry, and her comments are sincere. She helps each boy find reasons for admiring his own painting.

## You Can't Sit by Me

It is lunchtime, and Maggie is sitting at the table. Brad, the least favorite of Maggie's friends, sits down next to her. Brad is younger and less mature than most of the group. He is also a messy eater.

MAGGIE:  You can't sit by me. I hate you.

BRAD:  I can sit here if I want to.

'MAGGIE:  No, you can't sit here.

*Brad starts to cry and complains to the teacher.*

BRAD:  Maggie won't let me sit here.

TEACHER:  It seems to be upsetting to you, but I see that you're still sitting there.

BRAD:  But Maggie says I can't.

TEACHER:  It's up to you to decide where you sit.

BRAD:  I'm sitting here, Maggie; it's my choice.

## I'm the Prettiest

Danielle and Gretchen are wearing fancy dress-up clothes. They try on an assortment of short nighties (they serve as dresses), high heels, superhero capes, and wigs.

DANIELLE:  I'm the prettiest.

GRETCHEN:  I'm pretty, too.

DANIELLE:  No, you're not. You're ugly!

GRETCHEN:  I'm the prettiest!

DANIELLE:  No way. I'm the only pretty one!

*Gretchen approaches the teacher.*

GRETCHEN:  Danielle says I'm not the prettiest. She says I'm ugly.

*Gretchen begins to cry.*

TEACHER:  Sounds like she hurt your feelings when she called you ugly. Do you want to talk to her about it?

GRETCHEN:  (to Danielle) That hurts my feelings.

DANIELLE:  OK. You can be pretty, too.

*The girls continue playing with each other.*

## My Daddy Will Chop Your Head Off

Tanya and Michael are standing next to each other at the sink, washing their hands before lunch. Michael accidentally splashes some water on Tanya. She retorts quickly.

TANYA:  If you splash me again, my daddy will chop your head off.

*Michael, who takes things literally, looks terrified and runs to hide behind the teacher.*

TEACHER:  Is there a problem, Michael?

MICHAEL:  Tanya scared me.

TEACHER:  You look pretty scared. Do you want to talk to Tanya about it?

*Tanya is still at the sink, smiling smugly at her accomplishment.*

TEACHER:  I can go with you to talk to Tanya.

*When Tanya sees the teacher coming with Michael, her expression changes.*

TANYA:  Michael, you can come to my house.

*Michael grins with relief as they go to lunch.*

## You Can't Come to My Party

Tracy and Meredith are best friends. They really care about what the other thinks. While playing with the doctor kit, Tracy tries to get the stethoscope from Meredith.

TRACY:  Can I have the stethoscope?

MEREDITH:  You can have it after me.

TRACY:  I need it now. My dolly's sick.

MEREDITH:  No. I'm not done with it.

TRACY:  If you don't give it to me, you can't come to my birthday party.

*Meredith looks anxious and tries to decide what to do. Threats about birthday parties are taken seriously in the preschool.*

TRACY:   I really mean it. You can't come to my party if you don't give it to me.

*Meredith is very quiet. Her lower lip begins to quiver, and tears come to her eyes. She goes to the teacher and stands next to her.*

TEACHER:   Meredith, you look very sad. Do you want to talk about it?

*Tracy watches Meredith go to the teacher. She looks guilty and speaks in a lower voice.*

TRACY:   She can't come to my party.

TEACHER:   That's why Meredith looks so sad. Do you want to say something to Tracy?

*With tears running down her face, Meredith shakes her head no. Meanwhile, Cory, who is listening, speaks up.*

CORY:   Meredith can come to MY birthday party. Do you want to come, Meredith?

TRACY:   No. She can't. She's MY friend and she can only come to MY birthday party.

*Tracy puts her arms around Meredith. Meredith obviously enjoys being wanted by both girls. Tracy and Meredith continue playing.*

## Don't Say That to Me

Brian and Robin are building with blocks. They have made several different structures when the teacher announces that it is time to go outdoors. Brian, who likes to procrastinate, continues to build. Robin takes his cue from the teacher.

ROBIN:   Come on, Brian; we have to go outside.

BRIAN:   Don't say that to me.

ROBIN:   We have to put our blocks away.

*Brian continues to play.*

BRIAN:   Don't say that to me.

*Robin tells the teacher.*

ROBIN:   Brian won't put his toys away.

TEACHER:   You must be concerned about him going outdoors with the group. Why don't you put your share of the blocks away? Then you'll be ready.

The teacher again announces to the group that it is time to go outside. Everyone except Brian is ready. He now quickly gets his blocks put away in time to join the group.

## You're a Poop

With children imitating adults and hearing profanity on television, it is not surprising that they bring certain "tabu" words to the preschool. Use of these words is more and more common in school-age children, and it is not unusual among the younger set. Generally, the most effective approach is to pointedly ignore offensive language. But if a child is being called names by another child and does not like it, he certainly has every right to object.

Benjy and Andrew are good friends. On the playground, they are climbing and sliding on the climbing structure.

BENJY:  Let's slide down together.

ANDREW:  No, I want to play by myself. I'll go first.

BENJY:  You're a poop!

ANDREW:  I'm not a poop!

*Benjy chants loudly.*

BENJY:  Andrew is a poop. Andrew is a poop.

*Andrew responds, screaming.*

ANDREW:  No, I'm not. I'm not a poop.

BENJY:  You're a poop! You're a poop!

*Andrew comes to the teacher.*

ANDREW:  Benjy's calling me a poop. He won't stop.

TEACHER:  How frustrating. You must hate being called names. Did you tell him that?

*Andrew turns back to Benjy.*

ANDREW:  Stop calling me names. I hate it!

*Benjy continues his name-calling.*

TEACHER:  I hear Andrew saying that he doesn't want to be called names. It's important to listen to him.

ANDREW:  Stop, Benjy. I don't like it.

BENJY:  Okay. I won't call you a poop. Let's go down the slide together.

## You Can't Play with Us

Exclusion of a child by other children is a problem that may require a bit more teacher intervention than other control issues. To be the only one excluded from a group activity is more than many children can tolerate without feeling more pain than is good for their self-esteem. Although the teacher should always be there to protect children from emotional as well as

**Figure 4.12** *When a child's feelings are hurt, active listening can help.*

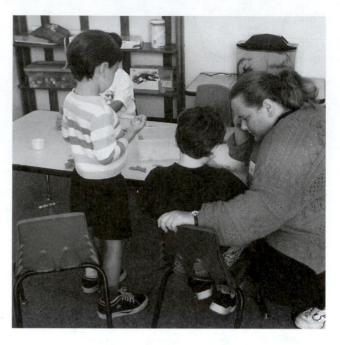

physical harm, she does not need to use a heavy-handed approach. Active listening can play an important role (Figure 4.12).

Three children are playing house in the dramatic play area. They are pretending to cook and take care of their dolls. A fourth child, Jenna, joins the group and begins to cook.

KATIE:    Go away. You can't play with us.

SOPHIE:   Yeah, go away. Don't touch the dishes.

TYLER:    We're playing here. No one else can play with us.

JENNA:    I want to play house, too.

KATIE:    No. Go away. We don't like you.

SOPHIE:   Yeah. We hate Jenna, don't we?

JENNA:    I can play if I want to.

TYLER:    No, you can't. We won't let you.

*The group starts yelling at Jenna, telling her she cannot play.*

TEACHER:  I can hear that there's a problem here. Do you want to talk about it?

JENNA:    They won't let me play.

TEACHER:  That must be upsetting. It hurts your feelings, too. What would you like to say to them?

JENNA:  I want to play, too.

SOPHIE:  We want to play by ourselves.

TEACHER:  I hear Jenna saying she wants to play here, and I hear Sophie, Katie, and Tyler saying they want to play by themselves.

TYLER:  Yeah. We don't want her to play.

TEACHER:  One thing we do at our school is allow kids to decide for themselves where they want to play. I see that Sophie, Katie, and Tyler have decided to be in the kitchen area. I see that Jenna has also decided to play here. Looks like everyone has made his own decision.

KATIE:  But we don't want to let Jenna play with us.

TEACHER:  This is Jenna's decision to play here, and it's your decision, too. If anyone wants to leave this area, that's also that person's decision.

The original three look at one another, deciding what to do. They all remain, including Jenna, and are soon playing together.

## This Is Boring

This morning the preschool group is working on a project that requires waiting for turns. They are tape-recording their voices. Each child takes a turn talking about his or her family. Some children are slow starters and take some time opening up to the tape recorder. Tiffany and Michelle are sitting next to each other. They have had their turns and are now acting silly and noisy.

TEACHER:  Tiffany and Michelle, I know it's hard to sit quietly when you've had your turn, but it's important to let other kids have their turns, too.

TIFFANY:  This is boring. I don't want to listen to them talk.

TEACHER:  It is hard to sit quietly and wait. You must be pretty restless by now. I wish we were finished, but I do want to hear what the other kids say, too.

MICHELLE:  But I'm bored with waiting. I want to play.

The teacher decides whether it is important for everyone to listen to the child who is now speaking or whether those who have finished might quietly look at books or work on puzzles. Either solution is appropriate. Whatever she decides, she has let the children know that she does understand how hard it is to wait.

## Summing Up Active Listening

Active listening is part of the process that is problem solving. By itself, it fills a deep need held by all of us: to be heard, understood, and accepted. When used with negotiation, explained in Chapter 5, and with setting limits, explained in Chapter 6, active listening adds a priceless dimension: empathy.

Active listening can be nonverbal or verbal and may be used with children of all ages. When used with a nonverbal infant, active listening consists mainly of the "guessing game": interpreting the baby's crying, expressions, and body language. The process is similar when used with non–English-speaking children. Verbal active listening is the process of interpreting the feelings behind the child's words, reflecting them back, and waiting for confirmation by the child. The teacher gives a name to the child's feelings and accepts all feelings as valid.

The active listening examples in this chapter cover a wide range of emotions and responses. All were taken from real situations with real children and teachers. As a teacher, you will encounter and respond to many similar situations. Here, in brief form, are the steps to use for active listening with the children in your care.

1. The teacher is open, approachable, and accessible to the children.

2. When infants and toddlers express their feelings nonverbally, the teacher calls on her knowledge of the child and makes an educated guess.

3. All feelings are accepted as valid. They are never discounted; teachers do not try to distract children from their emotions.

4. The teacher reflects back to the child what he thinks the child is feeling, using phrases such as "It sounds like," "I hear you saying," or "It seems to me that."

5. Feelings are given names that describe them as accurately as possible.

6. The teacher uses a warm, accepting, and empathetic tone of voice.

7. The teacher encourages and allows children to solve their own problems.

## Practice and Discussion _____

1. What does the phrase "acceptance and trust" mean to you as a teacher of young children? Discuss or write a paragraph about how to convey acceptance and trust to a young child both nonverbally and verbally.

2. Make a poster using words that express strong feelings that are often confused with or covered by anger. If you are already working as a teacher, hang the poster in your center.

3. Choose any topic for discussion, and have two students in your class-room role-play active listening. Use Figure 4.5 as a guide. Practicing with a number of students may be helpful.

4. What is the guessing game? What are some things to look for when playing the guessing game with infants?

5. How does active listening relate to a child's self-esteem? Pick one of the examples in this chapter to demonstrate the relationship.

6. Pick an example of a power issue from the section "Active Listening with Toddlers" in this chapter. Rewrite the example using an authoritarian approach. How would the outcome differ?

7. Write your own example of active listening with a toddler of limited verbal skills. Does this approach feel comfortable to you?

8. Write your own example of active listening with a preschooler with good verbal skills. Analyze your need to control or not control what the preschooler says.

9. Evaluate your current feelings about active listening. Do you have strong feelings about using it or not using it? Does it feel natural or contrived?

10. Practice active listening on someone in your family or a close friend without telling him or her what you are doing. Do you notice any particular reaction? Is it positive or negative?

---

## Notes

1. John Gottman, *The Heart of Parenting* (New York: Simon & Schuster, 1997), pp. 111–12.

2. William Pollack, *Real Boys* (New York: Henry Holt and Company, Inc., 1998), pp. 32–33.

3. Mary Sheedy Kurcinka, *Raising Your Spirited Child* (New York: HarperCollins, 1991).

4. Pollack, *Real Boys*, p. 40.

5. Pollack, *Real Boys*, p. 43.

6. Michael Gurian, *The Wonder of Boys* (New York: Tarcher/Putnam, 1997), pp. 20–21.

7. Thomas Gordon, *P.E.T.: Parent Effectiveness Training* (New York: New American Library, 1975), chapter 3.

8. Daniel Goleman, *Emotional Intelligence* (New York: Bantam Books, 1997), pp. 104–106.

9. E. H. Erikson, *Childhood and Society* (New York: W. W. Norton, 1985), pp. 247–74.

10. Richard M. Restak, *The Infant Mind* (New York: Doubleday, 1986), p. 212.

11. Restak, *The Infant Mind*, p. 207.

## Recommended Reading

Goleman, Daniel. *Emotional Intelligence.* New York: Bantam Books, 1997.

Gopnik, Alison, Andrew N. Meltzoff, and Patricia K. Kuhl. *The Scientist In the Crib.* New York: William Morrow and Company, 1999.

Gordon, Thomas. *P.E.T.: Parent Effectiveness Training.* New York: New American Library, 1975.

Gottman, John. *The Heart of Parenting.* New York: Simon & Schuster, 1997.

Greenspan, Stanley I. *The Essential Partnership.* New York: Viking Penguin, Inc., 1989.

Gurian, Michael. *The Wonder of Boys.* New York: Tarcher/Putnam, 1997.

Kurcinka, Mary Sheedy. *Raising Your Spirited Child.* New York: HarperCollins, 1991.

Pollack, William. *Real Boys.* New York: Henry Holt and Company, 1998.

Restak, Richard M. *The Infant Mind.* New York: Doubleday, 1986.

Sanger, Sirgay. *Baby Talk—Parent Talk: Understanding Your Baby's Body Language.* New York: Doubleday, 1991.

# 5

# *Negotiation*

Imagine that you are sitting comfortably in your living room watching your favorite television program. You are thoroughly engrossed in the story; in fact, the most exciting part is coming up. Suddenly, there's a knock at your door. When you answer it, you find a neighbor, one you know only casually. She says, "My TV just broke and I'd really like to borrow yours to watch. My favorite program is on tonight and I'd hate to miss it." What would you do?

When you refuse to lend your television set, your spouse (or roommate) hears what happened and says, "Shame on you for not sharing. How could you be so selfish? You're supposed to share!" These words do not make you feel kind and generous. They make you feel hurt and resentful.

Sharing is something we as adults do only when we are in control of a situation and are willing to make a sacrifice for a person or cause of our choice. Giving or losing our possessions to others through coercion, force, or threats could not really be called sharing, could it? Yet people do choose to share possessions and money with friends, relatives, and those in need. Most of us, under the right circumstances, do share.

## The Process and the Steps

Children are, by nature, possessive, territorial, and egocentric. All this is a natural part of development. They must first establish and feel secure in their own identities before being able to take the great leap to empathy, consideration, and generosity toward others. In the example above, even the most generous adult would refuse to automatically share a possession as ordinary as a television set. This is why the insistence that toddlers share their precious toys with friends is unrealistic and seems cruel to them.

It is safe to say that all parents want their children to share. Over and over, I observe parents forcing their obstinate and frustrated child to give up a toy to another child. "Good boys and girls share their toys," they say. If the child refuses and throws a tantrum, the parents look embarrassed and guilty, perhaps even punishing the child. Why do we expect so much more of our children than of ourselves?

Sharing is a concept that is totally foreign and perplexing to infants and toddlers. Somewhere between three and four years of age, however, children who have been allowed total control over their belongings will begin to enjoy a limited amount of voluntary sharing. Again, this must be their own decision. If children have always had the right to say no to sharing, they will acquire the maturity and desire to say yes. This is partly because by the time they are three or four years old they discover that sharing is more fun than playing alone.

How does problem solving deal with the question of sharing? In a children's program, the circumstances are obviously different from those in a child's home setting. The toys are there for everyone to play with, and they belong to no one. If a child brings a toy from home, it is definitely his or hers. But what about the center's toys?

If you've cared for young children, you know that they are capable of fighting over the most insignificant object. With a group of toddlers and preschoolers, you could find yourself refereeing all day long. Most adults feel that it is easier and less trying simply to step in as the authority figure and tell kids what to do. This solution may be easier for adults, but it certainly fails to address the long-term process of helping children learn to get their needs met in a positive, productive way. It also fails to give children the skills they need to form close, lasting relationships with other children.

The term in problem solving that refers to resolving conflicts is "negotiation." Like everything else in problem solving, it is part of a process. When the teacher uses authority and decides who is right and wrong, the conflict is, theoretically, over, and everyone abides by the ruling. With negotiation, the children involved participate equally in solving the problem, then decide on the preferred solution and abide by their own decision. This approach is more time-consuming for the adults in the center. It requires attention and patience, and sometimes the children cannot reach a mutually satisfactory solution. The process of negotiation, however, is more important than the outcome. Children are learning during this process.

Negotiation is not a matter of finding an instant answer to a problem. It is about children learning social skills, such as assertiveness, that will last a lifetime. It is about learning to see another person's point of view. It is also about learning to be a good listener as well as a clear communicator. And it is about taking responsibility for your own actions. Adults are always relieved when kids solve their problem and stop fighting, but for a long-term goal, the learning process is much more important.

To understand the process of negotiation, reread the opening pages of Chapter 1, the example of the red tricycle. Two children wanted the red tricycle even though there were other trikes. Their tugging and yelling were leading nowhere, so the teacher assumed the role of facilitator and helped them solve their problem. In the course of facilitating, the teacher followed certain steps (Figure 5.1):

1. She helped the children identify their problem. Both children wanted the red trike.

2. She encouraged them to contribute ideas for solving the problem and gave them enough time to think of ideas. Any idea was okay.

3. She restated their ideas in a positive way. Each child wanted the other to find another tricycle. Then they said they could take turns.

4. She helped them decide which idea they preferred. They preferred taking turns.

5. She helped them carry out their solution. She told them when five minutes were up.

6. She reinforced the process by telling them how well they had solved their problem.[1]

Notice what the teacher did *not* do. She did not place any blame, try to figure out who really had the trike first, order the children to take turns, separate them, scold or lecture them about sharing, ask why both wanted the red trike, or redirect, threaten, cajole, distract, or discount their feelings. None of these tactics is used in problem solving.

Teacher facilitates

1. Helps children identify the problem
2. Encourages children to contribute
   ideas; suggests ideas if children get stuck
3. Restates ideas in a positive way
4. Helps children decide on the best
   idea
5. Helps children carry out their
   solution
6. Reinforces the process when the
   problem is solved

Children negotiate

The role of the teacher in negotiation is to make
it easier for children to communicate their ideas
for solving problems.  She follows steps 1 through 6
without interfering with the children's own flow of
ideas. Nonverbal and non–English-speaking children
need more help; verbal children need less help.

**Figure 5.1**    *Resolving conflicts through negotiation.*

Negotiation is appropriate whenever there is a conflict between children—that is, when the relationship "owns the problem." Negotiation is also appropriate between teachers and children when the problem belongs to them together. All children should feel that they have a part to play in resolving conflicts and that they will be listened to and respected. They should also know they will never be forced to negotiate. At times, children may decide a situation is not worth their time and effort. They may choose simply to walk away from it. This is every bit as acceptable as sticking with the situation.

A prerequisite to effective facilitating on the teacher's part is to get to know each child as well as possible. It is important to know which children

**Figure 5.2**    *The teacher's use of her body contributes to the negotiation process.*

are more powerful physically and emotionally and which are weaker. It is important to know how verbal children are and how well they understand what is going on. A teacher must also learn each child's capacity for frustration. Knowing the children's level of skills and limitations helps the teacher in facilitating.

The way the teacher uses her own body while facilitating also contributes to her effectiveness. She must establish eye contact with each of the children involved. This technique helps build trust between all parties and focuses attention on the problem. It requires the teacher to get down to the children's eye level by bending, kneeling, or squatting. This act of lowering her body also equalizes the situation; the teacher is no longer a large force looming over the children but rather a person of their stature (Figure 5.2).

Tone of voice is extremely important, as it is in all aspects of problem solving. For the teacher to remain a helper, rather than an enforcer, her voice should be neutral, nonjudgmental, and respectful. The teacher's role is not to take sides or become emotionally involved in the problem, but rather to be there and to be helpful if and when she is needed.

If the teacher knows that two children are unequally matched—for example, one child is physically larger, more aggressive, or more intellectually powerful than the other—the teacher can choose to be positioned next to the weaker or victimized child, facing the more powerful or aggressive child. Without a word, this gives added power, confidence, and moral support to the smaller or weaker child. This strategy is called equalizing.

The goal of negotiation is always to help children get their needs met appropriately. Both children should be satisfied with the solution, and no child should ever "win" simply because she is able to overpower her playmate, whether physically, mentally, or emotionally.

Often during negotiation, children direct their comments and ideas to the teacher rather than to each other. The teacher who fails to recognize this may end up arguing with the children or trying to solve the problem herself. It is therefore essential to consistently direct the children to each other. A phrase such as "you can tell Billy about it" or a reminder to "talk to each other" will help. Many children have been taught by their parents to rely on adults to rescue them. A problem-solving teacher helps steer children away from this habit and encourages them to deal directly with each other.

Time is an important element in negotiation, and the teacher should allow sufficient time for children to think of their own ideas. The "right" amount of time is a matter of judgment that comes with experience. If a conflict continues for too long, however, and the teacher feels that her attention is being taken away from the others in the group, she may decide to remove the cause of the conflict, usually a toy, and let the children know that when they have decided on a solution she will gladly return to toy to them. If the conflict turns into a fight and there is hurting, the action should be stopped so that no one gets hurt, but in a way that allows communication to continue. The teacher's hand outstretched between the fighters helps them curtail their aggression but still allows them to face each other and talk or scream. The teacher can say, "I can't let you hurt each other, but you may use your words and talk." This technique is described later in the chapter in the section "Fair Fighting."

A practice currently popular with many teachers is called redirecting. This strategy consists of diverting a child's attention away from a conflict or problem and getting him interested in something or someone else. It may offer a temporary solution, but it does not help children learn to negotiate. If, however, the teacher offers this only as a suggestion by saying, for example, "I have an idea; would one of you like to play with a different doll?" or if children come up with this idea by themselves, then redirection can play a part in problem solving. The difference is significant. Teachers who depend heavily on redirection are teaching children to evade negotiation. Teachers who suggest redirection as one of many possibilities in the negotiation process are facilitating problem solving.

During negotiation, the teacher has an opportunity to provide children with tools that help them negotiate more assertively and confidently. Even a very young child can learn to put her hand up in a gesture that means "stop" and say the word "stop" to the other child. I have seen children at twelve months use this signal successfully to protect themselves and make a point.

Some very young children may also move their hand as if to slap at the other child, but the teacher can show them how to gesture without hitting. Sometimes both the victim and the aggressor will say "Stop," but they eventually catch on to how it works. The teacher who is facilitating should always make sure that the aggressor really does stop when the victim makes this gesture so that children will trust this process as one that can work for them.

When they are given the chance to participate equally in problem solving, children do cooperate. They really want approval, acceptance, and a sense of belonging to the group. The rewards of playing cooperatively become more appealing than the rewards of keeping a toy someone else wants. Somewhere within all children a little seed of altruism is growing. That is why negotiation works so splendidly with young children. It makes them feel lovable and loving.

Another reason negotiation works so well is that children who learn to negotiate are also learning to be assertive. Assertiveness is a quality most people respect and admire. Assertive people communicate self-confidence, strength, and power and compel others to listen to what they say. Assertive children will not be abused, ridiculed, or excluded. Everyone wants to play with them. Assertiveness is a quality children will carry throughout life. It will open many doors for them. It is to be nurtured, valued, and learned through negotiation.

Control, altruism, and assertiveness are some reasons why negotiation works. Try it with your own group of children, and they will amaze you. Remember, however, that negotiating requires time and a willingness to really allow children to solve their own problems.

There are several differences in negotiating with verbal and preverbal children. For that reason, this chapter includes separate sections for dealing with those two categories and numerous examples of negotiation applied to a variety of circumstances. There may be some overlapping, but the differences should be relatively clear. First, let us look at the moral implications of negotiation and some gender differences.

## *The Moral Implications of Negotiation*

The negotiation process does not depend on absolutes of right and wrong or on adult authority. Instead, it relies on the budding sense of fairness and altruism in normal children and their deep desire for acceptance by their peers. A child who negotiates learns what other children will tolerate and what they consider fair and acceptable. The child also learns how far he or she can push other people before invading their boundaries. During negotiation, children face each other and deal with their strengths and weaknesses. They learn what kind of impact their behavior has on other children and how to evaluate the consequences of their behavior. They test themselves to find out when to be flexible and when to stand their ground. Inevitably, they also learn to confront their own emotions and recognize that these emotions are transient and not fatal.

This complex process of making decisions, respecting the needs and desires of other children, considering the consequences of their actions on their playmates, and seeing themselves as other children see them contributes to the building of children's character, their moral quality. Not only does negotiation allow children to solve concrete problems, it also provides a framework for seeing the world as a place filled with possibilities. Children see that they can choose from a vast array of options if they can master the skills of negotiation. This positive outlook on life equips children to tackle whatever comes their way with self-assurance and optimism. Later in school, they will encounter rules, authority, and absolutes. Children armed with a sense of trust in their own decision-making powers will make morally sound choices on the basis of their own knowledge and experience as well as the dictates of society.

## Gender Differences in Negotiation

Whenever we address gender differences, we are dealing with generalities. Of course, a generalization does not apply to every child, and we don't want to set up stereotypical expectations. You may seldom come across these stereotypical situations. However, the more we accept potential gender differences, the better we can help children accept themselves and others.

Generally speaking, there are differences in the ways boys and girls negotiate. Boys often have difficulty looking at each other during a negotiation. They are more prone to become physical and threatening with each other, yelling and clenching their fists. If they do look at each other, it's to scream in the other boy's face. Some boys are extremely competitive and determined to outdo any challenger, whatever the issue. The facilitator's role is first to help them find at least a few words that will state the problem, then to help them focus on solving the problem instead of fighting or yelling. This is not always easy, and sometimes the facilitator must restate the problem frequently to focus attention on solutions (Figure 5.3).

Girls might be more willing to look at each other, but some are also more likely to expect the teacher to solve their problems. Girls may tattle and whine more than boys, but they also value reconciliation above competition. When girls negotiate, they seem to consider the effect that fighting will have on their relationship. The ultimate and most powerful threat is "I won't be your friend any more if. . . ." The facilitator must resist being drawn into an emotional diatribe; again, the negotiation should focus on solving the problem.

When a conflict is between a boy and a girl, the teacher may have to consciously remain neutral, remember that each has a source of inner

**Figure 5.3** *When boys negotiate, they often display angry body language.*

strength, and avoid making the assumption that the boy is the aggressor and the girl the victim. If the girl seems intimidated and gives in too readily, the facilitator should check with her to make sure this is what she really wants to do. If the boy gives in because the girl starts to cry, the facilitator should check with him as well. A successful negotiation should end with both parties voluntarily agreeing to a solution. Both boys and girls gain self-confidence and trust in the negotiation process when the outcome is mutually beneficial.

## Negotiating with Preverbal Children

When facilitating the negotiation process with infants or preverbal toddlers, the teacher has a special role to play. It is her job to put herself in the place of the child, try to guess what the problem really is, and express it verbally for each child. It is the same procedure as in active listening, with the addition of a conflict involving two or more children. Unless the children are clearly showing a preference for a solution, the teacher also provides them with ideas from which they can choose. A teacher's tendency may be to provide those ideas too quickly, without waiting for a cue from the children. It is therefore important to exercise restraint and patience, so preverbal children will have time to indicate their wishes. Otherwise, they may be denied the chance to work out their own solutions.

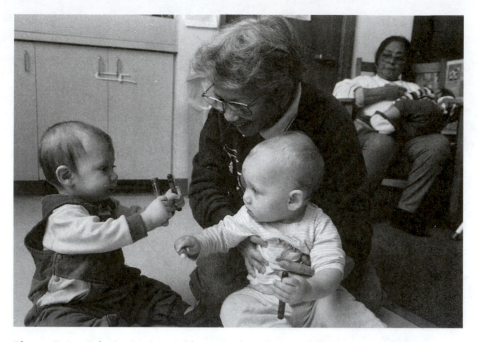

**Figure 5.4**    *Substitution is a viable option for infants and facilitates negotiation.*

Generally, only a few typical situations are appropriate to negotiation with infants, and they apply only to older infants. When babies begin to be mobile, they also begin to grab things from each other. This is a natural function of a healthy curiosity, a curiosity we certainly want to encourage as much as possible.

For older infants and young toddlers, substitution is often a viable option. At this stage, children often do not care about keeping a particular toy, especially if it is quickly replaced by another. Their short attention span allows them to change their focus frequently. To facilitate substitution, the center should have at least some duplicate or similar toys for infants and toddlers (Figure 5.4).

## Negotiating with Infants

Following are several examples of the most typical negotiation situations involving infants.

*What Can We Find for Ryan?*    Nine-month-old Ryan is sitting on the floor, contentedly shaking a wooden rattle. Cory, who is eleven months old and just beginning to walk, walks over to Ryan and grabs the rattle. Ryan begins to whimper and looks expectantly at the rattle. The teacher sits on the floor with both boys.

TEACHER:  Ryan, it looks like Cory took your rattle. Is that okay with you?

*Ryan looks at the rattle and whimpers some more.*

TEACHER:  Cory, I hear Ryan saying something. It sounds like he wants the rattle.

*Cory looks unconcerned and is happy with the rattle. The teacher brings him back to where Ryan is sitting.*

TEACHER:  Ryan, I wonder if you would like a different rattle. Cory, let's see if Ryan would like another rattle. I'll help you find one for him.

*The teacher and Cory look in the plastic tub for another rattle and bring it to Ryan.*

TEACHER:  Ryan, would you like to play with this rattle?

*Ryan takes the new rattle and tries to shake it. He seems satisfied.*

TEACHER:  Cory, it looks like that solved the problem. Ryan likes this new rattle, and you like yours.

What if Ryan had really wanted to keep his first rattle? Let's try it that way.

TEACHER:  Ryan, looks like Cory took your rattle. Is that okay with you?

*Ryan looks at the rattle and begins to cry.*

TEACHER:  Cory, I hear Ryan saying something. It sounds like he really wants his rattle back.

*The teacher brings Cory back to where Ryan is sitting.*

TEACHER:  Ryan, I hear that you really want that rattle back.

*Ryan continues to cry and look at the rattle.*

TEACHER:  Cory, I'll help you give this rattle back to Ryan; then we'll look in the tub for another rattle for you. That way you and Ryan will each have a rattle, and the problem will be solved.

Cory may object to returning the rattle to Ryan. Active listening will help until he finds another rattle he will accept.

***You Can Say "Stop"***    Tina, age ten months, is crawling on the floor and happens to crawl on top of twelve-month-old Georgie, knocking him over. Georgie is startled and reacts by crying. The teacher removes Tina from on top of Georgie.

**Figure 5.5**   *Even a preverbal child can learn to put up his hand and say "Stop!"*

TEACHER:   Georgie, what a surprise, having Tina knock you over. Looks like that startled you.

*The teacher helps Georgie sit up. He begins to calm down.*

TEACHER:   Georgie, is there something you want to tell Tina? You can tell her to stop.

*The teacher holds Georgie's hand up in front of him and says "Stop" for him.*

TEACHER:   Tina, Georgie wants you to be more careful and stop pushing him over.

The babies in this interaction are beginning to understand more every day. Although they are still young, the word "stop" seems to have meaning for them (Figure 5.5). It is one of the first words some infants learn to understand, and with it they learn the concept of protecting themselves from aggressors. The powerful word "stop" is usually enough to ward off a potentially harmful aggressor. Babies love to use this word and, in fact, sometimes try it out on their parents!

***Two Kids in the Same Spot***   Alexander, twelve months old, has crawled up the ramp to the infant climbing structure. He is followed by Cathy, who is eleven months old. Somehow they end up wanting to sit in the same spot. They push each other and cry. Cathy becomes very frustrated and screams loudly.

TEACHER:   Looks like you both want to be in the same place.

*They are not hurting each other, so the teacher watches closely but does not intervene.*

TEACHER:   Looks like you've decided to push each other. If that's okay with both of you, I'll just watch. But if one of you wants to move, I can help you move.

The infants continue to push and cry angrily. The teacher watches to see that they are not being hurt. Intermittently, she reminds them that they can stop if they want to. The teacher has a choice to make. She may watch them until one decides to crawl away, or, if she must care for other children, she can say, "I have other children to watch, so I'll have to move both of you to another place." Chances are good that they will not push and cry for very long; if she does remove them, they are unlikely to return to the same spot together.

These are the most common negotiation situations with babies under one year of age. Let's move on to young toddlers, who are still preverbal.

## Negotiating with Young Toddlers

Depending on program organization, young toddlers between twelve and twenty months may be in their own classroom or may be mixed in with older toddlers. The examples provided for preverbal toddlers include some for negotiating with toddlers close to the same age and others for negotiating with older toddlers. Although the examples for younger toddlers may be similar to those for infants, we must assume that children between twelve and twenty months are bigger and stronger and have larger vocabularies and better understanding than infants.

Some toddlers, especially younger ones, resist learning to negotiate. They may be new to the program and therefore not understand what is happening or what is expected of them. They might feel intimidated by the process or by a particular child. Whatever the reason, if the toddler cries, screams, and pulls away, it is best to avoid making an issue of it. You can simply say, "I can see that you're upset now. Maybe later you'll want to talk." Then tell the other child, "It looks like Natasha doesn't want to talk right now. Let's find another way to solve the problem."

If a child constantly and persistently reacts negatively to negotiation, observe her to try to learn why. Is she shy or upset about separating from her parents, or is this her way of evading confrontation? Her behavior may be an indication that her parents punish her or make her feel guilty when she is assertive or demanding about getting her way. It could also mean that no limits are set for her at home. Help her become involved in social interactions in less confrontational ways until she feels comfortable expressing her feelings within the group.

If this same child hurts or frightens other children and then refuses to listen to them, it is important for the other children to be able to express their feelings. You can hold her briefly so they can at least have their say, even if she refuses to listen. Eventually almost all children decide to cooperate with negotiation; they see it working for others and are willing to give it a try.

Toddlers frequently slap at each other with their hands during negotiation. This is almost a reflex and seldom hurts. There are, however, differences of opinion among caregivers as to whether children should be permitted to hit one another. On one hand, hitting is a fairly safe way for children to learn for themselves that fighting can hurt. As long as only slapping is involved and not more harmful aggression, it can be permitted for its value as a learning experience.

On the other hand, many people feel that any act of aggression by children should be prohibited. The level of violence in our world certainly makes this point of view understandable. Exploring this aspect of children's behavior, Clarke-Stewart in *Daycare* examined numerous studies of the difference in the level of aggression between children in day care and those who stay at home with a parent. The research indicates that children in day care are generally more aggressive but that much aggression in day care is eliminated when children are taught social skills. "Programs in which children are taught social problem-solving skills are least likely to promote aggression," she concluded.[2]

There is no proof, however, that allowing mild aggression in conjunction with teaching social problem-solving skills will result in violent behavior in a child's later life. A connection can be determined only by conducting long-term research on comparable groups of children, for example, (1) one group allowed to exhibit mild aggression while learning social problem-solving skills, (2) another group allowed to exhibit mild aggression without learning social problem-solving skills, (3) an additional group allowed to exhibit no aggression while learning social problem-solving skills, and (4) a final group allowed to exhibit no aggression at all and not learning social problem-solving skills. To my knowledge, no such research has been attempted.

I respect the opinion of some parents and teachers that no aggression should be permitted in a children's program, and I include examples that prohibit hitting. In my years of experience, however, I have observed that children who learn the problem-solving skill of negotiation come to depend on their words instead of aggressive behavior. They achieve this by being allowed to discover what strategies are most effective and tolerated by their peers, rather than by being prohibited from hitting. Therefore, I also include examples that allow hitting as long as it doesn't escalate to hurting. The section "Fair Fighting" relates primarily to older preschoolers. Individual teachers may exercise their options according to their own beliefs.

In negotiation, we encourage children to use their words. It is important to remember that infants and toddlers have few words at their disposal. They understand much more than they can say, so teachers must provide meaningful words that are easily spoken and get the point across. Words such as "stop," "move," and "mine" serve the purpose.

## Mine! I Want It!

Colin, age eighteen months, and Rachelle, age sixteen months, are rummaging around in the toy toolbox. Hammers are a great favorite, and there are several, but as usual there is one favorite: the red one. Colin finds the red hammer and walks away with it. Rachelle follows, trying to take the hammer from him. She grabs it and pulls, but Colin hangs on. They begin to cry loudly.

TEACHER:  Colin, I see that you want to keep the hammer. Can you say something to Rachelle about it?

*Colin just cries more loudly.*

TEACHER:  Rachelle, I can see that you want it, too. Do you want to say something to Colin?

*Rachelle also keeps crying and tugging.*

TEACHER:  Colin, do you want to say "Mine"?

*Colin stops crying long enough to say "Mine."*

TEACHER:  Rachelle, I hear Colin saying "Mine." Do you want to say "I want it"?

*This is a harder phrase to say, but Rachelle makes an attempt.*

TEACHER:  Good talking, Rachelle. Colin, I hear Rachelle saying she wants it. Colin is saying "Mine," and Rachelle is saying "I want it." Sounds like you both want the same hammer. What can you do when two kids want the same hammer? Any ideas?

Both toddlers recognize the word "ideas." They relate it to their past experience. To them, it means "go find another one." Colin thinks about it for a few seconds, then runs to the toolbox and pulls out another hammer, which he offers to Rachelle. The teacher says, "Wow, Colin had a great idea. He brought another hammer. Rachelle, is it okay with you to play with a different hammer?" Rachelle thinks about it. If she accepts the new hammer, the teacher says, "Looks like you've solved the problem. You each have your own hammer." If Rachelle refuses the offer, the teacher says, "Colin, it looks like Rachelle still wants the red hammer. Do you want to keep the green one?"

If Colin feels generous and cooperative, he will probably be satisfied with the green hammer. But because problems are not always so easily solved, let's carry through with the alternatives. Colin throws the green hammer on the floor and returns his focus to the red one. He tries to get it back. The teacher says, "Colin is showing that he still wants the red hammer. Any other ideas?" Being limited by their lack of verbal skills, the toddlers keep tugging on the red hammer. The teacher offers a suggestion: "I have an idea. I remember that sometimes you like to use the toy saw, too. Would either one of you like to use the saw or even the toy screwdriver?"

By now with children this age, it is almost certain that one or both have lost their urgent need for the red hammer and will take a different toy. It is even likely that both will want something totally different and quickly abandon what they were fighting for. The teacher may continue making any suggestions she thinks will work. If, however, Colin walks away from the conflict without getting what he wants, it is important that the teacher ask, "Is it okay with you that Rachelle keeps the red hammer?" Both children should feel satisfied with the outcome of their negotiation. If both are not, the process continues until they are. This is a very basic example of preverbal negotiation with toddlers.


## I Hear Only Screaming

Meghan and Laura are both about twenty months old. They are sitting next to each other at the table. Each has a board with playdough on it. There are several potato mashers at the table for using with the playdough. All but one are being used by other kids. Meghan reaches for the remaining potato masher and begins to pound on her playdough. Laura wants a potato masher, too, so she tries to take Meghan's. Soon both are crying and pulling on that potato masher.

TEACHER:    I see that two kids want the same tool. Meghan wants it, and Laura also wants it. Can you talk to each other about it?

*The girls continue to scream loudly.*

TEACHER:    It's important to talk to each other when you want something. Can you say "Mine" or "I want it"?

*The only response is more screaming.*

TEACHER:    I hear only screaming; I don't hear anyone talking.

*Rather than talk, the girls begin to hit each other.*

TEACHER:    Hitting can hurt. It's important to use your words.

Without moving them, the teacher puts her hand between them and repeats, "I can't let you hurt each other." Because these girls do have some vocabulary, the teacher expects them to communicate in ways other than hitting or screaming. If, however, they choose only to scream, the teacher may respond, "I don't hear you talking to each other, so I'm going to hold the potato masher. When you're ready to talk about it, let me know. I have to watch other kids, too."

The girls may continue to scream, which is okay unless it disrupts the group, in which case they may be moved to a more "screamproof" area. When they do quiet down, the teacher may ask again if they want to talk about the potato masher. Chances are that they will have lost interest, but they may be ready to pursue it further. If they seem to have lost interest, the teacher discreetly replaces the tool in the container with the other tools.

## Paint on Your Own Easel!

Twenty-two-month-old Renee and seventeen-month-old Evan are painting side by side at two separate easels. Renee is intensely covering a corner of her paper with red paint. Evan has one brush in each hand and is not only painting his paper, his hands, and the plastic wall covering, but periodically also dabbing his brush on Renee's paper. Renee becomes upset about this, hits Evan with her brush, and screams.

TEACHER:   Evan, I hear Renee telling you that she doesn't want you to paint on her picture. Renee, hitting Evan with your paintbrush can hurt him. It's important to use your words. Can you ask him to stop?

RENEE:   Stop!

*The teacher takes Evan's hands and guides his brushes back to his own easel.*

TEACHER:   This is your painting, Evan. Your brush stays on your own paper.

Evan may try to paint on Renee's paper again. Once Renee has said "Stop," however, the teacher's role is to remind Evan that it is important to listen when someone asks you to stop. If he continues to ignore Renee, the teacher will have to move Evan to another area, saying, "When you're ready to listen to Renee, you're welcome to return to the easel," (Figure 5.6).

## My Trike!

Matt and Josh are around two years old. They can say many phrases, including "Stop!," "Mine," "I want it," and others necessary for expressing their needs.

**Figure 5.6** *Toddlers do not yet recognize boundaries; your paper is my paper.*

The boys are happily riding little tricycles in the yard. Suddenly Josh sees a toy truck that interests him. He gets off his wheel toy and goes to get the truck. While he is gone, Matt quickly changes to Josh's trike. When Josh returns, he wants his tricycle back.

JOSH:   My trike!

*He tries to push Matt off the trike.*

MATT:   Mine. I want it!

*He pushes Josh away. Both boys are pushing each other as the teacher approaches.*

TEACHER:   Looks like there's a problem. Can you talk about it some more?

JOSH:   Me have trike. I want it!

*Matt pushes Josh again.*

TEACHER:   Is that okay with you if Matt pushes you? You can say "Stop."

*Josh puts one hand up in front of him and says, "Stop!" Matt keeps pushing.*

TEACHER:   I heard Josh say "Stop." It's important to listen to him.

JOSH:   I want my trike.

TEACHER: I hear Josh saying he wants his trike back, and I hear Matt saying he wants it, too. You both want this trike. Any ideas of what to do?

JOSH: Matt get that one.

*He points to another trike. Matt is still sitting on the trike that Josh had.*

MATT: Josh ride that one.

*Matt points to the trike Matt had been riding. Josh thinks about it and gets on Matt's former trike.*

TEACHER: Looks like you solved the problem.

## No Help Wanted

Nicole, age twenty-six months, is working on a puzzle at the table. She concentrates intently on where to put the pieces. As she is working, Adam, age twenty months, sees her puzzle and wants to help. Nicole grabs some of her puzzle pieces.

NICOLE: No, mine!

*Adam looks at her and picks up a puzzle piece and chews on it.*

TEACHER: The puzzle piece is not for your mouth, Adam. It goes in the puzzle.

NICOLE: My puzzle.

TEACHER: Adam wants to help with your puzzle. Do you want to say something to him?

NICOLE: No help. My puzzle. Adam get puzzle.

TEACHER: Adam, I hear Nicole saying she wants to work on her own puzzle. She suggested that you find another puzzle to work on.

*The teacher helps Adam choose a puzzle he likes.*

TEACHER: Now you can each work on your own puzzle.

## Move!

Trevor and Carrie are among several children on the outdoor climber and slide (Figure 5.7). Trevor is twenty-one months old, and Carrie is twenty-three months old. Trevor is at the top of the slide, ready to come down. Carrie is sitting at the bottom, swinging her legs. Trevor has waited for several minutes for her to move and finally starts to go down the slide.

TEACHER: Trevor, looks like Carrie is on the slide, too. I'm afraid someone will get hurt if you go down now.

**Figure 5.7**   *A backup on the climber is solved through negotiation.*

*Trevor becomes frustrated and begins to kick his feet.*

TEACHER:   Looks like you're getting frustrated. Is there something you can say when you want someone to move?

TREVOR:   Move! Move!

TEACHER:   Carrie, I hear Trevor saying "Move." He's waiting to go down the slide.

*Carrie turns and looks up the slide at Trevor. She wriggles off the slide.*

CARRIE:   Come down, Trevor.

*Trevor slides slowly down the slide. At the bottom, both are excited about Trevor coming down.*

TEACHER:   I like the way you solved your problem.

What if Carrie had not moved off the slide? It might have gone like this.

TREVOR:   Move! Move!

CARRIE:   I sitting here.

*Trevor continues kicking his feet, and others are also waiting to come down the slide.*

TEACHER:  Carrie, I see Trevor and other kids waiting to come down the slide. I'm afraid someone will get hurt if they slide down on you.

*Carrie continues to sit at the bottom of the slide, swinging her legs.*

TEACHER:  Carrie, it's important to listen when someone asks you to move. You may get hurt if you don't.

*Kids waiting at the top are getting restless and begin pushing. The teacher talks to them about the danger of pushing children on the climber. She returns to Carrie.*

TEACHER:  This is not a safe situation. I'm really afraid someone will get hurt. I'm going to help you get down.

*The teacher takes Carrie's hand and helps her get down. Carrie is actually ready by now.*

TEACHER:  Thank you, Carrie.

This situation offers a good time to remind children to let each other know when they're going up or down the slide by saying "Move" or "I'm coming down (or up)" or "Excuse me," then waiting for others to move. The more children can learn to verbalize their intentions and wait for a response, the safer the playground will be.

## Stuck

Landon, age two and one-half, and Hal, almost two, are riding big wheels on the bike path. As they pass each other, the wheels on their riding toys stick together. Landon screams.

HAL:  No! No! No!
TEACHER:  Looks like you have a problem.
HAL:  Stuck!

*Landon pushes on the wheel toys, still screaming.*

TEACHER:  Hal says his bike is stuck. Do you know what to do when a bike is stuck?
LANDON:  Move, Hal.

*The boys move their wheel toys around until they come apart.*

TEACHER:  You sure solved the problem.

*The boys are beaming as they continue down the bike path.*

## *The Non–English-Speaking Preschooler*

Between the nonverbal and the verbal child is the child who is verbal but in a language other than English. For this child, negotiation is perhaps the most difficult aspect of problem solving. The child may be old enough to have ideas for how to solve the problem but not have the vocabulary. Depending on the child's temperament and personality, he or she may be willing to take a chance and try the words you've been teaching or may withdraw passively or just cry. As mentioned in Chapter 1, some words needed for getting along include "stop," "mine," "I want," "more," "wait," "come," "take turns," and "trade." Teach these words as you would teach them to a toddler; an older child will learn them quickly and figure out how to use them in negotiation.

As in any negotiation, you will be the facilitator, but the non–English-speaking child may require more accommodation on the part of the other negotiator. This is a good way for children to learn compassion and empathy for their playmates. Look for ways to explain "Juan Carlos doesn't know our words, so we have to take more time and help him learn." Younger children may not have the capacity to respond with kindness, but older children can empathize to a certain extent. The child will eventually learn enough vocabulary to get along.

## Negotiating with Verbal Toddlers and Preschoolers

As children gain vocabulary and become more articulate, they also provide more sophisticated and complex situations for negotiation. They begin to play in groups and form closer relationships with selected children in their peer group. They also begin to exclude or "pick on" some children and take advantage of smaller, less powerful ones. Many children discover that they can overpower others by screaming loudly. A certain amount of this behavior is normal and not necessarily an indicator of future behavior problems.

The following examples include classic negotiating situations in which children are unevenly matched, negotiation becomes fighting, a child is excluded, or safety issues are involved. Examples later in the chapter examine aggression and fighting.

### I Want the Tambourine

Chelsea and Kevin are among a group of three-year-olds playing rhythm instruments and marching around the room. Chelsea watches Kevin with his tambourine and decides it looks more interesting than her bells. She approaches Kevin.

CHELSEA:  I want the tambourine now. You can have the bells.

KEVIN:  No. I want to keep the tambourine.

*He begins to play it again.*

CHELSEA:  But I want it.

*She tries to grab it from Kevin's hand.*

KEVIN:   You can't have it; it's mine.

*Chelsea continues to grab at the tambourine.*

TEACHER:   What seems to be the problem?

CHELSEA:   I want the tambourine.

TEACHER:   Can you talk to Kevin about it?

CHELSEA:   I want it.

KEVIN:   No. I want to keep it.

TEACHER:   It looks like the problem is that two kids want the same instrument. Kevin wants to keep the tambourine, and Chelsea wants to play it. What can you do when two kids want the same toy?

CHELSEA:   I want it!

*Chelsea grabs the tambourine again.*

TEACHER:   I'm afraid that the tambourine could get broken if you pull on it.

CHELSEA:   But I want it!

TEACHER:   Two kids want the same toy. Any ideas of what to do?

KEVIN:   I want to keep it.

TEACHER:   I hear Kevin saying he definitely wants to keep the tambourine. Can you think of a way to solve the problem?

KEVIN:   When I'm done, Chelsea can have it.

TEACHER:   Sounds like Kevin's willing to take turns. Chelsea, how does that sound to you?

CHELSEA:   OK. I want it in three minutes.

TEACHER:   You've agreed to take turns, and Chelsea thinks three minutes would be a good turn. What do you think, Kevin?

KEVIN:   No, I want five minutes.

CHELSEA:   OK, five minutes.

TEACHER:   Great. You two solved the problem. I'll let you know when five minutes are up.

## When Best Friends Fight

Stephanie and Lindsey are two and one-half and three years old. They are the best of friends and play together constantly. They also know how to push each other's buttons to get the desired reaction (Figure 5.8). They pick at each other, tease, and get very silly. This morning Stephanie arrives with a certain look in her eyes, and the two are off and running. Stephanie grabs Lindsey's doll and runs away with it. Lindsey catches her and yanks on her shirt. In a flash, they are hitting each other. The teacher intervenes (Figure 5.9).

**Figure 5.8** *Friends sometimes tease and push each other's buttons.*

**Figure 5.9** *This teacher intervenes and stops the fight.*

TEACHER:   Is this okay with both of you? Do you both want to fight?

*Lindsey starts to cry.*

TEACHER:   If you don't want to fight, you can say "Stop."

LINDSEY:   Stop hitting me!

STEPHANIE:   You stop hitting ME!

TEACHER:   I hear you both saying "Stop." Looks like you both want to stop. If Stephanie stops hitting and Lindsey stops hitting, you can stop fighting.

*The hitting slows down.*

TEACHER:   Do you want to talk about your problem now?

LINDSEY:   No!

STEPHANIE:   No talk.

*Suddenly, without any apparent reason, the girls go off together happily and play. What if they had continued fighting? Let's watch.*

TEACHER:   Is this okay with both of you? Do you both want to fight?

*Neither girl responds, but they keep hitting.*

TEACHER:   It seems that you both want to fight, so I'll stay close to you until you've finished.

If the girls are an equal match and want to continue hitting and if the group size and activity level allow, the teacher stays right there with them to see that they do not harm each other. Hitting with hands does not usually cause harm. If, however, they begin to kick, pinch, pull hair, bite, scratch, or hit with a hard object, the teacher intervenes. She places her hand between the girls without interrupting their fighting and says "Kicking hurts; I can't let you kick" or "Pinching hurts; can you find another way to solve the problem?" The teacher may remove a child who continues to hurt another. If there is other activity that must be closely supervised in the area, the teacher may have to stop the hitting even if it is going on with mutual consent. She can explain, "I can't watch you while you hit right now."

This chapter contains a separate section on fair fighting and the teacher's role in a fight. For now, it is important to emphasize that simply "winning" a fight physically does not mean that the problem is solved. After the fight, there is still a need to negotiate.

## Two Against One

Three toddlers, around age two and one-half, are sitting on the floor playing with a small train and track set. Jason sees a piece of the track that he needs to complete his part. He reaches over to Justin and takes the piece from his hand. Justin cries but makes no attempt to get the piece back. When Erin sees what is happening, she follows Jason's lead and grabs another piece from in front of Justin, making Justin cry more loudly.

TEACHER: It looks like there's a problem. Justin, do you want to talk to someone about it?

*Justin just cries. The teacher sits down next to Justin, facing the other children.*

TEACHER: Justin seems to be upset. I wonder if you two want to talk to him.

JASON: I want the train track.

*Justin cries more loudly.*

TEACHER: Jason is saying he wants this piece of track. Justin, are you ready to talk yet?

*If Justin continues to cry, the teacher may let him cry while she watches other children.*

TEACHER: Justin, I know you're upset. It looks like you want to cry now, and that's okay. Let me know if you decide to talk and if you want help. Right now I have to watch other kids, too.

The child who cries when there is a problem should be allowed to choose crying without criticism or cajoling. In a few days, or perhaps a few weeks, this child will learn that it is much more effective to talk to get what he wants. If Justin decides to speak up this time, the negotiation may go like this.

TEACHER: Justin, do you want to talk to Jason and Erin about the train track?

JUSTIN: It's my track. I had it first.

TEACHER: I hear Justin saying he wants his train track.

*Jason and Erin return the pieces they took. After that, the three play together. Suppose Jason and Erin refuse to give back the train track.*

TEACHER: Looks like all three of you want these pieces of train track. Do you have any ideas about what to do?

ERIN: Justin can have this piece.

*Erin gives Justin a different piece of track. Justin takes it and smiles.*

TEACHER: Is that okay with you, Justin?

*Justin looks satisfied.*

TEACHER: Great. It looks like Erin found a solution to the problem. Thank you, Erin.

## You're Never Getting This Swing

Situations involving limited space and too many children make for common negotiation opportunities. A teeter-totter or a tire swing fits this description and can lead to conflict. Let's consider the tire swing. There are three spaces for children on the swing. Jamie, Amber, and Chris are already on it. Along come Joseph and Sean, demanding to get on.

JOSEPH: I want to ride on the swing.

JAMIE: You can't get on it. We're on it now.

CHRIS: We're going to stay on for two hours.

AMBER: You're NEVER getting on this swing!

SEAN: I want to get on, too.

JOSEPH: (to the teacher) They won't ever let us on the swing.

TEACHER: Did you talk to them about it?

SEAN: They're gonna stay on for two hours.

TEACHER: Looks like three people are on the swing and two others want to get on. Do you have any ideas?

JOSEPH: We want a turn.

TEACHER: Did you talk about taking turns?

SEAN: (to the kids on the swing) We want a turn.

*Jamie, Amber, and Chris continue swinging and taunting Joseph and Sean.*

TEACHER: I hear Joseph and Sean trying to talk to you about taking turns. It's important to listen to them.

*The teacher may stop the swing so the children can listen to each other.*

JOSEPH: We want a turn on the swing.

AMBER: OK, in twenty minutes.

TEACHER: Sounds like Amber agrees to taking turns. What about the rest of you?

*Everyone joins in and agrees to take turns.*

TEACHER: You're all agreeing to take turns. Now you just have to decide how long the turns will be.

SEAN: I want six minutes.

CHRIS: I want five minutes.

TEACHER: One person wants six-minute turns, and one wants five-minute turns. What do the rest of you think?

*After several minutes of dickering, everyone agrees to six-minute turns.*

TEACHER: Looks like you solved the problem. I'll look at my watch and tell you when six minutes are up.

## Big Guy and Little Guy

In a program where the age span between toddlers is a year or more, there are bound to be times when a larger, verbal child confronts a smaller, less verbal one. In this sort of confrontation, the younger child may be just as powerful as the older one, and you may consider them an even match. In this example, however, pretend that the older, larger, more verbal child has a definite advantage. In this case, the teacher's positioning is critical. It gives support and power to the little guy.

Nathan, age two, is pushing a small car around the room. Kenny, three and one-half, spots the car and decides he wants it. Kenny takes the car from Nathan.

NATHAN:  My car. My car. I want my car!

*Nathan begins to cry.*

TEACHER:  Nathan, do you need to talk to someone?

NATHAN:  Kenny taked my car.

*He continues to cry.*

TEACHER:  Do you want to talk to Kenny about the car?

*Nathan hesitates, a little wary of the larger boy. Nathan begins to suck his thumb.*

TEACHER:  Would you like me to go with you?

*Nathan holds the teacher's hand as they walk toward Kenny. The teacher kneels down next to Nathan, facing Kenny.*

TEACHER:  Kenny, Nathan would like to talk to you about something.

*Nathan freezes up, sucks his thumb, and says nothing.*

TEACHER:  Nathan, it's important to tell Kenny how you feel.

*Nathan says nothing.*

KENNY:  He's not talking.

TEACHER:  I think Nathan may be afraid, but I believe he wanted to talk about the race car. Is that right, Nathan?

*Nathan nods his head yes.*

TEACHER:  Nathan, can you tell Kenny what you want to say about the race car?

NATHAN:  I want it.

*The teacher immediately reinforces Nathan's statement.*

TEACHER:  I hear Nathan saying he wants the car back.

KENNY:  No, I want to keep it.

**Figure 5.10**  *Negotiation usually begins with active listening. Both the more powerful and the less powerful child express their feelings.*

TEACHER:  Looks like you both want the same car. Do you have any ideas of what to do?

Depending on how cooperative the older child is, the teacher may allow him to hold the toy while they negotiate, or she may decide to hold it herself. At this point, either child may get another toy and offer it to the other or suggest playing with it together or taking turns. Any idea is accepted and reinforced, but both children must agree on the solution. If, however, the older child insists that he keep the toy and refuses to negotiate, the teacher can say, "I can't let you keep it just because you took it. It's important to talk about it and solve the problem." A more powerful child should not believe that by grabbing toys from younger children he will win the toys. He must learn that problems are solved through negotiation, not by brute force (Figures 5.10 and 5.11).

## I Want to Play Alone

Four-year-old April is sitting at the table playing with a container full of magnets and magnetic items. Jeff, also four, arrives and is interested in the

**Figure 5.11** *The teacher facilitates, allowing the less powerful child to face the more powerful child. The children can then work on solving their problem together.*

magnets. He sits down next to April and begins to play with one of them. April quickly grabs the magnet from him.

APRIL:  I want to play alone by myself.

JEFF:  I want some magnets, too.

They both hold on tightly to the one magnet and struggle to pull it away. The struggle takes them away from the table and across the room, still holding on tightly, still trying to pull the magnet away. They begin to cry in frustration. The teacher stays close without intervening. A third child brings a similar magnet from the container and offers it as an alternative to one of them. Neither wants it. They continue to cry and struggle until April finally pulls the magnet away from Jeff. She tries to leave, but the teacher reminds her to stay and talk.

APRIL:  (crying) I want to play with it alone. Leave me alone!

JEFF:  (crying) I want them, too. You're not nice!

*Over and over they cry out these same phrases. As they become calmer, the teacher is able to facilitate.*

TEACHER:  Looks like this is a tough problem to solve. April is still saying she wants to play alone, and Jeff still wants some magnets. Are you ready to think of some ideas to solve the problem?

*The children ignore the teacher and continue struggling over the magnet.*

TEACHER:  I have an idea. What if you divide up the magnets and each have half?

APRIL:  No! I want all of them to myself!

JEFF:  I want some, too!

TEACHER:  April really wants to play by herself. Have you thought about taking turns?

APRIL:  I'll NEVER be finished with these.

TEACHER:  I have other kids to watch, so I'm going to let you two talk about this by yourselves.

Because this is an even match between children, the teacher feels that they can work on a solution alone. Both children are getting tired, and Jeff sees other kids playing house. He goes to play with them, and April returns to the table to play with the magnets. A few minutes later, April has finished playing with them. The teacher suggests that she ask Jeff if he still wants the magnets, but by now he is busy and says no. He has lost interest.

## Don't Follow Me Around

Two children, Leslie and David, age four, are on the playground with others. Both are playing close to each other in the sand. For some reason, Leslie no longer wants to be near David. She gets up and walks away. David gets up and follows her.

LESLIE:  I'm going for a walk. Don't follow me around.

*Leslie keeps walking, and David keeps following.*

LESLIE:  Stop following me! I don't want you behind me!

*Leslie keeps walking, and David keeps following. Leslie approaches the teacher.*

LESLIE:  David keeps following me around.

TEACHER:  Did you talk to him about it?

LESLIE:  I told him to stop following me around.

Because there is no conflict over a toy and there is no fight, the teacher in this and similar cases has no reason to facilitate. An appropriate response might be "It's up to each of you to decide where to walk." The same principle applies when one child does not want another child to sit next to her at the table or stand next to her during a game or play on the same climber. It is each person's decision to be where he or she wants to be, as long as someone else's rights are not infringed. It is okay to be annoyed by another person's presence, but we cannot decide for another person where he or she should be. If there is space made for privacy in the room or playground, the child who wants to be alone may be able to go to that place.

## They Won't Let Me Play

Young children attribute magical powers to words, even words spoken by their peers. The phrase "she won't let me" means to one child that another child doesn't want her to do something. Sometimes these are negotiable situations; often they are not. This is demonstrated by the following example.

Valerie and Kim are sitting on top of the climbing structure. Debbie is on the ground and begins to climb up.

VALERIE
AND KIM: We don't want Debbie up here, do we? Debbie can't come up here.

DEBBIE: I want to come up, too.

VALERIE
AND KIM: You can't come up here.

*Debbie goes to the teacher.*

DEBBIE: They won't let me play. I want to play on the climber, and they won't let me.

TEACHER: How are they stopping you from climbing up?

DEBBIE: They said I can't come up.

TEACHER: Do you have to do what they say?

DEBBIE: Yes, because they won't let me come up.

TEACHER: It's your decision to go wherever you want to go. If you want to climb up, it's up to you to decide. Their words can't stop you.

*Debbie thinks about it and goes back to the climber.*

DEBBIE: I'm coming up. It's my decision.

Four-year-olds can easily learn to be assertive when they hear statements such as "It's your decision," "You can decide for yourself," and "You don't have to do what they tell you." All persons need to be able to say such things to themselves and realize that only they themselves are in control of their own actions.

## Look What He Did

Four-year-olds are extremely law abiding when it comes to ensuring that the other child behaves properly. The child who exceeds a limit or makes a mistake and is reminded of this by the teacher will lose no time "telling" on the next child who commits the same error. "Tattletales" can become quite a nuisance unless their behavior is nipped in the bud by a combination of negotiation and ignoring. The teacher should avoid becoming involved in tattling. Here is an example.

Scott was recently reminded that his coat had been left in the middle of the preschool floor. He hung it up, and a little later, when Walter left his jacket on the floor, Scott was quick to tell the teacher.

SCOTT: Walter left his jacket on the floor.

TEACHER: Oh.

SCOTT: But he has to pick it up.

TEACHER: Do you want to talk to him about that?

SCOTT: No, you tell him.

TEACHER: If it's a problem for you, you can certainly tell him.

SCOTT: Pick up your jacket, Walter.

*Later, Walter finds a reason to tell on Scott.*

WALTER: (to teacher) Scott didn't put away the crayons.

TEACHER: Oh.

WALTER: He left them on the table.

TEACHER: Is that a problem for you?

WALTER: He didn't put them away.

TEACHER: Would you like to talk to him about that?

WALTER: Scott, put away the crayons.

In such cases, the teacher should deal with the limit that has been exceeded but not as an immediate response to the tattling. That would only reinforce the tattletale.

## You're Stupid!

Preschoolers are experimenting with words and sounds and are discovering the power in their words. For the most part, this is desirable, but they will inevitably use their newly acquired verbal skills to exert power over and elicit reactions from other children. Name-calling at this age is common and generally best ignored. When mutual name-calling is done mainly for fun and effect, the teacher can turn a deaf ear to it. If, however, there is a victim of the name-calling and that child is unable to ignore it or make it stop, the child should not be forced to put up with it, especially if it is obviously aimed only at her. The following example shows ways to empower the victim of name-calling.

Elisha and LaToya are coming in from the playground when they notice Juan sitting in the book corner looking at books.

ELISHA:   Hi, stupid Juan.

JUAN:   I'm not stupid.

LATOYA:   Say stupid again.

ELISHA:   Stupid, stupid, Juan.

JUAN:   I don't like that. (He looks distressed.)

TEACHER:   Juan, if you don't like being called a name, you can tell Elisha to stop.

JUAN:   Don't say that; stop it!

ELISHA:   I can say stupid. Stupid, stupid, stupid.

TEACHER:   I heard Juan say "Stop" to calling him names. It's important to listen when kids ask you to stop.

Elisha stops the name-calling, and he and LaToya find another activity. It is likely, however, that name-calling will happen again, with different children and different words. If it becomes harassment directed at certain children, the teacher can take further steps to curtail it (see "Special Behaviors"), but most name-calling is done for fun and experimentation.

## Special Behaviors

Until now, all the examples given have demonstrated negotiation techniques being used with typical, appropriate childlike behavior. These examples have shown that, when two or more people are willing to communicate and seek a solution, negotiation can be successful. A few types of behavior, however, are a bit beyond everyday childlike behavior and require special handling. (I am not referring to chronic or destructive behaviors. These are discussed in Chapter 8 with specific techniques for addressing them.) The behaviors discussed next are within the range of typical behaviors displayed by young children, but they require close attention by the teacher to prevent them from becoming problematic. These behaviors are harassment, anger and aggression, fighting, and biting.

### Harassment Is Not Okay

Harassment is a behavior that is characterized by repeated attacks, whether verbal or physical. Under this category we find behaviors such as teasing, annoying, nagging, and otherwise attempting to wear down someone's defenses. Harassment is always unfair and inappropriate, and children especially need protection from harassment because it is too threatening or distressing for them to cope with reasonably left to their own resources.

Teasing is probably the most common form of harassment among children. When a child or several children consistently threaten and hurt children younger or less powerful than themselves, they are usually considered

**Figure 5.12** *Teasing is a common form of harassment but is not as serious as bullying.*

"bullies." Bullying is more severe than teasing and calls for a parent conference (Figure 5.12). I discuss the true bully in Chapter 8; in this chapter, the focus is on the more common forms of teasing.

Teasing is often done by two or more children. Most children would be afraid to tease by themselves. Typically, a couple of bigger children who are a little bored and in need of extra stimulation think up ways to annoy younger children. There is not really a problem or conflict to negotiate, because their goal is to stimulate and call attention to themselves, not to find solutions. The harassers may go around taking toys from younger children or pushing them down. The younger children have no idea what is going on, so they cry. Their crying is the response the teasers desire.

*General Strategies*   How do you handle teasing and other harassment? First, do some examining. All behavior is motivated by a need. What do these teasers really need? Are they being given enough opportunity to work off their energy? Can a teacher round them up with others in their age group and take them to a part of the playground where they can play games, ride trikes, run, and scream? Do they need more structure at certain times of the day, when they do most of their teasing? What about their self-esteem? Are they children who need more positive reinforcement for their good qualities? Do they have any particular fears? Role playing with three-, four-, and five-year-olds may help them express their fears and help adults give them some direction. When a teacher suspects that the problem arises because a child's home may be too restrictive or chaotic, a parent conference may be in order.

What about victims of harassment? They should always have the opportunity to tell the teaser how they feel and to stop the teasing behavior. It is important that children learn to handle teasers. Someday on the playground, every child will be forced to confront a teasing child, and there may not be a teacher around to rescue the victim. Role playing may also be possible with children who are victimized, if they are sufficiently verbal. At the very least, they should be taught how to put up a hand and firmly say "Stop." Surprisingly, this is extremely effective for younger children.

Teasing is generally a passing phase. Some children simply try it on to see how it feels. Most do not seem to enjoy it enough to suffer the consequences. Take care not to overreact to teasing and make it seem more important than it really is.

*Using the Contract*    Another strategy to use with preschool-age children who harass is the contract. The child and teacher sit down with a piece of paper and together write down what the problem behavior is and what consequences are appropriate for that behavior. The child must have unlimited input and decide on consequences that the teacher feels are adequate to curb the child's behavior. For example, the contract may state that the child will perform certain tasks as a consequence of teasing or spend a certain amount of time sitting apart. Included as a consequence should be a way for the teaser to rectify any damage done to the target child by the teasing.

In addition to consequences for problem behavior, there should be consequences for positive, nonteasing behavior. The child should be able to choose the "rewards" for his positive behavior. The most appropriate consequences for desirable behavior are privileges such as having an extra five to fifteen minutes of play with a special toy, being allowed to run an errand to another part of the center, or helping pass out materials during an activity. These "rewards" should be given after a relatively short period of time, such as an hour of appropriate behavior. Here is a sample contract between four-year-old Jay and his teachers. The boy thought up all the consequences with the help of his primary teacher.

> This is a contract between Jay Jones and his teachers, Eleanor, Joan, and Debbie.
>
> Every time I knock down a little kid, I'll help him get up and give him some ice for his head or wash off his owie.

Every time I take a toy away from a little kid, I'll give it back and find him some more toys.

If I do it again, I'll go sit by myself for five minutes.

If I do it three times, I'll go to the toddler room for one hour, and I'll have to be a toddler.

If I don't knock down any little kids for one hour, I get to hold the guinea pig for five minutes.

If I don't take any toys away from little kids, I get to pass out the cups at snack time.

signed ——————————— signed ——————————— ————————

signed ——————————— signed ———————————

With this contract posted on the wall, it didn't take long for Jay's behavior to change for the better.


## Understanding Anger and Aggression

Anger and aggression in young children are the cause of great concern in parents and teachers. We are amazed and puzzled by the fierce crying of a nine-month-old infant; we are concerned when a toddler grabs a friend's toy and hits her over the head with it. What is really going on when young children behave aggressively?

In Chapter 4, I depicted anger as an umbrella covering up fear, hurt feelings, frustration, disappointment, jealousy, and other so-called negative emotions. Think of your own angry situations and look beneath your anger for a primary emotion. The same process occurs whenever there is angry behavior. A primary emotion triggers the anger. If we, as teachers, can work on staying in touch with those primary emotions and expressing them openly, we can set an invaluable example for our children in dealing constructively with their own "negative" emotions. They can learn that all emotions are normal and acceptable and, when expressed authentically, can help build empathy toward others.

The expression of anger is essentially physical. What do we as adults do when we are tense or angry? Some adults permit themselves to drink a cocktail, take a tranquilizer, curse and swear, yell, throw things, hit someone or something, drive a car fast, or smoke a cigarette. Other adults deal more positively with anger and may go out dancing, run around the block, or do an exercise workout. Compare these adult options with the options we as a society allow our children. Based on their observations, children may be confused when we tell them that it isn't OK to be angry, that they must not cry, scream, or hit. For them, throwing a tantrum may bring punishment, as may swearing, jumping, hitting, or throwing things.

How can we help the young child deal positively with anger? First, listen for the hidden feelings behind the anger, and use active listening to reflect those feelings back to the child. Even the child too young to understand the words will sense our empathy. Soon the words will come and will enable the child to identify and express the feelings behind the anger.

Then give the child many options for expressing anger physically. Punching on playdough or on a pillow, throwing or kicking a ball, jumping on a trampoline, going into an empty room to scream, and running around outdoors are just a few ideas. These options do not always help, however, especially if the anger is chronic and stems from the child's home life.

What happens to a child's anger when he or she is prevented from expressing it positively? Frequently, it is channeled into aggression. Aggression emerges in various forms and kinds of behavior. There are two main categories of aggression, each different in meaning and behavior. They are called instrumental aggression and hostile aggression.[3]

Instrumental aggression is a goal-directed attack usually aimed at obtaining an object, such as a toy; a territory, such as a space on the slide; or a privilege, such as attention from an adult. This is the most common type of aggression among preschoolers and decreases as they grow older. Individual children have their own styles, which may vary depending on the situation and the child's stage of development. Let's look at three styles commonly found in boys and girls under age five.

First, aggression is an expression of anger. Without help, young children cannot discriminate between their primary emotions and anger. The child who is scared, frustrated, upset, disappointed, or hurt may attack a parent, teacher, sibling, friend, or pet. Anger, which seeks a physical outlet, combines with the goal of getting a toy, space, or attention. Generally, the more a child is denied legitimate ways of expressing anger, the more anger he or she will express through aggressive behavior.

Second, aggression is a means of overpowering another in order to gain control. This situation may resemble an expression of anger, but in this case you have one child who is physically or psychologically more powerful than the other child trying to gain control of an object, territory, or privilege by using that power.

Third, aggression is a way of testing one's own power. This usually happens when a previously powerless child such as the youngest, smallest, or most passive in the group suddenly walks over and very proudly pushes another child, sometimes wearing a big grin. This is a normal part of a child's growth and development and will run its course and pass.

All three styles of instrumental aggression are effectively treated by the use of negotiation techniques described in this chapter.

Hostile aggression, an attack on another person, is the second category of aggression. Often it is an attempt to damage that person's self-esteem.

This type of aggression is often referred to as bullying and is discussed in Chapter 8.

## Fair Fighting: Steps for Supervising a Fight

Most fights between young children consist of slapping rather aimlessly at each other. There is little chance that one child will harm the other. Usually, the children are vying for a toy or space, and the fighting breaks out spontaneously. They seldom intend to hurt another person. The goal is simply to get what they want.

When a teacher sees a fight, it is important to give it immediate attention. If another teacher is available to watch the other children, the first teacher should signal for that teacher to do so during the fight. It is also extremely important that the teacher stay close to the action to keep the fighting children from harming each other and to encourage communication between the participants.

If there is no hurting taking place, the teacher asks, "Is this okay with both of you? Do you both want to fight?" If either does not, the teacher reminds them that either can say "Stop." The teacher then waits for the child to say "Stop," so that it is the child's own decision to cease fighting. If one child does not stop fighting when asked, the teacher says, "I hear Tammy saying 'Stop.' It's important to listen." The teacher places a hand between the children to halt the action but not the communication.

If both children want to fight, the teacher remains close to watch for hurting, intervening only when necessary and never disrupting communication. The teacher may, from time to time, ask questions such as "Do you feel like you're solving the problem?" or "Is there another way to try to solve the problem?"

Kicking, pinching, scratching, biting, hair pulling, or hitting with a hard object is considered hurting. When hurting occurs, the teacher stops it immediately. She places her hand between the children and says "Kicking hurts. I can't let you kick" or "Pinching hurts. It's not okay to hurt kids." If either child continues hurting, the teacher may say, "It looks like you're having a hard time fighting without hurting. I'll have to stop you and ask you to solve your problem another way." A child who refuses to stop hurting is removed from the fight. If possible, the teacher removes the child by verbal instructions, but if the child persists in hurting his playmate, she may pick him up and remove him physically (Figure 5.13).

When the fight is over, there is still work to be done. Fighting is never the solution to a problem. Whether someone "wins" or "loses" has no bearing on whether or not she keeps the toy or the space over which she and her playmate have been fighting. Both children are still equal participants in the negotiation process, and the teacher's next job is to encourage them to continue negotiating. If one child feels he has "lost," the teacher lets him know that fighting did not solve the problem or determine the outcome. If kids get

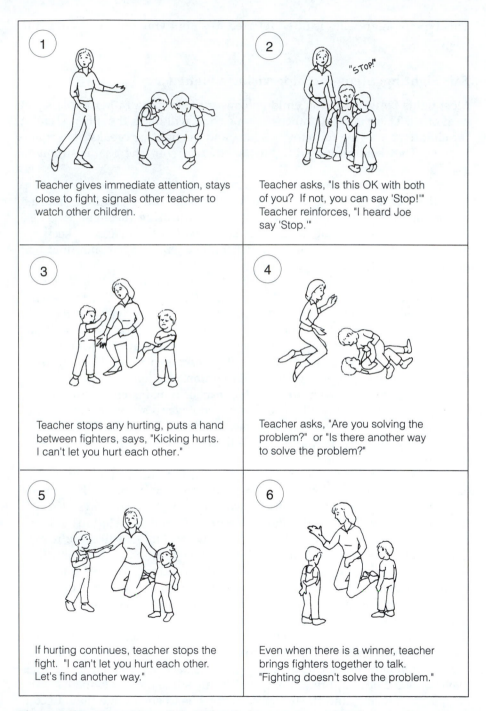

**Figure 5.13** *Supervising a fight. Although the steps are numbered, events do not necessarily occur in this order.*

their way by fighting, fighting becomes more attractive. They need to know that, whether they win or lose the fight, their rights will be respected and the solution will be mutually satisfactory. Following are a few examples.

*My Wagon!*    In the playground, Eden and Aaron, two-year-old toddlers, are sitting in the wagon, being pulled by another child. Because the wagon is small, they are crowded and begin to push each other. Because the wagon is moving, this situation looks unsafe to the teacher.

TEACHER:   It looks pretty crowded in that wagon. I'm afraid if you push each other, someone will get hurt.

*The teacher stops the wagon from moving. The children continue to push, then begin to slap at each other and are soon kicking with their feet. The wagon topples over. Now Eden and Aaron are even more furious and continue to slap and kick. The teacher alerts another teacher to watch the other children so that she can supervise the fighting.*

TEACHER:   Eden, Aaron, looks like you're both upset, but I can't let you hurt each other.

*She kneels down and stretches her hand out between the kicking feet.*

TEACHER:   Kicking hurts. I can't let you kick.

*Eden and Aaron sit on the ground screaming but no longer fighting. They scream for a while and then get up and, with the teacher's help, negotiate for the wagon.*

*Do You Both Want to Fight?*    Brent, Gary, and Phil, all three years old, are jumping on the gymnastics mat. Brent and Gary decide they want to put the mat next to the climber so they can jump from the climber to the mat. Phil, however, wants the mat to be next to the table so he can jump from the table to the mat. There is a tug of war as the boys pull the mat from one destination to the other. Finally, Brent becomes extremely frustrated; he begins to scream and cry and then attacks Gary. Brent waves his hands wildly, slapping at Gary. Gary returns the slaps. Phil watches the fight from the sidelines.

TEACHER:   Is this okay with both of you? Do you want to fight?

*Both boys continue hitting without responding.*

TEACHER:   I see both of you hitting. If one of you wants to stop, you can say "Stop."

*The boys keep hitting, then grab each other and wrestle on the mat. The teacher changes positions in order to watch the other children in the room and stay close to the fighting at the same time.*

TEACHER:   Is this still okay with both of you?

**Figure 5.14**  *If both children want to fight and are not hurting each other, the teacher remains close and asks, "Is there another way to solve this problem?"*

*They respond by continuing to wrestle. Suddenly, Brent grabs Gary's hair and pulls. Gary lets out a scream. The teacher quickly reaches out a hand and places it over Brent's hand.*

TEACHER:  Pulling hair hurts Gary. I can't let you pull his hair.

*Seconds later, Brent starts to cry again.*

TEACHER:  Brent, are you ready to stop fighting now? If you are, you can say "Stop."

BRENT:  Stop!

TEACHER:  Gary, I hear Brent asking you to stop. Looks like he doesn't want to fight anymore.

*Brent and Gary are still on the mat but sitting facing each other.*

TEACHER:  Looks like you've finished fighting. Are you ready to talk?

PHIL:  I know; we can jump off the climber, then jump off the table.

TEACHER:  Phil has an idea. You could take turns moving the mat from the climber to the table.

*The boys jump and begin pulling on the mat again. There is still some friction between them, but they manage to do their jumping without another fight. Figures 5.14 and 5.15 show two boys fighting and a teacher supervising.*

**Figure 5.15**     *If there is hurting, such as kicking, the teacher uses her hand to stop the hurting. She continues to encourage the children to communicate and negotiate. During a fight, she stays close and asks, "Do you both want to fight?" If not, she stops the action.*

*I Just Want This One*     Lisa, age four and one-half, is sitting at the table, all dressed up in her dress-up clothes. She is setting the table with toy dishes and food. Pam, also four and one-half, arrives, approaches the table, and watches for a few minutes. Suddenly, Pam reaches out and grabs a cup.

LISA:  I'm playing with these dishes.

PAM:  Well, I just want this one.

LISA:  No, I need that one, too.

PAM:  But I want it. Just this cup!

LISA:  I need it for my dinner.

*The girls continue to scream loudly. In her frustration, Lisa reaches over and tries to scratch Pam's face. She makes a small scratch mark, and Pam screams even more loudly.*

TEACHER:  Pam is hurt. Let's go wash off that scratch. Lisa, you can help.

*As they wash off Pam's face, the teacher talks about hurting.*

TEACHER:  Scratching can hurt badly. It's not okay to use your nails to hurt kids.

*Lisa puts her arms around Pam.*

LISA:   I'm sorry. I won't do it again.

*The girls return to the dramatic play area and play together with the dishes.*

**It's My Rock**   The preschool group is on the playground. Several boys are playing together in a gravel area, filling dump trucks with gravel. Craig and Taylor both spot an all-white rock at the same time, and each reaches for it. Craig grabs it first, and there is a fight.

TAYLOR:   I found it first. It's my rock.

CRAIG:   Uh, uh, it's mine! I found it first.

*The boys grab each other, clutching at their bodies.*

TEACHER:   Is this okay with both of you?

TAYLOR:   Yeah, I wanna get my rock.

TEACHER:   How about you, Craig? Is this okay?

CRAIG:   It's my rock, and I'm gonna keep it.

*The boys wrestle on the gravel for a few minutes. Then Taylor becomes very frustrated and suddenly tries to grab the rock from Craig's hand. Craig is surprised, and Taylor grabs the rock and runs. Craig begins to cry.*

TEACHER:   Looks like the fight is over, but the problem is not solved. Do you want to talk to Taylor about the rock?

*Craig nods his head yes.*

TEACHER:   Let's go together.

*The teacher and Craig wait for Taylor to stop running away, then approach him.*

TEACHER:   Taylor, Craig still wants to talk to you.

CRAIG:   I want my rock!

TAYLOR:   I got it. I won, so now it's mine!

TEACHER:   You did get the rock away from Craig, but the problem is not solved. Winning a fight does not solve the problem. Now it's time to use your words.

*The boys now negotiate successfully.*

## Biting—Never Bite Back

Children who bite other children present an issue that is emotional for everyone involved. Above all, the parents of both the biter and the bitten become upset, and understandably so. The sight of a bite mark on a young child brings out all the protective parental urges in full force. And the thought that your own child left hideous marks on another child is embarrassing as well as distressing.

Relatives and friends sometimes advise parents to bite their children if the child bites. This is unnecessarily harsh as well as ineffective. Children who bite often get bitten in return, and being bitten does not stop the confirmed biter. If it worked, it might be worth the try, but biting a small, helpless child only teaches that we condone such behavior. Teachers would, of course, risk all sorts of repercussions if they went around biting children.

Why do some children bite? We don't really know. Biters are usually children under age three who are beginning to talk but cannot yet express their feelings verbally. They may become frustrated and use what is always handy and always works: their teeth. Or they may even be trying to imitate kissing. Only a small percentage of children ever bite; most never do. Parents who fear that a bitten child will then become a biter have no grounds for their fears. In my experience, there is no evidence to support the idea that a child can be transformed into a biter. A child either bites or does not.

What can be done about biting? There is no sure cure except time. Children do grow out of biting, usually by age three at the latest. There may be an occasional reversal during a moment of stress, but generally by age three it is over, much to everyone's relief. When a biter is very young, under eighteen or twenty months, all you can do is say firmly, "Biting hurts kids. I can't let you bite," then remove the child to another part of the room. A young child will not understand sitting apart because she does not make the connection between her mouth and inflicting pain. Giving a biting child an object made for biting does not usually work because biting is about communication and frustration rather than the need to bite.

A toddler over two years old should always be involved with the pain he has inflicted. He should face the bitten child, who is usually crying with pain, and help put ice on the bite to reduce the swelling. It is important that the teacher repeat often that biting hurts and it is not okay to bite kids. If this procedure seems to become a game for the biter, then all you can do is sit the biter apart until he is ready to play without biting. It is always the child's decision to return to the group when he feels ready.

Even though bites do hurt terribly and one that breaks the skin may even be dangerous, children seem to get over being bitten as quickly as they get over anything else. It is the parents you will have to deal with most gently, with compassion and understanding. A policy of not revealing the name of the child who bites will keep angry parents from glaring at and lecturing the child who bites their child. Such confrontations could end in very hurt feelings and confused children. The teacher must sometimes be the facilitator for parents as well as for their children, and this may be the most difficult issue.

## Summing Up Negotiation

Negotiation is the process used for helping children deal with their own conflicts in the problem-solving philosophy. The process itself is always more important than the outcome. Through the process, children learn the skills they need to interact with their peers and to assert themselves in order to meet their own needs. They learn to consider the needs of others as well, a moral necessity. The skills learned in negotiation also equip children to handle the larger, more aggressive children they may encounter. Learning to put up a hand and firmly say "Stop!" is a simple yet powerful tool.

Negotiating may be used with both preverbal and verbal children and with children who do not speak English. With the teacher as facilitator, even young toddlers feel free to express their needs and wants to other children. The older and more skilled the children become, the less help they need from the teacher and the more capable they are of resolving conflicts without any help. Following are the six steps of negotiation in an abbreviated form:

1.  Help children identify their problem.
2.  Encourage children to contribute ideas for solving the problem. Any idea is accepted.
3.  Restate their ideas in a positive way.
4.  Help the children decide which idea they prefer.
5.  Help the children carry out their solution.
6.  Reinforce the process when the problem is solved.

The examples in this chapter are taken from real situations. As a teacher, you will encounter many situations that are not specifically addressed by these examples. This should not be cause for concern if you remember the six steps. Learning to solve problems is an ongoing process that is never fully perfected or made automatic. It is, however, a goal and an ideal worth our effort.

## Practice and Discussion

1.  What are your feelings about children's sharing? Can you recall an instance when you were required to share? How did you feel about it? How would you feel now if you were forced to share your possessions?
2.  Name some lessons children learn during the process of negotiating with other children. Why is the process more important than the outcome? What are some of the moral implications of negotiation?
3.  What steps does the teacher follow while facilitating the process of negotiation between children?
4.  Describe how the teacher uses his or her body and voice during negotiation between children.

5. How do you feel about assertiveness in children? Can you accept a child who is assertive with you, the adult? Can you respect the child's right to disagree with you? What are your own limits?

6. Name several situations in which negotiation would be appropriate for infants. Give your own example.

7. Pick an example of preverbal negotiation from this chapter. Have two or more students in your college class role-play the example, using their own dialogue. Did the outcome resemble the outcome in the example?

8. How would you help a non–English-speaking child negotiate?

9. Do the same exercise as in question 7, using an example from the section on verbal toddlers or preschoolers. How does it feel to be a child in the role playing? How does it feel to be the teacher? Did you gain any insight from role playing?

10. If you are already teaching, try out negotiation with two children the next time there is a conflict. Report back to the class how it worked out.

11. Describe several ways to handle teasing. Why is it important for children to learn how to handle teasing?

12. What are the three styles of instrumental aggression? What are some constructive ways for children to express aggression physically?

13. How does the teacher supervise when there is a fight between children? Name the steps the teacher will follow.

---

## Notes

1. Adapted from Thomas Gordon, *P.E.T.: Parent Effectiveness Training* (New York: New American Library, 1975), p. 237.

2. Alison Clarke-Stewart, *Daycare* (Cambridge, MA: Harvard University Press, 1993), p. 133.

3. These terms are taken from Willard W. Hartup, "Aggression in Childhood," *American Psychologist* (May 1974), pp. 336-41.

## Recommended Reading

Smith, Charles A. *The Peaceful Classroom: 162 Easy Activities to Teach Preschoolers Compassion and Cooperation.* Mt. Rainier, MD: Gryphon House, 1993.

Wichert, Susanne. *Keeping the Peace: Practicing Cooperation and Conflict Resolution with Preschoolers.* Philadelphia: New Society Publishers, 1989.

# CHAPTER
# 6

# *Setting Limits*

Once, long ago, when I was substituting at a child care center, a very capable and agile preschool girl proudly showed me that she could walk all the way up the slide, standing up, using no hands. As I stood admiring her achievement and applauding her tenacity, the head teacher approached and barked at the beaming child, "Jenny, you know better than that! The rules are that you climb UP the ladder, then go DOWN the slide. Those are the rules."

I, too, felt chastised and resentful as her accomplice. I never forgot the feeling of humiliation that Jenny and I shared that day. The "rules" had made us feel small and unimportant and had taken away our option to make our own decisions.

In recent years, child care providers have discussed at length ways to achieve acceptable behavior from children in programs and schools. I hope that corporal punishment, such as spanking, shaking, slapping hands, and pinching, is gone forever; but some of the replacements for this punishment, such as yelling, scolding, shaming, and punishing, are equally destructive of a child's self-esteem.

The current trend of using behavior modification is also disturbing. Behavior modification may be helpful for some extreme behavior problems when it is used in a clinical setting by highly trained therapists. When practiced by teachers and caregivers in a classroom with normal children, it amounts to no more than rewards and punishment. The adult controls the rewards and the "time outs"; children must "behave" to please adults, not to get their needs met or to develop the inner controls we call self-discipline.

Another commonly used method is called "redirection." As discussed in Chapter 5, redirecting consists of diverting a child's attention away from a conflict or problem and getting him interested in something or someone else. This practice also eliminates the need for a child to accept responsibility for his behavior.

Problem-solving techniques are being adopted in schools for children in primary grades through high school, with many claims of success. When these techniques are adapted for preschool-age children, however, there is a tendency toward a great deal of adult control and manipulation along with interrogating ("Why did you do that?") and moralizing ("How would you like it if someone did that to you?"), as well as lecturing and placing blame. None of these are appropriate techniques to use with preschool children.

Throughout the many methods runs a common thread—that of "rules." Many people think that without rules and punishment children will be wild and uncontrollable; they believe that children who do not behave properly should be punished. We accept this way of thinking so automatically that we may never stop to question whether it is really best for children or whether it helps them improve their behavior.

In his book *A Good Enough Parent,* Bettelheim discusses rules in the context of parent-child relationships. I feel that the same principles apply to the teacher-child relationship. Bettelheim says, "Trust in rules saves us the trouble of having to think through each problem situation and feel responsible for its good resolution."[1] Problem solving has the opposite effect. It forces the child to think through a situation and accept responsibility for its resolution. In this chapter, I examine the differences between rules and limits and describe the problem-solving method for setting limits with infants, toddlers, and preschoolers.

Because I use the term "I-message" frequently in this chapter, I provide a brief description of an I-message here.[2] The term "I-message" describes the most desirable method for setting limits when limits are needed. The I-message consists of a statement formulated in three parts. The first part is an expression of the teacher's feeling about a child's inappropriate behavior.

The second part describes what the teacher sees happening. The third part explains the reasons for the teacher's feelings. A typical I-message is "It worries me when I see you throw rocks at the window because I'm afraid the window will break."

## Rules Versus Limits

When applied to children, the words "rules" and "punishment" usually relate to making the children behave according to an arbitrary adult standard. Rules are made by adults and broken by children; when rules are broken, punishment follows. Rules place all the power in the hands of adults. Sometimes a rule is made on the spot to fit a unique situation that arises. Then this rule is applied equally to everyone, with no acknowledgment that all children and all situations are not identical. Rules often place artificial, illogical restrictions on the natural and logical behavior of children and rob them of their option to think for themselves. Punishment then tends to make them angry and resentful and teaches them that when they do act on their own instincts it is best not to get caught.

Return to the example of Jenny and the slide. Most climbing structures made for children have a slide that is reached by climbing up stair steps to the top. Does this mean there should be a rule that this is the only way to use the slide? What would happen if there were no rules about the slide, only a limit that children use the slide safely? Each child would have to judge and decide what was safe for him. He might not feel the need to hold onto the railing. He would choose to take only risks for which he felt ready. If he were at the bottom, trying to walk up the slide, he would be sure no one was coming down. If he were at the top, ready to slide down, he would warn those at the bottom and wait for them to move. If two children wanted to be at the top or at the bottom, they would negotiate with each other to resolve the dilemma. All this can be done without imposing a single rule.

Rules are rigid and may be broken, but limits are flexible and may be adjusted to fit the individual situation. Limits respect children as unique and capable yet expect them to act responsibly. With limits, the slide may be used any way children can think up as long as they consider their own as well as other children's safety. Control is given to the children, and they learn through their own experience what they can accomplish safely on the slide. Although rules may restrict activity, limits enhance it.

## "Limit" Defined

Pretend you are a horse in a large meadow with other horses. Each horse is tied to a tree so that each has shade. Water and food are brought to each horse, so the horses have no responsibilities. You can eat, sleep, and walk around your tree. You are safe, comfortable, and free from conflict. You might become quite passive in this setting, or you might become so frustrated that you're waiting for a chance to explode.

Now pretend that your owner built a fence around the entire meadow. He untied all the horses and let them run free. You would have to be responsible for going to a central feeding place, and you might have to compete with other horses for the best shade tree, but you could run, jump, and romp, doing what horses do. Your only limitation would be the fence, which would keep you safe from outside hazards. Of these two, which environment would you choose?

Limits are like that fence. They keep children within the boundary of safety, respect, and responsibility without tying them down. When a program is governed by rules, teachers often seem to be quoting rules and referring to them; when there are limits, the "limit" never seems to be mentioned. Rather than talk about a limit itself, teachers discuss the reason for setting the limit. Rather than receiving a dictate, children participate in a learning experience. Limits are therefore more compatible with the process of development. Although children living with limits instead of rules may not realize they have boundaries, they are most certainly developing the most enduring boundary of all: the internal boundary called self-control.

## The Teacher's Attitude

In years of training teachers, I have found that the most difficult concept to teach is that of using limits rather than rules. Some teachers rely heavily on absolutes such as good and bad, right and wrong, and nice and naughty. They feel lost without these crutches, and when they are asked to give up these absolutes they are in a quandary. It does take more time, skill, creativity, and respect for children to use limits instead of rules. The teacher must be willing to communicate both verbally and nonverbally and to accept the child's opinions and ideas as valuable, worthwhile, and workable.

For anyone who has the will to give up rules and turn to limits, the rewards are enormous. Limits not only benefit the child but also liberate the teacher, allowing him or her to join the child in the processes of thinking, questioning, wondering, and, of course, solving problems. Teachers no longer feel like authority figures who must always be right but instead are able to relax and see themselves as friends and advocates of children. It is well worth the effort to make the transition.

## Consistency or Authenticity

There is apparently an almost universal belief that parents and teachers should be consistent in their application and implementation of rules. This has been called "putting up a united front." This belief is based on the idea that, if adults have differing styles and opinions regarding behavior, children will perceive this as weakness and "divide and conquer." When child care is based on enforcing rules, perhaps this is true. A system of rules requires that each adult suppress his or her own feelings to stay in line with what other adults are saying and doing. With limits, however, the word "consistent" may be replaced by the word "authentic." Here is why.

In a preschool or child care setting in which a rule is made and upheld consistently by every teacher, what do children learn? First, they learn that adults are all alike; grown-ups believe the same thing, have the same tolerance level, and always obey all rules. This seems to be something our society wants children to believe, although it is anything but true. Second, children learn that big people are powerful and little people are powerless, no matter what the extenuating circumstances may be. Even if a small person has a clever idea, a different way of perceiving a situation, or a more logical way of doing something, the bigger, powerful person is always right, and the smaller, powerless person is always wrong. This makes the big person an authority figure. Third, children learn that rules are more important than ideas. All children can do about that is hide their ideas and try them out when there are no rule enforcers around to catch them.

Do children really need consistency? In its truest form, yes; they do need it in certain ways. If consistency is defined as harmony, cohesiveness, and living out one's beliefs, we all need it. But when consistency is applied to a set of rules for young children, authenticity is preferable. What do young children learn in a preschool or child care center in which there are limits instead of rules and teachers who are authentic rather than autocratic? First, they learn that adults are different, believe in a variety of things, have varying levels of tolerance, and sometimes like to change things, too. Second, they learn that, although bigger people may in fact be more powerful, some of them are willing to give up power or share it with smaller people in order to nurture clever ideas, encourage new ways of perceiving a situation, or try out a more logical way of doing something. This makes the bigger person a friend and fellow seeker. It creates a climate for closeness and empathy. Third, children learn that ideas are more important than restrictions and that children can do their experimenting in front of their teachers, not behind their backs. Teachers are real and genuine, diverse and adventurous, open and worthy of trust. This describes the kind of person needed for our young children to imitate, admire, and love.

*Routines and Transitions*    There are two areas in which consistency is extremely important. One area is routines and transitions. For toddlers and preschoolers, routines such as eating and napping at the same time every day keep the program running smoothly. Transition times are often stressful for young children, and they need the comfort and security of knowing what will happen at a certain time. As simple a change in routine as the mother instead of the father dropping the child off at day care can be upset-

**Figure 6.1**   *Routines run smoothly when they are organized and consistent.*

ting to the child. That child may be clingy or cry easily all day long. Routines such as meal and nap times should be kept predictable; they should also be kept to a minimum. The benefit should be to the children as well as to program organization. In addition, children can be given a great deal of control during transition times. Children can wash their own hands, serve themselves at meals, decide what to eat or not eat, undress themselves for naps, dress themselves after naps, and decide whether to walk or be carried to a diaper change (Figure 6.1). When children feel secure with routines that are consistent and predictable, they are usually willing to cooperate. Infants, however, need routines that are flexible and fitted to their individual internal schedules.

*Avoiding Responsibility and Problem Behavior*   The other area in which consistency plays a role is in the application of strategies used for avoiding responsibility and chronic problem behavior. When a child is not responsive to the limit-setting methods described in this chapter, that child's behavior may be considered chronic problem behavior. The strategies used in the section "Avoiding Responsibility" do require consistency, as do the strategies used in addressing some of the chronic behavior problems discussed in Chapter 8.

## Limits for Infants

The role of process in the development of young children has been mentioned often in this book. I repeat it here because process plays an integral role in setting limits. Developing the positive qualities we all value in human beings is an ongoing, lifelong process, beginning in infancy. Infants are not capable of willfully causing harm or destroying materials, yet they certainly have the capacity to inadvertently cause pain, break things, and make messes. An infant may be fascinated by another's hair and experiment by pulling on it. He may discover his ability to pinch and therefore pinch whoever comes close. She may bang a toy excessively on the wall or on a window. All these actions are motivated by natural, healthy curiosity, a curiosity to be nurtured, not inhibited. It is possible, however, to demonstrate to an infant that certain behavior is inappropriate without causing that infant distress.

Infants are extremely sensitive to the facial expressions, tones of voice, and body movements of the adults in their world. They spend a great deal of time studying adults and becoming familiar with their characteristics. Even an unintentional angry look, harsh voice, or abrupt movement may bring a sudden outburst of tears from an infant. A baby knows by the way she is held if the adult holding her is feeling tension or discord. Because very young children are so sensitive, there is no need for negative words like "no" or slaps on the hand in order to elicit appropriate behavior from them.

A process usually indicates movement from less to more. Regarding infant behavior, there is less behavior that warrants setting limits, and the limits themselves are less demanding. The most effective limit setting for infants is, in fact, done nonverbally. As infants proceed in their development and become toddlers and preschoolers, limits can be expressed more verbally, with greater responsibility placed on the child to respond appropriately. As with any age group and any process, setbacks and mistakes are to be expected and provide rich opportunities for learning.

There are two ways to set limits nonverbally with infants: removal and substitution. Removal simply means that when an infant is behaving in an unsafe way or harming another, he is bodily removed from the situation. Whether he is kicking an adult or hitting another child over the head with a toy, the infant is moved to a place where he will no longer be causing harm. At the same time, he will need a substitute activity on which to focus his attention. A different toy or another area in which to play, being taken outdoors or placed in a sensory tub—whatever will give him a new occupation or outlook is helpful. If words are used for setting limits with infants, they should be spoken in conjunction with the act of removing or substituting. A simplified "I-message" or information may be given in a neutral tone of voice. Anything stronger may frighten the baby. Because infants require so few limits, in the remainder of this chapter I provide information, discussion, and examples of setting limits related to toddlers and preschoolers. If you need to set limits for infants, refer to the sections on younger toddlers.

## Limits for Toddlers and Preschoolers

As the process of development continues, children are able to accept more responsibility for their actions and understand more of what we say to them. As their physical, intellectual, and emotional growth proceeds, their skill level rises, and they are ready to take greater risks in their experimentation. The more risks a child is willing to take, the more he learns, but sometimes it is more difficult for his teacher to watch and supervise him.

It is important that teachers remain flexible and grow, so to speak, along with the child. The child at fourteen months may dump toys on the floor but is not attempting to jump off the top of the climbing structure. The preschooler may be capable of making that jump and needs an environment that provides the safest possible ways for her to take reasonable risks. Being the child's teacher is, of course, different from being her parent. Some parents allow their children to try almost anything. Caregivers, however, are legally responsible parties and must be cautious about safety matters while allowing children to try their wings. It is, at times, a delicate balance.

The teacher's physical presence can often make the difference in whether a child takes the risk she wants to take. A young toddler may want to jump six inches from a log to the grass. She may be willing to risk it only if a teacher stands next to her. Proximity assures the teacher that if the child falls her parent can be accurately given the details of the fall. Another preschooler may not necessarily want the teacher to be close by, but the adult must stay close enough to assure the child's safety.

### Guidelines for Setting Limits

Limits in a problem-solving program are based on guidelines that encompass program goals. Following is a set of four guidelines that address and include all types of behavior. These guidelines could apply equally to adults and children; indeed, they serve as a foundation for interactions between teachers as well. Limits are set to accomplish the following:

1. Assure the safety of each child and adult

2. Prohibit the destruction of nondisposable materials and equipment

3. Assure individual acceptance of responsibility for one's actions

4. Assure equal and respectful treatment of all people

The four guidelines are statements of the values found in the problem-solving philosophy. These guidelines are applied to each situation as it occurs, and the individual child is considered along with the circumstances. In situations that do not involve immediate danger, there is a great deal of flexibility. Limits are also needed during routines and transitions. Limits are always based on these guidelines and are not contrived simply to make things more convenient for adults. The teacher's role is to inform children of the limits but not criticize or punish. Inappropriate behavior is treated as a problem to be solved by those involved in and affected by it.

The teacher has a choice of five methods for setting limits, depending on his or her assessment of the situation: (1) using I-messages, (2) giving information, (3) allowing natural consequences and devising logical consequences, (4) using contingencies, and (5) giving choices. These methods allow the teacher to consider the needs of all children involved, based on his or her knowledge of them. The teacher is not constrained by a need to put up a united front with other adults or conform to other teachers' judgments. Every child feels free to present his case to the teacher, knowing that his ideas and opinions will be seriously considered. This liberates the teacher to join the child in the processes of thinking, questioning, evaluating, and solving problems. I discuss the five methods for setting limits later in this chapter. In addition, I discuss removing and sitting apart, which are methods of last resort.

Limits are set in positive ways, using techniques found in this chapter. Phrases such as "That's not nice," "That's naughty," "Shame on you," or "Say you're sorry," which induce guilt or shame, have no place in problem solving. The goal of setting limits is to help children learn for themselves that some types of behavior are unacceptable to others and that the children are responsible for changing that behavior. They may also be able to convince others that their behavior is, indeed, acceptable. In so doing, they will gain the respect of their teachers, their peers, and themselves.

Limits depend heavily on trust. When rules are used, there is generally punishment for those who break them. But a limit is essentially saying "Your behavior is unacceptable as it is, and I trust that you will change it." There is no threat attached, and no punishment required. If a child chooses to ignore or evade the implied request for change, the message is restated, the tone of voice is strengthened, and the expectation is made clearer. The child is given every opportunity to make the change out of consideration for others.

## Limits and Morality

How do limit-setting strategies aid the development of morality and character? Do limits have the same effect as rules on a child's sense of right and wrong? These questions are impossible to answer or prove in any concrete way. However, we can draw some reasonable conclusions. The more opportunity a child is given to try out and depend on inner controls, the stronger those controls will become. Morality, like all developmental growth, is a learning process that occurs with the passage of time and with firsthand experience. Limits are flexible enough to allow for time and experience yet challenge the child to apply his or her own level and degree of self-discipline to everyday situations.

Each of the four guidelines for setting limits deals with what is, in part, an underlying moral issue without resorting to an accompanying threat. The most powerful incentive for compliance is acceptance by the teacher and the group. All children want to belong, and belonging requires approval. Children learn that they gain approval from adults and other children by treating them with fairness and respect. This approval motivates them to continue acceptable behavior.

Here, briefly, are the underlying moral issues addressed by each of the four guidelines.

1. *Assuring the safety of each adult and child.* Each child learns that her life and well-being are precious and it is her duty to keep herself and others from harm. She learns to discern which activities are safe or harmful to herself and her peers.

2. *Prohibiting the destruction of nondisposable materials and equipment.* The child learns to value the possessions of other people and to understand the impact that destroying someone's property has on that person.

3. *Assuring individual acceptance of responsibility for one's actions.* A child learns that his behavior has consequences. He puts away his toys to avoid peer pressure. If he hurts someone, even by accident, he listens to that person express his or her feelings or risks losing the group's admiration. If he feigns helplessness, he fears the loss of his friends' respect.

4. *Assuring equal and respectful treatment of all people.* Practically every child at some time is excluded from the group, if only for a moment. Exclusion can be devastating to a young child. Every child, whether the excluded or the excluder, needs to know that exclusion and disrespect are considered morally unacceptable.

## Gender Differences and Limits

Most complaints about the behavior of children in programs are related to the behavior of boys. As noted in Chapter 2, this predicament is based on the fact that many programs are set up and arranged to meet the needs and behavior of girls. When we attempt to fit boys into an environment made for girls, problems are inevitable. In order to make boys fit in and conform, we must make rules that prohibit normal boyish behavior, followed by effective punishment to enforce the rules. Since punishment cannot really change the basic nature of a boy, it fails to bring desirable results. Left with virtually no power to remedy the situation, we continue to helplessly and ineffectively complain.

If we seriously want to help boys gain self-control, we must be willing to make changes in both the environment we provide and the attitudes we hold. The environment must offer indoor active play for both sexes—climbing and jumping equipment, space to ride trikes and other riding toys, and

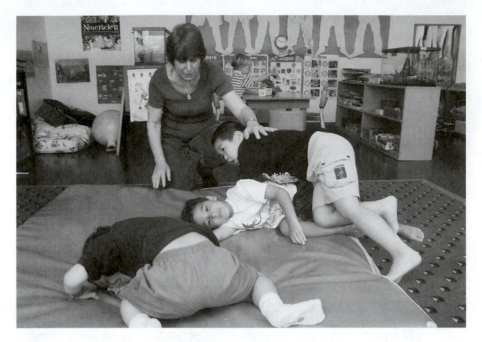

**Figure 6.2**     *A limit for wrestling: "Kids stay on the mat."*

designated areas such as a mat on the floor where kids can wrestle—and the choice of as much outdoor time as needed (Figure 6.2). It also must provide built-in challenges and relatively safe risks that can be effectively supervised by the average teacher. A stimulating environment is the best antidote to unacceptable boy behavior. Setting reasonable limits is not possible in the absence of reasonable alternatives for normal, active boys.

Once the environment meets the needs of boys, the teacher can use the limit-setting strategies described in this chapter. In setting limits for boys, joining physical cues with verbal cues is helpful. For example, when teaching tasks such as putting away toys, the teacher should demonstrate the task at hand, and then take the child's hand to guide it through the motions until the child catches on. We already do this with toddlers, but boys need physical cues even when they are preschoolers. If a boy leaves an area without putting away his toys, the teacher should not simply remind him verbally but should lead him back to the mess and wait close by until he picks it up. Matching a physical action with a verbal request will get a more favorable response from the average boy.

## Limits for Non–English Speakers

Setting limits with a non–English-speaking child can be awkward and requires some shifting of gears. Unlike negotiation, setting limits is not a dialogue that requires a verbal response from the child. A child who has exceeded limits needs to understand what is expected in order to comply. Problem-solving strategies are based on the premise that most children will comply when a limit is conveyed with respect and confidence in the child. When the child does not understand nuance or subtlety due to a language barrier, the respect and confidence of the teacher will not be enough. A more authoritative voice and simpler phrases are needed to set limits until the child's language has progressed.

An I-message, for example, will be bewildering to a child who doesn't recognize the words for feelings. A contingency might be confusing, and making a choice is useless unless the child understands the nature of the choices. Giving information lends itself more to visibly showing the child what you mean; consequences can also be demonstrated visually to a certain extent. In the end, setting limits with a non–English-speaking preschooler will most likely require expectations as with a younger child. For example, the teacher may need to show or point to where a toy should be put away, gently take the child's hand and guide him or her through routines, or remove the child physically from unsafe situations. Most children are motivated to become part of the group and quickly learn what is expected of them.

## The Teacher's Voice and Movements

Teachers can communicate in many different ways when they are setting limits. They can learn to observe and monitor their own communication skills. This is important for any part of the problem-solving philosophy, but particularly for setting limits. When teachers are setting limits, the goal is usually to change a behavior. To make the appropriate change, the child must receive a clear message with no doubt or confusion about the meaning. When sending an I-message, teachers should use their voice and words to convey a sense of expectation and trust. If, instead, a teacher uses a voice that sounds apologetic, weak, or pleading, the message may be "I don't really expect change." If the teacher's voice is demanding, scolding, or critical, the teacher is using authority rather than problem solving, no matter what words are used.

To send an effective I-message or set a limit using other problem-solving methods, the teacher's voice should stay neutral, that is, it should not judge right or wrong or place blame. However, the voice should be firm, direct, and easily heard. By bending or squatting, the teacher can make eye contact at the child's level, maintaining a pleasant facial expression. A teacher who is upset or frustrated about something is free to express feelings with eyes, voice, and facial expression. These expressions should, of course, be kept relatively mild so children do not become frightened or intimidated. Children do respect genuine feelings if they are expressed with authenticity and restraint.

**Figure 6.3**    *To remove a child from an unsafe situation, lift the child by his trunk, not his limbs.*

Body movements also must be as neutral as possible when teachers are setting limits. If a child needs guiding from one area to another, do this without pulling on a hand, grabbing an arm, or dragging a child by any part of the body or clothing. Walk behind the child and guide him with your hand on the child's shoulder or back. When "herding" a group of children, keep them on the right track with your outstretched arms behind them. A child who must be bodily removed from an unsafe situation should be lifted by the trunk of his body, with the teacher putting both hands on the child's trunk rather than lifting him by his limbs (Figure 6.3).

## Phrases to Avoid

Before discussing positive ways to set limits, I provide some phrases that are negative and should be avoided. They fall into four main categories:

1. "You need to. . . ." For some reason, this phrase is used constantly with children and is really a way of giving orders. Adults seldom use it with each other. Aside from being simply a command in disguise, it also teaches children a poor usage of the word "need." Most of the commands that follow "You need to . . ." are not

anything children really need; they are more likely things adults want them to do.

2. "I think. . . ." Adults sometimes use "I think . . ." instead of making a clear, direct statement. Instead of "I think it's time to eat," it is better to say "It's time to eat." That statement is simple and direct.

3. Prohibitions such as "Don't," "Don't touch," "No, no," "Keep your hands to yourself," and "Behave yourself." These provide a negative role model for the child to imitate and fail to give positive guidance.

4. Attacks on the child, such as "You're a bad boy," "You're naughty," or "You should be ashamed of yourself." Such statements are destructive to the child's self-esteem.

Similarly, arguing over limits should be avoided. Although limits may be negotiated, they should not be debated. Some children are adept at involving teachers in their problems. When a child begins to argue with the teacher about a limit, a good response is "The problem is. . . ." Then repeat the limit. This keeps both child and teacher on the right track. Something else to avoid is chasing. If a child runs away when a limit is being set, the teacher might say, "I'm not going to chase you," then position herself so that the child cannot leave her area. When the child is calmer or more ready to listen, the limit may be set again, clearly and firmly.

Limits should not be given ahead of time. If the teacher anticipates that a child will behave inappropriately, the child may feel there is little trust in his intentions. He may also get the idea to exceed a limit he had not intended to exceed. A limit is just that, an outer boundary of acceptable behavior. Only when the child's behavior reaches the boundary should the child be given a limit.

## The Child's Response

Children respond to the problem-solving methods for setting limits in their individual ways, but most react logically and appropriately. Those who consistently react negatively may have a behavior problem that warrants special attention. Here we will look at typical responses.

Young children who have learned problem solving since infancy are in tune with the intent of an I-message. Because the I-message conveys respect and trust to children, they do not feel as if power and control are being imposed on them. Unless there is a safety issue, the children are not forced to comply automatically. They comply not out of fear, but out of goodwill and their need to be an acceptable part of the group. This is why limits are explained and are based on logic and reason.

It is important that a preverbal child understand what is being said and what is expected. This may require showing her, for example, how to pick up toys and put them on a shelf. The teacher can make this a game. The teacher puts a toy in the basket; then the child puts the next one in. The adult might also go through the motions with the child, putting a hand over hers while both teacher and child put the toys away.

Because children are real people and not perfect, it is important to recognize that their responses will reflect their diverse temperaments and backgrounds. Following is a variety of levels of response to setting limits.

1. The highest level is the ideal response. The child stops the inappropriate behavior and quickly makes a change. This is actually a very common response in a program based on problem solving.

2. The child hears the limit-setting message and procrastinates. Perhaps she is involved in her play or work and hates to be interrupted. The teacher then evaluates the situation. How soon must the behavior change? If the situation is unsafe or destructive, the action should be stopped immediately. The teacher explains the reasons to the child. If it is a matter of putting away a toy, the teacher may allow more time for a response. In either case, the limit is restated, and the child is informed of how soon the change is expected.

3. The next level is resistance. The child may feel that his behavior is just fine or simply not want to change it. If the teacher is sure that a change is needed, the most effective course of action is to restate the limit firmly, making eye contact, if possible. It may be time to make a transition from an I-message to giving information or using one of the other strategies.

4. The least desirable response from the teacher's point of view is outright refusal. Everything has been tried, and the child still refuses to comply. Even at this level, there are strategies to try. I describe them in the examples given later in this chapter. It is also important to try to understand why a child refuses to comply. Her logic and reasons may be valid from her point of view.

## The Teacher's Response

There are times when a child's behavior is very upsetting or frustrating to a teacher. Behavior such as biting, tearing books, spitting in someone's face, or destroying materials may be offensive. Every teacher has a tolerance limit. At such times, a teacher should be authentic enough to express her strong feelings to the children. This is a good way for her to release tension and to allow the children to know the teacher as a real human being. An I-message such as "I am so frustrated when I see kids tearing books" or "I feel indignant when someone's painting is destroyed" tells the children that the teacher has strong feelings, too, and serves as a role model for expressing those feelings without hurting people.

## I-Messages

The most desirable method for setting limits is the I-message. It is used to convey the teacher's feelings when a child's behavior becomes inappropriate. We say that the teacher "owns" the problem because exceeding a limit is not a situation for negotiation between children. The teacher, not the other children, is dissatisfied with the child's behavior.

An I-message is an expression of feelings stated as a problem. When we send an I-message, we should get in touch with how we really feel about the child's behavior. We may think we are angry about it yet may really be only annoyed or frustrated. We may actually be worried or concerned about a certain behavior rather than irritated by it. The anger umbrella in Chapter 4 gives a variety of feeling words from which to choose. It is important for us, as adult role models, to express our feelings authentically to children.

An I-message consists of three parts, which may be put in any order. I will dissect and rearrange the following example to illustrate how it works: "It scares me when I see you climbing on the table because it's not strong, and you could get hurt."

The first part, "It scares me," tells the child how the teacher feels about the behavior. There are many feelings that may legitimately belong in this part of the I-message. The teacher states his or her feelings as authentically as possible. The umbrella of feelings can help the teacher choose the most appropriate word to fit the feelings.

The second part, "when I see you climbing on the table," tells what is happening that the teacher finds unacceptable. A clear statement of what the child is doing fits into this part.

The last part, "because it's not strong, and you could get hurt," tells the child why the teacher is so concerned that the limit is being exceeded. This part may also convey the message that, under different circumstances, the same behavior might be appropriate.

Here is a diagram of an I-message arranged in three possible ways:

1. *It scares me* when *I see you climbing on the table*
   (your feelings)      (what's happening)
   because *it's not strong, and you could get hurt.*
                      (the reason)

2. When *I see you climbing on the table, it scares me,*
         (what's happening)              (your feelings)
   because *it's not strong, and you could get hurt.*
            (the reason)

3.  *This table is not strong, and you could get hurt.*
              (the reason)
    That's why *it scares me to see you climbing on it.*
              (your feelings)   (what's happening)

In this example, climbing on the table, the I-message may be followed by a question: "Is there another place for you to climb?"
Here is another dissected example:

1.  When *I see kids running indoors, I worry* that
              (what's happening)   (your feelings)
    *they could fall and hit their heads.*
              (the reason)

2.  *I worry* when *I see kids running indoors;*
    (your feelings)   (what's happening)
    *they could fall and hit their heads.*
              (the reason)

3.  *Kids could fall and hit their heads when running indoors;*
        (the reason)                    (what's happening)
    *that worries me.*
    (your feelings)

After this I-message, the question "Where else could you run?" may be asked.
Here is one more example:

1.  *I feel frustrated* when *there's so much noise.*
    (your feelings)        (what's happening)
    *I can't read the story.*
    (the reason)

2.  *There's so much noise* that *I can't read the story.*
    (what's happening)        (the reason)
    *I feel frustrated.*
    (your feelings)

3.  *I can't read the story* with *so much noise.*
        (the reason)        (what's happening)
    *I feel frustrated.*
    (your feelings)

More in-depth examples of I-messages appear later in this chapter under the headings of each of the four basic limits.

## Information

Giving information is also an effective way to set limits. Although I-messages are best because they express the teacher's feelings as well as the limit, it sometimes seems more appropriate simply to give children the information they need and wait for them to react appropriately. There may also be times when a mixture of limit-setting techniques is most effective.

When giving information to set limits, begin with the smallest amount of information the child would need to respond appropriately. The goal is always to trust the child to act responsibly. If children receive more information than necessary, their responsibility is diminished, and the teacher's words begin to sound like directions rather than information. Here are some examples of giving information progressively, according to the child's response.

"I see that your puzzle is on the floor." (Wait for a response. If no response comes) "Do you remember where the puzzle belongs?" (If no response) "The puzzle belongs on the shelf."

"Windows may break if you pound on them." (Wait) "Windows are not for pounding on." (Wait) "Can you think of another place to pound?"

"I'm watching kids in this area." (Wait) "I can't see you when you leave the room." (Wait) "It's important to stay where I can watch you."

"It's time to get ready for lunch." (Wait) "The toys get put away." (Wait) "I can't take you to lunch until the toys are put away."

"Kids take their shoes off at nap time." (Wait) "It's time to take off your shoes." (Wait) "Shoes belong next to your sleeping mat."

## Natural Consequences and Logical Consequences

Natural and logical consequences are an outgrowth of the child's behavior, and the result always follows the action immediately. This is a concrete, tangible way to teach children the principle of cause and effect as it applies to their own behaviors as well as to teach them the need to accept responsibility. As explained by Dreikurs,[3] natural consequences are those that occur without any adult intervention, such as a child's tripping over an object and being more careful the next time, touching a hot surface and remembering not to touch it again, or hitting someone and being hurt when the person hits back.

Adults cannot allow children to learn certain things through natural consequences; it would be too dangerous. For this reason, adults arrange what we call "logical consequences" that are tailored to fit the precise situation.

Here are some examples:

"Looks like your milk spilled; here's the sponge."

"When kids throw their toys, they pick them up."

"When I get kicked, I put kids down on the floor. Kicking hurts me."

"When I see you playing with your toothbrush, it makes me think you're finished. The toothbrush gets put away."

Dreikurs warns that adults frequently use logical consequences inappropriately, either by implying "I told you so" or as outright punishment. When this happens, the result can only be resentment, rebellion, and hostility on the part of the child. The effective use of consequences depends primarily on the attitude of the adult. It is critical that the teacher remain neutral, friendly, and uninvolved. His or her tone of voice should indicate that the child's inappropriate behavior and the resulting consequence are the child's responsibility and that the teacher is only a bystander and resource. When children are confronted with the consequences of their behavior, the experience should be one of learning rather than punishment.[4]

## Contingencies

A contingency is a situation in which a second action depends on a first action's being performed. The first action may be putting away a toy, finishing crying or screaming, or stopping hurting another child. As with consequences, a contingency should be stated in a neutral, nonpunitive way. The statement usually begins with the word "when." This implies that the child will cooperate. The first half of the statement tells what is expected of the child. The second half assures the child that he will have what he wants after he meets the expectation (Figure 6.4). Here are some examples:

"When your puzzle is put away, you may have another toy to play with."

"When you've finished screaming, you may come back into this room."

"When you're ready to be with kids without hurting them, you may come back and play."

"When your shoes are on, you'll be ready to go outside."

## Choices

The technique of giving choices may be used when other limit-setting techniques have not produced satisfactory results. It also works especially well with children who are strong willed and in need of a great deal of control.

**Figure 6.4** *A contingency: "When the blankets are picked up, you may take your doll for a walk."*

Giving choices to this type of child avoids a power struggle and helps ensure that neither teacher nor child is backed into a corner from which there is no escape. Choices are also helpful for the child who is learning to say "No!" to everything, because a choice does not usually encourage a no answer.

The choices that are offered should always be acceptable to the teacher as well as the child, so that with either selection both the child and the teacher have their needs met. Again, a neutral tone of voice will communicate this to the child. If the child refuses to make a choice and previous limit-setting responses have not worked, the teacher will have to make the choice for the child and explain why. Here are some examples:

> All the children are putting on boots to go outside because the grass is wet. One child objects to wearing boots, so she dawdles until everyone else is ready. The teacher finds it appropriate to give her a choice. "You may wear the blue boots or the red ones. Then you'll be ready to go outdoors."

> A child continues making too much noise indoors. When all else fails, the teacher may say, "You may be noisy outdoors or stay inside and play quietly. Which do you prefer?"

> A child does not want his diaper changed. He sits on the floor and refuses to move. "You may walk to get your diaper changed, or I can carry you." If the teacher must pick up the child, she should do so in

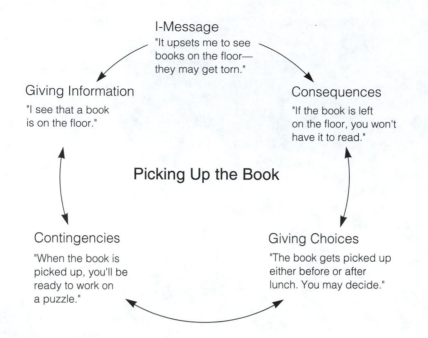

**Figure 6.5**   *Methods for setting limits. The I-message at the top of the diagram is the ideal method for setting limits. The other methods are options to be used when they fit the circumstances.*

a neutral way so the child does not feel reinforced for inappropriate behavior. A good technique for this purpose is the "football" hold: The teacher holds the child's body horizontally under her arm—like a football—with head forward and feet behind, to avoid being hurt if the child kicks.

## Removing and Sitting Apart

I do not include the method of removing and sitting apart with the five methods for setting limits because it is not interchangeable with the other five. Since this method is a last resort for children displaying chronically unresponsive, aggressive, or harassing behavior, there should be a clear distinction between this method and the five limit-setting methods previously described (see Figure 6.5). In addition, the abuse of "time out" has been so prevalent in children's programs that I must clarify any confusion between "time out" and "removing and sitting apart."

There are times when you are dealing with procrastination, resistance, or refusal when the less said, the better. After several repetitions of the limit, words lose their value, and action is much more effective. Children who are nonverbally removed from a situation will understand the reason. They are bright and know when they have overstepped the bounds and taxed the teacher's patience. No teacher should be expected to repeat a limit endlessly. It is demeaning to her and not at all helpful to the child. Actions often truly do speak louder than words. Removal from the source of inappropriate behavior gives children a chance to exercise their own inner controls and use their inner resources.

The second part of this method is called "sitting apart." The child who is harassing or hurting other children, throwing toys or materials, or destroying things is usually out of control. She needs some time to regain control and compose herself. Sitting apart is not a punishment, nor is it a time-out, because in sitting apart the child is not isolated but generally remains in the room. The child is also still in charge of her behavior. In sitting apart, the child is told, "It looks like you're having a hard time playing with other kids without hurting them. I'm going to have you sit by yourself until you feel ready to play without hurting kids. When you're ready, come back and join the group." Children will sit for varying amounts of time and almost always rejoin the group in a state of improved control. This sense of self-control makes sitting apart very different from time out. Of course, the behavior may be repeated later, but the more control the child has over sitting apart, the sooner she will master her own behavior.

## Examples of Setting Limits

This section presents examples of setting limits using the four guidelines. Numerous examples, responses, and alternatives are presented for each guideline. Here again are the four guidelines. Limits are set to accomplish the following:

1. Assure the safety of each child and adult
2. Prohibit the destruction of nondisposable materials and equipment
3. Assure individual acceptance of responsibility for one's actions
4. Assure equal and respectful treatment of all people

Although children are generally responsive to setting limits using problem-solving techniques, the examples provided here include children who procrastinate, resist, and refuse more than usual.

### Assuring Safety—Guideline Number One

I have mentioned the subject of safety in child care in various sections of this book. I cannot mention it too often. Above all, parents expect their children to be kept safe in any child care situation. All professional caregivers must

**Figure 6.6** *Children use equipment in unexpected ways. A limit: "It worries me when I see you hanging on the ball. It might break."*

make safety the highest priority. Yet, no matter how safe a facility, children are experts at finding unsafe activities, some of which have little to do with the level of safety in the environment. Such activities include fighting with each other and misusing equipment.

Children learn through their experiences, so it is important that they be expected to take responsibility for keeping themselves safe from harm. This is the only way for them to become independent and self-sufficient. They must learn to judge the risk involved in their actions and find safe ways to experiment and challenge themselves. Problem solving provides a framework for this experimenting. It does not, by any means, release the teacher from the responsibility of keeping children safe.

Whenever possible, teachers should provide an alternative to an unsafe situation and point it out to the child. Part of establishing a safe environment is anticipating unexpected ways that children may use equipment (Figure 6.6). Riding toys, for example, invite crashing and bumping into other children as well as objects (Figure 6.7). A row of discarded automobile tires (usually obtained free) makes a safe, appropriate target for "crashing."

**Figure 6.7**   *Safety comes first: "Crashing can hurt kids." Another limit: "Kids wear safety helmets when they ride outdoors."*

A movable gymnastics mat makes almost any area safe for jumping, and children are at less risk climbing on a specially made structure than climbing on a high shelf.

   The following examples deal with safe behavior. They may give the impression that the teachers are, at times, a bit overprotective. Keep in mind, however, that these scenarios represent situations in which limits are needed. Most play in a good center is very safe and calls for no limits or intervention by the teacher. Think of these examples as unusual cases.

***Tasting the Paint***   Julie, age eighteen months, is painting at the easel. Because she learns through her senses, she decides to experience paint with her mouth. She dips her hand in the paint cup and then sticks it in her mouth.

TEACHER:   It worries me when I see paint in your mouth, Julie. It could make you sick.

*The teacher guides Julie to the sink and washes her hands. Julie returns to the easel and uses the brush. But soon the paint becomes irresistible again, and the brush goes into her mouth. The teacher speaks more firmly.*

TEACHER:  Julie, the paint can make you sick. It's not good for your mouth. It belongs on paper.

*The teacher repeats the washing up, then shows Julie how to use the brush on the paper. When Julie tries a third time to eat the paint, the teacher removes her from the easel.*

TEACHER:  Looks like it's hard for you to paint without eating the paint. How about drawing with crayons instead?

*The teacher brings Julie to the table and gives her paper and crayons.*

At Julie's young age, she will forget easily that the paint is not for eating. Her fascination with paint is for the feel and taste of it rather than the results of painting. If given every opportunity to learn, however, she will come to appreciate the strokes and shapes she can make with paint.

***On Top of the Trike***    Two-and-one-half-year-old Dawn is fascinated by tricycles. She loves to try different ways to get on and off. Today she has managed to climb all the way up on the seat and stands there, wobbling.

TEACHER:  Oh, Dawn, it scares me to see you stand on the trike seat. The trike could slide out from under you, and you could fall off.

*The teacher lifts Dawn down from the seat and places her on the ground. Dawn climbs back on the trike and rides away. Soon she is crashing her trike into the climbing structure.*

TEACHER:  Crashing may hurt you and the trike, Dawn. Crashing is not safe.

*The teacher bends down to make eye contact with Dawn.*

DAWN:  I like to crash.

TEACHER:  I'll bet it is fun, but I worry about you getting hurt. If you want to crash, you can crash into the tires.

*Dawn agrees and rides away; this time she crashes into the tires.*

***Sand Can Hurt Kids' Eyes***    Jeremy, twenty-two months, is playing in the sandbox. Other children are playing nearby, but he isn't playing with them. Suddenly, Jeremy begins to throw sand up in the air.

TEACHER:  I'm afraid the sand will get in someone's eyes. That could hurt.

*Jeremy stops throwing sand, but when the teacher moves away he starts again.*

TEACHER:  (firmly) Sand can really hurt kids' eyes. I'm worried about that.

*Jeremy stops, but starts again when the teacher leaves.*

TEACHER:  Jeremy, throwing sand can hurt kids. I'll have to move you if you insist on throwing sand. You may choose. Either stay in the sandbox without throwing sand or move to another area to play. It's up to you.

*Jeremy is preverbal, so he makes no immediate response.*

TEACHER:  Would you prefer that I move you?

*Jeremy frowns and shakes his head no.*

TEACHER:  Are you ready to play without throwing sand?

*Jeremy smiles and nods yes.*

This time Jeremy plays appropriately with the sand. If, however, Jeremy did throw more sand, the teacher would simply remove him from the sandbox without further discussion. The teacher could also suggest an alternative. Jeremy might be willing to throw a ball instead of sand, if offered the choice.

***Kids Walk Indoors***  Emily and Grant are two-year-olds. Both are very active and often forget to walk instead of run indoors.

TEACHER:  Emily, Grant, kids walk indoors. When I see kids running, it worries me. There is furniture you might bump into and hit your head on. I'm afraid you could get hurt.

EMILY:  I a choo choo train.

GRANT:  I an airplane.

TEACHER:  That sounds like fun. The problem is that indoors is made for walking. If you run, you might get hurt.

EMILY AND
GRANT:  We want to run.

TEACHER:  Kids walk indoors, but there is a place where you can run and be choo choos and airplanes. Can you think of where that is?

EMILY:  Run outside?

TEACHER:  Good idea. It's much safer to run outside. There's much more open space.

GRANT:  I stay inside.

TEACHER:  It's OK with me if you stay inside. But kids walk inside. You can decide whether you want to stay indoors and walk or go outdoors and run.

*Both children decide to go outdoors and run.*

***Hard Toys Can Hurt***    Twenty-month-old Travis has recently learned how to throw objects. Although there are some soft objects for throwing indoors, he prefers throwing metal cars or wooden blocks.

TEACHER:    Travis, it makes me anxious when I see you throwing hard toys. Someone could get hit.

*Travis smiles proudly at the teacher. He thinks throwing is a great accomplishment.*

TEACHER:    I can tell that you enjoy throwing, and you're learning to throw so well, but throwing hard toys can hurt kids.

*Travis reaches for another block and starts to throw it. The teacher puts her hand in front of his to keep him from throwing it.*

TEACHER:    I can't let you throw the block. Someone could get hurt. But let's see if we can find something else for you to throw.

*Together the teacher and Travis look for and find some foam rubber balls to throw. Travis is satisfied for now.*

***The Sink Is Not for Climbing On***    Molly is an eighteen-month-old dynamo. She is always on the move and loves to run, jump, and climb. Today she has climbed on a chair to reach the top of the play sink and is precariously perched on top, ready to fall. The teacher moves in quickly and catches her.

TEACHER:    Molly, that was a close call! I'm very glad you didn't fall. But it bothers me to see you climbing on the furniture. It isn't safe, and I'm afraid you'll get hurt.

*Later, Molly is trying to climb the bookcase.*

TEACHER:    Molly, it's not safe to climb on the bookcase. It might topple over and fall on you. We have a climber for you to climb on. It's in the playground, so I'll help you get ready to go outside.

*Molly objects to going outside. She lies on the floor and kicks her feet.*

TEACHER:    It looks like you want to stay indoors. But I can't let you climb on the furniture. When you're finished crying, we can talk about it.

*Molly cries and kicks for a little while, then becomes quiet.*

TEACHER:    Are you ready to talk now?

*Molly looks expectantly at the teacher. At her age, she has very little vocabulary, but she can smile.*

TEACHER:    I'll let you decide. You can either go outside and climb on the climber or stay inside without climbing.

*Molly goes to the door and indicates that she wants to go outdoors.*

TEACHER:  Great. Looks like you're ready to go outside and climb.

*An indoor climbing structure might also be an option.*

**Windows Can Break**    Two-year-old Shane loves the plastic tools, especially pounding with the toy hammer. Most places are okay for hammering with a plastic hammer, but it's not a good idea to allow children to pound on windows, even the unbreakable ones required in children's centers. They may then pound on regular windows at home and end up breaking one and cutting themselves. Today Shane is pounding on a low, unbreakable window.

TEACHER:  Shane, it disturbs me to see you pound on a window. Windows can break, and you could get cut.

SHANE:  My hammer.

TEACHER:  You really enjoy hammering. It's okay to use the hammer, but windows aren't for pounding on. They can break. Can you find another place to pound?

*Shane ignores the teacher and continues to pound on the window.*

TEACHER:  It's not safe to pound on the window. I feel frustrated that you're ignoring me. I'm going to take the hammer until you're ready to listen to me.

SHANE:  My hammer. I want my hammer!

TEACHER:  I'll save it for you. Let me know when you're ready to pound somewhere else. When you're ready, I'll give you the hammer.

*The teacher moves away to watch other kids. Shane sits by himself, looking angry. Suddenly, he gets up, goes to the teacher, and says he's ready for the hammer. Then he goes off to pound on walls, floor, door, and furniture.*

**Watch Out for the Teeter-Totter!**    Teeter-totters can be dangerous for toddlers, but preschoolers can learn to be cautious and use them safely. Today four-year-old Shannon is trying to talk to the children who are on the teeter-totter. She approaches and gets very close to it as it moves.

TEACHER:  Shannon, it troubles me to see you so close to the teeter-totter. You could get hit in the head.

*Shannon moves away, but while the teacher is watching other children she gravitates back to the teeter-totter.*

TEACHER:  Shannon, it's important to stay away from the teeter-totter when you're not on it. It's dangerous.

*Shannon moves away again. When a child gets off, Shannon gets on. Soon she is waving her hands around and bouncing jerkily.*

TEACHER: Shannon, it's scary to see you bouncing and riding with no hands. You could fall off.

SHANNON: But it's fun with no hands.

TEACHER: I'm worried about you falling off. It's important to hold the handles.

*Shannon ignores the teacher. The teacher wordlessly lifts Shannon from the teeter-totter.*

SHANNON: (angrily) My mommy says I don't have to hold on. I'm gonna tell her.

TEACHER: Kids hold the handles when they ride the teeter-totter. You can choose to ride and hold on or to play somewhere else.

SHANNON: I'll hold on, but I'm gonna tell my mommy.

TEACHER: Okay, maybe we could tell her together.

**The Daredevil on the Climber**    Andrea is a very athletic and daring four-year-old. She is good at taking risks she can achieve, but sometimes she scares the teacher. Today she has climbed to the very top of a high climber and is balancing on a beam.

TEACHER: Oh, Andrea, I'm frightened to see you up there! What if you lose your balance?

ANDREA: I won't. I can do this.

TEACHER: You probably can; you're such a good climber. I'm the one who's terrified.

*Andrea climbs down, visibly proud of herself.*

TEACHER: That was exciting! I wish it didn't scare me to see you up there so high. If you could balance on a lower beam, I could stand close to you. Then I wouldn't worry so much.

*Andrea indulges the teacher by showing her other tricks that aren't so frightening.*

TEACHER: Thanks for helping me to not be afraid. I feel much better now, and I love seeing you do your tricks.

**Using the Real Tools**    Most preschoolers love to use real tools. They can handle small saws, small hammers, pliers, files, wrenches, and sandpaper quite well. Some are skilled at pounding nails, and, if the teacher gets it started for them, they can saw into a log or beam. Today the group is using real tools.

**Figure 6.8**    *By setting limits, the teacher instills a sense of safety in the children.*

TEACHER:  It's very important to hold the saw with both hands. That way you can't cut one of your hands. Also, everyone who is sawing stays on the same side of the log. That way you can't saw each other.

*The group is using several of each tool. A number of children are hammering.*

TEACHER:  It's important to pound the nails all the way in so no one will get scratched on them. Also, the files are only for using on the wooden beam.

As she watches for safety hazards, the teacher gives information to the children. Seldom, if ever, does anyone get hurt (Figure 6.8).

## Prohibiting Destruction—Guideline Number Two

Common sense dictates that young children have extremely durable toys, especially in a group setting where playthings are so well used. Children also need a certain amount of destructible material. This is sometimes overlooked. They love to change the shape or form of a material, pull it apart, tear or crumple it, and otherwise render it unrecognizable. Activities such as covering a blank piece of paper with crayon or watercolor; pounding on playdough; pouring sand, water, cornmeal, or beans into and out of containers; taking apart a puzzle and putting it back together; banging on rhythm instruments; throwing foam rubber balls; hammering and sawing with toy tools; and jumping on an old mattress help satisfy some of these destructive urges. If there are enough such activities, children have little need to destroy materials. Nevertheless, at least a small amount of destructiveness generally takes place in any children's facility. The following examples provide effective ways to curb destruction.

*Books: Handle with Care*    For many teachers, books are objects deserving of great respect, almost reverence. Because of the value we place on books, children should be given books at the earliest age so they can learn how to handle them with care. There are programs in which children may handle books only when they become preschoolers. Even then, the books are often old and ragged, a poor image of books to give children. A quality program provides books to the youngest infants. Cloth and hard board books are virtually indestructible. Books should be placed in the eager hands of toddlers and older children with no restrictions other than to treat them with care. There may be a torn page from time to time, but tears can be repaired. Books are an irreplaceable source of learning and pleasure, and, with libraries and bookmobiles everywhere, they are accessible to any center.

The next two examples demonstrate one approach with a young toddler who may destroy a book and another approach with a preschooler who has had much experience with books.

Derek, age fourteen months, is sitting on the floor with a book on his lap. Trying to turn the pages, he swats at the book with his hand, wrinkling the pages.

TEACHER:    Derek, it makes me sad when books are treated roughly. They tear so easily. I'm going to sit with you for a minute and show you how to turn the pages.

*The teacher sits next to Derek and puts her hand over his hand. She guides his hand so he can locate the edge of the page and shows him how to turn the pages carefully. Because his coordination is not well developed, turning pages may be difficult for Derek, but he is learning that a book is to be cherished. What if Derek tears the book?*

TEACHER:    Oh, Derek, it looks like the book is torn. I'm sorry that happened. I'll get the tape, and you can watch me repair it. Then you can look at it more carefully.

*Amy is a preschooler. After reading a book, she leaves it lying on the floor. Along comes Brett, who walks right on top of the book.*

TEACHER:    It upsets me to see a book on the floor, and I really feel sad when books get walked on. I hate to see a book damaged. It's important to take good care of books so we can have them to read. Amy, books belong on the shelf. Brett, when there's a book on the floor, it gets picked up.

*The teacher's voice reflects her genuine feelings, including her distress at seeing a book damaged and her respect for books.*

**Posters Are Not for Tearing**   Kelsey, age two, loves to look at posters that are attached to the wall. Because they are at her eye level, she can also pull on them. Today Kelsey is exploring the edges of the poster to see if there is a place to pull. She finds a spot where the tape is torn, sticks her finger under it, and pulls. Predictably, the poster begins to tear.

TEACHER:  Kelsey, I'm sorry to see the poster being torn. I really like it, and I think you do, too.

*Kelsey looks guilty and tries to smooth the poster back on the wall with her hand.*

TEACHER:  I'll get the tape. I'll give you a piece of tape, too, and you may help me fix the poster.

*Kelsey looks relieved. Later Kelsey is picking at another poster.*

TEACHER:  It really irritates me to see another poster being torn. The posters are for kids to look at and enjoy. When posters are torn down, kids don't have them to look at anymore. I'm going to move you to an area where there are no posters.

*The teacher guides Kelsey to another area or room. Kelsey begins to cry.*

TEACHER:  When you're ready to be near posters without tearing them, you can talk to me about returning to this area.

*When Kelsey indicates that she is ready to return, she is welcomed back.*

**Walking on the Blocks May Crush Them**   Shanna and Candice, both four-year-olds, are building a house with the cardboard blocks. They have worked cooperatively together for quite a while. They are getting a bit tired of their project but are not ready to put away the blocks. They begin to sit on and then walk on the blocks.

TEACHER:  Cardboard blocks aren't strong enough to walk on. You could stand on the wooden blocks, but the cardboard blocks will cave in.

SHANNA:  This is our street. We're walking on the street.

CANDICE:  Yeah, we don't want to make any more houses. We want a street.

TEACHER:  I wish these blocks were stronger. They would make a nice street, but they're only cardboard. They're like little boxes; standing on them will crush them.

**Figure 6.9**   *Breakable equipment requires limits for careful handling.*

*The teacher guides the girls off the blocks.*

TEACHER:   It looks like you've finished building with the cardboard blocks. When you're finished playing with toys, they get put away.

***Handle With Care***   Keelin and Tannah are pushing little cars around the preschool room. When they come to the typewriter, they not only push the cars across it but discover interesting sounds when they bang on it with the metal cars (Figure 6.9).

TEACHER:   This typewriter has keys that are easily bent. I worry that they won't work if they get bent.

KEELIN:   We're just driving our cars on it.

TANNAH:   Well, actually we're crashing them, too.

TEACHER:   That's the problem. When the keys get bent, they don't work. That's what happened to our last typewriter.

KEELIN:   Well, I wasn't crashing my car. I was just driving it.

TANNAH:   Oh, no. You were crashing, too.

TEACHER:   The problem is that typewriters are easily broken and need careful treatment. Where else could you drive your cars and crash them?

*The girls take their cars to the block area and build a wall out of wooden blocks to crash their cars into.*

**Game Pieces Stay Together**   Preschoolers love playing table games, even when they don't remember the rules. They love to make up their own rules or have no rules at all. The problem with such games is that they often have small pieces that get lost easily. It is usually best, therefore, to have children play table games at a specific table or area where the pieces can most easily be kept with the game. There will be times, of course, when preschoolers, such as Kyla and Todd, "forget" where to play games. Kyla and Todd have taken the checkers game off the shelf and have "secretly" carried it to the housekeeping area, where they are using the checkers to make soup.

TEACHER:   Looks like you're cooking the checkers! I guess you need some ingredients to put in your pot.

KYLA:   We're making soup. It's almost cooked.

TEACHER:   Your soup looks great. The problem is that it's important to keep the checkers game together. The pieces get lost so easily.

TODD:   But we have to use them for the soup.

TEACHER:   I see that you need ingredients, but I'm concerned about losing the checkers. Then the game would be ruined.

*Kyla and Todd look distressed.*

TEACHER:   It must be disappointing to have to change your whole plan for cooking. I wonder what else you could use for the soup. Let's look around.

The teacher helps the children find a substitute for the checkers. There may be some plastic food in the housekeeping area or even a set of Duplos or Legos nearby. A piece or two missing from those toys wouldn't render them unusable. Or the teacher may decide to allow the use of the checkers with the limit that the children count the pieces to make sure they are all returned. Limits are considered flexible. Creativity should be nurtured along with responsibility.

**Doll Furniture Is for Dolls**   Despite all the attempts to provide sturdy toys for young children, certain items are not quite sturdy enough to be climbed on or sat in. Although some doll furniture, such as high chairs, cradles, strollers, and dollhouses, may be built especially for nursery schools and is more durable than commercial brands, it is not strong enough to hold real children.

Billy and Vicki, two-year-olds, are playing with dolls in the housekeeping area. Billy puts his doll in the high chair, and Vicki puts hers to bed in the rocking cradle. Suddenly, they decide to join their respective dolls. Billy tries to climb up into the high chair, and Vicki crawls into the cradle. Both items are too small to hold the children.

TEACHER: Looks like you two want to be really close to your dolls.
  BILLY: I eating.
  VICKI: I sleeping.
TEACHER: I see. And you're enjoying it, too. The problem is that the doll furniture is only strong enough for dolls. It isn't made for children.

*The teacher lifts the children off the furniture. Vicki begins to kick and scream, and Billy, who is observing her, begins to cry.*

TEACHER: That must be pretty disappointing. You were having such a good time. I wish I could let you stay on the doll furniture, but it just isn't strong enough.

*Billy and Vicki continue their noisy protest. When there's a breathing spell, the teacher quickly interjects a few words.*

TEACHER: I wonder if there's another way to eat and sleep with your dolls. Can you think of a way?

*There is no immediate response. The children continue to cry and scream.*

TEACHER: When you're finished crying and screaming, maybe we could think of some ideas.

*Soon the children have calmed down.*

TEACHER: Looks like Billy wanted to eat with his doll and Vicki wanted to sleep with her doll. Can you see other ways to do that?

The children and the teacher share ideas. The children decide that Billy and his doll can sit on a chair at the table and pretend to eat. Vicki and her doll can lie down together on the floor with a pillow and a blanket. They resume their play, satisfied.

*The Colors Stay in Their Own Cups*  Every young child deserves the opportunity to use an easel and cups filled with clear, bright, or creamy pastel colors. The act of filling an empty sheet of paper with living color is obviously a delight to any child. There is, however, a flip side to easels. Children do tend to mix the colors together, and after several days all the colors have a brownish cast to them. Yet it is well worth the effort to teach children how to use each color with its own separate brush and keep from muddying the colors. This is, at best, a long process, so the teacher should be prepared to mix new colors at least once a week. Keeping each child's painting on his or her own paper and off the walls also calls for close supervision. Covering nearby walls with washable oilcloth helps because it is relatively easy to change. A painted-over oilcloth, however, shows the creativity that is being expressed.

Kirsten is eighteen months old and is fascinated by the process of painting. She has tried everything, including putting the paintbrush in her mouth, sticking her fist in the paint cups, painting with a brush in each hand, and painting her hair green. At present, she is mixing up all the brushes, putting each brush in a different color paint.

TEACHER:   Kirsten, it's important to keep each brush in its own color. Otherwise the paints all turn brown, and there are no other colors to paint with.

*Kirsten looks questioningly at the teacher, wondering why this matters at all. The teacher puts each brush back into its own cup.*

TEACHER:   See, the red brush stays in the red cup, the blue brush stays in the blue cup, the yellow brush stays in the yellow cup, and the green brush stays in the green cup. Now the colors will stay clear and bright. Can you remember to put each brush back in its own cup?

The teacher moves away from Kirsten to watch other children while Kirsten happily continues painting. The teacher will probably return to remind Kirsten about keeping the colors separate, but as long as Kirsten is not eating the paints or pouring them on the floor, the teacher is satisfied.

When setting limits that relate to misuse of materials or equipment, it is sometimes necessary to reassess a situation and decide whether the child is really being destructive or simply finding an alternative, unconventional way to use a toy. In fostering curiosity and creativity, the teacher walks a fine line and always approaches a problem with the most positive attitude. Children are very capable of being creative and responsible if they are treated positively and respectfully. Their creativity will not be squelched by balancing it with responsibility.

## Accepting Responsibility—Guideline Number Three

The concept of giving responsibility to young children may seem vague to some readers. For that reason, this section is longer than the other introductory sections in this chapter. The process of growing up includes accepting responsibility. It is natural for children to want independence and freedom; it is not necessarily natural for them to behave responsibly. When responsibility is expected, however, and approached with problem-solving techniques, children are willing and sometimes eager to cooperate.

What kind of responsibilities can be given to an infant, a toddler, or a preschooler? Admittedly, infants can take on practically none at all. As they near age one, however, they can begin to learn about putting away their toys. Teachers act as role models for putting things away and also make a game out of having the baby help. The teacher puts one block on the shelf; the baby puts one on the shelf. As they take turns, the teacher uses words like "pick up" and "put away" to help the baby make the connection.

When children reach toddler age, they can begin to put toys away by themselves. The teacher begins teaching this by going through the motions with the child. She places her hands over his and moves his hand from the toy to the container or shelf and back again. As she moves his hand, he will naturally grasp the toy and deposit it in the appropriate place. As with infants, the teacher uses the words or phrases that go with putting away toys. It is important that the teacher stay alert, as always, to notice which child played with which toy. As soon as a child finishes playing with a toy, it is put away. Writing on a piece of paper or on a chalkboard a list of children and their playthings can help the teacher remember who had which toy. Older infants and younger toddlers are natural "dumpers." Part of their learning experience is dumping a container full of toys onto the floor. This is a perfectly appropriate way to learn certain concepts and should be permitted. Allow only one dumping at a time, however; then toys are picked up and put away.

Toddlers and preschoolers are able to hang up their coats, dress themselves (more and more), take part in routines, listen to other children when there is a problem, scrape their plates after meals, wipe up spilled milk, and take responsibility for other appropriate actions. Putting things away, in any event, is the primary responsibility for toddlers. With items the children use personally, they easily make a connection between using an item and putting it away. The association between using and putting away cannot be made so directly in any other activity. Toddlers also recognize cause and effect when they put away items they have used.

Putting things away also accomplishes other worthwhile goals, such as keeping the play area safe. Both children and teachers are liable to trip over toys left on the floor. Putting away also keeps the area orderly and appealing. Children can be overstimulated by a cluttered, messy play area and may respond with inappropriate behavior. A neat, orderly play area is a more inviting place to play. Children may also be overwhelmed by having taken out several toys and then being expected to put them all away. It is unrealistic to expect a young child to put away a floor full of toys.

When a child puts things away, she is also involved in a cognitive process. She learns that toys may be sorted into various categories according to type, size, color, shape, and other properties. As mentioned, she is learning cause and effect on a very personal level. She may also learn something about ordination and numeration. When toys are put away after their use, each one represents a mathematical unit.

Children learn social lessons by putting away toys. There may be a disagreement about who took out which toy. That calls for negotiation. Or one child may be able to talk another child into helping her put her toys away.

Many children actually delight in being helpful and will always offer to help other children put away their toys. Sharing responsibility is part of the process of growing up. It also gives children a sense of camaraderie.

Like limits involving safety, limits involving responsibility are set with the help of I-messages, information, consequences, contingencies, and choices. It is best to begin with the least amount of verbal direction and help and offer more only if the child is unresponsive. There is a progression for helping children accept responsibility. It is demonstrated by the steps to responsibility shown in Figure 6.10. The least amount of help is found at the bottom, and more direction is given as the steps are climbed.

The following examples of setting limits for accepting responsibility include appropriate limit-setting techniques as well as techniques for dealing with children's responses such as procrastination, resistance, and refusal. They apply to older infants, toddlers, and preschoolers.

***Dumping, Dumping, Dumping***     Fourteen-month-old Paul seems convinced that the baskets of manipulative toys are there for him to enjoy dumping out. He is very fast and can cheerfully dump several baskets on the floor before the teacher can reach him (Figure 6.11).

TEACHER:  Paul, it looks like you have several different toys out at the same time.

*The teacher sits down next to him.*

TEACHER:  I know you like to dump toys on the floor. The problem is that now there are so many toys to put away. Which toy would you like to keep out and play with?

*The teacher watches for a clue from Paul. If there is no clue, the teacher may decide to leave out the last toy he dumped and model for him how to put the others away.*

TEACHER:  Paul, it looks like you might want to work on this puzzle. We'll leave the puzzle out and put the spindle toy and the pegs away. Let's start with the pegs.

*The teacher divides up the pegs.*

TEACHER:  Here are some for you to put away, and here are some for me to put away.

*The teacher puts some of the pegs in the basket, using words that describe what is happening.*

TEACHER:  I'm putting away the pegs. Now it's your turn. Which one can you put away?

The teacher waits for Paul's response. If he puts a peg in the basket, she gives him positive reinforcement using "putting away" words such as "You

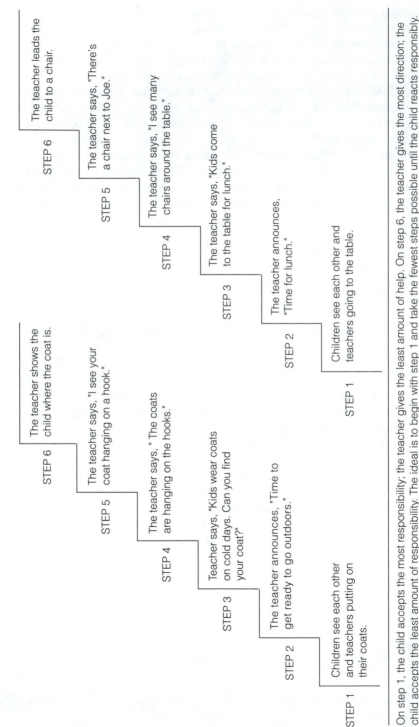

On step 1, the child accepts the most responsibility; the teacher gives the least amount of help. On step 6, the teacher gives the most direction; the child accepts the least amount of responsibility. The ideal is to begin with step 1 and take the fewest steps possible until the child reacts responsibly. Younger children require more steps; older children require fewer steps.

**Figure 6.10** *Steps to responsibility (continues on next page).*

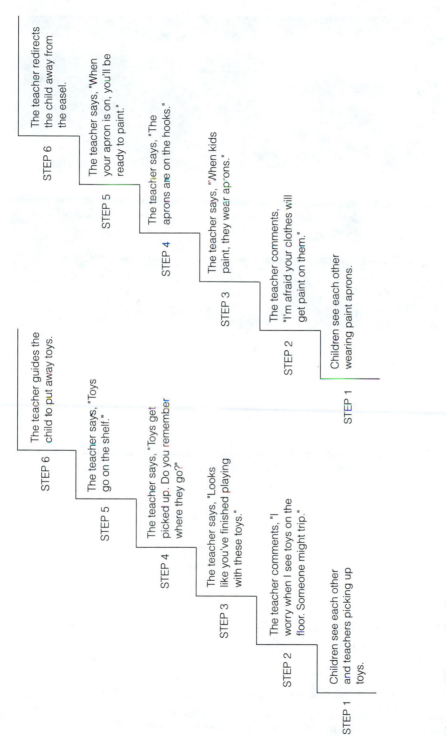

STEP 1 | Children see each other and teachers picking up toys.

STEP 2 | The teacher comments, "I worry when I see toys on the floor. Someone might trip."

STEP 3 | The teacher says, "Looks like you've finished playing with these toys."

STEP 4 | The teacher says, "Toys get picked up. Do you remember where they go?"

STEP 5 | The teacher says, "Toys go on the shelf."

STEP 6 | The teacher guides the child to put away toys.

STEP 1 | Children see each other wearing paint aprons.

STEP 2 | The teacher comments, "I'm afraid your clothes will get paint on them."

STEP 3 | The teacher says, "When kids paint, they wear aprons."

STEP 4 | The teacher says, "The aprons are on the hooks."

STEP 5 | The teacher says, "When your apron is on, you'll be ready to paint."

STEP 6 | The teacher redirects the child away from the easel.

**Figure 6.10**  *(continued)*

**Figure 6.11**  *Young toddlers like to dump toys but may be easily overwhelmed when they have dumped too many.*

did a good job putting away the red peg." They continue to take turns until the pegs are put away. The next step is putting the basket "on the shelf." The teacher helps Paul hold the basket and place it on the shelf. If Paul ignores the teacher or becomes distracted by other toys, she can help him focus on the task by taking his hand and placing it over a peg until he grasps it. Then she moves his hand to the basket and holds it while he drops the peg. These movements involve reflexes, and the child normally grasps and drops objects automatically. Once momentum is built, the child may continue without help, and the teacher becomes an appreciative audience. Many children like to applaud themselves for such achievements. Young toddlers seldom resist this procedure. They are fascinated by their growing ability to do things for themselves and are delighted by a new set of skills.

*Take Your Time*    Tara, age two, has been playing with dishes in the kitchen area. When her friend, Alden, beckons to her, she leaves her dishes to play with him.

TEACHER:  Tara, looks like you forgot about your dishes. They're still on the table.

TARA:  I don't want to.

TEACHER:  The dishes get put away before you leave the kitchen area.

TARA:  I playing with Alden.

TEACHER:  Sounds like you want to play with Alden.

*Tara nods her head yes.*

TEACHER:  You and Alden seem to be good friends. I see that he's waiting for you.

TARA:  I going.

TEACHER:  I know you want to go play with Alden, but I see that the dishes are still on the table.

*Tara starts to leave.*

TEACHER:  I wish I could let you go with Alden right now, but first the dishes get put away.

*The teacher guides Tara back to the kitchen area.*

TEACHER:  When the dishes are put away, you may play with Alden.

TARA:  I can't.

TEACHER:  There's no hurry. Take your time. You can put them away when you're ready. When I see you trying, I'll be willing to help you.

*Tara begins to whine and move away from the dishes. The teacher brings her back.*

TEACHER:  You can put them away now or later, but they get put away. I'll stay near you until you're ready.

The teacher stays nearby but watches other children, too. If she must leave, she tells Tara that she'll be right back. Tara may cry, scream, or throw a tantrum, refusing to put away the toys, but the teacher simply watches and stays neutral. If Tara tries to move away, the teacher brings her back with no further comment. Tara knows why she is there and needs no additional words to tell her. Tara's refusal to put away her toys is a common response but not so common in a problem-solving philosophy. There is a power struggle going on, however, and the teacher should meet this resistance with a calm, neutral attitude.

When Tara becomes bored with her predicament, she picks up the dishes, one by one, and puts them on the shelf. Then the teacher says, "It looks like you've decided to put away your dishes. Good for you. I think Alden still wants to play with you."

***Sand, Water, and Cornmeal Stay Where They Are***   At eighteen months, Artie is fascinated by tactile materials. He is discovering water play, the sandbox, cornmeal, and anything else he can sink his hands into. But part of the fascination is in pouring or dumping these materials out of their allotted containers. Almost every child goes through this stage. When all else fails, removal seems the best approach.

TEACHER:    Artie, I can see how much you're enjoying the water table. You're pouring water from this pitcher to that bottle and pouring really well.

*Artie continues pouring. Suddenly, he pours a whole cream pitcher full of water on the floor.*

TEACHER:    Artie, when the water is on the floor, I'm afraid someone will slip and fall on it. Water stays in the water table. Here are some paper towels to wipe the floor with.

*Artie helps clean up, then returns to playing. Before long, he is pouring more water on the floor.*

TEACHER:    Artie, the water stays in the water table. The choice is to keep the water in the water table or play somewhere else. It's up to you to decide.

*When Artie pours more water on the floor, the teacher moves him away.*

TEACHER:    Looks like you've decided to be moved away.

*Artie may leave without protest, or he may try to stay. If he keeps returning to the water table, the teacher reminds him firmly but respectfully.*

TEACHER:    You had a choice and decided to pour water on the floor. Now it's time to play somewhere else.

If Artie is persistent, the teacher may have to direct him to another play area. Eventually, Artie will learn appropriate ways to play with water as well as sand, cornmeal, and other materials (Figure 6.12).

***Kids Drink Their Bottles on the Mat***    When toddlers are still drinking from bottles, it is important that they be responsible for their own bottles. There are ways to facilitate this, such as assigning to each child a bottle of a different color or character. Bottles come in many colors and styles. The child who always has the same bottle can be more independent and responsible for it. There should be one place in each room where children are permitted to drink bottles. Not only is it not safe to walk around with a bottle in the mouth, but doing so allows milk to drop on furniture and the floor, causing unpleasant odors.

Maria, age twenty months, has asked to take her bottle from the cooler. She heads for the mat but becomes distracted.

TEACHER:    Maria, remember, kids drink their bottles on the mat.

*The teacher guides Maria toward the mat, where she may drink her bottle.*

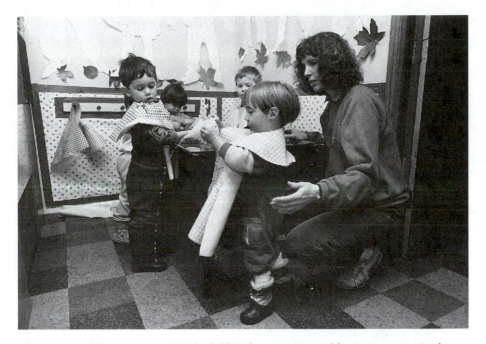

**Figure 6.12** *Limits are set to help children become responsible. "Water stays in the water table."*

TEACHER:  Here's a nice, comfortable place to drink your bottle. There's a pillow here, too, if you want to lean back and relax.

Maria sits down and drinks her bottle. She may forget and wander around with it. If she persists, she may have to decide between walking around and having her bottle. Most toddlers, however, are responsible about their bottles.

*Kids Dress and Undress Themselves*   By the time they are about two and one-half, children usually have the necessary skills and dexterity to dress themselves. Many children are capable of dressing themselves long before parents expect them to. Many parents continue to dress and undress their toddlers until they have become preschoolers. In a group situation, however, most children want to keep up with their peers and therefore eagerly dress and undress themselves with amazing speed. Yet, in any given group, there is the one child who resists taking on that much responsibility.

Sammy is two and one-half. He and his friends are getting ready for their nap. All the children except Sammy have removed their shoes and pants. Sammy sits looking helpless.

TEACHER:  Sammy, it's time to get undressed for story and nap.

SAMMY:  I can't. I can't do it.

TEACHER:  It works best if you start with your shoes. Can you untie the laces?

SAMMY:  You do it.

TEACHER:  I let kids undress themselves, Sammy. But if I see you trying, I'll help if you ask for help.

SAMMY:  You take off my shoes.

TEACHER:  I don't see you trying yet.

*Sammy makes a helpless sort of gesture toward untying his shoes.*

SAMMY:  I can't.

TEACHER:  Here's the end of the shoelace. Can you pull on it?

*Sammy pulls the end of his shoelace, and the shoe is untied.*

TEACHER:  You did it. Can you take your shoe off now?

*Sammy makes another helpless attempt and the teacher talks him through the procedure of removing his shoes, then his socks.*

TEACHER:  Now your pants, then you'll be ready for a story before your nap.

As Sammy makes more attempts at taking off his clothes, the teacher gives as little help as possible and gives it mostly verbally. She may get his zipper started or place his hands appropriately on his waistband. When he has finished, she reinforces his efforts positively. Once Sammy has established his skills in removing his own clothes, the teacher no longer talks him through the procedure. Her expectation is that Sammy will, indeed, undress himself.

TEACHER:  Sammy, it's time to get undressed for story and nap.

SAMMY:  I can't. You do it.

TEACHER:  I let kids undress themselves. I'm sure you can do it.

SAMMY:  I don't want to get undressed.

TEACHER:  The story is starting now, and all the kids in your group are listening. When you're undressed, you may join them. If you're not ready soon, you'll miss the story.

It does not usually take many times of missing out on something to motivate the dawdler to keep up with the group. The same procedure applies to getting dressed. Children who are physically capable should be expected to dress themselves. They may move slowly and miss out on some playtime or activity, but learning to dress themselves and to accept responsi-

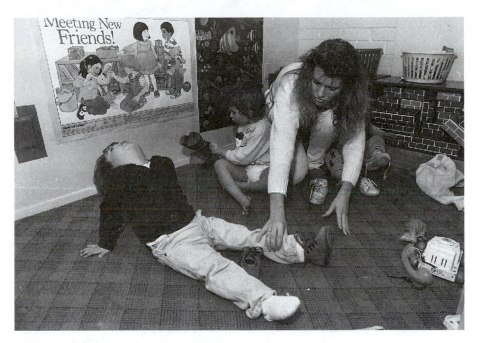

**Figure 6.13** *The dawdler may miss out on story time.*

bility is as important as any other lesson. It is a key step for children in reaching independence (Figure 6.13).

*I Can't Find My Shoe*   Richie and his four-year-old friends have been playing dress up. He takes off his own shoes and plays in cowboy boots. When it is time to get ready for outdoor play, the children put on their own shoes and clothes, but somehow Richie has misplaced one of his shoes.

RICHIE:  I can't find my other shoe. It's lost.

*Richie walks around the room looking in the middle of the floor.*

TEACHER:  Have you checked your cubby?

*Richie looks in his cubby.*

RICHIE:  It's not there. It's lost.

*He lifts up his hand helplessly.*

TEACHER:  Looks like you're having a hard time finding that shoe. Can you think about where you took it off?

*Richie returns to the dramatic play area and stares at the dress-up clothes.*

TEACHER:  Do you think your shoe is mixed up with the dress-up clothes?

RICHIE:  I don't know. I don't see it.

TEACHER:  I see that everyone else is ready to go outdoors.

At this point, the teacher has a decision to make. She can keep the other nine restless children waiting, she can look for the shoe herself, she can ask the group to help find the shoe, or she can apply logical consequences, which in this case would mean keeping Richie indoors until he finds his shoe. None of these choices is perfect. To keep nine preschoolers waiting while one searches aimlessly for something is certainly undesirable. But if the teacher finds the shoe herself, she is teaching the group that she will rescue them when they shirk responsibility. She may counteract that somewhat by verbalizing her feelings, such as, "I'm going to help find Richie's shoe because everyone is waiting, but it is irritating that the shoe was not put away in his cubby." This message lets the group know that the teacher is displeased when children do not accept responsibility. Applying logical consequences is the most effective way of handling this situation. The teacher can say, "Richie, you haven't found your shoe, so it looks like you'll be staying indoors until it's found. The rest of the group is going outside to play."

The major drawback here is that there may not be a way for the coordinator or another teacher to keep an eye on Richie while he looks for his shoe. If the outdoor play area is adjacent to the preschool room, however, Richie's teacher may be able to check on him easily through a window or door. If there is any safe way to manage it, Richie will learn more from facing the consequences of not putting away his shoe than from any lecture or criticism the teacher could give. This strategy is not recommended for a toddler unless a teacher can stay with him and give him verbal clues.

*Who Had Which Toy?*  When several children are playing together, it is hard to keep track of which child is playing with which toy. Younger toddlers go from toy to toy, usually alone, but as they grow older their play is more organized and social. Two- and three-year-olds are able to identify those toys they had out, and preschoolers even remember which toy everyone else was playing with.

As children grow within a problem-solving philosophy, taking responsibility becomes second nature. They also feel secure knowing that there is no punishment or scolding when toys are left out. There is a simple solution: putting them away. There are, of course, times when many kids have played with many toys, and some children may have drifted away, leaving the toys out. Following is such a situation.

Briana, Caitlin, Rory, and Charles, ages four and five, are playing house in the kitchen area. They have set the table with dishes and play food. They have dolls out to play with and some of the dress-up clothes, too. Briana notices a friend playing with something else and drifts away from the group.

TEACHER: Briana, I see that you're leaving the kitchen area. Do you have toys to put away?

BRIANA: The other kids are still playing with them.

TEACHER: Did you ask them if they're willing to be responsible for your toys, too?

BRIANA: (to the others) Do you guys want to play with my dishes and my doll?

RORY: I will.

BRIANA: Will you put them away, too?

RORY: Yeah, I'll put them away.

TEACHER: I guess Rory is willing to be responsible for your toys, too.

*The three children who are left continue to play. Soon Marissa and Brooke join the group. All five now play for a while. Then Rory and Charles decide to join some other children building with blocks.*

TEACHER: Boys, did you remember to ask if the other kids are willing to put away the toys you were playing with?

CHARLES: Will you put our toys away when you're all finished?

MARISSA,
BROOKE,
AND
CAITLIN: No, you put them away yourselves.

CHARLES: Don't you want to play with them anymore?

MARISSA: No. We're all done playing. Come on, let's go play with something else.

TEACHER: Looks like everyone's finished playing. I see dishes and dolls and dress-up clothes that haven't been put away.

*The children all look at each other, accusingly.*

TEACHER: Before anyone leaves the area, the toys get put away.

*Marissa begins to put some dishes away.*

TEACHER: I see Marissa working. Can the rest of you remember which toys you were playing with?

RORY: Briana had these dishes.

TEACHER: I remember that Briana asked if you were willing to put away her toys because you wanted to play with them. You agreed to put them away.

RORY: (reluctantly) Okay. Come on guys, let's put these away.

*Everyone works to clean up the area, and it is quickly straightened up.*

TEACHER: What fast workers! Everything is put away. You did a great job.

**Figure 6.14**
*Sometimes it is necessary to call the whole group together to put away the toys.*

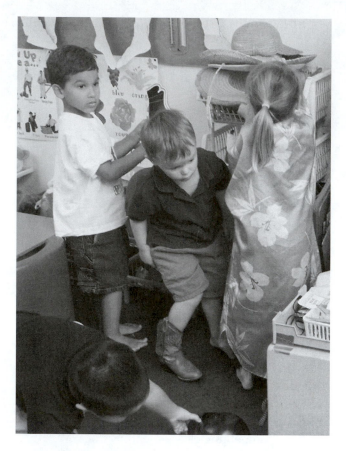

Sometimes it is very difficult to keep up with the children who are coming and going during an activity. Perhaps it is time to clean up for lunch or before going outdoors. It may be necessary to call the entire group together and ask everyone to find one or two toys to put away (Figure 6.14). This often reminds them of who actually had the toys out, and peer pressure may encourage those children to put away their toys.

*Can You Help Him Feel Better?*   Responsibility involves more than dealing with things; it involves interactions with other people. When one child hurts another, it is important that he listen to the hurt child's feelings about what happened and respond in some way. Many parents force their children to say "I'm sorry" whether or not they really mean it. This teaches children that a hurt person is easily dismissed by a few words and that sincerity doesn't matter very much. It also teaches them to lie about their feelings. The following example shows one way to help a child deal responsibly with someone he has hurt and develop empathy in the process.

Eddie and Curtis, age four, are chasing each other around the outdoor climbing structure. As they run, they catch up with each other, and soon there is a collision. Eddie is knocked to the ground, crying, but Curtis is standing up, looking unconcerned.

TEACHER:  Are you OK, Eddie? Let me see where you're hurt.

*Eddie has no bumps or bruises.*

TEACHER:  I'm sorry you were hurt. Do you want to say something to each other?

EDDIE:  (crying) Stop! Stop knocking me down!

CURTIS:  You bumped into me. I didn't do it.

EDDIE:  (still crying) You pushed me down!

CURTIS:  I couldn't help it.

TEACHER:  It seems that this was an accident. Neither of you meant to hurt the other.

*Curtis begins to walk away. Eddie is still crying.*

TEACHER:  Curtis, I'm not sure Eddie is finished talking. Eddie, do you want to say anything else? Maybe you could tell Curtis a way to help you feel better.

*Eddie keeps crying.*

TEACHER:  Curtis, can you think of a way to help Eddie feel better?

*Curtis thinks for a few seconds, then goes to Eddie and puts his arms around him for a big hug.*

TEACHER:  That looks like a wonderful way to make someone feel better. Do you feel better, Eddie?

*Eddie smiles. The boys go off to play.*

Although many children are openly affectionate with their friends, not all are as responsive as Curtis. A child may accidentally hurt herself, and the children who see it may laugh. Some things just look funny to young children, and no malice is intended. Such a response may also be an expression of relief that the hurt did not happen to them or an expression of their own fears, which they need to keep under control. The teacher should provide a role model for compassion and may also involve the children in sympathetic and empathetic behavior by asking the observers for ideas to help the hurt child feel better. The hurt child should also be encouraged to say what would make her feel better. This enables her to keep in touch accurately with her own feelings.

## Rescuing from Responsibility

Many of us have the urge to rescue children from unpleasant situations that they really could handle themselves. When a child falls to the ground, has a conflict with a more powerful child, is trying to perform a difficult task, or cries to avoid responsibility, the teacher's immediate reaction may be to rescue the child. But too much help given too quickly may rob the child of an experience that can contribute to her independence. Unless there is a question of safety or injury, the teacher should offer the child the least amount of help possible and allow plenty of time for her to help herself. Always begin with verbal cues, including active listening. When appropriate, progress to offering a finger, then a hand. In other words, give the least amount of help and the greatest amount of encouragement.

*Will a Finger Help?*   Doug is fourteen months old and has been walking for two or three months. He is a good walker but is easily frustrated, so when he falls he just lies where he is and screams. He has just fallen on the grass and, as usual, is lying on his tummy screaming, making no effort to get up.

TEACHER:   Doug, looks like you tripped and fell. That must have been pretty scary. Can you get up by yourself?

*Doug screams and waits to be picked up.*

TEACHER:   I don't think you hurt yourself, Doug, but it seems very frustrating to you. Would a finger help you?

*The teacher reaches out a finger to Doug. He has the choice of pulling himself up with the help of the finger or staying on the ground. If Doug uses the finger to help pull himself up, he will soon be upright and walking again. But what happens if he refuses the finger and hopes someone will pick him up?*

TEACHER:   Doug, I hear you screaming, and I know it's frustrating to fall. But you didn't want my finger for help, so I'm going to watch other kids. Whenever you're ready, I'm sure you can get up all by yourself.

If left to his own resources, Doug will, indeed, take responsibility for himself and will get up. It will be hard for teachers to resist swooping down and picking him up, but Doug will be the loser if they do not resist.

*Fear of Sliding*   Eighteen-month-old Karen climbs up the ladder of the toddler slide. She sits at the top with a look of anticipation and fear. Another child climbs up behind her, and she feels pressured to go down the slide. Karen freezes at the top of the slide and begins to cry.

TEACHER:   Oh, oh, looks like you're stuck at the top of the slide. Sounds like you're afraid to come down.

**Figure 6.15**  *The teacher offers the least amount of help needed. Sometimes a finger is enough.*

*The teacher shows Karen how to hold onto the slide, but Karen is too frightened to slide down by herself. After giving Karen time to come down by herself, the teacher offers a finger. Karen stops crying and holds the offered finger. As Karen holds it, the teacher walks beside her as she slides down (Figure 6.15).*

TEACHER:  You can be so proud of yourself. You made it down the slide.

When Karen gains more self-confidence, she will no longer need or want even a finger to hold. If Karen had been so frozen with fear that she had refused the finger, the teacher might have had to pick her up and move her from the slide, saying, "It looks like the slide is scary for you now. Maybe you'll be ready to try again later."

## Responsibility During a Conflict

Previously, I discussed rescuing in terms of a less powerful child negotiating with a more powerful one. In a conflict, the teacher can give the victim more power by positioning herself next to him, lowering herself to the aggressor's eye level, and helping the less powerful child face the more powerful one. She can also advise the victim to put up his hand and say "Stop!" The teacher reinforces the child's words, such as, "I hear him saying 'Stop!' It's important to listen to what he's saying." The teacher's role is never to rescue the less powerful child from such a confrontation but rather to equip him with the tools to take care of himself. Harassment by a larger or older child toward a smaller, younger one calls for problem solving among teachers and a plan for all teachers to use in dealing with the harassing child.

## Gaming to Avoid Responsibility

A tactic many children learn and use for avoiding responsibility is called "gaming." It works this way. The parent or teacher asks or informs the child about a task (such as putting away toys), a routine (such as getting ready for a nap), or a transition (such as going outdoors). Rather than responding in a compliant way, the child plays a "game" with the adult. The game consists of trying to distract, dissuade, or avoid doing what the adult expects by being cute or funny or ignoring the adult in some way. The most common game is to run away and wait to be caught.

The more attention of any kind a child receives for playing evasive games, the longer gaming will continue. Parents are often embarrassed when their child plays these games in public. The parent may become angry at the child, but because others are watching he or she hides her anger and joins the game. Following are some game-playing tactics and ways to handle them.

*Enjoying the Audience*    Two-and-one-half-year-old Aaron has been playing with the Legos. He wanders away from them and is brought back by the teacher. He puts several away, then giggles and dumps them on the floor again. Several other children see this and laugh. Enjoying the audience, Aaron repeats the game several times.

TEACHER:    Aaron, looks like you're dumping the Legos again. That's one way of playing with them, and when you're finished they get put away.

*When Aaron's friends are tired of his game, Aaron still has the Legos to pick up. He wanders away again.*

TEACHER:    Aaron, I'm going to bring you back to the Legos. There are still some on the floor.

*Aaron giggles a bit anxiously and dumps them again. He looks around to see who is watching.*

TEACHER:    It seems that you're really finished playing with the Legos. Time to put them away.

If Aaron continues the dumping game, the teacher sits down next to him, and although he is two-and-one-half years old she may have to take his hand, place it on the Legos, and have him pick them up one by one. There should be no verbal interaction during this time. It should be strictly business so that Aaron gets no mixed messages. The less attention he is paid, the better it will be, until all Legos are put away on the shelf.

***Twirling for Attention***    Stacy, age three, has been in the program all her life. She knows the routines well, including the routine after lunch. Children her age go to a rug, where they undress for a nap. When undressed, they look quietly at books until story time. Stacy, however, plays the game of running from the table and twirling around the room after lunch. This happens sporadically, several times a week, so the teacher can never predict when it will occur. Although this is not a serious problem, it is an inappropriate way to get attention and also encourages other kids to do the same.

Without speaking, the teacher goes over to Stacy, puts her hands on her shoulders, and silently guides her back to the table or to the rug. Any verbalizing would only reinforce Stacy's attention-getting tactics and prolong the game.

***Hide and Seek***    The group of preschoolers is getting ready to go outside to the playground. Everyone is putting on coats, shoes or boots, and perhaps mittens, but Greg, age four, is hiding under the table. He either does not want to go outside or wants to call attention to himself.

TEACHER:  Greg, it's time to go outdoors. Everyone is almost ready to go.

*Greg huddles under the table and laughs nervously.*

GREG:  I'm not going outside. I'm staying in here.

*As the teacher approaches, Greg springs from under the table and hides behind a cupboard.*

TEACHER:  I wish I could let you stay in by yourself, but there won't be a teacher in here when we leave.

*Greg scoots under the easel.*

GREG:  I don't want to go out.

TEACHER:  I hear that you don't want to go out, but I can't give you that choice this time. I have to take you with me so I can watch you.

*Greg gives the teacher a defiant grin and moves under the table again.*

TEACHER:  Greg, I can't let you stay here alone, and I'm not chasing you. If you're not ready to go out when we go, I'll have to ask someone else to come and stay with you.

Changing the players often feels like a threat to the gaming child. He really wants the attention of his own teacher and peer group. If at all possible, the teacher should send someone who is not as involved with Greg. It is unlikely that he will continue the game with a less familiar player. If Greg does not get ready and leave with his group, the coordinator or another teacher may easily be able to walk up to Greg, say "hi," and guide him outdoors. If not, she may have to sit silently, ignoring him totally until he becomes bored with the lack of an audience and goes outdoors. This does not mean that teachers should become dependent on others to solve their problems, but others are, indeed, there to help when needed.

*Dawdling to Avoid Responsibility*    Another, albeit more passive, tactic young children use to avoid responsibility is dawdling. The dawdler is the child who is never ready for an activity or routine and who constantly leaves a trail of toys lying around, forgetting to put them away. The same child often turns around and harshly criticizes other children for doing the same thing. The difference between the dawdler and his peers is that, although they may be late or forget once in a while, the dawdler's behavior is chronic. Dawdling seems to be a way of controlling situations passively. It may be a learned behavior, a response to an overcontrolling adult, or perhaps an imitation of an adult with the same habit.

Until a "cure" comes along for dawdling, the best remedy seems to be using natural or logical consequences. Nagging, reminding, cajoling, lecturing, or scolding does not seem to affect the dawdler because he has learned to tune out what he doesn't want to hear. The stark reality of facing the consequences of his behavior seems to impress him most. In order to work effectively, consequences must be applied consistently by all teachers and by parents, too. A meeting of teachers and parents is strongly advised to work out strategies.

*Disrupting the Group*    It is circle time in the preschool, and the children are seated on the floor, ready to sing. Cooper plops down on top of his friend, Abey. Abey complains and pushes Cooper off. Both boys are shoving and disrupting the group.

TEACHER:  Boys, it's time for circle. Are you ready to sing?

ABEY:  I'm ready, but Cooper keeps pushing me.

TEACHER:  Did you tell him to stop?

ABEY:  Stop it, Cooper!

*Cooper quiets down, and the group begins to sing. Halfway through the first song, Cooper leans over against another child, who also pushes him away. Not wanting to stop the singing, the teacher chooses to ignore this episode. After the song, the teacher talks to Cooper.*

TEACHER:  Cooper, this is circle time, not time to play rough. Two kids have asked you to stop. Are you willing to sit and sing, or would you rather sit outside the circle?

COOPER:  I want to stay here.

TEACHER:  Good, let's sing another song.

**Figure 6.16** *Removing and sitting apart allow the children to stay in control. They return when they are ready to be with the group.*

A few minutes later, Cooper is at it again, this time shoving and leaning against the child on his other side. The teacher gets up silently and moves Cooper to another part of the room. He stays there voluntarily, taking time to regain his self-control (Figure 6.16). After circle time, Cooper rejoins the group and plays appropriately.

## Treating People as Equals—Guideline Number Four

Discrimination is a concept of adults, not children. Unless they are imitating adult behavior, children who are preschool age do not usually single out another child because of race, religion, gender, handicap, or another societal reason. Bigotry is a learned behavior and, even when practiced subtly, is communicated to young children.

Children are, of course, curious about differences and, unless inhibited by adults, will readily ask what we consider embarrassing questions such as "Why is your skin so dark?" or "How come your legs don't work?" or "Why don't you have a penis?" There is no underlying motive but simple curiosity and the need children have to make sense of their world. Children's questions should always be answered honestly and with sensitivity. Truth is rarely harmful, but deception almost always is.

Teachers are role models, not only for the children in their care but in many cases for the parents as well. They have considerable power to influence young and also older minds. Teachers, however, like everyone else, are subject to stereotypes that are imprinted on our minds at an early age. Do we have different expectations for the child of parents who are of a different race from ours? Do we respect parents who cannot speak to us in English? Do we feel superior about our own religion, sexual orientation, or culture? Does our upbringing cause us to treat children of different genders in different ways? Do we perceive a child with a disability as somehow defective?

I believe that each of us has experienced inner conflicts about these and other issues, if only fleetingly, and these thoughts can in turn determine our behavior and the beliefs we communicate to children. I do not believe we can wish away such thoughts, but we can become aware of them, confront them honestly, and deal with them consciously. To do so may require us to read, educate ourselves, become personally involved with the families of children who are "different," and, above all, open our hearts and minds to all children.

Meanwhile, in the classroom, the teacher may be confronted with what we might call discrimination or unequal treatment of a certain child. Some children feel powerless and can feel more powerful if they can find a scapegoat or someone to make them feel superior. Sometimes an entire group will join in and, for no apparent reason, pick on one child. This is not usually indicative of societal prejudice but more likely something about the child that others find "unlikeable."

The child who is picked on may be the one who is less mature and therefore acts babyish. The child may not be as clean as the others or may smell bad. She may be acting out more problem behavior; be shy, fearful, or bossy; or have a speech impediment. It is fairly difficult to predict which child will be picked on. Many children with the characteristics just mentioned are popular and well liked by other children. Many who are kind and loving may be intensely disliked.

No group of children should be permitted to ridicule or ostracize a child. Preschool children are not emotionally equipped to withstand that sort of treatment. Their self-esteem is at stake. It is up to the teacher to set the example and, without calling attention to the child, counteract harmful remarks. Without preaching, the teacher can show affection and respect for the picked-on child and talk about her positive traits. In so doing, she should avoid making other children jealous, because they will then take out their hostility on the already beleaguered child.

Such a situation also warrants a meeting or two with the child's parents. It is important that they be made aware of what is going on and tactfully given some ideas for helping their child. If, for instance, the child is dirty or has a constant runny nose, the parents could work with him on ways to keep himself cleaner. Parents can also use role playing with their child to teach the immature child some social skills. These strategies are not meant to compromise the child's authenticity, but rather to equip him to meet his peers on their level.

Time and maturation will usually fill the gap, but meanwhile a child's self-esteem may be seriously damaged by being the class "victim." If the problem becomes intense, serious consideration should be given to placing the child with a different group of children. Perhaps this child would feel more mature and self-confident with a younger group. Perhaps the bossy or domineering child needs to spend time with older children. Whatever the solution, it should be sought before harm is done to the child.

The most common type of discrimination practiced by unaware or insensitive teachers may be gender discrimination. They may still think in terms of boys' or girls' activities or toys. They may compliment girls' appearance while forgetting that boys need as much complimenting. They may think and act in terms of "strong boys" and "weak girls" or "active boys" and "passive girls." They may, verbally or nonverbally, imply that boys are "little devils" and girls "little angels," or that girls are brighter (or less bright) than boys. The problem with stereotypical thinking is that, as a result, teachers may treat boys and girls in ways that promote societal stereotypes. There is a difference between accepting gender characteristics and actively reinforcing them. During these young, formative years, every child deserves the chance to try to be all that he or she can be, unhampered by gender stereotypes.

If children make statements such as "No boys allowed" or "Only boys can play here," the teachers can state firmly, "In our school, boys and girls decide for themselves where they can play" (Figure 6.17), or "All the toys at school are for both boys and girls."

*No Girls in the Tent*    This morning in the preschool, the teacher has set up a "tent" by draping a large bedspread over several tables. As children go in and out of the tent, the teacher watches and listens for problems. About mid-morning, Ariana crawls out of the tent, crying.

TEACHER:    Looks like you're really upset.

ARIANA:    Those boys said "No girls can come in the tent."

TEACHER:    Do you want to talk to them about it?

ARIANA:    No, they're mean.

TEACHER:    It's hard to talk to people when they're acting mean. How about if I hold your hand. It's important to tell them how you feel.

*The teacher takes Ariana's hand, and they kneel down and lift up the bedspread. Ariana starts to say something, but the boys start yelling.*

BOYS:    Go away! No girls in the tent!

**Figure 6.17** *"In our school, boys and girls decide for themselves where they can play."*

This is a clear case of discrimination. Ariana's behavior is not the issue but simply the fact that she is a girl. This fact cannot be negotiated or changed. In such a situation, the teacher should intervene and set a limit.

TEACHER: Ariana tried to talk to you about how she feels, but I want to talk to you, too. This tent and all the toys in our center are for all children to use, both boys and girls. Kids decide for themselves where they want to play.

In most cases, stating this limit is enough and kids will cooperate. Sometimes, however, there is resistance.

BOYS: We don't want to play with girls.

TEACHER: That's your choice. You can choose to play in the tent, but Ariana can choose to play in it, too. Or you can choose to play somewhere else. It's up to you. Boys and girls can choose where they want to be.

This principle applies to other situations, such as which child another one sits by at the table or in the circle. The emphasis should be on everyone's right to make his or her own decision and the fact that everything in the center is there for every child. At this level of the children's development, this message should be sufficient.

## Routines and Transitions

As noted in Chapter 3, there are times of the day when certain activities must take place to keep the program running smoothly and to meet the needs of the group. Routines are those times when everyone performs the same task every day in the same way—for example, hand washing before meals, having diapers changed, or lying down on a mat to nap. Transitions are those times when changes take place, such as going outdoors or indoors, moving from the sink to the table, or moving from free play to circle time. There is, obviously, much overlapping.

All the methods for setting limits may be applied during routines and transitions, but these are usually times when consistency and predictability are especially needed. Often there is little time for negotiating, and circumstances may prohibit teachers from giving children choices. The most effective limit-setting method may be giving information clearly, firmly and positively. Following are four phrases that are helpful for setting limits during routines and transitions, as well as a way to say "I can't give you a choice, but I can explain."

IT'S TIME TO: wash hands, go outside, get ready for lunch, rest quietly.

I NEED YOU TO (*not* "you need to"): look at books while I clean up the table, wait for me before going outside (or inside), help me get the room ready for lunch (nap time, etc.).

IT'S IMPORTANT TO: use soap to remove germs, brush to get food out, ask someone to trade to another area, stay where I can see you.

WHEN KIDS: play at the table, food might get spilled; are noisy during stories, I can't read; are finished going potty, they lie down on their mats.

I CAN'T GIVE YOU A CHOICE BUT I CAN EXPLAIN:

We all go outside after breakfast (so someone can clean up the room).

Kids come to the table for "activity time" (but don't have to participate).

Kids sit on their bottoms during meals (so they don't fall off their chairs).

When diapers are wet or poopy, they get changed (so your bottom doesn't get sore).

Kids stay on their mats at nap time (so everyone can rest).

## Summing Up Setting Limits

This chapter, of necessity, is long and complex because it deals with concepts that are fundamental to the problem-solving philosophy. It begins with the essential element that sets this philosophy apart—the difference between limits and rules. It then offers guidelines for setting limits and, finally, provides the five methods of setting limits, showing teachers how the philosophy can be translated into practical, everyday solutions to the problems they confront in working with children.

Limits, in the context of problem solving, are seen as boundaries that are flexible and often negotiable. For some teachers who have worked with rules and punishment, the change to setting limits may be the most difficult part of problem solving. It requires both mental and emotional adjustments in the teacher's attitude. This adjustment may take only a few moments as the teacher hears and eagerly embraces this new philosophy, or it may take months of self-monitoring to make the needed inner changes. The day will come, however, when setting limits instead of enforcing rules will feel comfortable and natural to teachers.

The four guidelines for setting limits are stated as a set of values. Limits are set to accomplish the following:

1. Assure the safety of each child and adult

2. Prohibit the destruction of nondisposable materials and equipment

3. Assure individual acceptance of responsibility for one's actions

4. Assure equal and respectful treatment of all people

When teachers are setting limits, their voice and body movements should remain neutral, unless they have genuine feelings to express. Such expression of teachers' feelings should be authentic yet not overwhelming to the children. An I-message is the preferred way for teachers to express their own feelings. Negative phrases should be avoided so the teacher is providing a positive role model. The child's response to the teacher's feelings or to setting limits may range from compliance to refusal. Whatever the response, the child deserves respect.

There are five methods for setting limits in problem solving: sending an I-message, the most ideal method; giving information; allowing natural consequences; using contingencies; and giving choices. As a last resort, teachers may use a method called "removing and sitting apart," which differs from the behavioral "time-out." In a few situations, using a contract, discussed in Chapter 5, may be appropriate. Examples of all types of behavior and methods of setting limits are included in this chapter.

## *Practice and Discussion*

1. Describe the difference between rules and limits. Give several examples showing the difference.

2. Give examples of the two ways to set limits for infants nonverbally. What role does the teacher's body language play?

3. What are the four guidelines for setting limits? Do you feel they are adequate? Would you add to or subtract from the list?

4. Which words and phrases should the teacher avoid? Why?

5. When you are setting limits, what four types of responses should you expect from children? How should you react to the different responses?

6. Name the five methods for setting limits in the problem-solving philosophy. Give an example of each. Which is most desirable?

7. Choose an example from the section "Assuring Safety—Guideline Number One." Experiment with using the five methods for setting limits. How many of the five methods might fit the example you have chosen?

8. Repeat question 7 choosing an example from the section "Prohibiting Destruction—Guideline Number Two."

9. Repeat question 7 choosing an example from the section "Accepting Responsibility—Guideline Number Three."

10. Choose examples from each of the sections named in questions 7–9 and use them to role-play setting limits in your college classroom.

11. How do you feel about children's accepting responsibility? Do you find it easier to do things for them? Can you train yourself to allow them to take responsibility for their own behavior?

12. Discuss the ways children try to avoid responsibility. What is the teacher's role in encouraging children to become responsible?

13. What is the difference between "removing and sitting apart" and "time out"?

14. How can teachers encourage children to treat one another as equals?

15. What strategies might be helpful when setting limits with boys? With non–English-speaking children?

## Notes

1. Bruno Bettelheim, *A Good Enough Parent* (New York: Alfred A. Knopf, 1987), pp. 37, 38.
2. From Thomas Gordon, *P.E.T.: Parent Effectiveness Training* (New York: New American Library, 1975).
3. Rudolf Dreikurs and Loren Grey, *Logical Consequences* (New York: Dutton, 1990), Chapter 4.
4. Dreikurs and Grey, *Logical Consequences*.

## Recommended Reading

Crary, Elizabeth. *Without Spanking or Spoiling.* Seattle, WA: Parenting Press, 1993.

Dinkmeyer, Don, and Gary McKay. *Parenting Young Children: Systematic Training for Effective Parenting (STEP) of Children Under Six.* New York: Random House, 1997.

Dinkmeyer, Don, and Gary McKay. *The Parent's Handbook.* Circle Pines, MN: American Guidance Service, 1997.

Dreikurs, Rudolf. *Maintaining Sanity in the Classroom.* New York: Accelerated Development, 1998.

Faber, Adele, and Elaine Mazlish. *How to Talk So Kids Will Listen and Listen So Kids Will Talk.* New York: Avon Books, 1999.

Ginott, Haim. *Teacher and Child.* New York: Macmillan, 1972.

Gordon, Thomas. *Teaching Children Self-Discipline.* New York: Random House, 1989.

Gottman, John. *The Heart of Parenting.* New York: Simon & Schuster, 1997.

# 7

# *Affirmations*

Sometimes when I am training a new teacher, I ask the teacher to pretend to be the host at a cocktail party at home. What is the role of the host? It's to welcome the guests and put them at ease, to facilitate the flow of interactions between the guests, and to make everyone feel important. The "perfect" host greets the guests, circulates among them, helps get conversations started, and finds something complimentary to say about each guest. Without imposing on the guests, the host remains easily accessible. More than the refreshments, more than the decorations or entertainment, the presence of the host makes a party a success.

How does the role of a host relate to the teacher in a children's program? Playing the same role and performing the same functions as the successful host, the teacher greets each of the children every day and welcomes them individually. After introducing new children to the group, the teacher may even suggest a toy or an activity to get them started. Using restraint and patience, the teacher allows children to enter the group at their own pace. As the children interact, the teacher circulates among them and, without imposing, lets each child know that he or she is important.

## Tools for Helping Children Feel Important

The teacher's tools for helping children feel important are given various names but serve similar purposes. In this book, they are called "affirmations" and include positive I-messages, reinforcement, noticing, strokes, and narration. These are perhaps the most underused yet most effective tools available to both teachers and parents. One of the greatest human needs is the need for attention. How often is it reported that someone has taken a dangerous risk in order to get attention from relatives, friends, and the public? Children also will frequently do certain things, usually perceived as negative, "just to get attention." Without acknowledgment and validation, a human being hardly seems to exist. People will go to great extremes to reassure themselves that they do, indeed, exist.

Too many children are noticed only when they are acting out inappropriate behavior. In a group setting, especially, the squeaky wheel is likely to get the oil. It may seem that focusing on inappropriate behavior is necessary in order for teachers to maintain control. This is what most of us have learned by example from home and society. How often is good news found in the headlines? How many of today's role models are people who simply do their jobs well, are kind and considerate, and accept responsibility? How many of those who do act responsibly are merely taken for granted by families and friends? How much crime is committed as a direct result of neglect? Although there are no definitive answers to these questions, every teacher of young children can answer one question: "How many children in my group were virtually unnoticed today?" If even one child who played cooperatively, listened attentively, and was helpful and dependable came and went without recognition, the teacher has work to do.

Teachers should train themselves to be aware of the child who is quiet or shy, who may spend a good deal of time playing alone and causing no problems. This child may not want to have attention called to herself but nevertheless deserves gentle recognition for existing and being there. Teachers needs systematic ways to remind themselves that there is a child or two who would welcome a smile, a casual touch, or a simple "hi." Some ways to keep track of the "quiet ones" include scheduling strokes into the daily lesson plan or routine, writing the names of these children on a note that the teacher, but not the children, will see, or setting certain times of the day aside for noticing. Songs, games, posters, and other materials are useful for calling attention discreetly to each child. This habit of keeping track should eventually become part of the teacher's natural teaching style.

## Relating Through Affirmations

Relating with young children occurs, at its best, through comfortable and relaxed dialogue. Some newcomers to the early childhood field, however, have little experience actually talking to children and consequently feel awkward and self-conscious conversing with them. Teachers sometimes feel as if they are conducting a monologue and question whether infants and young toddlers even understand. My belief is that, because we do not really know how much babies understand, we should always assume they understand everything and speak to them accordingly.

In this chapter, I attempt to make it easier for new teachers to become comfortable and relaxed while talking to children by providing examples of affirmations that teachers can use to get started. These positive comments incorporate inherent benefits such as raising children's self-esteem, engaging them in problem solving, and eliciting their cooperation in the classroom. I begin this section by presenting some varying opinions regarding affirmations that are held by other writers in the field.

The popularity of behavior modification (rewards and punishment) has caused many teachers to hand out stickers in place of freely given affection and verbal affirmation. Such rewards either become meaningless in time or teach children that their own value depends entirely on how many rewards they can acquire. These children are not involved in a process that enables them to develop their own inner sense of self-worth. The problem-solving philosophy in this book is aimed at developing children's self-esteem, independence, and sense of responsibility. The relationship between the teacher and the child is the key element in the problem-solving process.

One common way of rewarding children verbally is the use of praise. The *Random House Dictionary* defines praise as "an expression of approval and admiration." This description sounds positive and benign, yet there are many interpretations and opinions about the use of praise. In Chapter 5 of *How to Talk So Kids Will Listen and Listen So Kids Will Talk,* based on the teachings of Haim Ginott, authors Faber and Mazlish discuss "descriptive praise." Rather than commenting on the child, descriptive praise teaches us to comment on the process, that is, on what the child is doing, and to be specific and sincere.[1]

Also building on the work of Ginott is John Gottman, who in his book *The Heart of Parenting* uses the term "scaffolding" to describe a certain type of praise. In Gottman's research experiment, parents who were already identified as "emotion coaching" taught their children a new game by giving them small increments of information and praising the child after each successful move. The key element of their praise was that it was specific to the child's action; in other words, parents praised the behavior, not the child. This is called scaffolding "because parents use each small success to boost the child's confidence, helping her reach the next level of competence."[2] Scaffolding is similar to reinforcement, as described later in this chapter.

Does praise change or modify behavior? Think of the last time you received a compliment. How did it make you feel? Do you remember what was said and by whom? Does it pop up in your mind from time to time? Did it motivate you? Do you feel warmth and affection toward the one who gave you that compliment and make an effort to maintain that person's high opinion of you? The chances are good that compliments motivate you more than criticism and that relationships are more satisfying with those who show you their respect and admiration.

However, some compliments make the receiver feel uneasy. If the words seem insincere, undeserved, or inaccurate or are given grudgingly, compliments may evoke feelings of distrust, embarrassment, guilt, or resentment. Your reaction to compliments like these may be similar to the following: "I'm not really that good. What did he mean by that?" "If she honestly thinks that was so great, she must have poor judgment." "That was so overdone and in front of other people, too. What must they think?" That kind of compliment may even make you want to prove how wrong the giver is!

In *Teaching Children Self-Discipline,* Gordon expands on the negative results of rewards, including praise. His focus is on the use of rewards to control behavior. He defines praise as "a verbal message that communicates a positive evaluation of a person, a person's behavior, or a person's accomplishment." In place of praise he suggests the "positive I-message,"[3] defined in the following section.

According to Gordon, praise becomes negative when it is used as a way to control a person's behavior or as an evaluating mechanism. These are valid concerns and ones that should cause teachers to look closely at their own motivations when they interact with children. Sincere compliments make us feel more worthwhile and valued than does criticism; however, a compliment given for the purpose of making us "better behaved" can feel exactly like criticism to a child. Children know when they are being controlled, evaluated, and manipulated.

In *The Parents Handbook: S.T.E.P.,* based on the work of Dreikurs, writers Dinkmeyer and McKay use the word "encouragement" to describe positive comments made about children's behavior. The purpose of encouragement is to recognize effort and improvement rather than achievement and to help children believe in themselves. These writers also warn about the problems inherent in using praise with children, such as setting up competition, unrealistic expectations, and reliance on external evaluation. Like Gordon, they are concerned with the use of praise as a method of control. Their "language of encouragement" closely resembles many of the positive statements found in this chapter.[4]

**Figure 7.1**    *Encouragement helps children develop positive self-esteem.*

The common concern of these writers is that praise, as we have known it in the past, may be damaging to children rather than helpful. Instead of raising children's self-esteem, facilitating problem solving, and eliciting cooperation, praise that is given ineffectively or with control as a motivation can do more harm than good. For this reason, it is important that teachers learn to use the affirmations of positive I-messages, reinforcement, noticing, strokes and narration in such a way that the child feels deserving, knows the words represent an accurate depiction of her behavior, and consequently is not embarrassed by or distrustful of the teacher or her words. The goal is to help the child recognize in herself those unique characteristics that make her lovable, valuable, and capable (Figure 7.1).

## The Positive I-Message

Unlike the I-message used for setting limits, the positive I-message may have two or three parts: your feelings, what is happening, and (optionally) the reason you feel as you do. These parts should be stated authentically, communicating the way the child's behavior makes you feel. An I-message is accurate and nonjudgmental; it is not a disguised attempt at changing behavior. Here are some examples of positive I-messages:

**Figure 7.2** *Noticing is the simplest yet powerful act of acknowledging the child's existence. No excuse is needed for noticing.*

"I appreciate getting so much help clearing off the table. We can get ready for lunch so much quicker with the paints put away."

"I like the way you got those blocks put away so we can have circle time."

"I enjoy watching you work on your project. It looks like fun."

## Reinforcement

Reinforcement generally refers to a particular positive behavior that is affirmed verbally. The child first takes the action; then the teacher immediately comments, telling the child that the action was perceived positively. The child feels instant approval of the action. The child may choose to repeat the same action in the future, perhaps hoping for the same sign of approval. Approval is a necessary ingredient in building a child's self-esteem.

## Noticing

"Noticing" is the simple yet powerful act of acknowledging the child's existence (Figure 7.2). The child may not be performing any particular act or behaving in any special way. Noticing is often a physical gesture such as a smile, a wink, a pat on the back, a touch of the hair, or a hug. It may also be verbal, given by a passing remark such as "You're looking happy today" or

"Wow, are you ever energetic this morning!" When appropriate, noticing may include commenting on a new haircut, a toy the child has brought, or a special pair of shoes. No excuse is really needed for noticing. The fact that the child is there in the group is a good enough reason for noticing him. Noticing should be nonsexist; boys enjoy having their clothes and haircuts noticed as much as girls do.

## Strokes

"Strokes" is a term from transactional analysis that has come to overlap reinforcement and noticing. For teachers and children, it signifies any or all positive communication coming from the teacher and received by the child. Its main focus is recognition of the child as an individual worthy of love and approval. Strokes are also part of the socializing process referred to as "rituals." Rituals include greetings, such as "Hi, how are you today?" and "I'm so glad to see you here." Once a ritual is begun, the child comes to expect it, reacts to it, and feels disappointed when it is forgotten or overlooked. Children love rituals because these acts are so reassuring. They teach children that some things can always be depended on. That reassurance also brings children a sense of safety.

## Narrating

Narrating is a way of putting into words what is happening when an activity is noteworthy. This technique is especially appropriate for infants and toddlers who are not yet able to say "Look at me!" and do not have the vocabulary needed to say "I'm coming down the slide" or "I'm drawing with crayons." Verbalizing an activity not only gives attention to the child but also gives words to fit the action. At the same time, it can make a new or self-conscious teacher feel that she is talking to herself. If narrating feels embarrassing to you, try to remember that the children do not think you're strange when you narrate; they think your behavior is quite normal. The more you are willing to narrate, the more it will seem normal to you, too, and the children will love your connecting with them in this way.

Here are a few phrases to help teachers narrate:

"I see" (John going up the ladder and down the slide; jumping on the mat; painting at the easel).

"I hear" (Aiko pounding on playdough; shaking her rattle; singing a song).

"Look at" (Marco taking some steps; putting away his toys; staying on his chair).

It is less important to remember the differences or similarities of these techniques than to know how to use them appropriately. Many adults have

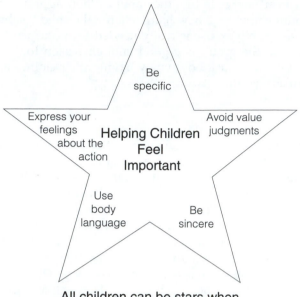

**Figure 7.3**　*Guidelines for giving affirmations.*

difficulty finding ways to give affirmations. When overused, phrases such as "That's a good girl" or "Isn't that nice?" become meaningless. Adults seem to do much better in interactions with other adults. Perhaps they find them more interesting, are not afraid of "spoiling" them, or are afraid to appear patronizing to them. Under what circumstances would one adult say to a friend "Good man" or "Good woman"? If an adult proudly shows a friend a new dress she made herself or a painting he spent months working on, what kind of friend would casually remark, "Oh, isn't that nice"?

## Five Guidelines for Giving Affirmations

Children need and want the same kind of recognition given to adults. To simplify how it works, here are five guidelines for giving affirmations. Some will overlap a bit, but this is not a problem. The guidelines are summarized in Figure 7.3.

1. Be specific. If the child paints a picture, comment on what you see. Rather than guessing what it is (you may be wrong) or asking what it is (how embarrassing!), talk about colors used, brush strokes, brightness, or darkness. If a child has paid attention to

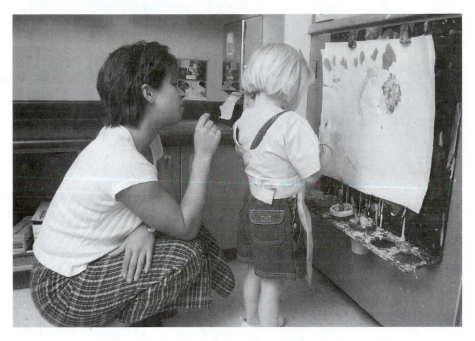

**Figure 7.4**    *Comments should be specific and sincere. "Look at those fluffy blue splotches!"*

directions, comment on how he has paid attention, such as remembering to put the puzzle on the right shelf. Comments should not be vague, general, or arbitrary. The child knows whether teachers mean what they say (Figure 7.4).

2. Express your feelings about the action, not the person. Many children are shy. Even if they are not, they often find direct praise hard to take. Saying "You're wonderful" or "You're such a good boy" may raise the question "Why?" in the child's mind. And if someone can be so wonderful or so good, what happens when he is not so wonderful or good? This can be a bit scary for a child (or an adult), who might feel the words are undeserved and insincere. A positive I-message, such as "I like the way you asked him to stop pushing you," focuses on the behavior, not the child.

3. Avoid value judgments. Telling a child that she has done something "right" or "correctly" may tell her not only that you approve but also that her work should be judged by you, using standards she does not yet understand or value. When children focus on the rightness or wrongness of their work, they may lose spontaneity and may feel inhibited from exploring freely. The fear of being "wrong" is very strong in young children. When an infant

shows his teacher he can now turn over a container of toys and dump them out, he is exhibiting a new skill. The skill is neither "good" nor "bad" but is another step in his development, and he has every reason to be proud of himself. Children can sense that a positive value judgment can easily become a negative value judgment. Value judgments should be omitted from affirmations.

4. Use body language. As mentioned, a child feels noticed and approved of by the use of touch. The word "stroke" had a predominantly physical meaning before it became a popular psychological term. Touching can be so fleeting, so unconscious, that it may be barely noticed by the adult, but it is significant to the child who receives it. It is important to remember, however, that touching is an invasion of the child's personal space. Although most children welcome and reciprocate touching, some may not. The child's response should be sufficient for the sensitive teacher. Because touching is so important to human development, the child who resists appropriate touching deserves some follow-up by the teacher. The parents may be asked if touching is done freely within the family or if the child has always resisted touching. The teacher and parents will want to consider all aspects of the child's personality and may decide to seek counseling for a child who withdraws altogether from touching. For such children, as well as all others, remember that a smile is a form of stroking that is always appreciated.

5. Be sincere. Nothing feels worse to an individual than insincerity. Affirmations are not meant simply to fill time or gaps. They are also not meant to manipulate people so they will behave like robots. Indeed, sincerity perceived as flattery will cause the opposite effect: rebelliousness. The child who feels flattered and manipulated learns to mistrust even those whose affirmation is authentic; he may learn to mistrust his own perceptions as well. His mistrust of himself and others will make him doubt his own self-worth and be damaging to his self-concept. One possible result may be a child who is constantly testing limits, expecting the punishment he thinks he deserves.

## Affirmations and Behavior

How do affirmations contribute to children's problem-solving skills? Whatever builds strong self-esteem in children will automatically help them have more confidence in their abilities. Children who feel good about themselves believe that they can at least try to solve whatever problems life presents. Adult encouragement only motivates them to try harder. As they develop and mature, the encouragement they have received externally becomes internalized. This facilitates their ability to work toward and wait for the solution to a problem. By affirming themselves for their positive behavior, they become independent and competent. As the process continues, such children will also begin to give affirmations to their friends.

Affirmations also play a unique role in the group setting. From an early age, children want what other children have. The infant sees another infant holding a bright, shiny object and goes after it. The toddler wants the biggest truck even though it is being used by another toddler. The preschooler wants whatever new toys her friends have. But children are not unique in this reaction. Our entire economy is based on our wanting what other people have. Television, a powerful force in the lives of children and adults, teaches us all to want what we don't have.

Wanting what others have includes recognition. Imagine a room with a group of three-year-olds in it. Every child has a toy out and is playing with it. The teacher has just announced, "It's time for lunch." Most of the children continue playing as if the teacher had said nothing, but one child begins to put her toys away. The teacher says, "Beth, I like the way you remembered to put your toys away at lunchtime. Thank you for listening to me so carefully." Jared, sitting several feet away, looks over at Beth, hears the teacher, and immediately says, "I'm putting my toys away, too." And he does. "Good work, Jared," says the teacher. "I appreciate your cooperation. Beth and Jared remembered to put their toys away." "Me, too," chimes in Melanie, then Luke and others. Soon all the toys are put away, and the children are sitting proudly at the table, ready for lunch.

Does this sound too easy, too improbable? Will children really respond so cooperatively and comply so readily? Most will. In this group, there may be a dawdler or a limit tester, but, by and large, children who receive encouragement and whose self-esteem is high are more cooperative and compliant than those lacking encouragement and self-esteem. If the teacher follows the five guidelines in this chapter and uses this technique only when appropriate, children will respond positively. If this technique is used primarily to manipulate the group, however, children will eventually become indifferent to the teacher's words, and this method will lose its effect. To remain effective with a group, affirmations must be used authentically and appropriately.

## The Morality of Affirmations

Guideline number three asserts that value judgments are incompatible with affirmations. Does that mean that affirmations play no part in moral development? Not at all. Active listening contributes to the development of empathy by giving children the freedom to discover their inner strengths. Affirmations represent the attributes that the world around them finds worthwhile. While active listening helps children develop empathy for others, affirmations, in a sense, help children develop empathy for themselves.

By viewing their strengths through the eyes of those who appreciate and admire them, children come to appreciate and admire themselves.

Empathy and compassion are closely related, and both play a part in morality. A narrow definition of morality is conforming to the rules of conduct dictated by society. In a broader sense, we think of a moral person as one who is capable of inward righteousness and outward compassion, in other words, a person of integrity. It is obvious that a person who commits crimes or other immoral acts against other people is sadly lacking in empathy and compassion and, therefore, integrity. We have only to delve into the childhoods of criminals to understand that most grew up with little or no sense of self-worth. Healthy self-esteem can shield a child from the temptation to take part in immoral behavior. Think of how many lives could be changed if we gave more affirmations!

## Gender Differences in Affirmations

In recent years, we have become so aware of gender issues that it hardly seems necessary to mention the importance of giving affirmations to both boys and girls. However, it is worth reminding ourselves from time to time that all children enjoy being noticed, for similar reasons. Boys want to be noticed for their new shoes and haircuts just as girls want to be noticed for their physical strength and risk-taking activities. Try developing the habit of greeting each child with a brief but sincere personal comment such as "You and I are both wearing blue today" or "Those boots look snuggly and warm" or "I'll bet your mom is happy that you help her with your baby sister." Remember, too, to let go of any preconceived ideas that certain classroom tasks should be done by one particular gender. Young children are ready to try anything if you give them the chance.

## Affirming the Non–English-Speaking Child

As you might suspect, giving affirmations to a child who does not understand your language is primarily a matter of using gestures, tones of voice, and facial expressions. Use the same words you would use with other children, but be sure to smile when you are pleased. A smile and a light touch go a long way toward making any child feel valued. Infants and toddlers require ongoing touch as a part of nurturing. On the other hand, if an older child is fearful or if the culture from which he comes is less receptive to casual touching, just use your smile until you're sure the child is ready to be touched. It would probably be beneficial to ask parents new to the program how much touching their child will tolerate from a stranger. Wait until you and the child are more familiar with each other before trying a hug.

## *Improper Uses of Affirmation*

There are some improper ways to apply affirmation of which teachers should be especially aware. Much of children's inappropriate behavior is done for the purpose of seeking attention. The child is not necessarily aware of this goal, but, in fact, practically every action he makes may be directed toward getting attention. Much, if not all, attention-seeking behavior originates with the child's home life and may be continued in the classroom. When this is the case, the teacher may actually be reinforcing undesirable behavior by using affirmation. The attention-seeking child plays "games," tests limits, may behave aggressively toward other children, and generally engages in disruptive or irritating antics. If the teacher pays attention and responds to this type of behavior, she is encouraging more of the same. For an example of attention-seeking behavior, see the section "Seeking Attention" in Chapter 8.

There is also the risk of using affirmation to promote competition. When a teacher says "Let's see who can pick up the most blocks" or "Who can finish his drawing first," she may be reinforcing the "winner" but causing resentment among the other children. This is an improper use of affirmation and may damage the self-esteem of those who cannot compete well. Competition is natural to boys, but it is not helpful when cooperation is needed. Boys and girls can find appropriate ways to compete when they are not working as a group. The purpose of affirmation is not to tell the child "You are better than the others," but rather "You are capable of being the best 'you' there can be."

## *Examples of Affirmations*

Sometimes teachers get stuck saying the same phrases over and over. This becomes boring, not only to the children but also to the teacher herself. Hearing the same words come out of one's mouth day after day becomes tedious and eventually causes burnout. Then the teacher will forget to use affirmations altogether. To help avoid that situation, here are some examples you may want to post on the wall within eyesight. A creative staff will add more phrases to the list. New and descriptive words make affirmations more fun for everyone (Figure 7.5). Although this list is primarily verbal, remember to use body language, too.

CHILD: Watch me hang by my knees.

TEACHER: Great trick! Your muscles are working hard.

TEACHER: (to children sitting on the floor) I'm glad to see Holly and Jordan starting to sit in a circle just the way I asked them to.

**Figure 7.5** *Descriptive words make positive comments more fun: "That ice must feel cold and shivery."*

TEACHER: (to child painting at the easel) I see lots of green swirls and yellow dots.

TEACHER: (to children building with blocks) Looks like you made a structure to put your car in.

TEACHER: (to child starting to crawl) I'm so excited! Now you can move all over the room.

TEACHER: (to child learning to take off his shoes) You've figured out how to take your shoes off.

TEACHER: (to child waiting for a turn to wash her hands for lunch) You're waiting so patiently.

TEACHER: (to child working on a puzzle) You've found so many of the pieces that you've almost finished.

TEACHER: (to child proudly holding his own bottle for the first time) You've been trying so hard, and you did it. Terrific!

TEACHER: (to children solving a problem) Chad has an idea. I'd like to hear it.

TEACHER: (to child showing how she can write her own name) I'm impressed. Every letter is there. You can be proud of yourself.

TEACHER: (to child picking up a book from the floor) Thank you for picking up the book.

TEACHER:  (to child playing alone in the sand) Looks like you're enjoying the sand.

TEACHER:  (to child pounding on playdough instead of on the table) I like the way you're pounding right on that playdough.

TEACHER:  (to children at the table during a Spanish lesson) John is really paying attention. Nice going, John.

TEACHER:  (to child starting to walk) It must be fun to see everything from up high. You're really getting around.

TEACHER:  (to children working on an art project) Everyone's working so hard. This is really creative.

TEACHER:  I feel very happy when you pet the guinea pig so gently.

TEACHER:  (to child sitting alone on the swing) Hi. How's your day going?

TEACHER:  (to child arriving at school, shyly) Good morning. When you're ready, there are some new markers to try out.

TEACHER:  (to child trying to find her shoes) I appreciate that you're still looking. You're sure trying hard to find them.

TEACHER:  (to child sitting holding a doll) You're taking such good care of your doll.

TEACHER:  (to child completing a card-matching game) You worked for such a long time. Looks like your persistence paid off.

TEACHER:  (to child arriving at center) You have a new haircut. I'll bet it feels more comfortable.

TEACHER:  (to child in an infant seat, intently watching a moving mobile) I enjoy watching the mobile with you. You look so interested.

TEACHER:  (to child who starts to throw sand, sees teacher, and stops before he throws) Thank you for remembering that sand isn't for throwing.

TEACHER:  (to child leaving center) Bye, bye. See you tomorrow.

TEACHER:  (to child who talks in a normal voice in a group of loud talkers) It sounds so good to hear a normal voice (also in a normal voice).

TEACHER:   (to child playing at the water table) You're pouring so carefully. The water's staying in the water table.

In addition to spoken affirmations, singing can play a major role in giving recognition to children. Every teacher knows some songs that are sung in a circle, singing the name of each child in turn and focusing briefly on him or her. Here are some examples of such songs:

Mary's here today, Mary's here today
Let's all clap our hands and sing
Mary's here today.
(sung to "The Farmer in the Dell")

Billy wore his blue shoes, his blue shoes, his blue shoes
Billy wore his blue shoes, to come to school today.
(sung to "Here We Go Round the Mulberry Bush")

Where, oh where, oh where is Susy?
Where, oh where, oh where is Susy?
Where, oh where, oh where is Susy?
I see Susy here today.
Is she up on the mountain? No, no.
Is she down by the fountain? No, no.
Has she gone out to play? No, no.
I see Susy here today.
(sung to "Ten Little Indians." Note: The words "Ten Little Indians" are
considered racist and should not be sung in children's centers.)

Where is Joey, where is Joey?
Here he is, here he is.
How are you today?
(child's response) Very fine and thank you.
Come and play, come and play.
(sung to "Are You Sleeping, Brother John?")

Songs are especially good icebreakers for shy children. With the songs, children can get attention without being singled out; at the same time, they are learning appropriate ways to give attention to others (Figure 7.6). For older toddlers and preschoolers, games provide another way to give individual attention to children. Table games such as Lotto, Memory, and Bingo (preschool versions) require children to take turns; these games have built-in success when played cooperatively rather than competitively. The teacher's enthusiasm and encouragement will help all the children feel like winners.

## Affirmations in the Environment

The classroom environment is a rich source of nonverbal affirmations (Figure 7.7). At least part of the room should be designated as a self-esteem area. On a wall there might be a poster with photographs taken of all the children during their daily play and on special occasions. One such occasion can be the celebration of each child's birthday. In addition to the photographs, there should be a poster showing the birthday of every child (Figure 7.8). A birthday ritual can be easily established. Older children can bake their birthday cake with their group; parents can bring one for younger children. A simple crown of construction paper for the birthday child brings excitement. Children love rituals and soon know exactly what is supposed to happen and when, so once birthday celebrations are established it is best not to change the ritual to any great degree.

**Figure 7.6**   *Songs that focus on each child help children feel important.*

**Figure 7.7**   *A child should feel "This is my place, and there I am!" Every child has an outline and many photos.*

**Figure 7.8**    *A poster (upper right) shows the birthday of every child.*

Other photographs in the room can be put into small, easy-to-hold albums for every age group, including infants, and kept with the other reading books. Children enjoy reliving events that happened in the classroom or on a field trip and seeing pictures of themselves or of friends who have gone on to kindergarten or moved away. Figure 7.1 also shows children's handprints as affirmations in the environment.

Another poster can be one used for measuring the children's growth. Growth charts may be homemade or purchased at a school supply store. Begin by measuring all children in the fall, then again the following spring to mark their growth. Measurements can be saved and marked on a chart from infancy to kindergarten age by coordinating use of the charts with teachers of every age group (Figure 7.9). Children can be weighed as well, although most scales are inaccurate and a child's weight fluctuates at different times of day.

Children can also create their own storybooks. Whenever possible, the children should be allowed to give dictation to the teacher, telling their stories. The teacher then writes, word for word, exactly what each child says. Children can make up fantasy stories, describe the action they see in a picture, talk about members of their family or friends, or tell of an event such as a trip. Everyone loves reading children's narrations, especially those that are wildly imaginative. In addition to their stories, children's artwork should be displayed and rotated whenever possible.

**Figure 7.9** *Growth charts allow children to see their own growth.*

## Summing Up Affirmations

Everyone needs to be acknowledged and validated. A great deal of inappropriate behavior, low self-esteem, and pain results from the lack of attention paid to children. The tools for giving attention and making children feel important are called affirmations and include positive I-messages, reinforcement, noticing, strokes, and narrating. I-messages express the adult's positive feelings about the child's appropriate behavior. Reinforcing desirable behavior, noticing a child simply because he exists, and using strokes to make him feel welcome and accepted are ways to communicate to the child that he is important. Narrating the activities of children as they play gives them both attention and vocabulary. All affirmations build children's self-esteem when they are given effectively.

Affirmations should be given authentically in such a way that the child feels deserving and is not embarrassed. Guidelines for giving affirmations include being specific about the appropriate behavior; expressing your feelings about the action, not the person; avoiding value judgments; using body language; and conveying a sense of sincerity.

Affirmations can be and often are ineffectively given by unskilled and poorly motivated teachers. These tools for making children feel important should never be used to give attention to "game" playing or other undesirable behavior, nor should they be used to promote competition between children. Teachers should broaden their vocabulary for giving affirmations so they are not constantly repeating the same phrases. This chapter includes numerous examples of affirmations.

Songs, games, and other activities that focus briefly on the individual child without singling her out help even shy children gain the recognition they need. The environment should also communicate affirmation through photographs of the children, birthday celebrations, charts of the children's growth, stories the children create and dictate to a teacher, and displays of the children's art.

## Practice and Discussion

1. How does the teacher's role resemble that of the "perfect host"? What are the functions of a host?

2. What are the teacher's tools for making children feel important? How does the teacher use them with children?

3. Discuss different opinions regarding affirmations. What is your own opinion about praise, I-messages, and encouragement?

4. Are there other kinds of affirmations not mentioned in this chapter? As a research project, try to discover and write about at least one other kind.

5. If you are now working with children, try at least five positive I-messages with your group. How did you feel about using them, and what was the result?

6. Describe reinforcement, noticing, and strokes and give an example of each.

7. Write a scene with children playing, and then interject narrating into the scene. Does it seem natural to you?

8. Does behavior change when affirmations are used? If so, how does it change and why?

9. How can teachers avoid embarrassing or judging children when giving affirmations?

10. Make a poster of phrases used for giving various kinds of affirmations. Be original and creative. Post it in your own children's program.

11.  Begin collecting songs that build children's self-esteem.

12.  Look around your own classroom and evaluate the environment for affirmations.

---

## Notes

1.  Descriptive praise is described in Adele Faber and Elaine Mazlish, *How to Talk So Kids Will Listen and Listen So Kids Will Talk* (New York: Avon Books, 1982), Chapter 5.

2.  John Gottman, *The Heart of Parenting* (New York: Simon & Schuster, 1997), p. 112.

3.  Positive I-messages are described in Thomas Gordon, *Teaching Children Self-Discipline* (New York: Times Books, 1989), Chapter 3.

4.  Encouragement is described in Don Dinkmeyer and Gary D. McKay, *The Parent's Handbook: S.T.E.P.* (Circle Pines, MN: American Guidance Service, 1982), Chapter 3.

## Recommended Reading

Crary, Elizabeth. *Without Spanking or Spoiling.* Seattle: Parenting Press, 1993.

Dinkmeyer, Don, and Gary McKay. *The Parent's Handbook.* Circle Pines, MN: American Guidance Service, 1997.

Faber, Adele, and Elaine Mazlish. *How to Talk So Kids Will Listen and Listen So Kids Will Talk.* New York: Avon Books, 1999.

Ginott, Haim. *Teacher and Child.* New York: Macmillan, 1993.

Goleman, Daniel. *Emotional Intelligence.* New York: Bantam Books, 1997.

Gordon, Thomas. *P.E.T.: Parent Effectiveness Training.* New York: Peter H. Wyden, 1972.

Gordon, Thomas. *Teaching Children Self-Discipline.* New York: Times Books, 1989.

# 8

# *Problem Solving for Problem Behavior*

Max was born with a twinkle in his eye and a crooked grin on his mouth. He was the kind of wiry, restless baby who seems to bypass crawling and walking and goes directly to running. Although all infants love to dump things out of containers onto the floor, Max could dump things and move on to the next dumping faster than anyone.

At thirty months, Max remained a highly active toddler with a short attention span and intense curiosity about everything he saw. Although he no longer dumped toys on the floor, he did flit from toy to toy, activity to activity, constantly forgetting to put things away. When reminded to pick up his toys, Max acted as if he believed he had not taken them out. He gave the teacher a blank stare or insisted that another child put them away. Max's social interactions were intense and frequently explosive. He seemed to be either laughing ecstatically with a good friend or screaming with rage at the same good friend.

As a preschooler, Max still ran instead of walked, had difficulty sitting through any structured activity, and lost control easily, behavior that often led to highly charged conflicts with his friends. He also possessed a great deal of personal charm, including his still twinkling eyes and winning smile. Other children admired him and were likely to follow his lead. Max's teachers, however, found his behavior disruptive to the group and a trial of their patience. In other words, Max was seen as a behavior problem.

The conventional children's program is generally organized and structured for children thought of as normal. The ratio of teachers to children maintained in most centers or homes can be effective only if the children are reasonably cooperative and compliant. Conformity is a necessity. The child whose behavior is not easily managed may find himself spending long periods of time in "time out," being criticized, punished, spanked (where permitted), or asked to leave the program. Parents may be asked to make the child behave; this may lead to parental guilt, anger, and feelings of shame that result in harsh treatment of the child. After all, the parents' employment depends on care for the child.

## Defining Problem Behavior

What is problem behavior? Is it any behavior that does not fit neatly into what we consider normal? Is it behavior that is difficult for the teacher to manage? Does it cause a problem for the child herself or for her peers? Before attempting to apply problem-solving techniques to problem behavior, we need some guidelines for defining problem behavior.

This book is about a specific philosophy, problem solving. When we define problem behavior, it is therefore important to use guidelines that relate to the principles of problem solving. The definition would not be compatible with those principles if behavior were considered a problem simply because it did not conform, was inconvenient, or did not fit into a certain structure. The goal of problem solving is to enable children to solve their own problems and to "do what kids do" in an atmosphere of freedom with responsibility. In such an atmosphere, children's needs and rights are of primary importance. They are treated with respect by teachers who put their trust in the natural processes of growth and development.

To support and facilitate normal growth and development, the problem-solving philosophy uses the tools of active listening, negotiation, limit setting, and affirmations. This philosophy encourages communication between teachers and children and the use of limits rather than rules to enable children to function in an atmosphere of freedom with responsibility.

In this atmosphere of freedom and responsibility, what constitutes problem behavior? Because there are no rules, the definition of problem behavior cannot be based on whether the child is breaking rules. There are, however, limits—limits that prohibit a child from causing harm and destroying equipment and materials, encourage him to accept responsibility, and eliminate discrimination against any children. Limits can serve as one guideline for defining problem behavior. If a child exceeds limits constantly, might this be considered problem behavior? It might. Yet there are many circumstances to be considered. Is the child capable of exercising the control necessary to operate within limits? Is he actually making an effort to stay within the limits? How often does he exceed the limits? Which limits is he exceeding? When a teacher reminds him of limits, is he defiant or simply unaware?

Although exceeding limits may be used as a tool for defining problem behavior, it is only one of several tools. Some behaviors that cause problems have little to do with limits. The behavior may be turned inward and harm only the child himself. The child who is painfully shy, for example, is probably the most cooperative, compliant child in the group. The chronic tattletale may also work hard at being so good that no one can, in return, tattle on her. If the result of such behavior is that the child's self-esteem is diminished or his ability to exercise freedom and accept responsibility is inhibited, this behavior may be considered a problem.

The child's teacher or teachers will be the first to encounter inappropriate behavior and respond to it. Is the behavior disrupting the group such that other children cannot play, work, and interact in a normal way? Is there the possibility of a personality clash between the teacher and the child? Is the teacher giving this child more negative than positive reinforcement? When a teacher responds negatively to a child, there is a risk of damaging the child's self-esteem. In addition, the teacher probably feels frustrated and inadequate as well. If the teacher's feelings cause resentment toward the child, the child will know it.

There is one last guideline for defining problem behavior. There is a saying that behind every behavior is a need to be met. People, including children, act and react in order to get their needs met. Those of us who have observed young children on a daily, long-term basis have learned that most of the time children figure out ways to have their needs met appropriately. If the need is for attention, they cry appealingly, smile winningly, do adorable tricks, hug and kiss, tell funny stories, or use any of a number of attention-getting devices. If they can get their own needs met in a positive way, they gain in competence and self-esteem. They may then go on to fill other needs.

Some children, however, have needs that neither they nor the adults in their lives understand. Because the need itself is vague or intangible, these children do not know how to satisfy it. They also may not yet have developed the skills necessary to effectively get their needs met. Getting needs met does require a certain amount of assertiveness, manipulation, and matu-

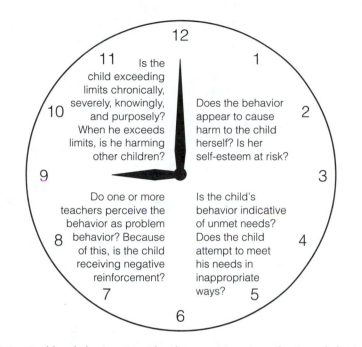

**Figure 8.1** *Problem behavior. Consider these questions in evaluating a behavior problem. All the questions should be asked in the context of time. Will the passage of time alleviate the problem behavior?*

rity. If the child has not yet sufficiently developed those characteristics, he must use whatever skills he does have. The resulting behavior may be inappropriate for meeting the particular need he is trying to meet. The attempt will probably end in failure and frustration. When this type of behavior becomes part of a pattern and is repeated chronically, it contributes to a child's problem behavior.

By applying the tools and guidelines discussed here, teachers in a problem-solving program should be able to judge whether a behavior problem actually exists. Not every guideline will apply to every suspected problem, but collectively these guidelines should help teachers gather sufficient information to make a realistic appraisal (Figure 8.1). By asking four sets of questions, they should have their answer. Those questions are:

1. Is the child exceeding limits chronically, severely, knowingly, and purposely? When he exceeds limits, is he harming other children?

2. Does the behavior appear to cause harm to the child herself? Is her self-esteem at risk?

3.  Do one or more teachers perceive the behavior as problem behavior? Because of this, is the child receiving negative reinforcement?

4.  Is the child's behavior indicative of unmet needs? Does the child attempt to meet his needs in inappropriate ways?

## When Is Behavior a Problem?

In the chapters on active listening, negotiation, and setting limits, I gave examples that encompassed a diversity of normal and typical childhood behaviors. I described "kids doing what kids do." Sometimes the child's behavior interferes with the rights of other children or causes them harm. Sometimes a child is upset or frustrated about something that has affected only her. In the examples, children responded to problem solving in fairly appropriate ways, as do "kids who are doing what kids do." In Chapter 2, in the section on modifying the environment, I discussed factors in the relationship between behavior and environmental factors. Examples in that chapter described ways to modify the environment's influence on children's behavior.

For the sake of clarity, a chapter on problem behavior must state as strongly as possible that every child has the right to be accepted as an individual human being without labels or tags to identify him as a problem child. Children are in a constant state of transition. They are changing more rapidly than we can imagine. It is extremely damaging to a child to stick him with an identity that may be here today and gone tomorrow. Every child should have the right to try out as many roles and identities as he chooses so that he alone can decide which ones feel comfortable and may be worth keeping.

No one can predict accurately what a child will be like a year from now. Temperament is formed at an early age and remains stable (refer to the section "Understanding Temperament" in Chapter 4). Most of us grow up to be adults very similar to our own parents. If they are good parents, this should be a reassuring idea, one that gives us a sense of awe and humility, because it tells us that the old metaphor of the garden and the gardener still applies to caring for children. We can only give them nourishment, protection, and the freedom to grow. With these things, they will blossom and become beautiful flowers. The most important ingredient in the process is time.

Time. How precious it is! It is what every child must have yet is being robbed of mercilessly. We want children to grow up, memorize numbers and letters, know how to work computers, and do "serious" work. They must learn to compete, perform, do it all, and have it all. What enormous pressure we put on them and how we rationalize away their childhoods! Children deserve and need time to be children, free from pressure and stress and competition. Children need time.

Such an emphatic statement is needed because adults are sometimes too quick to classify behavior that is difficult to manage as problem behavior. This leads immediately to the next step, which is "fixing" the behavior. Adults have so much power over children that the temptation to "fix" them can be overwhelming. If nothing else, the problem-solving philosophy demonstrates that most children are perfectly capable of fixing themselves. They can solve problems, including the problem of their own behavior, if they are only given the tools and the time.

Behavior is a problem when neither time nor the child's own problem-solving skills are working effectively for her, when the child needs extra individual help to gain back her own control over herself, when the child is causing harm to herself or to others, when the child is losing self-respect and the respect of her peers, or when the child's self-esteem is at stake.

## Causes of Problem Behavior

The goal of this chapter is to help teachers identify and help children whose behavior is considered to be causing problems for themselves and others. Because the focus of this book is caring for children in programs of all kinds, there will be no major attempt to dissect and psychoanalyze the entire life of every child with a behavior problem. There are too many possible causes: societal, environmental, developmental, and genetic. Most teachers are not psychologists or physicians and cannot know the case history of each child. However, some events in the life of the child are obvious contributors to stress and inappropriate behavior. Figure 8.2 illustrates some of the most common of these. Many of their relationships to behavior are explored more fully in the examples later in this chapter.

### Separation from Parents

The major cause of problem behavior in programs, separation from parents, pertains specifically to day-care centers or day-care homes, where children usually spend more waking time than they do in their own homes. The phenomena of two-working-parent families and single, working-parent families are relatively new to our society. We are just beginning to conduct research that may give families some meaningful information regarding what is best for young children. We know that divorce and the loss of a parent, usually the father, or the absence of a father altogether due to out-of-wedlock birth can be devastating to a child. Such loss inevitably results in further separation when the child is subsequently placed in day care with virtual strangers. When the family is intact and there are two parents, if both parents work full-time the child experiences a similar loss and may even feel rejected and abandoned. In view of all we know about infant bonding, it is

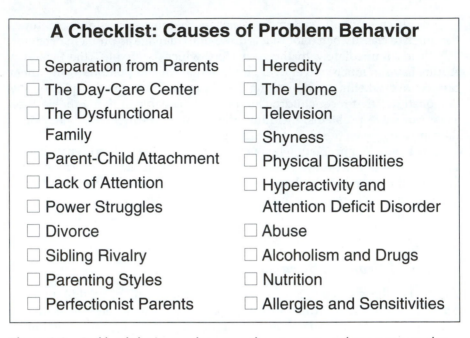

## A Checklist: Causes of Problem Behavior

☐ Separation from Parents
☐ The Day-Care Center
☐ The Dysfunctional
   Family
☐ Parent-Child Attachment
☐ Lack of Attention
☐ Power Struggles
☐ Divorce
☐ Sibling Rivalry
☐ Parenting Styles
☐ Perfectionist Parents

☐ Heredity
☐ The Home
☐ Television
☐ Shyness
☐ Physical Disabilities
☐ Hyperactivity and
   Attention Deficit Disorder
☐ Abuse
☐ Alcoholism and Drugs
☐ Nutrition
☐ Allergies and Sensitivities

**Figure 8.2**    *Problem behavior may have more than one cause, and causes may overlap.*

safe to say that separation from parents, especially during infancy, presents a risk to both child and parent.

Every morning millions of children are separated from their parents. Some go through a daily process of grieving; some face the day with hopeless resignation; some will be criticized, abused, and neglected; some will benefit simply because their day-care environment is healthier and more supportive than their home; some will choose to rebel rather than conform; and some, I hope more and more, will joyfully encounter those of you who are reading this book. They are the lucky children who will find trained, skilled teachers ready to give them the love and acceptance they need to deal with their tumultuous world.

To children, the world revolves around their needs for nurturing, usually provided by mommy or daddy. Siblings, grandparents, day-care teachers, and friends may play an important role, but above all every child wants and needs her parents. And the feeling is mutual. Parents themselves feel a great deal of pain and loss when reconciling their financial and self-fulfillment needs with their sense of love and duty to their children. In addition, new mothers experience strong hormonal influences on their emotions. These parents transmit to their children their feelings of guilt and anxiety and their fears surrounding day care itself. Their ambivalence is confusing to their children and adds to their conflicting emotions.

Separation from parents, for many children, is the underlying cause of problem behavior. They may experience a variety of emotions, including loss, rejection, abandonment, fear, resentment, helplessness, and aggression. Although most children are able to adjust to a caregiving program, form new attachments, and respond cooperatively, many children cannot completely control their feelings. Their behavior is a symptom of their inner conflict.

## The Day-Care Center

Much of what is labeled problem behavior in day-care centers is actually behavior that is not only normal but necessary to the child's survival as an individual. A child who finds herself in a restrictive, regimented, adult-centered environment has no choice but to rebel or surrender. A child who finds herself manipulated and controlled by stickers and "time outs" will do all she can to maintain her individuality and integrity. Sometimes the child who is causing so many problems can teach us the most if we are willing to listen, observe, and search for solutions.

Day care as an institution is also caught in the country's societal transition. As a nation, the United States has not yet recognized day care as a necessity for much of its work force and so offers little support. Countless well-intentioned and caring day-care workers receive minimal or no training and earn extremely low wages. As a result, a significant portion of the day-care industry is controlled either by big business corporations who model their centers after fast food chains or by smaller absentee owners with no education in child development. Children in these programs learn that only the most passive, conforming behavior is acceptable.

Fortunately, there are also individuals with high ideals and standards for quality who are skilled professionals, willing to swim upstream and make the sacrifice in order to run programs where kids can do what kids do. I suspect there are far fewer cases of problem behavior among children in such centers and homes because the teachers there recognize that normal children behave normally and adapt their programs to fit the developmental needs of the children. Far too many programs, however, have day care that is not child centered and staff who are poorly trained and underpaid.

## The Dysfunctional Family

Many factors may impair the ability of a family to provide a healthy, supportive environment for a young child. Some of these are unemployment of a parent; poverty; discrimination; marital distress that results in fighting, abuse, withholding of affection from the child, or blaming the child for the parents' troubles; too many children; unsupportive relatives; illiteracy and lack of education; substance abuse; and medical or other physical disabilities of the child or another family member. A family that is dysfunctional is likely to produce a child who is also dysfunctional.

## Parent-Child Attachment

Attachment is the bonding together of mother and child (or father or other primary caregiver) as a reciprocal unit. This process begins during pregnancy and continues during the child's first year of life. Biological factors, such as the mother's hormones; behavioral factors, such as holding, making eye contact with, and breast-feeding the infant; and psychological factors, such as compatibility of mother and child temperaments, play a major role in the normal development of attachment. If certain elements are missing, such as the mother's ability to breast-feed or a blind mother's ability to make eye contact, special care must be taken to use alternative ways of bonding.

Attachment is the single most critical event in the life of every child; some researchers believe it is a determinant of future relationships. Although the research on attachment is far from definitive, many studies suggest that insecure or faulty attachment may produce a child who is emotionally needy, fearful, dependent, explosive, or aggressive.

## Lack of Attention

When two parents are working outside the home or there is a single working parent, time is a scarce commodity. Parents may come home from work and attend to dinner and other duties or drag the child to the market or shopping mall. Some parents engage in other activities that require them to be away from home in the evenings. In our society, too many children are existing on crumbs of time from their parents. Whatever is left over at the end of a long, tiring day may go to the child. By this time, the child is too tired and cranky to be receptive. Children will go to any lengths to get attention, even when it becomes negative and punitive. This negative attention-seeking behavior is typically carried to the day-care center.

## Power Struggles

Power struggles are the source of numerous behavior problems, especially in two- and three-year-olds. Adults are likely to give unconditional love and acceptance to a baby, who appears helpless, vulnerable, and generally compliant. Babies do not say "no," "mine," and "I want to do it myself." But as children approach age two (many begin much earlier), they seek autonomy and identity as separate people. At the same time, parents begin to have expectations about what children are supposed to do. Some of these expectations relate to issues of control over the child's body, and a struggle for power begins. Much of this struggle is aggravated by opinions of relatives, friends, and doctors. The pediatrician may choose a certain age for all his patients to be weaned from the bottle or breast. Parents tend to acquiesce without really consulting the child. Seeing a neighbor's child toilet trained by age two, parents may put pressure on their own child. The toddler who once ate large amounts now needs less food, bringing about coaxing, bribing, and endless comments by grandparents. Bedtime battles also ensue when the three-year-old no longer needs as much sleep, thereby robbing parents of their much needed private time together.

The day-care program may also be a primary cause of power struggles by having arbitrary rules about bottles, toilet learning, eating, and sleeping. The attempt to put all children on the same schedule for their bodily functions runs counter to the best principles of child development and exacerbates power struggles. Teachers themselves may be responsible for this attempt to fit children into slots in order to make the teachers' jobs easier. As with any behavior problem, all factors involved in power struggles should be examined as objectively as possible.

## Divorce

Divorce has rapidly become a part of our society and is apparently here to stay. Although the option of divorcing is clearly beneficial to adults and in the long run to many children, it is usually devastating to children when it occurs. Life with two warring parents is, of course, unbearable, yet few children would actually choose divorce as a solution. The greatest loser is the child, who is caught in the middle and forced to take sides. Even when divorce is handled with the greatest sensitivity, children generally suffer one of life's most profound losses—that of one parent. Often accompanying the sense of loss is the child's belief that he was to blame. If only he had been different, the child tells himself, his parent would not have left. The trauma of divorce will certainly influence any child's behavior.

## Sibling Rivalry

For many children, the arrival of a new brother or sister marks a turning point in their lives. If the child is the oldest, she will probably perceive the baby as a threat to her place in the family. She may become more clinging, possessive, and tearful during the mother's pregnancy. Imagine that one day your spouse announces, "I have great news: A new spouse is coming to live with us. It will be fun having someone new in our family, and you'll enjoy the relationship. I'll love you just as much, but I've always wanted another one like you. You won't mind sharing me, will you?" Now imagine being two years old and hearing this from your parents. Wouldn't you be afraid of losing their love? Could you share the most important people in your world? If they really loved you, would they need someone else? Aren't you good enough for them?

Even when the child is not the oldest, sibling relationships can be disturbing. Perhaps the child feels overshadowed by an older, more accomplished brother or sister. How does she find positive ways to get attention? Or perhaps the child is somewhere in the middle and feels lost in the crowd.

Although not all sibling relationships are based on competition, and many are positive, enriching experiences for children, they do influence a child's behavior and are worth discussing with parents when they seem relevant to a behavior problem.

### Parenting Styles

Most parents try hard to be the kind of parents they want for their children. The number of available parenting books, classes, and seminars indicates that at least some parents feel they need help doing their job well. Many others, however, are content to rear their children as they were reared, even if their childhood was unhappy. They feel that because they survived their own parents' inadequacies, their children will survive theirs. They may have forgotten the heartbreak and disappointment of their childhood and the lack of a close, loving parental relationship. Parents may also have disparate parenting styles that confuse or polarize their children. Parents with different parenting styles may rear happy, well-adjusted children, but much depends on how the parents view their own differences.

### Perfectionist Parents

Young children naturally believe their parents are perfect. Because parents are the people that children love, trust, and depend on for everything, children need to believe that their parents can do no wrong. This changes, of course, as children grow and come in contact with other significant people, such as teachers, doctors, and ministers. For some children, however, their view of their parents as perfect people creates in the children a feeling of inadequacy. This feeling frequently develops when a parent is perfectionist and therefore critical in general. The child may interpret the parent's critical attitude to include the child. Many parents are also larger than life to their child. If they are especially accomplished in their career or talents, the child may feel overshadowed and withdraw into shyness and self-deprecation.

### Heredity

When a behavior problem appears for which there is no apparent cause, it may be traceable to one of the parents or a close relative. This is not to imply that there is specifically a genetic link, but the child may have inherited a behavior pattern from a family member. Time after time, when asked tactfully "Has this kind of behavior ever been seen in your family?" parents will look as though a light had been turned on. They may remember hearing their own parents describe very similar behavior. Some even recall parents saying, "Someday you'll have a child just like you, and you'll know what I'm going through." If the parent acknowledges the connection, it may prove very helpful to the teacher who is working with the child. It may also bring a greater sense of tolerance to the parent-child as well as the teacher-child relationship. After all, if the parent turned out well, the child probably will, too.

## The Home

Although the stereotype of the middle-class family is based on four people in a comfortable house, many children grow up in a confining or inhibiting home. It may be an apartment, a condominium, or an overcrowded tenement. Much of this type of housing does not provide a safe outdoor area where children can run, play, and socialize freely without constant supervision. Because children are meant to be active, when they do not have adequate space their normal activity level may be severely curtailed or even punished. When they arrive at day care and release their energy, there may be problems.

## Television

Television and its offshoots, such as videos, video games, and promotional toys, have become invasive and pervasive parts of our daily lives and most certainly a contributor to children's problem behavior. The fact that children in the United States spend more time watching television than attending school is, by itself, disturbing. Even more unsettling is what children are watching on television and the impact this viewing has on their lives.

In August 1999, the American Academy of Pediatrics issued a policy statement regarding the effects of exposure to mass media on young children. The statement made many recommendations, including that children under age two have no television-watching time at all. This recommendation was based on the child's need for interaction with other human beings, which is the foundation for normal brain development. Previous research showed five areas in which television watching has harmful effects on children:

1. Media violence increases aggressive behavior in some children, desensitizes children to violence, and makes the world look "meaner and scarier" than it is.

2. Sex in the media is rarely shown as responsible or as having risks or negative consequences.

3. Alcohol, tobacco, and illegal drug use is normalized and glamorized; in popular movies, it is shown as harmless fun, without negative consequences.

4. Increased passive television watching is "a significant factor leading to obesity."

5. Time spent watching television robs a child of more important, enriching experiences such as "involvement in creative, active or social pursuits."[1]

**Figure 8.3**    *The shy child seldom causes problems for teachers or other children.*

When we look for causes of problem behavior, it is easy to forget that television may be a primary factor or at least one of many. It is a mistake to overlook such a powerful influence.

## Shyness

Shyness may be the outward symptom of a child's low self-esteem, it may be a behavior that is learned from a parent or close relative, or it may be both. Shyness runs in families, so there may be a hereditary factor as well. In its extreme, shyness can be the underlying cause of social withdrawal, anxiety, fear, depression, and self-hatred. Shyness is often reinforced by teachers because the shy child harms only himself and seldom causes problems for the teacher or other children (Figure 8.3).

## Physical Disabilities

Children who are born with or develop physical impairments may also suffer from low self-esteem and have a low tolerance for frustration. Their low self-esteem probably comes from being compared or comparing themselves with other children as well as from the way they are perceived and treated by their families and society. Some of their frustration may stem from their inability to keep up with other children or to accomplish what they set out to do. If the environment is not suited to their needs, their frustration may be constant. With today's tendency to include in regular classrooms children who are physically challenged, there is a greater need for teacher training in working with this population so that the children's self-esteem can be raised and their possibility of success increased.

## Hyperactivity and Attention Deficit Disorder

The term "hyperactive," sometimes shortened to "hyper," has become a catchall to describe the child with an unusually high activity level. In the strictest sense, hyperactivity is a biological condition that probably begins in the brain and affects the nervous system. The behavior we observe as hyper may or may not be true hyperactivity, a condition that requires medical diagnosis. According to Brazelton in *Touchpoints*, "A truly hyperactive child has a short attention span, is driven by frenetic activity, uncontrollable impulsiveness, and emotional volatility. These problems interfere with the child's life."[2] This description tells us that most children who are highly active are not truly hyperactive; they are within the normal range of childhood activity.

The term "attention deficit disorder" (ADD) has also become a catchall for behavior problems such as aggressiveness, short attention span, antisocial behavior, destructiveness, distractibility, ceaseless activity, severe excitability, temper tantrums, uncooperativeness, negativism, and poor verbal skills. Many of these same behaviors are also found in hyperactivity. A case study of a preschool child diagnosed with ADD as well as hyperactivity is found in Singer's *Playing for Their Lives,* and I recommend this book as reading for all teachers of young children.[3] Singer's example helps put into perspective the differences between children who are highly active and difficult to manage and those who are clinically diagnosed with hyperactivity and attention deficit disorder. Another highly recommended book is Kurcinka's *Raising Your Spirited Child,* which describes "difficult" yet normal behavior and provides effective strategies.[4] Gurian and Pollack also include sections on ADD (see Recommended Reading).

## Abuse

Child abuse, whether physical, emotional, sexual, or verbal, happens to many children in our country. Because it occurs in all socioeconomic groups, no day-care center or preschool is immune. This is yet another argument for maintaining lower ratios of children to teachers. The teachers should get to know the parents as well as possible and become trusted friends with whom the parents feel comfortable discussing problems. In some cases, this may even be enough to keep parents from abusing their child. One form of abuse that is often overlooked is criticism. Frequent and harsh criticism, just like physical abuse, causes pain and destroys self-esteem.

## Alcoholism and Drugs

A plague of misery and pain is attacking our society and our children in the form of parental addiction to alcohol and other drugs. The confusion, destruction of trust, sense of shame and guilt, and subsequent loss of childhood are enormous. We are just beginning to address this problem as it relates to children, a relationship that lasts a lifetime and continues to destroy lives. Alcoholism and drug use among parents also know no socioeconomic boundaries, and the chances are great that every teacher will be forced to deal with the effects at some point.

## Nutrition

Often overlooked as a cause of problem behavior, the type of food a child eats is believed by many to influence behavior directly. Although there is much controversy within the medical profession regarding sugar, milk products, grains, and other foods and their relationship to behavior, teachers who observe their children carefully can form their own opinions. If a child reacts consistently to a certain food with an undesirable behavior, it is at least worth asking the parent to monitor it, too, and bring it to the doctor's attention. The other aspect is lack of proper nutrition. The child who arrives without having eaten breakfast (unless breakfast is served at day care) or brings candy, chips, or cookies for a daily snack may show signs of listlessness and lack of energy. The center itself may contribute to poor nutrition by serving sugary drinks and food high in fat, sugar, or salt.

## Allergies and Sensitivities

Aside from food, irritants such as cigarette smoke, dust, pollens, detergents, chemicals, and hundreds of other common substances may affect children's health and therefore behavior. Some medications may also affect behavior, although usually only temporarily. Children and parents alike should be educated about the hazards of secondhand cigarette smoke. The American Cancer Society has produced teaching kits for young children that may be obtained free or for a donation in some areas. Other suspected allergies usually require testing by a physician.

## *Is There Always a Solution?*

Working with young children within the problem-solving philosophy is an education in itself. One thing, paradoxically, becomes more and more apparent to the experienced teacher: Every problem does not have a logical solution. Sometimes the best solution to a problem is no solution at all. To put it in more positive terms, the best solutions may be time or even change. As previously emphasized, time may be the main ingredient in solving a behavior problem. In rare cases, however, when a behavior problem does not respond favorably to the problem-solving approach, it is conceivable that another approach, perhaps more structured, would better suit the child and parents.

Conditions that primarily require the passage of time to abate include transitions, such as a family's moving from one home to another, a vacation (children may think they're never coming back to day care), a visit to relatives or friends, a change in parents' working schedule, a parent's being away on a business trip, a new weekend babysitter, or a sibling's going off to school. These and other changes in the life of a young child can seem monumental and permanent because children are unable to put such events into perspective. Behavior changes due to such transitions may last from two to four weeks. I often tell parents that by the time we figure out why the child is behaving differently, the behavior will be over and the child will be back to normal.

If a child's behavior falls within the previously stated guidelines for problem behavior, and if the behavior does not respond to problem-solving strategies, it is also conceivable that the child has a condition, whether physical, emotional, or intellectual, that warrants a more specialized treatment. Such a condition may require diagnostic testing by a physician, psychologist, or learning specialist. The prescribed treatment may be one that can be carried out in the child's present program or may require a referral to a different program. Sometimes the child may remain in the program and spend several hours a week at a treatment center nearby.

Conditions that might benefit from a change in program or outside treatment include Down's syndrome; hyperactivity; attention deficit disorder; severe developmental delays in physical growth, speech, intellect, and other areas; neurological diseases; and other conditions that might prevent a child from communicating with other children. Because problem solving is built substantially on communication skills, the child who cannot communicate with at least the youngest in his group would be at a great disadvantage. He may feel isolated and frustrated, and his self-esteem would certainly suffer.

All this does not indicate that a child should automatically be "expelled" from a program. Young children are extremely accepting and flexible, and it is not necessarily harmful for them to be exposed to children who are different. To the contrary, it may provide the opportunity to call on their budding empathy and compassion and teach a lesson in love. They will also learn to relate to people as people, not as problems, and to accept them as diverse but not threatening. As long as no harm is being done to the special child's self-esteem and she, in turn, is causing no harm to the other children, a great deal of good may come from some types of problem behavior.

If, however, the child's problem behavior is so severe that the class is frequently disrupted, nothing has helped the child, and teachers are experiencing extreme stress, it may be best for the child as well as the class for the parents to seek other arrangements. Some children do not thrive in groups, and it is important for the child's sake for you to be willing to communicate this honestly to the child's parents. Perhaps the child would be happy with a nanny in a one-on-one situation, or in-home with a smaller group, or with older children or younger children. Perhaps parents are able to rearrange their work schedules to allow one of them to spend more time at home with the child. Parents might substitute other group activities such as a cooperative preschool where parents remain with their children at least part of the time or a gymnastics class where the child will benefit from social interactions.

## Types of Problem Behavior

Now that we have established a set of guidelines for defining problem behavior and explored some causes, it is time to examine some specific behavior problems. This section provides examples of how the problem-solving philosophy can be applied to the behavior problems presented here. This is not to imply that all possible solutions are found in this section; other approaches may also work. The focus of this section is on approaches that are compatible with the goals and principles of problem solving.

Some of the behaviors in the following examples have been the subject of entire books or may be found in various books on child development, child psychology, and child care. It is always beneficial to investigate a problem from many points of view, especially to learn more about its causes. Advice on how to solve a given problem may vary a great deal; readers must decide which approaches they can use comfortably. It is important to resist being intimidated by those who offer "the only correct solution."

As with all other problem solving, the process of solving problem behavior is one in which the child is included whenever possible. Although it is frequently best to meet with parents without the child in order to seek out causes for the behavior, in many cases the child who is three or older should be included in a separate meeting in which he participates in the process of finding solutions. If a meeting with parents is not needed, the teacher or teachers who are most involved with the child should meet privately with him to look for solutions.

Following are twenty-one true cases taken from my own experience. They depict types of problem behavior commonly found in the day-care or preschool setting.

### Seeking Attention

Deanna is the youngest child in the preschool. She has been at the center since she was an infant, so it is her second home. She has a close relationship

**Figure 8.4**    *A child who disrupts the play of others is seeking attention in negative ways.*

with most of her teachers. Before Deanna was at the center, her older sister, Rose, had been there. Rose, who also started there as an infant, was gregarious, outgoing, and open and could be very impulsive at inappropriate times. But when Rose started kindergarten, she matured a great deal and became a model child. Rose is talented and sociable and receives a great deal of positive attention for her achievements.

When Deanna began to realize just how much admiration Rose was getting, she began to feel left out and perhaps inferior. Sensing that she could not compete with her older sister on her older sister's terms, Deanna intuitively began seeking attention in negative ways. At home, she was cruel to her cat, kicked her older sister, and tried to break Rose's toys. She dominated every evening by turning bedtime into a power struggle. She even hit and kicked her parents. At day care, Deanna began to hit and kick the children who were older than she and, after watching them play, would attempt to break their toys. Free-play times brought a series of Deanna's attention-getting pranks, and during the structured activity time she disrupted the group with every antic she could think of (Figure 8.4).

The adults in Deanna's life reacted to her behavior in predictable ways. They tried to be understanding, but in the end Deanna would push them until they lost patience. Often at preschool, Deanna was removed and sent to play with younger children. Anytime she could make her parents or teachers angry, she had won a victory. She then had their complete and total, undivided attention. Deanna was entangled in a pattern of negative attention seeking; this pattern could cause more problems for her as well as everyone else if it continued.

During a conference between Deanna's teachers and parents, some strategies for both home and the center were developed. At home, every evening Deanna's parents would take turns spending half an hour with only Deanna. This time was to be spent while her parents still had energy to give her. It would be given willingly (children know when their parents would rather be doing something else), without excuses or interruptions by phone calls, television, or Rose. The time would be spent doing whatever Deanna wanted to do. She would be in control.

Deanna's parents also agreed to try ways to help Deanna express her feelings. Whether her feelings were anger, sadness, or happiness and even if Deanna directed angry feelings at her parents, they would never judge her feelings as good or bad, right or wrong. They would never discount her feelings as being silly, unrealistic, or imaginary but would accept them all as belonging to Deanna and worthy of respect. Because Deanna was not as open and expressive as her older sister, her parents had to learn how to ask open-ended questions that could not be answered with a simple "yes," "no," or "I don't know." Instead they asked "what, where, how, why, and when," as would a reporter. At the end of the day, they asked Deanna what had been her "saddest" or "maddest" time that day and used active listening. They did not try to solve her problems for her or protect her from her feelings.

Other strategies included never allowing Deanna to hit, kick, or otherwise hurt anyone in the family. Without a long lecture, they let her know that hurting was not permitted and that if she hurt people they would not allow her to come close to them. But her parents were not to spank Deanna or punish her mentally or emotionally by name-calling, belittling, or inducing guilt or shame. They would look for a child-rearing approach such as P.E.T. to use with Deanna and take classes together.

Deanna's parents promised to eliminate any violent television programs or movies she may have been watching, including even many funny cartoons or sitcoms that use subtle violence. They would eliminate violent toys, too. Deanna's diet would be modified to eliminate snacks and foods containing sugar, flour, and chemicals, all of which have been suspected of causing negative reactions in some children. Recently, milk has also come under scrutiny as a possible influence on some children's behavior.

It was also decided that Deanna needed an activity of her own in which she could excel, gain admiration, and become a "star." Because Deanna's father spent less time with her than her mother, they agreed that he would enroll her in and take her to a weekly gymnastics class. Deanna had previously attended a gymnastics lesson with her class and had done extremely well, but her parents had not been involved in that class. This time she would gain recognition from those most important in her life.

The remaining strategies were to take place at day care. All teachers involved with Deanna were directed to do the following. At least every half hour (timed by the clock if necessary), the teacher would seek out Deanna and give her affirmations. These affirmations could be physical, such as a hug, kiss, or friendly pat; verbal, such as "I'm sure glad you're here today" or "I enjoy your company"; or both physical and verbal. The affirmations would not relate to Deanna's behavior but would be entirely unconditional. They were to let her know that she is noticed and accepted simply because she exists. Because Deanna was such a bright child, the attention given to her would have to be sincere and indirect or she would become suspicious and evasive.

The next part of the plan for Deanna was that teachers would ignore her attention-seeking pranks and antics unless she was hurting someone or disturbing a group activity. They would turn their heads away if necessary, making no eye contact when she was behaving inappropriately. This would be extremely difficult, but the teachers must not become involved in Deanna's negative attention-seeking behavior. If Deanna did hit, kick, or otherwise hurt another child, she was to be removed wordlessly and immediately to another area or corner of the room, where she would remain until she was ready to rejoin the group without behaving aggressively.

When teachers observed Deanna watching other children and obviously wanting to join their play, they would help her find words to use to attract their attention before she attempted to destroy their toys and disrupt their play. In the group, they would also do some role playing about how to make friends and play cooperatively. As a group, they would also talk about feelings and what makes them angry, frustrated, sad, and happy. As the children express their feelings to each other, they gain empathy and tolerance, and the teacher, who listens nonjudgmentally, gains insight and wisdom.

Changes do not occur overnight. Deanna, however, began to have better and better days. Eventually, she will need less special attention from her teacher and parents, so the scheduled affirmations can come farther apart. In the process, Deanna has become more likeable, is learning to seek attention in positive ways, and is regaining her self-esteem.

## Perfectionism

Several preschool children are sitting around the table working on art projects. Each is making a project in his own way: drawing, gluing, cutting, or painting. Some children are chatting as they work, obviously enjoying the process. One child, Alice, is using markers to draw a picture of her mommy. Unlike the others, Alice grows tense as she works. She constantly groans, contorts her face, and clenches her fists.

By anyone's standards, Alice's drawing is excellent. She can draw better than most children her age. Her representations are mature, realistic, and artistic. The teacher, who is visiting with each child, comments on the colors

Alice has used and the lines she has drawn, then remarks that her mommy will certainly enjoy seeing the drawing of herself.

As soon as the teacher moves to the next child, Alice crumples her picture and throws it in the trash. She returns to the table and begins drawing again. When the teacher notices her crumpled drawing, Alice says it was ugly. But starting over doesn't bring satisfaction for Alice either, and her frustration only grows. When the teacher tries to encourage her, she only becomes more frustrated.

Alice is a young perfectionist. This might seem humorous to adults, but for this child perfection is deadly serious. Getting things right is so crucial to her self-image that failing to be perfect can cause her to be paralyzed with fear. She sets such high and impossible standards for herself that anything less constitutes complete and total failure.

What makes a child become a perfectionist? We don't know whether perfectionism is inherited or learned, but there is usually at least one perfectionist parent involved. The perfectionist bases his self-worth on performance and constantly worries about performing well enough to gain approval. Perfectionism is also about being in control. If I am always right or always perform perfectly, no one can criticize me. This also allows me to be critical of others. Perfectionist children are often tattletales.

There is another side to perfectionism that has to do with beauty. Perfectionists see beauty as perfect and see perfection as beautiful. Have you ever been moved to tears by a song, a poem, an act of kindness, or a sunset? Have you heard the stories of artists who died trying to duplicate the Mona Lisa's perfect smile? This passion for beauty may be the force that drives the perfectionist.

How can we offer support to the perfectionist child? Active listening gives the child a way to express frustration and relieve some of the stress, but it probably won't convince a perfectionist child that it's okay to make a mistake. As long as the child can function normally, there is no valid reason to try to change her style. On the other hand, there are some ways to demonstrate that making a mistake is not the end of the world. For example, the next time you spill the juice or break something, casually talk about it. Say something like "Oh, oh, I spilled the juice; I'll go get the sponge" or "Look what I broke; I'll get the broom." If the children laugh at you, laugh with them to show that it is not a disaster.

You can also show approval of the child when he's playing happily and not performing. Say something like "I love to see you having fun." It might give him permission to appreciate his nonperforming self. The perfectionist needs to know that he is lovable and is accepted for himself even when he is not perfect.

Share your own love of beauty with the perfectionist child. Help her see the positive, constructive side of perfectionism. There is a sense of joy and satisfaction in doing something well and adding beauty to the world.

After all, where would this world be without its perfectionists? I, for one, wouldn't want to know!

## Shyness

It is nine o'clock on Monday morning. Several children in the three-year-old group are sitting at the table, painting and drawing. Another two are playing house in the dramatic play area. Some have not yet arrived. Courtney, age three and one-half, and her mother come in. Mother says good-bye and turns to leave. Courtney, thumb in mouth, clings to her mother. The teacher approaches as Courtney's mother leaves. The teacher says, "Good morning, Courtney. I'm glad to see you." The teacher speaks quietly and warmly.

Courtney looks down at the floor. She makes no response and continues to suck her thumb. The teacher says, "When you're ready to join the group, Courtney, there are children doing artwork at the table and some playing house. Or you may think of something else you'd like to do." Courtney continues to stand silently, looking down at the floor, sucking her thumb. The teacher moves away and allows Courtney to gain control over the situation. She may stand and watch the group for a very long time. The teacher refrains from coaxing, prodding, or pressuring her to make her move before she is ready. After the initial greeting and invitation to join the group, the teacher avoids any direct action that draws attention to Courtney. From time to time, however, a smile from the teacher lets Courtney know that she is still welcome.

Eventually, when she feels in control, Courtney joins another child, and they silently paint together at the easel. As she gains confidence, Courtney interacts with other children and joins their play. Later there is a circle time led by the teacher. The group sings a song that includes the name of each child. They sing, "Courtney's here today. Courtney's here today. Let's all clap our hands and sing, Courtney's here today." Courtney does not sing, and as the children sing Courtney's name she lowers her eyes and seems frozen. As the day progresses, there are other group activities. When the children work on a gluing project, Courtney watches but does not participate. She says that she cannot do the project; it is too hard for her even to try. The teacher invites but does not attempt to force her to try.

Courtney is not new to the group. For about four months, she has spent her days in the same way. When her mother comes to pick her up, however, Courtney tells her all about her day and how much fun she had. Courtney is one of the estimated 30 to 50 percent of children who are shy. Shyness, according to Zimbardo in *The Shy Child*, is above all fear—fear of being judged and rejected by others, fear of being unable to respond appropriately to social situations, and fear of intimacy (if they know what I'm really like, they won't like me).[5] In order to combat their fear, shy people worry constantly about the impression they make. They refuse to take risks that may bring criticism; they choose the safer role of being an observer rather than a participant.

A main issue in shyness is low self-esteem. To avoid risks that bring rejection, the shy child will often become "perfect" in every way possible. Everything she does must be done perfectly or not at all. There is little room for flexibility; failure is tragic. This perfectionist behavior is often reinforced by society because it produces "good" boys and girls. Shy children who are also extroverts may adopt a technique called role playing, which enables them to become someone else, such as Superman, who is powerful and in control. Playing various roles gives the shy child an identity with which to face the world without fear of rejection.

Because shy children seldom cause problems for the teacher, shyness is often inadvertently reinforced in the classroom. The shy child may go unnoticed while attention is given to the more assertive child. The teacher may mentally label the child shy and may even refer to him as shy. Labeling a child as shy simply because he is exhibiting some shy behavior is a major cause of chronic shyness in children. The sensitive teacher avoids mentioning the word "shy." If necessary, he or she may instead say, "Courtney is not yet ready to say hello to us. I'm sure she'll be ready later."

Another important factor in shyness has to do with expectations. Parents and teachers tend to think in terms of performance. When expectations are unrealistically high, a child is likely to fail. Children judge themselves harshly and may believe that the love they receive is based on their living up to parents' and teachers' expectations. When they fail, their self-esteem is diminished. There are also parents and teachers who expect little or nothing of a certain child, so the child remains dependent, clinging, and feeling helpless. This child internalizes the adults' feelings that she is incapable of dealing with most situations, and self-esteem is again at risk.

No one can know how much shyness is a result of inheritance, experience, poor parenting, or societal influences. Shy children often have shy parents, although the parents may be hiding their own shyness with perfectionism or role playing. Even the youngest child, however, can see through the facade and sense her parents' fears and insecurities. If, in addition, the parents are highly accomplished people who have learned to disguise their fears, the child has no way to receive authentic guidance from her parents, who may actually overwhelm and overshadow their children.

Shyness is a source of pain and harm to the child and, if ignored, may become a source of more visible behavior problems. It affects so many children that every teacher and parent needs to learn more about it and become sensitive to its manifestations. For the extremely shy child, such as Courtney, a private conference with parents is in order. Zimbardo's *The Shy Child* should give them a great deal of insight and perhaps even help them acknowledge their own shyness and perfectionism and encourage them to help both themselves and their child.

Shyness is probably not completely curable, but a problem-solving program can do much to give the child more confidence and higher self-esteem. The program should be a balance between predictable routines that give children a sense of control and opportunities to make as many choices as possible in order to encourage the children's independence. Children need acceptance for who they are and the freedom to be themselves. They should have a sense of belonging to the group, having their own role to play. The shy child should be in a small group, no larger than ten preschoolers, and have some younger, less powerful children available to play with.

The problem-solving philosophy emphasizes allowing children to express feelings such as anger, frustration, and resentment and encourages children to work out and solve their problems and conflicts by themselves with as little teacher intervention as possible. Limits are communicated in a positive, nonpunitive way such as through I-messages and giving information. The problem-solving philosophy also allows for time. Shy children, when given time, show a great deal of progress between the ages of three and five. The temptation to push the shy child to become more social before she is ready is hard to resist, but it must be resisted so she will have the time she needs to find her identity and gain self-confidence.

The teacher can do much indirectly to help the shy child. She should greet him discreetly every day and find something special to say to him. She should attempt to make eye contact, smile, and let him know he is welcome to join the group when he is ready. The teacher can notice and comment when the child is playing with a group yet avoid embarrassing him or calling too much attention to him. When there are special responsibilities to be given, such as sending a child to the office with a message, the shy child should not be overlooked. The message can be written down so the child can simply hand it to the appropriate person. The teacher can also be sure that any problems with the shy child are handled in privacy.

There are group activities to help shy children, too, such as singing songs that mention each child's name and using birthday calendars and other posters with children's names on them. Photo albums with their baby pictures in them help children feel good about themselves, too. Role playing in the form of telling a "hero" story is also excellent. The teacher starts a story about a child meeting a bear, flying a spaceship, swimming across a lake, saving a cat's life, or performing some other heroic deed. The children all contribute to the story, each including his own heroic deed. Children love telling these often outrageous fantasies about themselves, and they vicariously live out an experience that makes them feel powerful.

Shyness is a prevalent affliction in a society that values performance, assertiveness, and physical power. The fear of rejection is so strong among shy children that childhood may be a painful experience for them. The child's need for social relationships is going unmet, while the child seems unable to find appropriate ways to meet that need. In a problem-solving program, the shy child has an excellent chance of emerging as a self-confident kindergartner.

### Temper Tantrums

Austin is almost four years old but emotionally and socially is much younger. Although he has adequate language skills, he lacks internal control. Most children who have tantrums are between two and three years old, but some, like Austin, are still having them at age four. Here is a typical scenario that would bring about a tantrum from Austin. This morning, Austin greets his friend Keith as Keith arrives with something in his hand.

AUSTIN:  Is that your tractor?

KEITH:  It's mine. I brought it from home.

AUSTIN:  Can I play with it?

KEITH:  No. It's mine. I brought it from home.

*Austin tries to grab the tractor, but Keith holds it tightly.*

AUSTIN:  I want to play with it!

KEITH:  No! It's mine!

*The teacher approaches and kneels down between the two boys.*

TEACHER:  It looks like there's a problem. Austin wants to play with the tractor, but Keith says he brought it from home. Do you have any ideas for solving the problem?

KEITH:  It's mine. I want to keep it.

*Austin's face begins to quiver, and his body becomes tense. Suddenly, he throws himself down and begins to scream and cry loudly, gyrating around on the floor.*

TEACHER:  Austin, it looks like you've decided to scream instead of talking to Keith.

*Austin is not listening to the teacher. He appears to be in another world where only his overwhelming need and the sound of his rage exist. He is capable of continuing this behavior for up to thirty minutes, and no amount of active listening makes any difference.*

TEACHER:  Keith, it looks like Austin doesn't want to talk now. Maybe he will later.

*Austin's screaming soon upsets the other children in the room. They cannot interact because of his piercing screams. The teacher feels that she must remove Austin to an area away from the other children. She carries him (he refuses to walk) to an adjoining empty room and leaves the door open.*

TEACHER:  Austin, I'm going to watch kids in the next room, but I can watch you through the door. Your screaming is upsetting other kids, but as soon as you've finished screaming you're welcome to join us again.

*The teacher's voice is accepting and neutral. Austin continues to scream and jump around the room. After five or ten minutes, he is finished and emerges from the room calm and in control.*

TEACHER:   I'm glad to see you back, Austin. Come join the group.

Although temper tantrums are more common among two-year-olds and active listening usually serves to diffuse the tantrum, prolonged tantrums in older children may indicate a more deeply rooted problem. It is worth investigating the possible causes for the behavior. In a problem-solving program where children are accepted and active listening is used, the program itself is not likely to evoke this behavior. One area of suspicion may be disparate or ineffective parenting styles. One of the parents may have exhibited similar behavior as a child. A few words with the parents may provide clues. Whatever the reason, however, problem solving requires that Austin be treated with respect and given time to mature and develop better self-control. If the tantrums continue as he approaches kindergarten age, he may need some counseling by a child therapist.

## Aggression

Carl has just turned three but is very big for his age. Because of his size, Carl thinks he should be playing with the four-year-old boys. He follows them around, trying to imitate them, but does not have the social or emotional skills to meet them as an equal. He cries easily if his feelings are hurt but physically can hold his ground. Because of Carl's social immaturity, the older boys don't want to play with him. When Carl has had his feelings hurt, he heads for his own age group and those who are a bit younger. They are all smaller than Carl, and they all know how much stronger he is. When he is upset, Carl goes from child to child, pushing them or taking their toys. He is reacting to his hurt feelings by getting back vicariously at the older boys.

In previous chapters, I have discussed anger and aggression in some detail. Because the kind of aggression Carl demonstrates can be perceived as problem behavior, it is worth another brief discussion. Carl is exceeding limits chronically, harming others as well as himself, receiving negative feedback, and trying to meet his needs in inappropriate ways. The cause is apparently his frustration over wanting to play with children his own size while generally interacting negatively with children on his own social and emotional level.

Some children seem to grow and develop unevenly. They may be bright and capable in many respects yet appear to miss out on the basic skills for relating to other children and for normal give and take. They seem to have an invisible barrier around them that keeps other children at a tolerable

**Figure 8.5**  *When aggression becomes chronic, problem solving helps the child find acceptable ways to meet his needs.*

distance. All interactions with other children must be on their own terms with little room for compromise. These children usually have a low tolerance for frustration, and their frustration is manifested in aggression against others.

When aggressiveness becomes chronic in this type of child, there are several possible solutions. First, it is of the utmost importance that the less powerful victims of aggression be given support and tools for protecting themselves. Chapter 5 includes an example of negotiation between a more powerful and a less powerful child in "Big Guy and Little Guy." In such a situation, the teacher gives power to the less powerful child by placing herself next to him so that together they face the more powerful aggressor. She also lets the victim know that he can verbally express his feelings and does not have to do what the aggressor demands of him. It is important that children learn how to assert themselves effectively against those who pose a threat.

Second, the child who is chronically aggressive, such as Carl, has a need he is trying to meet. When Carl's feelings are hurt, the teacher should immediately use active listening to show acceptance and to enable Carl to accept himself. Then Carl should be helped to find acceptable ways to meet his needs (Figure 8.5). In Carl's case he needs a peer group of children close to his social-emotional level who will accept him as he is. Whether in a structured activity group, group games, singing, or other ways, Carl should be encouraged as often as possible to join his peers. It may even be suggested to his parents that he and another child or two visit with each other at home in order to form a closer bond. In Carl's case, he should be given a great deal of responsibility and control over solving his behavior problems. Carl's type of aggression will probably pass with time as his social skills develop and he finds more appropriate ways to express his feelings. Changing this kind of problem behavior usually takes time and patience.

## Bullying

Like Carl, four-and-one-half-year-old Amanda is a husky girl. For several months, Amanda has been acting very angry. When she plays with her friends, she must always be in control and be the boss, and she will hit anyone who disagrees with her. She especially picks on one child, Elizabeth, who is younger and more vulnerable. She tells Elizabeth she doesn't smell good, refuses to sit next to Elizabeth, and tells other children not to play with her. She looks smug when Elizabeth's feelings are hurt. Amanda has always been a strong-willed, domineering child. Her parents, who are both small in stature and quiet, gentle people, have always been in awe of their child. Amanda has pretty much ruled the roost at home and now is also beating on her mother. Her parents are worried.

Hostile aggression manifests itself with attacks on another person and attempts to destroy that person's self-esteem. This is commonly called "bullying" and is a result of low self-esteem in the bully herself. Hostile aggression can be verbal, physical, or both. It increases with age and is more prevalent in boys than in girls. Amanda, however, certainly fits the description. The bully most assuredly is a child in need of help. She is probably fearful, confused, and insecure. There is likely to be an overwhelming event or situation in her home that is behind her behavior (Figure 8.6).

In Amanda's case, there were several circumstances. Her parents had always bent over backward to give Amanda everything she needed or wanted. Without realizing it, they were permissive to the point that Amanda controlled the household. They thought they were being modern, progressive parents. Then the situation at home changed. Amanda's parents were in the process of separating. There was quarreling, crying, the disappearance of her father for several days, and finally his moving out. In all this, Amanda no longer had control. She could not make things stay the way they had been. As often happens with divorce, Amanda probably took responsibility and blamed herself. This was so frightening and confusing that she had to lash out at something or someone. At home, she beat her mother until her mother had to lock Amanda in her room to protect herself. At day care, Amanda hurt her friends and especially tried to humiliate Elizabeth.

**Figure 8.6** *The bully is a child in need of help. Parents must be involved in the problem-solving process.*

Normal negotiation methods, found in Chapter 5, did not work with Amanda. The real problems in her life were not solvable through negotiation with friends. The only real control she had was over Elizabeth, and she would not willingly give that up. When Elizabeth expressed her feelings to Amanda, Amanda stuck out her tongue, turned her head away, or made angry faces. The teacher worked closely with Elizabeth, using active listening so that her self-esteem would not be jeopardized, while at the same time meeting with Amanda's parents. The teacher in this case recommended counseling for the parents, including parenting classes to help them learn to set reasonable limits for Amanda. She also suggested several sessions of play therapy for Amanda to help her deal with the grief and loss in her life.

Amanda was fortunate; both her parents loved her and were willing to cooperate on her behalf. Amanda has come through her crisis and is no longer a bully. Her parents are divorced and sharing custody; Amanda seems to be adjusting well to her new home life. She is still bossy and self-righteous, as are numerous preschoolers, but she no longer needs to control everyone in her environment. She has even made friends with Elizabeth and has stopped harassing her.

Divorce is a major crisis in any child's life. Other common causes of bullying are child abuse, parental alcoholism and drug addiction, permissiveness, and critical parents. Much can be done for the bully if parents are willing to meet with and cooperate with a sensitive, knowledgeable teacher. Unhappily, many parents are intimidated by or even hostile toward the notion that there is something going wrong with their child and that they have anything to do with it. When parents refuse to cooperate for the good of their child, the teacher can only do her best to work with the child and build self-esteem in all possible ways. At the same time, the bully must be held responsible for her actions and kept from causing harm to other children. Bullying must not be permitted to continue, and if all else fails the bully must be expelled in order to protect the other children.

## The Victim

Jerry is a quiet child, small for his age and very cautious about taking risks When other kids want Jerry's toys, they don't ask, they just grab them. Jerry passively walks away from any confrontation. At home, he tells his parents that kids are mean to him, and his parents bring their anger and frustration to Jerry's teacher. How can the teacher help Jerry and his parents?

As teachers, we see this scene reenacted on a regular basis, and we often feel as if we should be doing something about it. But what can we do? Every human being has certain characteristics. Some of us are naturally more aggressive, some more passive. As we grow, we learn skills that enable us to function in society. Aggressive children learn how to restrain their urges in order to make friends; passive children learn how to assert themselves enough to get their needs met. The skills we learn don't transform us into someone else. They only permit us to lead reasonable lives in spite of our different tendencies.

When a parent or teacher sees a child behaving like a victim, there is a strong urge to rescue that child, but rescuing can actually damage a child. If the parent or teacher treats the child as a victim, the child will also begin to see himself as a victim; he may feel hopeless and helpless and just give up. The result is a self-fulfilling prophecy. The child, who might have been helped to assert himself, really does become a victim. Rescuing deprives a child of the chance to overcome obstacles and to become stronger by gaining self-assurance and self-esteem.

It is important to repeat that bullying must not be tolerated. However, the child who has become a victim does not require a bully to make him feel victimized. Almost any normal, assertive child can intimidate a willing victim. What the victim needs is self-confidence, which so far has failed to develop. This may be due to a combination of factors, such as temperament, disruption in the parent-child relationship, physical problems, or feelings of inferiority. There is also the possibility of childhood depression. A psychological evaluation may be beneficial if the parents are cooperative.

To a degree, we must accept passive children as they are, value them, and respect their right to walk away. Many very accomplished people consider themselves passive and see it as an accomplishment, not a failure. On the other hand, we are obligated to teach them how to protect themselves

**Figure 8.7** *We are obligated to teach passive children how to protect themselves: "You can put up your hand and say 'Stop!'"*

(Figure 8.7). The negotiation strategy called equalizing will help some children (see Chapter 5). Here is an example.

*Jerry is playing with a toy truck. Along comes Ryan, who is bigger and more assertive. Ryan grabs the truck and walks away.*

TEACHER:   Jerry, is it OK with you if Ryan takes the truck?

*Jerry smiles weakly and shrugs.*

TEACHER:   If you want to keep the truck, you can put your hand up and tell Ryan "Stop!" I'll go with you while you talk to him if you want me to. It's up to you.

*Jerry declines the teacher's help time after time, but one day Jerry comes to the teacher.*

JERRY:   Damon took my shovel.

TEACHER:   Do you want me to help you talk to him?

JERRY:   Yeah.

*The teacher kneels down next to Jerry, facing Damon.*

TEACHER:   Damon, Jerry wants to talk to you about the shovel. Jerry, what do you want to tell Damon?

JERRY:   I want the shovel.

TEACHER:  Damon, Jerry is saying he wants the shovel back. What can you
do when two kids want the same toy?

*At this point, the situation becomes a normal negotiation between two children who
want the same toy, and the teacher helps them find a solution that is agreeable to
both of them.*

Children who have been passive for a long time may eventually
become fed up and begin to act aggressively. Typically, this is only role playing. The child wants to know how it feels to be aggressive. Before long, this
child will return to behavior that is more natural and comfortable for him,
but now he is equipped with assertiveness skills. Hopefully, he will not
revert to being a willing victim.

## Chronic Crying

In "Chronic Crying" in Chapter 4, we met Timmy, who spent most of his
time in the infant care program crying. Timmy is a real child who is now a
student in elementary school. Using Timmy as a subject, I gave many examples of active listening for the chronic crier. Active listening let Timmy know
that he was accepted and also gave the teachers a way to express their own
feelings positively.

Is chronic crying by an infant a true behavior problem? Don't all
infants cry at times to express feelings for which they have no words?
Should crying be avoided, or is it a choice made by the child? Shouldn't the
well-trained, dedicated infant teacher be able to patiently accept crying from
so tiny a source? The answers to these questions are not always obvious and
do not always fit into neat yes and no categories. A small number of infants
do spend a great deal of time crying. I had such an infant of my own and
have had experience in day care with many others. Being able to follow
these infants as they grow and develop (my chronic crier is now forty-one) is
comforting and helps put things in perspective because these children do
become normal, well-adjusted people. They may be dramatic types, to be
sure, but they can be intelligent, sociable, and quite lovable. This is not a scientific statement but simply the opinion of an educated observer.

When an infant has been thoroughly examined by her pediatrician and
is loved, held, nurtured, perhaps breast-fed, and stimulated appropriately
yet screams every time she is put down, what is left to do? The humane and
responsible course of action is to approach the parents and ask them to
explore the possibility of keeping the infant at home with one of them. This
takes courage, but if we do not advocate for this infant, who will? The infant
is suffering. I believe that most parents want to do what is best for their
child. If there are two working parents, perhaps one of them can work part-
time or they can figure out how to live on one income for the time being. Perhaps one parent can find a way to work from home for a few months, or

**Figure 8.8** *When a baby's needs have all been met and the crying is still chronic, problem solving is needed for both baby and teachers.*

perhaps there is a close relative who can help by giving the child extra love and attention. While it is not your responsibility to solve the parents' financial and career problems, you can suggest alternatives that will help them fulfill their parental roles. Such suggestions may be met with shock and resentment, but at least you will have done your best for the child.

If the child has only one parent or the parents are poor and have no options, the strategy described below might help. But what can be done for the teacher? Even the most loving and dedicated infant teachers have limits to their tolerance for crying. Teachers are not saints and should not be expected to be. Caring for infants is for many an eight-hour-a-day job, even more for the home day-care provider. The teacher who is bombarded by constant loud crying is experiencing stress that is probably greater than that experienced in almost any other job. She may develop headaches, upset stomach, or other nervous symptoms. She may have difficulty relating to her family. She is also likely to carry a sense of guilt with her. She feels inadequate because she cannot make this infant stop crying (Figure 8.8). She also feels guilty because she is giving more attention to the crying baby than to those who are behaving more desirably.

There is another point of view to be considered. An infant who is crying constantly may be waking up other babies who are trying to sleep. The other babies may also become agitated and fussy due to the loud crying. Parents of the infants who are not crying feel quite uncomfortable and begin to believe that their own infant is being neglected in favor of the crier. Even if this is not true, they may feel strongly enough to withdraw their child from the program. At this point, a good relationship with the parents is essential, but it is also important to have a plan for alleviating the situation.

In several such cases, the plan described below was followed. It is not perfect, and there may be other, equally effective plans, but this one has worked especially well. It responds to the bonding needs of infants, which are sometimes disrupted by the separations inherent in day care. The baby's needs have all been met as much as possible, but in spite of all the love, nurturing, and patience, the baby still cries chronically. This plan works best if there are at least two infant teachers and more than one room or area available to the infant staff.

Leif is eight months old and has been in the program since he was six months old. Recently, he has become more aware of his parents' leaving in the morning. Although he has done his share of crying in the past, his crying has now become angry and incessant. His teachers feel that Leif is now going through a separation crisis. His crying is loud and piercing, causing sleeping babies to awaken before they are ready, making them cranky. His crying also upsets other babies, who begin to cry more easily. Leif's teachers have tried everything and are themselves showing signs of stress.

After discussing the problem in a staff meeting, the teachers tried the following strategy. Every time Leif's crying was above the normal range needed for getting his needs met, one teacher would take Leif to another area. It could be the bathroom, the playground, or a room not being used by another group. The teacher held Leif and said, "If you want to cry, it's okay with me. I'll hold you until you finish, then we'll go back to our area." She held him firmly, stroked him gently, talked to him affectionately, and made eye contact when possible. It was sometimes difficult to give Leif time to finish crying, but he was shown that his needs were important. If a teacher could not hold him for the entire time, she brought another infant who was unbothered by Leif's crying and sat with both of them until Leif finished crying.

Leif was especially attached to one particular teacher, so she was the likely choice to carry out this plan. If the strategy proved too stressful for that teacher, however, the other teachers could rotate to alleviate the stress. The teacher who was left with the remaining babies had extra work, but without Leif's incessant crying her work was easier. For a teacher who is alone with a group of infants, this plan would be much harder to carry out. She might have to enlist the temporary help of her director or an assistant to separate and hold the crying child.

With consistent carrying out of this plan, Leif's chronic crying diminished little by little. Infants who go through a separation crisis at around eight months of age usually recover within weeks if they are nurtured and held by their caregivers. After several weeks, Leif became a contented baby who cried only when he had a reason. By the time he became a toddler, Leif was a typical little boy. Meanwhile, the infant teachers had maintained their sanity and even enjoyed having Leif with them during the remainder of his infancy.

## Immaturity and Developmental Delay

Tamara was a different kind of child from birth. Doctors could not diagnose any specific cause, but it was evident that she had major problems. She had been a premature baby and was small for her age. Her muscles did not move normally; they lacked normal muscle tone. One of her eyes was crossed, requiring surgery, and her lungs were congested, requiring a process called nebulization several times a day. Tamara had almost no speech. As an infant, she uttered a single syllable. She did not cry or show facial expressions.

Because the cause of Tamara's problems was unknown, the course of Tamara's development was, understandably, unpredictable. She remained small, limp, and speechless well beyond her first year of life. At eighteen months, she was still not walking, but she showed signs of boredom and frustration with the infant program. After a meeting between Tamara's parents and teachers, it was decided that Tamara should be moved to the toddler section. No one knew if or when she would ever walk or talk, but she was accepted as she was and at least given the chance. At age two, she did begin to walk, and by three she was speaking short phrases.

Tamara's immaturity was due to biological causes. Many children, however, exhibit behavior that is appropriate for a much younger child, and there is no apparent cause. These children do not realize that there is a gap between them and others in their peer group. They may want very much to be like their friends but cannot manage or control their social interactions. The immature child may be unusually impulsive, may cry easily, or may explode when frustrated. She may be intellectually behind her age group; her language skills may be inadequate for expressing her feelings effectively. Her physical coordination may prevent her from mastering many skills.

There is a wide range of normalcy in every stage of childhood development. When a child is at the lower end of the spectrum, there is always the dilemma of deciding where she should be placed. If placed with a younger group where she fits in socially and emotionally, will she remain immature? Will her self-esteem suffer because she knows that she is not with her age group? If she stays with her age group, will she feel inferior, be excluded from their play, or be teased for her babyishness? There is no pat answer, and this decision should be made thoughtfully, with the child's best interest in mind.

In problem solving, trust in the normal process of development and respect for the feelings of the child are always the standard, along with acceptance of the child as an individual with her own unique strengths. Those strengths may be the key to placing her in the appropriate group. Often, when a child is immature, her strengths are inadvertently overlooked. She may, in fact, be advanced in an area such as mathematical concepts, manifested by her ability to match objects, work puzzles, duplicate designs, or sort buttons by size, shape, and color. A skillful teacher can encourage and broaden such a strength, building a sense of achievement in the child.

The only real solution to immaturity is time. While time is doing its job, the problem-solving philosophy, with its emphasis on expression of feelings, social interactions, and responsibility, will contribute enormously to the child's maturation process.

## High Activity

At the beginning of this chapter, we met Max, the high-energy, high-activity infant who proceeded to become a high-energy, high activity preschooler. Max was always on the move, his attention span was relatively short, and his social interactions were often explosive. Max was a difficult child for his teachers to manage, and they therefore considered him a behavior problem. Many children like Max are referred to by adults as "hyperactive." This term is overused and inaccurate. Hyperactivity is a condition that requires diagnosis and sometimes treatment by a medical doctor, child psychologist, or other qualified professional in the field of childhood mental health. Even among the experts, there is a great deal of controversy and acrimony over just what constitutes hyperactivity and the options for its treatment. Short of administering drugs, at this time there is little agreement about what really works, but many alternatives are being tried.

There is no intent here to dismiss the possible need for or potential benefits of such treatment in many cases. Nor can we diminish the real difficulties for teachers faced with the extremely active child. But this child, like others, may in fact respond enthusiastically to problem solving if given the chance. Max, for example, was considered a behavior problem by his teachers, yet they continued to show him acceptance, trust, and respect. His personal charm elicited affection from them as well as from his friends. As a preschooler, Max found more appropriate ways to express his frustrations. He also learned appropriate places for running and being active. When an activity interested him, Max's enthusiasm was contagious, and he could spend longer periods of time concentrating. Between the ages of four and five, Max developed by leaps and bounds. He then graduated to kindergarten and is now in elementary school; he is an enthusiastic learner (Figure 8.9).

## Hyperactivity and Attention Deficit Disorder

Lance entered the preschool class when he was about three and one-half. During most of his young life, he had been cared for by his grandparents, who were elderly, while his father attended college and his mother worked. The grandparents set few or no limits with Lance and found him unmanageable. He was extremely big and strong for his age. Now that Lance's father had graduated, the parents were able to pay for child care. When he called to

**Figure 8.9**    *A high activity level does not necessarily indicate hyperactivity, which must be diagnosed by the appropriate professionals.*

inquire about day care, Lance's father told the director that Lance was "a handful."

On Lance's first visit to the preschool, his father stayed with him. Lance moved rapidly around the classroom like a "whirling dervish," grabbing this and that and leaving a trail of toys behind him. His father followed him, picking up the toys and looking embarrassed. Whenever Lance encountered another child, he pushed the child aside. He did not seem hostile but appeared to be making contact in his own way. The teacher observed Lance and his father and finally asked the father whether he would mind if she showed Lance how to put his toys away. The father looked relieved and responded eagerly.

This turned out to be a more difficult act than the teacher had anticipated because Lance reacted wildly to any attempt at setting limits. The father liked the way the teacher handled the situation, however, and Lance was enrolled in the preschool.

In subsequent weeks, Lance managed to turn the preschool upside down. Several teachers worked as a team in the preschool, and Lance needed constant watching by all of them. His speech was very immature and he had a winning smile, so he had a kind of babyish charm and the teachers grew to like him. But Lance never stopped moving, grabbing, attacking both kids and teachers; he was so strong that other children began to run when they saw him coming. Lance also had a habit of erupting into loud shrieking at the most inappropriate times. Every attempt at having a circle time or group activity ended in chaos. Everyone was feeling the stress.

The director and head teacher arranged a meeting with Lance's parents. During the meeting they learned that Lance's father had been a highly active child who had been sent to a strict private school and resented the regimentation. He appeared to have outgrown his childhood behavior and had done well in college. He had fears that Lance would be like him and have to be regimented as he had been. The teachers also learned that Lance and his mother came to the center by bus every morning, a ride of forty-five minutes during which Lance was understandably restless and made his loud shrieking noises, embarrassing his mother.

The main impression the staff came away with from that meeting was that Lance's parents desperately wanted to believe that Lance's behavior was normal. They hoped and felt that Lance was making progress and that his behavior would improve even more. At the same time, Lance's mother admitted that she could not let him play with other children because he hurt them and that when she had taken him to a birthday party he had completely disrupted the party, making her feel hopeless and ashamed. She frequently asked, "Why does he act that way?"

Lance remained at the center for about four months. The teachers worked out a system whereby every day one teacher became his shadow, watching only Lance, so the classroom could function. Needless to say, this was not a practical solution. There were some minor improvements, and Lance seemed to be enjoying his experience. After several more meetings with Lance's parents, the center strongly urged that Lance be tested by his pediatrician to rule out any medical problems. Their next request was going to be psychological testing. Much to his credit, Lance's pediatrician contacted the center for more information about Lance's behavior and decided to refer him for further testing at a children's hospital.

Lance was diagnosed as having attention deficit disorder with hyperactivity. Doctors recommended a small, highly structured child care situation for him. His parents contacted their local school district, which accepted children at age three in its special education classes. Lance attends classes three mornings a week and is cared for at home by a nanny the rest of the time. He may someday also receive medication. Lance's parents sincerely thanked the child care staff for doing all they could for Lance. The staff remembers Lance because he taught them the difference between a highly active child like Max and a true case of hyperactivity.

A similar case with a different outcome was that of Clark. Clark enrolled in the toddler program at about fourteen months of age. From the beginning, he exhibited behavior like that of Lance. He never stopped moving; even his nap was very brief; he pushed children down as if they were bowling pins, and he bit children at every opportunity. After several months of trying to cope with Clark in the younger toddler class, the teachers decided to see whether Clark would behave more appropriately with older toddlers. They hoped that the bigger toddlers would discourage his aggression and that their more complex environment would alleviate what might be his boredom.

Before making this change, the teachers met with Clark's parents, who admitted that he was difficult to manage at home. They had two large dogs who were Clark's main companions. He constantly wrestled with, pushed, and jumped on the dogs, who didn't seem to mind. Clark had almost no limits set for him, and his parents described how he jumped on all the furniture, including the dishwasher. They also admitted that when his behavior became too unbearable they spanked him. Clark's parents were sure that his behavior was normal.

The teachers, however, made some suggestions. They suggested that Clark and the dogs be kept separate in order to break the pattern of roughhousing, which he generalized to the children in the center. They also suggested that the parents refrain from spanking Clark and discussed alternative ways to set limits. In addition, they tactfully suggested that a parenting class or some books might help the parents with managing Clark.

When a child is as young as Clark, any solution to problem behavior should include evaluating parenting skills, the environment, and the teacher-child interactions. Presently, it is extremely difficult to determine whether behavior in so young a child is simply an extreme phase of normal development or indicates the possibility of hyperactivity. In my opinion, it is irresponsible to label a toddler hyperactive unless there is a clear medical diagnosis. In Clark's case, a medical exam did not uncover any abnormalities, so the focus was on parenting, environment, and teachers.

After moving Clark to the older toddler class, there was a period of about two weeks when his behavior seemed to improve. In fact, it was a sort of "honeymoon" period that wore off when he became comfortable in his new class. His new teachers had high hopes but found that Clark returned to aggression and biting, of both large and small kids, continuously grabbing toys and moving constantly from toy to toy. The program in Clark's room was now suffering due to Clark's need for one-on-one supervision.

Clark's behavior was a major topic at teachers' meetings, and there were further conversations with his parents. Nothing changed, except that the toddlers were becoming more and more fearful of Clark and other parents were expressing concern. As with Lance, the staff had tried everything and had reached their limit. There was a strong consensus that Clark needed someone who could give him his or her full attention, take him outdoors for active play whenever he wanted it, and set clear limits for him. The center director prepared a list of resources for finding a nanny or a small day-care home that specialized in behavior problems, but Clark's parents protested that they only wanted him in a center.

After five months of trying unsuccessfully to keep Clark in the program, Clark's parents were asked to find another child care placement. The staff felt sad and, of course, somewhat guilty, but everyone hoped that Clark's parents would find the right place for him where he could get his needs met. Clark's parents were quite resentful, however, and they moved Clark to another center. Although everyone was disappointed, they wished the best for Clark.

## Rebelliousness

Marie is only three years old and has recently enrolled in the program. She is a child who already looks old. Her usual facial expression is one of suspicion and hostility. On arrival, Marie let everyone know that she had no intention of going along with the way things were. She absolutely refused to put away toys, negotiate with other children, stay at the table during meals, or join in any activities. She had a vocabulary of profanities that she did not hesitate to use on teachers and children alike. The director learned that Marie had been "expelled" from her previous child care arrangement for all the obvious reasons.

While interviewing Marie's parents, the director formed the impression that Marie's father used a strict, moralistic parenting style. (Later, she learned that the father was an active alcoholic.) Marie's mother was a quiet, condescending woman who seemed genuinely puzzled at her daughter's behavior. In spite of their previous experience, both parents had high expectations that Marie's new teachers would "straighten her out." While talking to the parents about the problem-solving philosophy, the director saw their eyes glaze over, as if they did not hear what she said. The parents had chosen the center because there was an opening for Marie and because it was conveniently located. They had no particular interest in the philosophy.

This is probably a rare occurrence. Parents who choose a program that uses the problem-solving philosophy are usually actively seeking a specific environment for their child. If they wanted strict rules and punishment, they would choose a different kind of program. If factors such as price, location, and availability are more compelling, however, it is possible that parents such as Marie's would enroll their child. It is also probable that their expectations would be quite unrealistic. Can a child such as Marie, who is already hostile at age three, fit into and be helped by a problem-solving program? Obviously, her treatment at home will be drastically different from her treatment at day care. Her treatment from each parent is, apparently, already disparate. Will she learn to behave appropriately under such confusing circumstances?

In spite of the obvious drawbacks, Marie deserves her chance, too. Children are amazingly resilient and flexible. They can learn to cope with a variety of situations—from visiting grandparents to eating at restaurants and going to the doctor. In Marie's case, however, more than ordinary flexibility is required. She is suffering from a severe lack of self-esteem, confusion, guilt, and anger. All these, plus childhood depression, are classic symptoms in an alcoholic family. Not only will Marie need large doses of acceptance, the building of self-esteem, and the planting of seeds of trust, but her family will also need the same sensitive treatment. Perhaps, if at some point trust has been established, her parents will be willing to cooperate with Marie's rehabilitation. This will probably require engaging outside help for the family, including, one would hope, alcoholic treatment programs for the entire family.

Although many children are simply born with a difficult temperament, rebelliousness and hostility are always signs of some deeper, more destructive problem usually traceable to the family. The day-care program that is willing to take on such a family and treat it with respect and sensitivity may be responsible for saving at least one precious life. It is asking a great deal, but the knowledge that the outreach was there is a tribute to those very special teachers of young children.

## Uncontrolled Rage

It's circle time, and Danny, age four, is having a hard time waiting for his turn to speak. He starts pushing and shoving Annette, who is sitting next to him. Annette tells him to stop, but he ignores her. Within seconds, he has hurt Annette. When she tries to talk to him about it, he reacts by yelling and waving his hands to drown her out. The teacher tries to talk to Danny, but he just yells more loudly. When she tries to move him away, he hits and kicks her. Afraid to make him angrier, the teacher backs off and lets Danny sit there yelling until he finally finishes his tirade. By then, circle time is in shambles, Annette feels cheated, the other children feel confused, and the teacher feels helpless.

Why was this teacher so intimidated by a child's rage? Is it because she doesn't know how to handle rage? Are strong feelings too frightening? Is she afraid someone will misinterpret her actions and accuse her of child abuse? Is she worried that the child's parents will sue her center? Is the situation too risky to handle?

Any large group of children is likely to include at least one child who is frequently disruptive and out of control. This is not necessarily the bully who gets his way through force or the average child who sometimes loses control. This is the child who cannot tolerate any limits being placed on his behavior and reacts to limits by lashing out at anyone in his way. His rage may stem from a variety of sources, usually related to the home, but it can be triggered by almost any event.

If such a child sees that all the adults in his life are so frightened by his strong emotions and too weak or unwilling to confront him, he will be terrified as well. He longs to be stopped and protected from himself, but instead adults reason and plead with him. Giving this much power to a small child can only encourage him to continue to push limits even more.

The question for teachers is what can be done about it. What you as a teacher cannot do is ignore it, cater to it, placate it, or be afraid of it. You have to confront rage and handle it. First, get to know the child, gain his trust, and teach him how to express his anger with feeling words by trying to find something really likeable about him and building a positive relationship on that. Once his trust is gained, he may eventually give some clues as to the root of his anger. This might enable you to get help for him from his parents and perhaps from a professional as well.

Next, meet with the child's parents, ask them what they do when he exhibits rage, and listen carefully to their response. It might give you some clues as to the source of the child's rage. Talk to them about how you will go about helping their child express his feelings and gain self-control. Let them know that you will confront their child's rage with respect but also with strength, determination, and resolve. You will not feel threatened by his rage, and you will not back down in order to keep the peace.

After that, talk to the child in private, making as much direct eye contact as possible. Your message should be simple, firm, and clear: "Danny, you have a choice to make. You can be with the group and use words instead of hurting kids, but if you hurt other kids or disrupt our group time I will remove you from the group. You can decide when you are ready to return, but if you return you must be ready to join the group without hurting or disrupting." You may have to describe what "disrupting" means.

Last, follow through. Always give the child a chance to gain self-control on his own; if he can't, remove him silently and bodily from the scene. If you are the only teacher, place the child where you can see him and where he cannot play with toys. The goal is for him to compose himself enough to return to the group. If he moves away, move him back. If he hits or kicks, carry him under one arm, like a football, back to where you want him to stay. Do not argue, threaten, or repeat yourself. Simply carry out what you said you would do.

You may be the only adult in this child's world who is not afraid of his rage. In a short time, he will come to respect you and depend on your strength. Someday, he may even be a child who brings you love and great satisfaction.

## Gaming and Testing Limits

Dustin was one of those babies who seem to know the score at birth. Intellectually bright and physically well coordinated, Dustin could apparently do everything. He also knew how to manipulate people. Even as an infant, he made his needs known and understood and found that his smile could get him anything. Learning was always easy for Dustin. His parents were both teachers who provided him with a wide variety of experiences. They also used parent effectiveness training as their parenting style, so Dustin's home life was compatible with his life at day care.

By the time Dustin was ten or eleven months old, he had passed up all the infants, even those months older. He was walking and constantly looking for challenges; this kept the teachers on their toes. As soon as possible, he was graduated to the toddler group, where his language skills at two years of age were remarkable. Dustin was articulate, artistic, mathematical, athletic, and on and on. He still had that sweet, charming smile, too. But something else was happening with Dustin. He had become a game player, a tester of limits, and a manipulator.

Dustin's best friend was Max, mentioned earlier in this chapter. They grew up together in the baby room and all the way through preschool. Knowing Max so well gave Dustin a great advantage. Although Max was emotional and explosive, Dustin was always in control and could, in fact, make himself "perfect." Dustin always knew exactly what to say to set Max off. The right word with the right inflection could reduce Max to tears, leaving Dustin smugly satisfied.

When Dustin was not being perfect, he was being disruptive. During circle time, he would clandestinely poke the child next to him, causing an outcry. Dustin's expression was angelic, and he always denied any harassing. During mealtimes, Dustin found excuses to crawl under the table several times. He always dropped something "by accident." This, of course, distracted the other children from the meal. During nap time, Dustin made noises without moving his lips, and the noises kept some children from falling asleep. When Dustin played with toys, he "forgot" to put them away and always got someone else to do it for him. Dustin had a whole repertoire of little games he played just to see how far he could go. The teacher's reaction was his reward, and he obviously enjoyed it. Dustin was getting too much negative feedback.

Many children, for reasons that are often unclear, become game players. Sometimes, like Dustin, they are extraordinary children who feel they have mastered everything and go on to riskier experiences, such as testing limits. Others may be children of average intelligence who seek attention through game playing and testing limits. Still others simply follow the first two types. Chapter 6 includes several examples of dealing with game players in "Gaming to Avoid Responsibility." If these strategies fail to work, there is another tactic to try: the contract. An example of a contract is found in "Special Behaviors" in Chapter 5. In that example, the contract was used for a child who was harassing other children. In the case of Dustin, however, a contract worked equally well (Figure 8.10).

As a preschooler, Dustin was able to immediately grasp the concept behind the contract, and he liked it. He enjoyed using his wit to compose the document. In private, Dustin and his teacher sat down with a piece of paper, and Dustin dictated the type of behavior he needed to change in order to receive more positive feedback. He also decided on appropriate conse-

**Figure 8.10**    *The chronic game player requires special strategies. Sometimes a contract is appropriate.*

quences. Dustin decided that he preferred getting stars on a chart to privileges, and his teacher respected his decision. While he was writing the contract, Dustin's attitude was no longer smug. Perhaps he really wanted more positive attention, or perhaps the process of constructing the contract was intellectually fascinating. Here is a copy of Dustin's contract:

This is a contract between Dustin and his teachers, Eleanor, Debbie, and Joan.

1. When I take out toys, I'll put them away by myself. If I forget, I can't play with any toys for five minutes. If I remember by myself, I get a star on my chart.

2. If I poke kids during circle time, I'll leave the circle and sit by myself. If I don't poke anyone during circle time, I get a star on my chart.

3. During mealtime, I'll sit on my chair. If I get under the table, I'll have to miss the meal. If I stay in my chair, I get a star on my chart. (Dustin insisted on the part about missing his meal; it was entirely his idea.)

4. If I make noises at nap time, I'll go sleep with the toddlers. If I lie quietly, I get a star on my chart. If I get ten stars, I get to choose a sticker for my chart.

Signed          <u>Dustin</u> <u>Eleanor</u> <u>Debbie</u> <u>Joan</u>

Dustin was very proud of his contract. The teacher limited the behaviors to only four at a time, and, for the most part, Dustin's behavior improved. For a while he became "perfect," but he gradually found a middle ground. In kindergarten the following year, Dustin was a star student and not a behavior problem.

## Tattling and Competing

Erica was once a painfully shy child. The first daughter of former student radicals, she may have felt intimidated by the loud, political arguments she heard when her parents' friends came to visit. When she first came to day care, she was paralyzed by fear, as was Courtney. After three years in a problem-solving environment, she has lost most of her shyness but has become a tattletale instead. Tattling itself is a normal behavior in preschool-age children. It gives them power over others and calls attention to their own "good" behavior. Although both sexes are known to tattle, girls seem to use this tactic more than boys. Boys generally, but not specifically, find more physical ways to compete and call attention to themselves. Girls do this, too, but those girls who are more verbal and competitive make greater use of tattling. It seems to fit their skills.

Is tattling a true behavior problem? On a normal scale, it is not. But when it becomes incessant and chronic, it may be a sign of some bigger problem. Perhaps the tattler needs more constructive ways to feel good about herself. Perhaps, unwittingly, the teacher has encouraged competition or has reinforced tattling by paying it the desired attention (Figure 8.11). In any case, if the teacher has four or five chronic tattlers in her group, she is probably tired of it and irritated by it.

Active listening is the usual problem-solving approach to tattling. The teacher reflects the child's feelings about what is happening and directs the child back to talk to the person she is tattling on: "It sounds like what she's doing is causing a problem for you. You can talk to her about it." When faced with numerous chronic tattlers, however, a teacher may want to go so far as to say "Today I'm not listening to any tattling. Everyone will have to solve their problems without telling me." The teacher should also explain how she feels about the tattling and why she plans to ignore it. It is important that she follow through and meet every approaching tattler with "I'm ignoring tattletales today." If the tattling actually stops after this approach, it's a relief for everyone involved.

**Figure 8.11**   *A teacher may encourage tattling by paying it the desired attention.*

## Parent-Child Attachment

Phedra had been a difficult child since early infancy. She was enrolled at the center at four weeks of age and was now about twenty-two months old. Throughout her time in the infant class, she cried a great deal and exhibited angry behavior numerous times a day. She seemed to choose one teacher and bond to that teacher alone. When that teacher had to leave the room for a break or any other reason, Phedra could not tolerate the separation; she fell apart, crying and screaming until the teacher returned.

Phedra was the second daughter of parents who had a special arrangement regarding child rearing. Phedra's mother did not really want children but her father did, so the mother agreed to give birth and then turn over the primary responsibilities to the father. He had grown up in a dysfunctional family and had no experience on which to base his fathering. Both parents worked long hours, often leaving their children in the child care center for eleven hours a day. In addition, the mother was gone for days at a time on business trips. The father loved his daughters, but his primary way of interacting with them was to sit in front of the television set with them every night until they all fell asleep.

Phedra's older sister had also been difficult as an infant and toddler, but by about age three she had become more social and could deal more appropriately with frustration. Phedra, on the other hand, seemed to grow more and more frustrated with time. She bit, cried, and threw tantrums in response to almost anything and demanded the undivided attention of any nearby teacher. She still fell apart when a teacher left the room, but now this behavior applied to any and all teachers.

There were numerous conversations with Phedra's father (her mother was never available), who had no idea why Phedra behaved as she did. Several teachers who knew the family well described their life as completely unstructured, with no limits set by the parents for the children. The staff noted that Phedra was always much more upset when her mother dropped her off, which was infrequent, than when her father did. Phedra's mother was finally urged to attend a conference to help the teachers better understand Phedra's behavior. During the conference, Phedra's mother casually mentioned that her job would soon require her to live in another state and that she would be home only on weekends. The staff were deeply concerned for Phedra but refrained from expressing their feelings.

When Phedra's mother began her new routine, Phedra's behavior went from bad to worse. When her mother dropped her off on Monday mornings (after which she flew off to another state), Phedra was fairly cheerful, but as the week progressed she spent most of her time crying, screaming, and throwing tantrums. She bit and pinched other children and wanted to be held constantly. By Thursday, Phedra could barely function; her mother returned Thursday evening and picked up Phedra; however, the mother wanted Friday to herself, so she brought her children to the center.

To the center staff, it was obvious that Phedra wanted her mother and nothing else would make her happy. Every teacher had some feelings and some opinion about the situation, and many felt pity for Phedra and anger toward her mother. Some teachers worried that Phedra's attachment with her mother was insecure at best and that her need for bonding was all-encompassing and overwhelming. Everyone shared Phedra's pain and fervently wished that Phedra's mother would change her job or her career, or at least her schedule, to give Phedra the attention she so desperately needed.

Phedra's case had nothing to do with whether fathers or mothers are better as primary caregivers. I have personally known fathers who were their children's primary caregivers and reared normal, healthy, and wonderful children. The difference is that those fathers were there for their children emotionally and the children also had a secure attachment to their mothers. When parents make an alternative arrangement, their children don't always understand the nature of the arrangement. From the child's point of view, a parent is there to provide love and nurturing, no matter what other understanding the parents have between them. In Phedra's case, her bond with her mother was insecure, and her father, although well meaning, was distant. Where was she to go?

Once again, staff met with Phedra's parents, both at the same time, and fully described Phedra's behavior progression, the intensity of her pain, and her needs. They tried hard to be nonjudgmental and simply present the facts. Phedra's parents gave it a great deal of thought and decided to hire a nanny so that Phedra would have fewer transitions and more stability; she would also no longer have to spend such long hours at the center. Coincidentally, a teacher's assistant who knew Phedra was at that time planning to become a nanny, so she took the position and looked after Phedra.

For several months, Phedra came to the center one day a week and spent her other days at home with the nanny. After those months, she completely dropped out of the program to spend every day at home. No one knows whether this arrangement is meeting Phedra's attachment needs, but everyone hopes it will help.

## Lying

Jillian was a preschooler who could construct a complex fantasy from almost any situation. One time a group of preschoolers was playing with baby goats at their center. The teacher pointed out that the goats were already butting heads with each other. The teacher wondered out loud how they had learned to butt heads because they had no older goats to imitate. Jillian responded immediately, "I know. My Daddy showed them how. He has goats at his office, and he butts heads with them." This child could produce an equally fantastic response to almost any question. Jillian's mother was concerned about her imagination. She was not sure whether these fantasies should be considered lies or if this abundance of imagination was appropriate and healthy for a child her age. Many parents, such as Jillian's mother, and teachers who may themselves have been products of a moralistic upbringing may confuse imagination with lying. Because this is such a critical issue in education and the building of self-esteem, I attempt to clarify the difference between lying and imagination by exploring both and comparing them.

Imagination is the key ingredient in the finest novel, play, movie, opera, musical composition, ballet, painting, or sculpture. It has triggered diverse and impossible ideas such as machines that fly, carry voices over thousands of miles, project moving images on a screen, and complete complex mathematical calculations in seconds. Before technology, education, or skill, there is always that most powerful, magic ingredient: imagination.

In adults, imagination is too often a buried treasure, highly sought after and prized. Yet children possess this treasure in abundance and share it freely with anyone who is willing to listen. Imagination has many manifestations. It is role playing, putting oneself in another person's shoes, trying on their feelings and their point of view. It is solving problems, especially those that present a conflict between the internal child and the external society. It is using symbols to represent overwhelming, frightening, or perplexing emotions the child may not understand. It is an important mark of distinction between humankind and other living species and is an inseparable part of intellectual development.

One sign of a healthy, young imagination at work is pretending, usually pretending to be one's own parent. In this way, children practice being the grown-ups they will someday be and try to cope with all the restrictions adults impose on themselves. The development of conscience is related to such pretending. The healthy, young imagination may also produce fear, especially fear of the unknown. During times of stress, such as the mother's pregnancy, a divorce, moving to a new home or child care center, or visiting a relative, a child may suddenly become quite clinging and dependent. He may act out his fears with a doll or another symbolic toy or treat his friends the way he wants to treat his parents or the new, unborn baby. He may overdramatize or embellish what he feels is happening to him. Some children, usually through loneliness, even invent imaginary companions who keep them company. This creative way of solving the loneliness problem is common to those who grow up to be literary people.

Imagination is nurtured through free, undisturbed play and by adults who value and appreciate imagination in children. Unfortunately, the importance of a nurturing environment for imagination is often overlooked. When programs are based on the adult concept of "work" and "learning," play is often thought of as wasted time. With the best of intentions, many adults correct or criticize children's fantasies, trying to make children understand the difference between fantasy and reality. Very young children mix fantasy and reality liberally; when they begin to know the difference, they often still find it more stimulating and fun to fantasize. That does not mean that the child will develop into a chronic liar. In fact, the freedom to fantasize may eliminate any need to lie.

What is lying as it relates to young children? Preschool-age children are still in the process of developing conscience, internal control, and morality, but these traits have not yet arrived. Generally, children have to grow for a few years before these concepts are meaningful to them. At this stage, children are simply trying things out to see how they work. The children's measure is usually the reaction they get from other people. Because fantasy and reality are still intertwined, the preschool child does not understand why adults make such a fuss over what adults call "lies" when the child is merely expressing something in one of the many ways she has available.

We generally think of a lie as a falsehood or untruth, anything that serves to deceive. From infancy, children in our society are surrounded by deception. Hundreds of times a day, they hear deceptive television or radio commercials. A great deal of so-called children's programming consists of a half-hour or an hour of selling products geared to children. These are often toys of violence, toys that are misrepresented and disappointing, or foods that are harmful or at least very low in nutrition; almost everything is overpriced and beyond the reach of many children.

Children are deceived in other ways by their own well-meaning parents. Santa Claus, for instance, has been so commercialized in the United

States that he almost seems sinister. He is seen on television pushing products; he is used as a threat to children, many of whom are forced, kicking and screaming, to sit on his lap. He is no longer a kindly, legendary figure, but parents feel compelled to make children believe he is real, only to admit several years later that it was all a lie. Why not treat Santa Claus as a fantasy figure and allow children to interpret him in their own way without the inevitable disillusionment?

Children are also surrounded by "white lies." They hear the phone ring and mother says, "If it's for me, say I'm not here." The same thing happens with the door-to-door salesperson or the charity collector at the door. Father may call in sick at work, then spend the day at the golf course. Grandmother tells a friend how nice she looks, then snickers behind her back. Big sister tells a boy she's busy because she doesn't want to go out with him. Big brother cheats on a test at school. Grown-ups say they love the gift they received but later throw it away. For the child who has not yet made a total distinction between fact and fantasy, these added social deceptions only make things more confusing. When the child forgets to put away her toys, what is so wrong with saying "I didn't do it" as long as she gets away with it? Or why not say "She hit me first" when the opposite is true if a lie gets the child what he wants or gets him out of a troublesome situation?

Children who frequently tell lies are probably afraid of something. Perhaps, in the home, there is too much criticism or punishment. Perhaps loss of love and approval is the price the child must pay for making mistakes or doing things the "wrong" way. Fear of criticism and punishment and fear of loss of love and approval are strong motivations for lying. Many parents and teachers have had the experience of a newly trained child messing his underwear and hearing him say innocently "I didn't do it." Fear is likely the reason behind the lie.

How are these types of lies handled in a problem-solving philosophy? To begin with, in problem solving, there is no threat of criticism, punishment, loss of love, or loss of approval. In problem solving, there is only acceptance of the child as he or she is. If the teacher consistently sends this message to the child, the child should eventually learn that mistakes are useful for learning and the consequences are reasonable. When the paint water is spilled, it gets wiped up. When a toy is left out, it gets put away. When someone messes his underwear, it simply gets changed. It doesn't matter who hit first or had the toy first. The important thing is to solve the problem. Children are naturally cooperative when they have no fear of negative consequences and when mistakes are treated as learning experiences.

In problem solving, the word "lie" is never mentioned or implied. Children are shown the same respect as adults. The teacher listens politely, then focuses on the problem to be solved, giving the responsibility for solving it back to the child. The distinction between truth and untruth can be taught in more positive ways, such as discussing whether a certain story was real or pretend. Puppets can be used to visualize real and unreal. Having the children role-play outrageous tall tales is another way. The teacher's own modeling of authenticity demonstrates more about honesty than any lecture, moralizing, or scolding could. A sense of humor and sensitive use of wit and irony by the teacher will also help children distinguish a joke from reality when everyone shares a good laugh.

If, after a teacher has evaluated the situation and finds that, in spite of the freedom and acceptance being given, a child still lies chronically, it is time for a serious meeting with the parents. The purpose of the meeting is to find the reasons for the child's fear of telling the truth. Is harsh discipline being used at home? Is there a perfectionist parent who criticizes and withholds love and approval when mistakes are made or limits are exceeded? This exploration can require extreme delicacy, because if the parent feels criticized the child may be punished even more. In the best circumstances, the matter will be handled sensitively, and trust will be reestablished between parents and child.

## Sibling Rivalry

Madison was two and one-half when his mother became pregnant. Before his teachers knew that his mother was expecting, they knew something was happening in Madison's life. His parents knew something was happening, too, but they didn't connect Madison's behavior with the pregnancy. Madison's mother complained about his whining, his demanding, and his clinging. When she dropped him off at the center, he cried when she left and threw a tantrum, something he had rarely done before.

At day care, Madison had become aggressive and possessive. He was easily frustrated and cried when confronted. He seemed unable to play cooperatively with other children and had tantrums throughout the day. These were changes in his classroom behavior, and the teachers were growing concerned. They requested a conference with Madison's parents, and it was during this meeting that Madison's mother casually mentioned that she was pregnant, "but I don't think Madison is aware of it yet."

During my years of working with children, I have seen this scene repeated numerous times. Parents do not always understand how deeply their own behavior affects their children or how much their children overhear. A young child may not fully know what pregnancy means, but he senses a threat in what he hears. The unknown seems so much more sinister than the reality that the birth of a sibling may almost be a relief. The months of pregnancy drag on endlessly, with parents blithely planning for the very person who will bring about their first child's loss of supremacy in the household.

After sharing in so many sibling experiences, I began to discreetly ask mothers if they were pregnant whenever I saw a drastic behavior change in their children. I always advise parents to discuss the pregnancy as fully as possible on their child's level, using books and pictures, making drawings, visiting other babies, taking the child shopping for infant equipment, touring the hospital, and talking about who will care for the child when the mother is giving birth. The child's greatest fear is the loss of her parents' love and her place in the family. By including and involving her, her parents can enable her to foresee a continuing role for herself as her parents' child and as a member of the family.

All of Madison's behaviors were normal under the circumstances. After the birth of his brother Manny, there was a period of about six months (this varies from child to child) when he remained extremely territorial and possessive. When his mother began bringing Manny to day care, she brought him to Madison's room and dropped off Madison first. Madison came into the classroom with an angry, defiant expression and warned everyone that they were not to talk to or touch either his mother or his brother. This behavior, in variations, continued throughout the day. The teachers noticed that Madison's mother seemed very uncomfortable when she brought Madison to the center. They suggested that it might be easier for everyone if the baby were taken to the infant room first. That way, Madison could go to the infant room and play a role in getting Manny settled in, then have his mom all to himself when he was dropped off. This strategy worked well and alleviated much of the morning stress, consequently making the entire day a bit easier.

The birth of a younger sibling is generally one of the greatest stresses placed on a child, and the ultimate outcome depends almost fully on the attitude of the parents. A teacher who finds out about a pregnancy should find a tactful way to inquire about what the parents are doing to help their child deal with the experience. Every teacher should be able to recommend at least one book on the subject so parents can educate themselves and give meaningful support to their children.

Teachers should also strive to understand how the child feels. There are many preschool books on the subjects of conception, birth, and early infancy, as well as stories about sibling relationships. It is important that you review these books before reading them so you can avoid ones that are evasive of facts, preachy about relationships, or unrealistic in expectations of young children. It is also important for teachers to consider the older child before gushing too ecstatically over the newborn sibling. Greet and notice your student first and let her introduce you to the new baby on her own terms. The baby won't care, but the older child will.

An additional strategy involves the parents at home; how they deal with the older child after the baby is born is probably the most important factor in enhancing family relationships. I advise parents to commit themselves to spending a scheduled uninterrupted block of time with each child at least three times a week, and more if possible. The block of time can be as short as fifteen minutes, but thirty minutes is better. The day and time should be consistent, and the child should be told that there will be no inter-ferences such as telephone calls, television, or visitors. The other parent is in charge of the sibling during this special time, and parents can alternate chil-dren so that each child has special alone time with both parents. During their time together, the child should be in charge, deciding what and how to play, read a story, or simply talk. The child who knows that she will have total access to her parent on a regular, predictable basis learns that her sibling is not a threat and also learns to defer some of her demands for attention until the scheduled time. This strategy by itself will improve a child's behavior and peer relationships both at home and at day care.

One last strategy for both parents and teachers is never to make com-parisons between siblings. No matter how well-meaning the comments, the child may interpret any comparison as showing him to be inferior. This is likely to set up competition with and resentment toward the sibling that may last a lifetime.

## Power Struggles

Spencer is almost three years old and is not yet using the toilet. Several months earlier, Spencer's parents voiced concern and spoke to Spencer's teacher. The teacher reassured the parents that many children do not show interest in toileting until after age three. Spencer's parents said that at home Spencer did use the toilet if they reminded him and took him. The implica-tion was that his teachers could assume that responsibility during the day. The teacher explained that she would be glad to ask Spencer periodically if he wanted to use the toilet but would take him only if he wanted to go.

Toileting is one of the major childhood power struggles and frequently marks the beginning of a pattern of power struggles between parents and children and between teachers and children. The most common power struggles revolve around eating, drinking bottles, toileting, sleeping, and saying offensive words. All of these issues involve ways that the child uses and controls his own body. Adults cannot win these power struggles except by force because the child can call upon his will power and win. It is of the utmost importance, therefore, to avoid power struggles. You accomplish this simply by allowing children to retain control over their own bodily func-tions to the greatest degree possible.

In a program, there is, of course, a need for routine and organization. A child will not be able to eat at will. On the other hand, when the child is offered a meal, he should have absolute control over whether he eats, what he chooses to eat from what is offered, and how much he eats. There is a des-ignated nap time when children are required to stay on their mats or cots, but no one can be required to sleep. After a period of resting quietly, about an hour, a child should be able to look at books, play quietly in a corner of the room, or go to another area with a teacher.

Power struggles over bottles are easily resolved by allowing children up to about age three to have access to their bottles in a cooler (see Chapter 9). Milk bottles can be replaced by water bottles at nap time, and children who are losing interest in bottles can be provided with cups as well. As for toileting, it is easily learned when the child feels totally in control and is encouraged rather than coerced. It is common for a child to get excited and want to use the toilet; then adults begin to expect it as the norm and the child rebels. Accidents are normal during toilet learning; children should be given the responsibility of removing their wet clothes and putting on dry ones without negative comments or expressions of disappointment.

When a child is engaged in power struggles over his bodily functions, his resentment is likely to be manifested in other areas of behavior, such as unwillingness to cooperate, put away toys, or pay attention in the classroom. Once a child has dug in his heels, the pattern is difficult to break and almost always requires that the adult let go of the struggle. A large ingredient of both effective teaching and effective parenting is the ability to allow children to develop and utilize their own power. There is nothing for us to fear, and watching a child's sense of power grow and develop is much more rewarding than engaging with him in a power struggle.

## Abuse

Cooper was adopted at the age of four by a childless couple and enrolled at the center. He had come from a childhood of physical and sexual abuse and would maintain some minimal contact with his birth mother as part of the adoption agreement. He was an intelligent child but had acquired no social skills, and because the attention he had received from his birth mother was primarily negative, he pushed limits to get attention. Cooper's adoptive parents were taking on quite a responsibility, one to last a lifetime, and they knew it. They wanted the best possible outcome for Cooper, so they were receptive to whatever guidance the center staff could give.

When Cooper was first enrolled, there was a honeymoon period during which he behaved perfectly while observing what was happening around him. At some point he must have felt relatively safe at the center, because the wall of perfection crumbled. Cooper began in sneaky ways to hurt kids, always denying what he had done and blaming the other child. He wore an angry expression that seemed to protect him from being hurt but also kept other children from making friends with him. He defiantly refused to cooperate with any activity that was going on in the classroom. When he left toys on the floor, he accused other children of having left them there. He lied for no reason because no one was going to punish him.

Cooper's adoptive parents tried to do what was right for him, but since he was their first experience at parenting they did not fully understand the impact of common events on Cooper's behavior. During the first few months of the adoption process, Cooper's new grandparents, whom he had never met, came to visit and to get to know him. They stayed at his new home for several weeks; Cooper's behavior indicated extreme stress. Soon after, his birth grandparents, whom he had known and loved, came from out of state to visit him. Having a second set of grandparents visit was confusing; he had nightmares and acted out aggressively at day care. His birth grandparents asked to see his day care, and, without realizing the impact, his adoptive parents agreed to let them come to Cooper's day care to take him out to lunch. All morning, Cooper was terrified, not understanding which set of grandparents was coming and worrying whether they were coming to take him away from his new parents.

The center staff saw their job primarily as one of helping Cooper build trust, the kind he may never have developed as an abused infant and toddler. Removing an abused child from an abusive environment does not automatically make him a trusting, normal child. Once certain patterns are in place, a child adheres to them because he has no positive experience to take their place. The pain and terror of Cooper's past were manifested by rage; this rage was now directed at his adoptive parents and others who offered him safety. From his perspective, he was being deprived of his biological mother, and he was furious at those he believed were depriving him.

Another job for Cooper's teachers was to help him learn the kind of social skills that would enable him to make friends and become more likeable. Having friends would indirectly serve to raise his self-esteem. This strategy was difficult, because the problem-solving philosophy requires that children listen to each other and contribute ideas. With Cooper's background of abuse, he had no expectation that anyone would respond to his needs or wants and had no faith in the words of other people. Rather than listen, when confronted he put his hands over his ears to shut out the words, contorted his face in an angry grimace, and yelled loudly at the other child. It took a great deal of time and patience on the part of the teachers to bring Cooper to see that he could get his needs met through negotiation. It was never easy for him and was always an effort, but little by little he found that he could endure the process in order to reap the benefits.

Aside from behavior that related to physical abuse, Cooper also acted out behavior that related to sexual abuse. This took the form of repeated and lengthy masturbation, which occurred mainly at nap time. For some of the teachers, this behavior was more disturbing than aggression; it was culturally and religiously unacceptable. For that reason, masturbation was scheduled as a topic for a staff meeting, and a public health nurse was enlisted to participate in the discussion. All the staff were given the opportunity to express their feelings and concerns. This resulted in their being able to pull together, overcome their deeply held feelings, and at least tolerate Cooper's masturbation nonjudgmentally. It was a learning experience for all, and in time the behavior diminished and practically disappeared.

Cooper spent almost two years at the center, and the problem-solving program had an enormous impact on his development. Very gradually, he formed affectionate bonds with the staff, and, although his peer friendships did not go very deep, he did acquire social skills, such as negotiation, that helped him play appropriately with other children and made him feel welcome in the group. In addition, Cooper was treated by a play therapist who kept in touch with the center staff; this helped him over the bumpiest transitions in his new life. There was evidence that he had learned to trust, although this is likely to remain a problem for him. It is now time for Cooper to leave the center for kindergarten, and he is ready to try his wings. He still has defenses to overcome and can still be defiant, belligerent, and aggressive, but his overall behavior has greatly improved. Everyone at the center wishes him luck in kindergarten.

## Absentmindedness

Wanda, age four, is a girl who, in the past, would have been called an absentminded professor. Nowadays, she might be called a space case. Wanda is extremely intelligent and talented and remembers everything she learns. The problem is that Wanda seems to be in another world, perhaps even in another time. When children are getting ready to go outside, Wanda cannot find her shoes. While she is playing with a toy, she wanders away, leaving the toy on the floor. During daily routines such as washing for meals, getting ready for naps, and coming to a circle time or table activity, Wanda is somewhere else, apparently oblivious. Although Wanda may grow up to be a physicist or discover a lost planet, her passage through childhood can put a strain on those who live with her.

Wanda has learned to tune out what she doesn't want to hear. There are very few strategies that work with her. Much of her behavior was either inherited or learned from at least one parent. When asked about their own childhood, one of Wanda's parents, her mom, embarrassingly admits, "I was just like that as a child. It drove my parents crazy." That parent may even admit that the same behavior is still driving her spouse crazy! The spouse may be a perfectionist who has expectations that neither Wanda nor the parent she resembles can live up to. Within the family, there is a tug of war. Wanda and her mom, creative and brilliant, move happily in their own world, while Wanda's dad is futilely trying to keep their home and lives organized. Wanda's dad tries to be patient, but he cannot always control his frustration and resentment, and Wanda keenly feels her father's lack of approval. To protect herself, she tunes it out.

Absentmindedness, which is similar to dawdling, seems incurable, but one strategy seems more effective than others: the use of natural or logical consequences. In this case, they must be used consistently and by all the teachers who have contact with Wanda. (This need for consistency is a digression from more standard problem solving.) If Wanda is not ready to go outdoors, she stays indoors with another group of children. If she fails to show up for circle time or an activity, she misses out on it. If she is not washed for lunch after a reasonable time, she is sent to eat with a younger group. This strategy may seem harsh, but Wanda is old enough to follow routines and will not miss more than a few activities before she learns that she would rather avoid the consequences. There is a chance that Wanda will not care about any of these consequences. If that is the case, the only course left to the teachers is to learn to love Wanda the way she is, accept her with a warm sense of humor, and remember that someday they will feel honored that they once knew and cared for Wanda.

## Conducting Parent-Teacher Conferences

Numerous times in this chapter, I have mentioned the idea of a conference between the teacher and parents. The purpose of the conference is to discuss what may be problem behavior in a child. It is, of course, important to get to know personally the parents of all children in the program before problems arise. The trust that is built and the rapport that is established between teacher and parents lay the foundation for future meetings. Whether the conference is private or part of a general meeting of parents and teachers, every parent is interested in his or her child's progress. Other occasions may help cement the bond between teachers and families. An annual picnic in the park, an open house at which friends and relatives may also visit, a party for Halloween, or the center's participation in a community event (such as a parade) helps everyone get to know one another informally.

When a problem that requires a meeting with parents does arise, preparation on the teacher's part is critical to the outcome. New or inexperienced teachers should not attempt such a conference on their own. If at all possible, the director or a more experienced teacher should accompany the new teacher, even if only for moral support. The older teacher may not necessarily contribute to the discussion unless called on by the younger teacher or unless she senses that things are going badly. The teacher or teachers should first do some background work. How does the problem behavior fit into the four sets of questions given in "Defining Problem Behavior" earlier in this chapter? Do other teachers work with this child? If so, how do they perceive his behavior?

An effective tool for conducting a conference is a written outline. The outline should begin with the child's strengths. It is extremely important to keep these in mind during the conference and to refer back to them. No parents want to believe their child is "all bad." After spending some time on the child's good qualities, move on to the parents' concerns. Always ask what the parents perceive to be the problem and the reason for the problem. It may be surprising to learn that the child's behavior at home is very different—maybe better, maybe worse. Allow the parents to express their concerns and views for as long as it seems comfortable.

Next, the teacher states the problem as she and her colleagues perceive it. This should be done gently, firmly, and with reassurance to the parents that this is a common behavior problem not unique to their child. The problem should also be stated with an attitude of confidence that it can be solved. As the atmosphere becomes more relaxed and less threatening to the parents, the teacher may sense that she can now broach the subject of the child's home life and relate ways that it may contribute to the problem. In practice, the parents may bring up problems at home long before the teacher does. The teacher must therefore be flexible and ready to change the course of the conversation.

Of course, a behavior problem is not always the product of a poor home environment. In fact, parents today are better informed than ever about child development; many are older, more mature parents than in the past; in many families, both parents are well-educated professionals. These parents may actually be providing an ideal environment for their child and be experiencing no difficulties whatsoever at home. Because teachers are not usually psychotherapists, they should avoid too much dissecting and analyzing of the child's home life unless there is an obvious connection with the child's behavior that the parents are willing to discuss.

If the teacher has done her homework, she will approach the meeting with some ideas for dealing with the behavior problem. She must, however, remain open to what the parents contribute and be willing to modify her approach if necessary. If she represents herself as an expert or authority figure, she is liable to alienate the parents and lose their cooperation. If possible, the teacher should present some options, at least one of which might appeal to the parents enough to engage their full cooperation. If there seems to be only one solution, she should state it with confidence and do her best to persuade them to allow her at least to try it.

What happens if the teacher is confronted by parents who are hostile, convinced that she is to blame for their child's problems and unwilling to listen to what she has to say? Unfortunately, this is a possibility, and the teacher should be prepared for it. This is the type of situation when having two teachers present to give each other moral support is very welcome. Parents who are hostile and rude may actually feel inadequate, guilty, or ashamed. They may suffer from low self-esteem, leading them to believe they *must* be right in all circumstances. A teacher who is tactful and sensitive to their needs may be able to give them support and nurturing, which is probably critical to the child's well-being. Many parents are themselves in need of good parenting.

Two or more conferences may be needed before an agreement about solutions is reached; the parents may remain uncooperative, leaving the teacher to her own resources; or this family may need far more than the teacher is equipped to provide. As a last resort, she should have available names and phone numbers of resources within the community. If she suspects abuse, she is required to report it to the appropriate agency. If there is family discord, addiction to alcohol or other drugs, mental or physical health issues, divorce, or lack of parenting skills, the teacher should have a list of appropriate agencies to which she can refer parents. Other issues, such as sibling rivalry, a new baby, and power struggles, may be helped by recommending appropriate books on those subjects. (The teacher should be familiar enough with the agencies and books she recommends to respect and trust their approaches.) No matter what the outcome of the conference, it is important to conclude on a positive note, reiterating the child's good qualities.

Teachers can use the following outline until they feel comfortable conducting parent-teacher conferences. As mentioned, these conferences should be kept flexible and open to all possibilities.

1.  Be prepared. Two teachers may be better than one. Have options ready to discuss with parents.

2.  Discuss the child's strengths and good qualities.

3.  Ask the parents what their concerns are for their child. What do they think are the reasons for the behavior?

4.  State the problem as perceived by the teacher and other teachers. State it with confidence and the expectation of a solution.

5.  If relevant and if appropriate, inquire into any problems at home that may be influencing the child's behavior.

6.  If the parents are cooperative, discuss ways the home environment could be modified.

7.  If the parents are uncooperative, give them support and nurturing and ask for another meeting.

8.  If needed, refer the family to an agency or suggest a book that may provide help.

9.  Reiterate the strategies that will be used at home and in the program.

10. Discuss again the child's good qualities. Keep the conclusion positive.

## Summing Up Problem Behavior

This chapter has been a discussion of a variety of children's behaviors that may be considered problem behaviors. The methods for finding solutions presented here are compatible with the problem-solving philosophy. A strong emphasis was placed on the child's natural growth and development as being the best solution to problem behavior; the importance of time in the process was also noted. Children should never be labeled "behavior problems," because their behavior is transitory and may change within days or weeks. A problem at home may be the cause of the problem behavior. In this case, if the home situation is resolved, the child's behavior will probably also improve.

Guidelines were given for determining whether a child's behavior should be considered a problem. The guidelines consist of four sets of questions to be asked by the teacher or teachers who best know the child. These questions help the teacher decide whether the child's behavior requires some kind of intervention or whether the best course to take is simply to wait and watch. Some of the major causes of problem behavior were also given. Many emanate from the child's home environment, but heredity, unrealistic expectations, and flaws in the program itself may be causes as well. In some cases, there may be no workable solution that can be implemented in a child care setting. For various reasons, some children do not fit comfortably into a problem-solving program.

Many examples of what may be considered problem behavior were given, and a variety of solutions was suggested. The solutions are not necessarily simple or final "cures" for problem behavior; there is not always a cure. Sometimes the objective must be to help everyone affected, including the teacher, get through a difficult time with his or her own self-esteem intact. Active listening and a sense of humor are great helps during these stressful times.

The necessity and usefulness of the parent-teacher conference was discussed in detail, and an outline to help the new teacher was given. Communicating with parents is usually more difficult than communicating with their children. Parents may have feelings of guilt and inadequacy that may overshadow the child's problem. The parent-teacher conference may require a great deal of tact and careful planning by the teacher or teachers involved. It is always best to develop a positive relationship and comfortable rapport with parents before problems arise.

Problem solving is a philosophy that puts trust in the natural process of growth and development. Time is the greatest solver of a child's problem behavior. Although intervention is sometimes necessary for the ultimate good of the child and the group, teachers should never lose sight of the child's right to be himself and to approach the world in his own unique way.

## *Practice and Discussion*

1. Describe the difference between the nonconforming child and the child with a behavior problem. How might both children be perceived as behavior problems?

2. Which four sets of questions should be asked to evaluate whether there is a behavior problem?

3. What is the danger in labeling a child a behavior problem? What might be the side effects?

4. Why is time an important factor in children's behavior?

5. Discuss several causes of problem behavior. As a teacher of young children, which causes do you think are the most common?

6. Choose one of the causes of problem behavior, and do more research on the subject. Share your findings with the class.

7. Discuss several types of problem behavior. Relate the type of problem to the possible causes.

8. Choose one type of problem behavior that you feel confident managing. What strategies would you use to treat and manage this behavior?

9. Choose one type of problem behavior that you feel you would have trouble treating and managing. Why do you feel this way? How could you change your attitude toward this behavior and improve your skills? If you wish, share your thoughts with the class.

10. With other students in your class, role-play a parent-teacher conference.

## Notes

1. American Academy of Pediatrics, "Media Education" (RE911) 104:2 (1999): 341–43.

2. T. Berry Brazelton, *Touchpoints* (Reading, MA: Addison-Wesley, 1992), pp. 305–11.

3. Dorothy G. Singer, *Playing for Their Lives* (New York: The Free Press, 1993), Chapter 4.

4. Mary S. Kurcinka, *Raising Your Spirited Child* (New York: HarperCollins, 1991).

5. Philip G. Zimbardo, *The Shy Child* (Cambridge, MA: ISHK, 1999).

## Recommended Reading

Biller, Henry B. *Fathers and Families: Paternal Factors in Child Development*. Westport, CT: Auburn House, 1993.

Brazelton, T. Berry. *Touchpoints*. Reading, MA: Addison-Wesley, 1992.

Campbell, Susan B. *Behavior Problems in Preschool Children*. New York: Guilford Press, 1990.

Elkind, David. *Miseducation: Preschoolers at Risk*. New York: Alfred A. Knopf, 1987.

Faber, Adele, and Elaine Mazlish. *Siblings Without Rivalry*. New York: Avon Books, 1987.

Frost, Joe L. *Play and Playscapes*. Albany, NY: Delmar, 1992.

Gardner, Richard A. *The Boys and Girls Book About Divorce*. New York: Bantam Books, 1985.

Goleman, Daniel. *Emotional Intelligence*. New York: Bantam Books, 1997.

Gottman, John. *The Heart of Parenting*. New York: Simon & Schuster, 1997.

Gurian, Michael. *The Wonder of Boys*. New York: Tarcher/Putnam, 1997.

Hallowell, Edward. *Answers to Distraction*. New York: Bantam Books, 1996. (on ADD)

Hallowell, Edward. *Driven to Distraction*. New York: Simon & Schuster, 1995. (on ADD)

Karen, Robert. *Becoming Attached: Unfolding the Mystery of the Infant-Mother Bond and Its Impact on Later Life*. New York: Warner Books, 1994.

Kurcinka, Mary Sheedy. *Raising Your Spirited Child*. New York: HarperCollins, 1991.

Pollack, William. *Real Boys*. New York: Henry Holt and Company, 1998.

Rapp, Doris J. *Is This Your Child?: Discovering and Treating Unrecognized Allergies*. New York: W. Morrow, 1991.

Sears, William. *Keys to Calming the Fussy Baby*. Hauppage, NY: Barron's, 1991.

Sears, William. *Night Time Parenting: How to Get Your Baby and Child to Sleep*. New York: New American Library, 1987.

Turecki, Stanley, *The Difficult Child*. New York: Bantam Doubleday Dell Publishing, 1989.

Welch, Martha G. *Holding Time*. New York: Simon & Schuster, 1988.

Whitehead, Barbara Dafoe. *The Divorce Culture*. New York: Vintage, 1998.

Zimbardo, Philip. *The Shy Child*. Cambridge, MA: ISHK Book Service, 1999.

# CHAPTER
# 9

# The Problem-Solving
# Approach to Curriculum

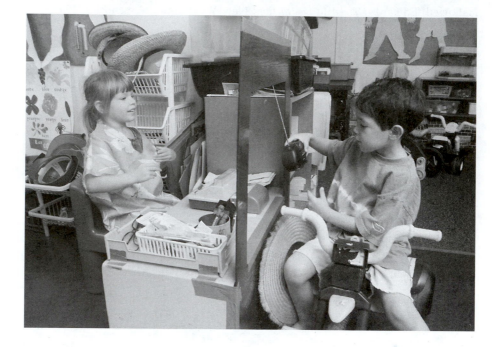

## *Acceptance and Trust:*
## *Building Self-Esteem*

Every morning, when three-year-old Alondra arrives in her classroom, she removes her outer clothing, quickly stuffs it into her cubby, and, wearing only her underwear, heads for the dress-up corner. There she finds her favorite long, striped skirt, the flowing scarf that is already tied and molded to the shape of her head, some shiny gold sandals, and a necklace of brightly colored beads. Magically, Alondra is transformed into a famous cartoon princess. Every morning for months, she has become this character; it is an important part of her identity and self-image.

In her costume, Alondra plays confidently with the other children. She builds with blocks, works on puzzles, plays at the sensory table, or, with other children, plays make-believe games. Sometimes Alondra wears her costume all morning. Other times, she wears it only briefly, then is ready to play as herself. Whether and how long she wears it is her own decision.

## Needs, Desires, and Curiosity

When Alondra arrives at her program, her first interaction is with the environment. She is one of a large minority of people who are considered shy. For this reason, Alondra begins her day by playing a role. In this way, she copes with the stress of entering the group. It is important to her self-esteem to make the transition from Alondra to princess to member of the group at her own pace. As the princess, she can feel confident. She soon forgets to be the princess and once again feels like herself.

The teacher in this class recognizes Alondra's need to enter the social group on her own terms and considers this a learning experience as important as any she could structure or plan. She provides an environment in which Alondra can fill her own particular need. She also provides an atmosphere of acceptance and trust, which contributes to the development of the child's self-esteem. Self-esteem is believed to be the single most important factor in the learning process. In this atmosphere of acceptance and trust, Alondra and her classmates are free to experience playing a role, to experiment with facets of their personalities, and to explore their world through interactions with their peers.

Someday, Alondra will discard her princess role completely and be comfortable as herself. Acceptance and trust in the classroom support children's risk taking, and if risk taking results in mistakes, these will be treated as opportunities for learning. In an atmosphere of acceptance and trust, Alondra is inspired to express her creativity and individuality and is given the priceless gift of time for long, uninterrupted periods of play.

What is the problem-solving approach to curriculum? Above all, it is the acceptance of children as individuals with needs, desires, and curiosity and the trust that they will learn by building on those needs, desires, and curiosity. Included is a deep conviction that children are whoever they are at the moment.

Every child is a complete human being with a personality and a set of characteristics that make him or her unique in countless ways. A problem-solving curriculum honors the inherent value of each individual child and demonstrates respect for each child's differences.

## *Problem-Solving Curriculum*

The word "curriculum," for many people, has come to mean structured teaching, the separation of learning from play, and lesson plans based on units or themes. This type of curriculum originates from and centers on the teacher. When we describe a problem-solving curriculum that is also child centered, however, we always begin with the child. Such a curriculum encompasses the whole child, her interactions with the environment, her relationships with teachers and peers, and the thinking process that transforms this experience into learning.

Throughout this book, the focus is on the problem-solving philosophy as it applies to children's social interactions and conflict resolution. Problem solving is an approach that is child-centered and built on the ideal of "kids doing what kids do." In this chapter, child-centered elements based on problem solving are integrated with curriculum, and both terms, child-centered and problem-solving, are used. These elements include the learning process, the child, the expanding environment, the teacher, open-ended learning, play, and creativity.

To visualize a curriculum that is child-centered and problem-solving, imagine that every child in your group is a pebble. Within this pebble are the child's inborn needs, desires, and curiosity. Every child's needs, desires, and curiosity revolve primarily around himself: every part of his body, everything he experiences with his senses, and everything he says and does. We have a great deal of information on which to build a problem-solving curriculum.

Our visualization does not end there, however, because if you drop the pebble in the pond of water, the ripples will move outward. These ripples represent the child's expanding circle of needs, desires, and curiosity, revolving around family, home, friends, the children's center or school, the community, the world, and eventually outer space. If you drop a handful of pebbles in a pond, their ripples will overlap (Figure 9.1). These pebbles and their ripples represent the group of children in your care. The constant movement of the ripples may remind us of what we know as the learning process. Curriculum that is child centered and problem-solving must catch the ripples, ride them, and somehow keep them energized so they continue moving outward.

## The Learning Process

In 1997, a major news magazine featured a cover story on the brain. Evidently, this story was in response to growing interest and research on the development of the brain. New techniques for tracking brain activity in even the youngest infant are only beginning to change the way we think about the learning process. In the years to come, new information is likely to lead to further debate and changes in the way we teach young children. There is also a danger that trends and fads, rather than basic experience and common sense, will guide the direction of early childhood education.

In *The Scientist In the Crib*, Gopnik, Meltzoff, and Kuhl describe three categories of learning that begin to take place even before birth: learning

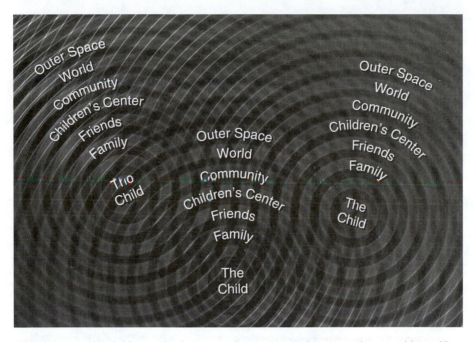

**Figure 9.1**   *The child's needs, desires, and curiosity revolve primarily around himself. The ripples represent the expanding and overlapping interests  of all the children in the group.*

about Other Minds (what children learn about people), the External World (what children learn about things), and Language (what children learn about language). They provide numerous examples from research, both their own and others'. They also describe how babies access information from these categories through three processes: Foundation (the genetic foundations that are already in place at birth), Learning (the experiences that stimulate and continuously reshape the brain), and Other People (the human interactions that promote and influence learning). Following is some of the information they share in their book.

Beginning at birth, babies remember, interpret, and form expectations from the input they receive through their senses. For example, they already know that their face resembles the faces of others and can imitate facial expressions. By experiencing other faces, they also experience emotions. An infant who "flirts" with another person expects a similar response. If the expected response doesn't come, the infant feels distress.

In addition to forming expectations, young infants can make predictions. For instance, they know that a toy car that disappears behind a screen should come out the other end, and they'll look for it to appear just where it should. At birth, babies can distinguish between the sounds of any spoken language, but within months they distinguish only the sounds of the language they hear spoken every day.

An infant's brain has been compared to a computer, but it is so much more than that. Think in terms of a computer that can reprogram itself daily, that makes its own connections, and that upgrades and updates itself—a computer into which you type in one word and out comes a complete book! Instead of a computer, Gopnik, Meltzoff, and Kuhl present an analogy that likens cognitive development to Ulysses' boat. While living and sailing on his boat over thirty years, Ulysses came into contact with external forces such as weather and gathered information through exploration, all of which caused him to continuously repair and rebuild his boat to adapt to various conditions. This is the process that allows infants to learn from their environment and their interactions with other people.[1]

As teachers, we have no influence on the infant's genetic foundations, but we certainly fit into the slots of Learning and Other People. It is our responsibility and joy to provide every infant, toddler, and preschooler in our care with enriching experiences and responsive human interactions. It is important to note, however, that the experiences needed by young children are not based on academics, what we normally think of as structured learning experiences. The experiences that every child needs are the everyday experiences in his or her environment. Young children learn by exploring home, neighborhood, and community while interacting with human beings who love and nurture them.

Infants especially need adults who speak "motherese," the baby talk we all do with infants. They need people who hold and play with them and introduce them to emotions, objects, and the world. Toddlers and preschoolers need grown-ups they can hug; kids to play with; and a place where they can watch, listen, touch, feel, taste, run and ride around, sing and dance, yell and shout, paint and pretend, make messes and clean them up, tell stories, and listen to stories being read. In other words, the best place for a child to learn is a place where he or she can be a child.

Students of early childhood education frequently hear the phrase "process, not product." In Chapter 1, "process" is defined as "change, actions leading toward a desired goal." This definition applies to learning as well as to socialization. In learning, the desired goal must belong to and emanate from the child rather than the teacher. It is the child's working with her own inner motivation that produces learning. Trust in this process is what inspires a teacher to respond in a problem-solving way.

Using an example of a small, plastic, nozzle-top bottle of white glue, we can follow the process through various levels of learning. If we gave the glue bottle to an infant, the infant's goal would be to put it in his mouth and experience it orally (Figure 9.2). A toddler who has seen glue being used might have a goal of getting the glue out of the bottle (Figure 9.3). He must, therefore, try to open the nozzle, squeeze the bottle, and aim the glue. This child has little thought of sticking something to the glue. He wants only to experience the process.

**Figure 9.2** *The infant perceives a glue bottle as an oral experience.*

Once a child has discovered the characteristics of glue for glue's sake, she will begin to experiment with uses for glue. Her goal might then be to stick things together in a random way, just to see what works. Eventually, she will explore more and more possibilities for gluing and use glue creatively. As a preschooler, she may begin to place more importance on the product, but this happens in the child's own time and way. It is important to the learning process that children find acceptance and trust at every level of the process and every action that leads toward their own goals. The freedom and time to experience, experiment, and explore are fundamental to the learning process.

## Experience

Experience is a personal encounter with an object or event and the knowledge gained from the encounter. Whether accidental or purposeful, the experience for a young child must relate to his needs, desires, or curiosity in order to have meaning. For younger children, information comes mostly through their senses; they must experience the encounter in a sensory way.

There is a saying that "experience is not the best teacher; it's the only teacher." For the learning process to be effective, even the youngest infant must be exposed to and stimulated by a rich environment in which his moment-to-moment encounters are meaningful. The application of this concept is found in the expanding environment, discussed later in the chapter.

**Figure 9.3**    *The goal of the young toddler is simply to get the glue out.*

## Experimentation

Experimentation is similar in meaning to experience, but on a higher level. Experience can be almost passive, as in an accidental encounter. Experimentation, however, requires initiation by the child. It is the act of making something happen, of trying out and testing ideas. Children are the greatest of all experimenters. To inspire a child to experiment, a material or an event must appeal to the child's senses; address his needs, desires, or curiosity; and be accessible. A priceless ingredient in experimentation is time. Children must be given enough uninterrupted time to carry out their experiments.

## Exploration

Exploration is similar to experience and experimentation but takes the process to an even higher level. To explore is to examine closely, to investigate, inquire, probe, search out, and pursue. More than an encounter or a trial, exploration is a commitment to seek out an inherent truth. An exploring child might ask questions that make adults uncomfortable. These queries may be unanswerable, or the answers may be difficult to explain to a young child. Teachers should always be prepared to set aside their own discomfort and become fellow seekers with an exploring child. We will never know how much exploration has been cut short by the attitude of an uncomfortable teacher with preconceived ideas, or what great discovery might have been made with the encouragement and support of a teacher who is child centered.

## The Child

At the center of the program is the child. It is important, therefore, to know what the child brings to the program. Each child is unique, yet we must plan a program that meets the general developmental needs of all children as well as those needs specific to individual children.

Every child has an inborn temperament, inherited characteristics, physical traits, and learned behavior. A child may be shy, compliant, fearful, responsive, affectionate, assertive, controlling, manipulating, aggressive, or any combination of these and countless other characteristics. At different stages, some children are more curious than others; some are problem solvers; some are more imaginative or creative; others are more physical. Some children develop language skills earlier than others, and those who develop later may be easily frustrated. Some children find it easy to get along with others, and some find social interactions difficult.

Temperament influences the way children learn, as does their stage of development. At every developmental stage, the child remains herself. Personality is sometimes overlooked when we try to determine a child's level of development, and too often children are assumed to be more predictable and more easily typified than they are. This assumption can lead to the belief that the nonconforming or atypical child must be "fixed," changed, modified, or in some way made to fit in. There is always a great danger that those children who do not fit fairly easily into the program will have their self-esteem damaged, perhaps permanently.

Any program that describes itself as child-centered is, in essence, making a commitment to put the needs of the child first. This means looking at every issue from the perspective of the children who are affected. In the following sections, I describe three problems I confronted as a teacher. Many programs deal with these problems by eliminating them entirely from the curriculum. The examples demonstrate, however, that a child-centered, problem-solving program will find ways to meet the needs of its children.

### Nursing Bottles

Trey has recently celebrated his first birthday and is ready to move into the toddler class. During his yearly checkup, Trey's doctor, who routinely recommends that children stop drinking from bottles at twelve months, suggested that Trey's parents stop his bottles. The parents then instructed Trey's child care providers that Trey would no longer be taking a bottle. Trey's

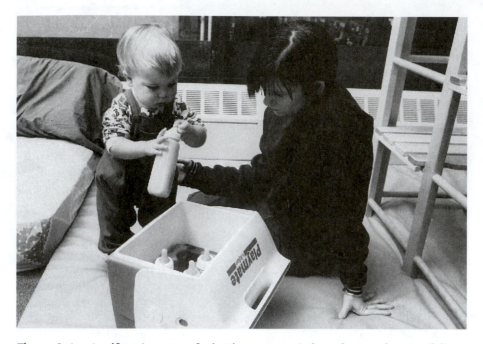

**Figure 9.4**    *A self-service system for bottles promotes independence and responsibility.*

teacher, who worried about such an abrupt change, asked for a conference with Trey's parents. During the conference, Trey's teacher explained the program's bottle policy and the reasons for it.

At home, a child feels most secure and might not need a bottle for comfort. Children in a program with several caregivers and a group of toddlers receive less individual attention than they probably do at home. There are times when a child who is upset might have to wait for comfort from an adult. During those stressful times, a child's bottle can provide that comfort. Humans are born with the urge to suck, and sucking fills a sensory need, providing pleasure, reducing stress, and bringing comfort. Observe adults sipping coffee, tea, soft drinks, or alcoholic beverages; drinking from sports bottles; or smoking various substances. The need for oral satisfaction becomes very clear.

At Trey's center, there is a self-service system for bottles; this procedure promotes children's independence and responsibility. Each child is issued a bottle of a specific color and style, labeled with the child's name. Every morning after breakfast, a caregiver puts milk or water in the bottles, places them in a portable cooler with blue ice packs, and places the cooler next to the designated bottle-drinking mat. Anytime a child wants a bottle, she asks the caregiver to open the cooler (an act that requires some coordination); then the child removes the bottle by herself (Figure 9.4) and takes it to the mat to drink. When she has finished, she replaces the bottle in the cooler.

Children who no longer prefer a bottle may have a cup with a lid, using the same system; this transition makes the shift from bottle to cup easier for the child. A teacher empties the milk bottles a half-hour before lunch and replaces them with water bottles only, which are used for naps. This avoids "bottle mouth," the condition in which a child falls asleep with a film of milk in his mouth. The lactose in the milk, left undisturbed while the child sleeps, contributes to tooth decay.

Trey's center has chosen age three for weaning. Most children have lost interest in bottles long before they are three, but those who are still attached to their bottles are old enough by that age to understand and participate in the weaning process. The child is given at least a month before his third birthday to adjust to the idea. During that time, his bottle is diluted more and more with water and he is issued his own cup. Most children respond positively to this type of transition and process it as a learning experience.

## Wearing Clothing

Lovenia, age two and one-half, hates wearing clothing. She loves the feeling of freedom she has when she can wear just a diaper. Every weekend at home, weather permitting, indoors and outdoors, Lovenia plays in her diaper. For a short time, Lovenia went to a children's center that had rules requiring children always to wear shoes and clothing. The center claimed this rule was for safety purposes, but Lovenia's parents felt it was for the convenience of the staff. After several weeks of conflict over this issue, Lovenia's parents enrolled her in another program, one that is child-centered.

In her new center, Lovenia can remove everything but her diaper at any time while she is indoors. The indoor temperature is kept at about sixty-eight degrees when heating is needed. Outdoors, there is a thermometer that is marked at sixty degrees. When the outside temperature falls below this, everyone wears clothing; below fifty-five degrees, everyone wears shoes. Lovenia and her classmates are learning to monitor and trust their own bodies to know when they are comfortable (Figure 9.5), but there are also some guidelines that allow teachers to set limits when these are needed.

In the summer, when the sun's rays are dangerous, Lovenia is covered with sunscreen and taught that when she is undressed she must stay in the shade. In parts of the playground where the ground is covered with bark, children are required to wear shoes; in parts where children are riding tricycles, caution is needed. Other limits hold children responsible for their own dressing and undressing, and for putting away their clothing. Lovenia is gaining invaluable knowledge about taking care of herself, knowledge she can acquire only through the process of being in control of her own body.

## Bringing Toys from Home

Yoshi, age four, attended a children's center that had rules requiring children to leave their own toys at home. The reason for this was that teachers and

**Figure 9.5**    *When children control their own clothing, they gain knowledge about their bodies.*

parents were afraid that children would fight over the toys, be jealous of them, break or lose them, and refuse to share. When the program's staff decided to become more child centered, children were permitted to bring their own toys. Yoshi's parents voiced their concerns to the director. What if Yoshi's toys got lost or broken? What should the parents do if Yoshi asked for toys his friends had and his parents couldn't afford them? What if other kids wanted Yoshi's toys and he didn't want to share them?

The director explained why she and her staff had changed the policy. When children bring toys from home, these playthings introduce more variety in the center. Children's interest and their playing are stimulated. The children who bring toys also gain a sense of ownership. When a child spends most of her day in a program, she may not have many opportunities to play with friends among her own toys at home. Without the experience of playing with her own toys around other children, a child may not learn how to deal with her own property. When children feel that they can control their own toys, they gradually become more willing to share. They discover that sharing is more fun than playing alone. In addition, it may be comforting to a child to have something personal close by when he is away from home.

For the child, bringing his own toys is a powerful learning experience that leads to higher levels of experimentation and exploration. Not all children want to bring their own toys, but a child-centered program will welcome the opportunity to meet the child's needs. After the conversation with Yoshi's parents, the director decided to write a set of guidelines to address the concerns of these and other parents. Here are the guidelines.

1. Toys depicting or encouraging violence should not be brought. These include guns, swords, bows and arrows, knives, books of a violent nature, and anything of this sort. Toys with pieces that can be swallowed should not be brought by children under age four, nor should anything that comes apart to expose a sharp edge or point

2. Children are never required to share their toys. Sharing is a purely voluntary act, the result of a process that brings a certain level of maturity. When children feel secure about ownership, they feel safer about sharing.

3. Anything new creates excitement. If your child arrives with a toy and other children overwhelm him, help your child say "I'm not ready for you to see it yet. Maybe later." Try to see the positive side of your child's learning to handle such encounters.

4. Toys are the child's responsibility. A toy that is considered so valuable that parents would be upset if it were lost or broken should not be brought. Teachers will encourage kids to put their toys in their cubbies when the toys are not in use, but it is not the teacher's function to take care of children's personal toys. Looking after their own playthings is one way children learn responsibility.

5. Children should bring in their own toys and not expect parents to carry them. This guideline reduces the size and quantity of what they bring and, again, teaches them to be responsible for their own toys.

6. The decision to bring a toy is between parents and child. Parents should exercise their veto when a toy is inappropriate or irreplaceable.

7. If a child is old enough to ask for a toy that parents can't afford because the child saw it at the center, parents can use this opportunity to impart their values, priorities, and choices to their child.

What do these examples concerning nursing bottles, wearing clothing, and bringing toys from home communicate to the child about the child-centered curriculum? They say, directly and indirectly, that this is the child's program; it is here to fulfill her real needs, desires, and curiosity. This message tells the child that she is important, valued, and accepted as she is. By strengthening the child's self-esteem, we give the child her most critical tools for learning.

These examples communicate respect for the child as a contributor to the program by building the program on the demonstrated goals of children rather than on adult interpretations. By allowing children to learn by their own experience, to make decisions relevant to their own well-being, and to feel in control of their own bodies and possessions, we empower them in every way and build on their ability to learn.

These examples also communicate teacher awareness that children can be trusted to take responsibility for their behavior. For children, the saying that "action speaks louder than words" is true. When teachers communicate realistic expectations to children, children are motivated to live up to the teachers' expectations. Collectively, all these messages open the doors for successful learning. The elements mentioned—a program built around children, strong self-esteem, respect, freedom to make decisions, control of oneself, trust and realistic expectations—are more fundamental to curriculum than all the teaching materials in the world. When it comes to the child-centered curriculum, only the child can lead us to what is meaningful.

## The Expanding Environment

In Chapter 2, the most effective environment for implementing the problem-solving philosophy is described in some detail. When the physical organization of the site is well-designed, both indoors and outdoors, it facilitates problem solving, decision making, risk taking, and learning through experience, experimentation, and exploration. It inspires creativity, play, and all types of social interaction by providing children with space, privacy, and time.

The problem-solving environment, as described, fulfills all the basic requirements for learning as well as socializing. Because Chapter 2 explained the environment thoroughly, this section about curriculum focuses on keeping the environment alive and expanding it to meet the developing needs, desires, and curiosity of children. The emphasis is on bringing vitality, constant challenge, freshness, and novelty to an environment already assumed to be child centered, developmentally appropriate, and adequately equipped.

The primary ingredient in the expanding environment is the teacher's awareness—awareness of the learning process as demonstrated by individuals in her group; awareness of children's various learning styles, developmental levels, attention spans, and interests. The problem-solving approach to curriculum always begins with the child; therefore, a large part of the teacher's job is to observe children as they are and anticipate where they are headed. The behavior, verbalization, and expression of emotions by children send out clues that the alert teacher can use for expanding the environment. Some examples follow.

Four-month-old Lexi is generally good-natured and easy to care for. Recently, however, when his caregiver lays him on his back with a mobile

**Figure 9.6**   *A change in position can expand the environment for an infant.*

overhead, he quickly loses interest, wriggles his body, grunts, stiffens, and begins to cry. Neither of his caregivers, who are feeding other children, can respond immediately. By the time one teacher is able to pick him up, Lexi is furious. The caregiver tries the "guessing game" and checks to see whether Lexi is hungry, sleepy, or in need of a diaper change. She holds him, rocks him, pats him, and, when he has quieted down, places him on his back again and rewinds the mobile. Within seconds, Lexi is furious again.

The other caregiver in the room recalls a similar incident with an infant a few months older than Lexi and tries something that worked with the older infant. In the room are small pillows shaped to support a child in a sitting-leaning position, a child-sized version of a bolster for reading in bed. The caregiver props Lexi up against the bolster so he can look around the room and see everyone. He is now content and alert, able to take in his surroundings from a different viewpoint. Lexi was ready for a new experience in his environment; he experimented with sitting up and explored the environment with his eyes. At first, caregivers were not aware that Lexi's needs, desires, and curiosity had advanced to such a degree at such an early age; once they understood, they made the environment expand for Lexi (Figure 9.6).

Lexi's needs were relatively easy to meet by the simple act of changing his position. The next example involves more complex needs.

Two-year-old Sayeko is one of ten in her group. For several weeks, about half-way through almost every morning, Sayeko has looked around the room and focused on something inappropriate to do. She climbs up on a chair to reach puzzles that are stored on a high shelf, grabs some pieces, and throws them on the floor, laughing. By the time the teacher reaches her, Sayeko has run away and "hidden" under the table. She laughs as the teacher brings her to where the puzzle pieces landed. By now, she has a small following, Lance and Alvin. In very little time, the three are chasing wildly around the room. Their teachers take them outside as frequently as they can, but the "gaming" continues.

Finally, the teachers become aware that these children have "used up" the environment. After spending almost a year in this room, they have experienced, experimented with, and explored everything that held their interest and are ready to move on. The problem is that there is no space for them in a room with older children for at least another six months. The other seven toddlers in the room are still engaging appropriately and with great enthusiasm in this classroom's environment.

For Sayeko, Lance, and Alvin, the environment must expand to meet their needs, so the teachers have worked out some strategies. Whenever possible, one teacher helps expose the three to a more complex and enriched environment. She has several options; she can borrow more challenging toys from the three-year-olds' classroom and take the toys and the three children to an unused area such as a hallway, teachers' lounge, or secluded part of the playground for twenty or thirty minutes. She can take her little group to the older children's more challenging playground for a time, or she can take them to the three-year-olds' classroom while the older children are outdoors. These are just a few of the ways to expand the environment.

Here is one more example of expanding the environment. A group of three-year-olds is eating lunch. The vegetable that day is corn, which is popular. The teacher mentions the color of the corn, and the kids talk about other yellow vegetables. Only one child, Halsey, remembers that he has eaten another yellow vegetable, acorn squash. On her way home that evening, the teacher stops at the market and buys an acorn squash, a carrot, a butternut squash, and a yam. The next day, the teacher cuts up the vegetables, allows everyone to examine and smell them, and then places them in an electric skillet with water. When the water begins to boil, the skillet is placed safely out of reach while the children are playing. In twenty minutes, everyone returns to the table to see the cooked vegetables, hot and steamy. The vegetables are placed on a plate to cool, then peeled and cut by the teacher and the children (sharp knives are not needed after the vegetables are cooked). Everyone tastes and smells, then the remaining vegetables are taken to the kitchen; they will be served to the children with lunch. At lunch, the conversation revolves around the vegetable experiment.

In the examples, expanding the environment is targeted to meet the specific needs, desires, and curiosity of individual children. In a wider sense, the entire environment is periodically in need of expansion. The environment, like a living organism, must evolve, grow, and mature with the children. This environmental expansion is accomplished through the teachers' vigilant and sensitive observation of the children. The role of the teacher is discussed more fully in the next section; here, let us repeat that the teacher is the key to opening and expanding the learning environment.

Assuming that the environment has been arranged in a problem-solving way (as described in Chapter 2), the teacher is free to determine the direction in which each learning center will move. Following are some ways to expand learning centers.

## Rotating Materials

A well-equipped program will keep at least two sets of items such as infant toys and rattles, puzzles, manipulatives, games, books, science objects, posters, and construction blocks. Each set should contain items that are different, yet in a similar category. When appropriate, one set can be in one classroom, the other set in another classroom. Periodically, the sets may be switched or rotated so the children have a new set of items with which to play. The teacher may have a flexible schedule for the rotation or might observe the children to see when they seem ready for something new.

The simple act of changing puzzles revives children's interest in working with them, especially if the existing puzzles have become too easy and boring. The public library can provide a new set of books every several weeks. Science objects can change with the season and region; these can be dried leaves, seashells, moss and fungi, fossils, bones, and seed pods.

## Rearranging Materials

While children enjoy the security and comfort of continuity and predictability, they are stimulated by change and novelty. Moving an area to a different location or rearranging toys within the room can sometimes cause children to notice something they have overlooked or taken for granted. The surprise of finding the bookshelf where the puzzles used to be will probably rekindle an interest in books. Moving dolls from the housekeeping area to the water table and providing sponges and soap for washing the dolls will spark the interest of both boys and girls. Moving new accessories to the block area will revitalize construction activity among the children.

## Accessorizing Materials

All types of construction blocks call for props such as small figures of people and animals as well as little vehicles; these extras will extend and expand the children's block play. Provide and rotate a variety of accessories. The home-making area should have basic cooking and eating accessories but also real telephones and appliances; the dress-up area can be accessorized with hair care materials, shoe-shining brushes, and real cameras (Figure 9.7). The

**Figure 9.7**   *Whenever possible, use accessories that are real.*

water table, sandbox, and other sensory bins need a never-ending supply of containers of all shapes and sizes for filling and emptying. Almost all of these can be donated by parents and teachers and replaced when they are worn out. The doctor kit should also contain real items such as ace bandages, a working stethoscope, blunt-ended medicine droppers, and any other safe medical items.

## Extending Materials

By observing the group, the teacher learns ways to widen the children's interests. For example, a story about baby animals may prompt one child to wonder if frogs come out of their mommies the way kittens do. The alert teacher makes a mental note of this expression of curiosity and looks for a book on frogs. When the appropriate season arrives, tadpoles may be caught or purchased and raised in a small aquarium. If the tadpoles are cared for diligently, they may develop into real frogs, which can be raised in a tank or set free in a local pond. Other small animals such as turtles, rats, guinea pigs, and birds may be introduced to the center after children read about them in stories or experience them in other ways (Figure 9.8).

In a toddler group, several children are interested in the toilet paper roll in the bathroom. Periodically, one of them comes out of the bathroom

**Figure 9.8**  *A tarantula adds a new experience to the environment.*

holding the end of the toilet paper with ten feet of paper trailing behind. A creative, problem-solving teacher brings out a wading pool, places it in the middle of the room, and puts a full roll of toilet paper in the middle. Toddlers climb in and unroll the paper, an activity that keeps them fascinated throughout the day.

An infant leans against a poster that is placed at her eye level and picks at the eyes of a baby's face on the poster. While picking at the eyes, the infant, Gina, vocalizes happily. The caregiver notices and joins Gina, talking about the eyes on the poster. The caregiver points to her own eyes, saying "eyes," turns Gina toward a nearby mirror and says "Gina's eyes," then finds a doll with eyes and lets Gina examine those. Almost instinctively, this caregiver has extended the learning environment.

## Field Trips

Leaving the center with a group of children is a real challenge for teachers and requires careful planning and organization, but every age group needs a periodic break from daily routine. Whether the outing involves putting infants and toddlers into multiple strollers for a walk around the block or forming a carpool of parents to take three-year-olds to a puppet show, the activity is worth the effort. The change of scene is stimulating to the children's senses and curiosity and represents the ultimate in expanding the environment.

For infants and toddlers, a field trip should be geared to their level of mobility, attention span, and interest, with the emphasis on pure enjoyment. Everything they will see is different from the children's center, and the experience of going anywhere as a group is itself enriching. A walk to a nearby park, supermarket, or neighborhood provides children with fresh air, a change of scene, and new sensory experiences. A car trip, however, is not generally beneficial for children at this age, and the stress might outweigh the enjoyment.

For children over age three, preparing them for a field trip to a puppet show, petting farm, visit to the dentist, or children's museum enhances their appreciation and sense of enjoyment. Children love to anticipate, and a week or two before the trip they can begin to talk about it, read about it, and experience it on many levels. For example, by reading and discussing the story of the puppet show before seeing it and acting out the story with puppets, the children will have a better understanding of what they will see. After the show, the discussion will be lively when they remember what they saw and which parts they liked most.

## Adding Materials

A dedicated teacher is always looking for materials that will stimulate children's interest and imagination. I can't count the times I went to the supermarket, hardware store, thrift shop, or office supply store to buy an item for myself and came out with a wonderful find to bring to my class. What teacher can walk through the woods, along a beach, or beside a river without something for the class catching her eye? Teachers seem to have an instinct and an awareness that help them see the possibilities in almost any item and keep them from throwing away anything that could have potential.

There are stores and catalogues that specialize in early childhood educational supplies and carry some items that are hard to find anywhere else, but many of their items are unimaginative and expensive. Some items described as "educational" actually appeal more to adults than to children and are limited in use and durability. Teachers who rely heavily on these commercial sources may miss out on the originality and creativity available from other, more unconventional sources.

For example, school suppliers sell dramatic play sets for dressing up as doctors, firefighters, police officers, and other workers. The props in these kits are specific to the characters they represent and leave little to the imagination. They are also extremely expensive. For a fraction of the cost, however, a teacher can find bags full of clothing at thrift or secondhand stores. These clothes are versatile and can inspire children to take part in all types of imaginative play as the children use them to become characters ranging from brides to pirates.

The best materials are multipurpose and open-ended so they can be used in a variety of ways by children at many levels of development within the group. A child becomes bored with a single-purpose toy. After experiencing its one use, he has little motivation for experimentation and exploration, and the toy may then be abused. Even the youngest infant will lose interest in a toy unless it is stimulating to many senses at once. A toddler, in addition, needs toys that endure pounding as well as their other uses. When you choose toys for all ages, it is important to consider and even try out the ways the children will use them. Avoid toys that require teachers to place too many limits on their use.

When feasible, find a real item instead of a toy replica. With supervision, children three and over can use real tools such as small hammers, pliers, wrenches, and very short screwdrivers; over age four, children can use small saws if the children are carefully supervised. In thrift stores, real telephones, cameras, and appliances (remove the cord) are easy to find and are less expensive than comparable toys. Real props for sets such as a doctor kit, hair care kit, and shoe shine kit can also be found at thrift stores. You can make an imaginative and inexpensive construction set by cutting PVC pipes into various lengths and buying a variety of joints with which to fit them together. As children use these materials, they learn skills that transfer to the real world and make them feel proud.

## Gender and Learning

In our discussion of environment and curriculum, it is important to add some thoughts about the relationship of the environment and the curriculum to gender, specifically, to boys. Throughout this book, I have pointed out areas in which there are differences between the ways boys and girls respond to their surroundings. In *Real Boys*, Pollack includes a chapter on schools with a section on the learning styles of boys. The research he cites and the conclusions he reaches indicate something we can observe in almost any group of mixed gender: Boys are generally more active than girls.[2] How does this impact the way we teach young children? Clearly, our commitment as teachers must be to meet the learning needs of children as they exist. If our goal is to create a positive, constructive, and effective learning environment and supplement it with meaningful curricula, we must accept the reality that children have varying learning styles and, in general, there are gender differences.

Boys need action; they prefer to learn by doing. Requiring most boys to sit still in a circle or in a chair at a table for more than a minute or two is an exercise in futility. Not only will you become frustrated, but a boy who is unable to keep still will begin to see himself as "bad." Constant reminders, removal from the group, and perhaps even punishment will lead to a cycle of defeat and to the boy's loss of self-esteem. This will only create more problems when he becomes the class clown or antagonist and disrupts everything you try to do. For this reason, look for ways to incorporate movement

**Figure 9.9**   *Rhythm instruments offer motion and action.*

into every activity you plan. Keep sitting and waiting for a turn to a minimum, and avoid lecturing as a way to impart information. Any activity must be engaging if you want to keep your boys busily learning.

As mentioned in Chapter 2, be sure to provide adequate physical activity in your classroom or nearby with a climbing structure, a mat to jump and wrestle on, riding toys, a rocking boat, and any other active equipment the program can afford (see Figures 2.1, 2.3, and 2.4). These will be used by all the children, but they will show the boys that you understand their needs. A few group activities boys enjoy include using real tools to hammer nails or screw screws into a board; dismantling old appliances, such as toasters, electric mixers, radios, clocks, and telephones; gluing together parts of dismantled appliances along with old wood scraps, mounting them on plywood or masonite boards, and then painting them; and singing, dancing, and playing instruments that require a great deal of motion (Figure 9.9).

## The Problem-Solving Teacher

In Chapters 1 and 2, I describe the characteristics needed by a teacher of young children who wishes to adopt the problem-solving philosophy. This teacher is one who accepts children as they are, with all their feelings, and trusts in the process that empowers them to deal with their feelings. This teacher respects the rights of children, enjoys children, and learns from them. She forms close relationships, openly communicates her own feelings, and takes time to listen to the children's communications. She is a facilitator, substitute parent, and loving friend. I call the teacher the heart of the center and a veritable treasure.

Although none of us can live up to this standard all the time, countless teachers fit this description most of the time. They possess knowledge of child development principles and have skill in applying these principles in their classroom. They are creative and bring an excitement for learning with them every morning. They are interested in the ideas, opinions, and complaints of their children; are aware of and sensitive to the children's needs, desires, and curiosity; and are flexible enough to make necessary changes in the center's environment. Sound judgment and a sense of humor that always uplifts and never derides are some of the best tools these teachers have.

All these qualities apply equally to the topic of this chapter: curriculum. One other characteristic should be added: organization. This may seem like a dull topic, but without organization the best efforts and talents of even the most creative teacher can be wasted and, consequently, chaos may reign in the classroom.

Every person has an individual level of tolerance for stimuli such as noise, motion, clutter, crying, and messes. As a teacher, you must know yourself and your tolerance level. If you are constantly frustrated, irritated, and annoyed by what is happening in your classroom, you will soon find yourself behaving irritably, feeling "burned out," and even getting sick. No one can function effectively while constantly out of step with his or her basic nature. I believe there is a place for the teacher whose temperament requires more order as well as for the teacher who requires very little as long as the children still feel free. The key for both is to be organized.

Organization is mainly subjective and should fit the needs of both teachers and children. There is no single way of organizing a classroom that suits everyone. Certain routines such as hand washing, meals, diapering, and napping apply to all children in particular groups and must be incorporated into the children's day. Teachers also need some systems for their own comfort and efficiency. These include adequate planning time for activities, equitable division of duties among teachers, scheduling of off-floor time to allow teachers to gather materials for expanding the environment, storage space that allows for easy access, and adequate time for cleanup. Such organization makes the day run more smoothly, helps avoid teacher stress, and leaves more time for the adults to have fun with the children.

A key factor in organization is the ability to prioritize. When everything is happening at once, as it does, a teacher must be able to make quick judgments about what is required first, second, and so on. Safety of the children is clearly the first priority, but many other situations are not so clear. Do you stop to change a diaper when another child is dumping toys all over the floor? Do you hang paintings on the wall while a child is crying for her mother? Do you stand closer to the climbing structure or to the sandbox? Your response to such choices will determine and reflect the organization in your room.

When two or more teachers work together, organization may be easier, but much will depend on their compatibility. Teamwork is essential, but the teachers must agree about the type and level of organization to be used. Strategies such as making a list of all daily tasks and dividing the list equally may be helpful. The lists might be rotated so the teachers' tasks do not become monotonous. The goal is to keep the classroom operating smoothly and provide the best possible environment for the children.

A last word about the characteristics of the teacher: As a new teacher, or one who has returned to study, you might be feeling a sense of awe and wonder about all there is to learn about teaching and guiding young children. When you are actually working with children, you will learn something new every day if you are open and receptive. I wish I could tell you how to keep your sense of awe and wonder intact, because too many teachers lose those childlike qualities and no longer identify with their children. My hope for every child is a teacher who sees the world through a child's eyes and communicates that sense of newness and wonder to every child.

## Open-Ended Learning

Open-ended learning is the part of problem solving that integrates the child's interaction with both the environment and the teacher. When a child enters the expanded environment, she is confronted with problems to solve, decisions to make, and a variety of choices. She also encounters a teacher who is skilled in encouraging and inspiring children to experience, experiment, and explore. Her thought process is stimulated, her curiosity is aroused, and the result is that she learns.

Learning that is based on the child's independent research and that leads him to his own conclusions is of the highest possible quality. Although the child's version of fact may not always coincide with what adults believe to be true, the perceptions and concepts forming within the child belong to him and are his version of truth.

When children arrive at their own truths through their own research, they feel excited. They have discovered something for the first time; for them, it never existed before their moment of discovery. Children's discoveries deserve to be treated with respect, excitement, and reverence. Such discoveries should be validated as the child's understanding of truth. There are very few facts that are so important that a child must be corrected and shown to be wrong. Instead, the teacher can help him think through the problem creatively and critically, with an open mind. Learning to think is more important than being right.

With so many children in programs where teachers constantly correct and even criticize, what happens to creative and critical thinking in our society? The child who makes a discovery only to be told it is wrong begins to distrust her intuition. If she is constantly exposed to correction and criticism, her self-esteem suffers and she is afraid to think for herself. Children believe what adults tell them about themselves. Children who feel compelled to ask permission to do almost anything or who wait for a teacher's direction before acting are products of the belief that children are unable to think for themselves.

How can we help children think for themselves, creatively and critically? We can do the following:

1.  Ask open-ended questions
2.  Encourage children to "try it yourself"
3.  Present problems to solve
4.  Support risk taking and mistakes
5.  Read stories
6.  Introduce cooperation and eliminate competition

## Open-Ended Questions

An open-ended question is one that cannot generally be answered by a simple yes or no. There is no right or wrong answer to an open-ended question; the goal is to provoke thought. Here are some examples of open-ended questions: "What can you tell me about that?" "What do you think would happen if . . . ?" "How do you think that works?" "When did you notice that?" "Where have you seen that before?" There is never a wrong answer to an open-ended question because the goal is not to obtain an answer that is factual but to enhance and exercise the child's thinking process. If the teacher feels that a child could gain more by extending his thinking, she can ask an additional open-ended question. Here is an example.

During circle time, a group of two-and-one-half- to three-year-old children are singing about the clothes they wore today. When it is Tait's turn, he says he wants to sing about his shirt, which is blue.

TEACHER:  Tait, what clothing would you like to sing about?

TAIT:  I want to sing about my red shirt.

OTHER
CHILDREN:  It's a blue shirt.

TAIT
(looking
uncertain):  It's my red shirt.

TEACHER:  Tait says his shirt is red, and some of you say it's blue. What other things in the room can you name that are red and blue?

*The children all talk at once, excitedly pointing to things that are red and blue.*

TEACHER:  It looks like you all found lots of red and blue. Tait, it's still your turn. What color did you decide to call your shirt?

TAIT:  I still want to call it red.

TEACHER:  Some of you say Tait's shirt is blue, but Tait would like us to call his shirt red, so we'll sing about Tait's red shirt.

This teacher knows that it isn't important that Tait learn that his shirt is blue on that particular day. He will certainly learn that fact in time. More important is that he and the other children become exposed to the process of thinking for themselves. The teacher did not tell Tait he was wrong; instead she asked all the children to think about colors. When Tait still insisted his shirt was red, she acknowledged that they might not agree but Tait had a right to his own belief. The same response might have caused Tait to change his mind and call his shirt blue. The teacher would accept this in the same way, without making him feel he had been proven wrong.

An important part of open-endedness is what I call "rebounding." This process entails catching the child's question and sending back a question instead of an answer, something like a game of tennis. Rebounding is not the appropriate response to every question, of course, but frequently it makes the difference between extending or ending the child's thought process. Often it empowers the child to find her own solutions to problems. Even such simple exchanges as the following help children do their own research and solve their own problems.

Eighteen-month-old Kiley likes to point at items and ask "What's that?" Her teacher makes a game of it by responding, "What *is* that?" The teacher and Kiley are looking at a book of animals and are soon joined by other children.

KILEY:  What's that?

TEACHER:  What *is* that?

KILEY:  Doggie. What's that?

TEACHER:  What *is* that?

KILEY:  Kitty. What's that?

TEACHER:  What do you think?

KILEY:  Horsie.

ANOTHER
CHILD
INTERRUPTS:  Cow!

*Kiley is calling a cow a horse. The teacher finds a picture of a horse.*

TEACHER:  Is this one a horse, or this one?

*Kiley and the other child point to the real horse.*

KILEY:  What's that?

TEACHER:  What says "Moo"?

KILEY:  Cow. What's that?

Here is another example:

LEAH

(age four):  Is this how to write my name?

TEACHER:  How does it look on your name card?

*Leah finds the card with her name written on it.*

LEAH:  What's this letter?

TEACHER:  What do you think?

LEAH:  Is it "h"?

TEACHER:  Here's the alphabet card with all the letters on it. Let's say the alphabet together until we find that letter.

This way of stimulating children to think for themselves should be distinguished from the more typical, relaxed, and intimate give-and-take of conversation between adult and child. Most adult-child conversation should be natural, responsive, and spontaneous. When we want children to seek answers and solutions, open-ended questions work effectively (Figure 9.10).

## "Try It Yourself"

In Chapter 4, I discuss helplessness in the context of active listening. Helplessness is sometimes a child's way of avoiding an undesirable task, such as putting on his clothing. In the context of curriculum, helplessness may have a similar meaning if a child feels he must perform in some particular way. If the environment encourages and motivates the child to experience, experiment, and explore and if risks are supported and mistakes used for learning, helplessness should be at a minimum. In other words, in a problem-solving environment, children naturally want to do things for themselves. There is no pressure to be right and no penalty for being wrong.

There are times, however, when a child wants something that requires extra effort and takes the path of less effort by asking the teacher for help. In some cases, the need is legitimate, and the teacher can help verbally or by giving the least possible amount of help. In the following example, a child wants the teacher to make something for him.

Vance and Brendon, age two, are at the table playing with playdough.

VANCE:  Make me a snake.

TEACHER:  I let kids make their own snakes. How do you think snakes are made?

**Figure 9.10** *Open-ended questions help children seek answers: "How much rice will fit in the pitcher?"*

VANCE
(making a
half-hearted
    attempt):   I can't. You make it.

TEACHER:   I wonder if anyone else is making a snake. Sometimes it helps to watch.

BRENDON:   I make a snake. See, I make a snake.

TEACHER:   Brendon says he's making a snake. Do you want to watch how he does it?

*Vance watches Brendon and imitates him.*

TEACHER:   Sometimes it does help to watch someone else.

## Presenting Problems to Solve

There are several ways to present problems for children to solve. One is by bringing a new toy or material into the room and presenting the new addition as a problem to be solved. Another way is by asking children to find their own toys or materials to bring to a group time and inviting the group to discuss them as problems.

When you bring in a new toy, game, or collection of materials, the way you introduce them to the group can influence how the children perceive and use the new items. Whenever possible, something new should be introduced when most of the children are present and can be gathered together. The teacher can ask for their ideas of where the item came from, what it is made of, and how it can be used and let children demonstrate their ideas. If there are any obvious limits, such as keeping pieces together or in a certain area, she can discuss them with the group at that time.

Periodically, the teacher can also introduce an item that is not a toy, such as something unfamiliar to the children and with no obvious function. The children can contribute their ideas of what it is and how it can be used. There are no rights or wrongs; there is only a problem to be solved through an exchange of ideas. This strategy works best with three- to five-year-olds, but you could try it with younger children by placing the focus on experimenting with the item rather than discussing it. Some children are eager to share ideas, and others are not; all should have the opportunity, and perhaps the quieter children will learn from the others.

Children might be asked periodically either to bring "problems" from home to discuss at circle time or to search the room for items for the group to discuss. It doesn't matter what items they bring; the goal is to elicit ideas from the children and stimulate their thinking. As each child shows his item to the group, the teacher asks open-ended questions about its possible use and other characteristics. This sharing of problem-solving ideas opens the child's mind to other possibilities and helps her become a critical and creative thinker.

## Risks and Mistakes

One of the most disturbing and serious elements in some children's programs is the lack of support for children to take risks and make mistakes. There are understandable reasons for this: Program administrators fear lawsuits if a child is injured; programs are organized to require conformity and compliance by children; teachers are themselves fearful of taking risks and making mistakes; many teachers lack knowledge about the learning process; children's curiosity is perceived as inherently "bad" or suspect; some teachers believe that children must be restricted to keep them from becoming "spoiled"; there is a general lack of creativity in the way adults interact with children.

The importance of taking risks and making mistakes, however, cannot be brushed aside for any of these reasons. Like challenge, risk taking is growth producing. The old saying "Nothing ventured, nothing gained" is absolutely true. Whether the risk is physical, intellectual, or emotional, a child needs support to reach out, stretch, try the unknown, and venture into another level of ideas and perceptions. Mistakes allow children to learn through the interplay of cause and effect in their own experiences and to solve the problems they encounter. There is no substitute for learning through one's own mistakes.

The basis for supporting children in their risk taking and in learning from mistakes is trust. Many of the reasons given above for denying opportunities for risk taking are based on a mistrust of young children, which comes from teachers' lack of understanding of normal development. The more teachers can learn about the child's learning process, the more likely they may be to support his taking risks and making mistakes.

The risks referred to here are not physically hazardous in nature. Safety is always the primary concern of any teacher. What is meant by risk is that the child has decided to try something new that might expose her to an unknown consequence. Usually, it is the act of trying something she feels ready to do but which may carry with it an element of fear. Children are normally extremely competent at calculating risks to match their current capabilities and will overcome their fears when they are really ready to try.

The teacher's role in risk taking is to support the child's effort, be ready to help if needed, and, if the risk turns out to be a mistake, observe the child's reaction. If the child wants to correct the mistake, the teacher can encourage him to find ways to do so, find an alternative way to achieve the same goal, or try again at another time. Natural and logical consequences help children learn from their own mistakes. The creative teacher finds many ways to encourage children to take risks and learn from their mistakes.

Jordan is eighteen months old and a rather fearful child. He often watches other children play in the water, wanting to join but too apprehensive to try. Today he is watching them splash and make bubbles, and this time he moves closer than ever before.

The teacher notices Jordan approaching, and bends down to talk to him about the water. She reaches her hand into the tub and brings out a handful of bubbles, holding them for Jordan. Cautiously, Jordan touches the bubbles and briefly smiles.

Taking Jordan's hand, the teacher gently leads him to the water. At first he resists, and she lets him know it's all right to be scared. Then she encourages him to reach in and touch some bubbles by himself. Gingerly, he begins to move his hand and is soon splashing, his fear forgotten.

"It looks like you're enjoying the water, Jordan," the teacher remarks, "and you look so proud of yourself. I'll bet it feels good."

Jordan smiles broadly.

**Figure 9.11**    *Children who are exposed to reading at an early age are likely to become motivated readers.*

## Reading to Children

One of the gravest problems all educators face is illiteracy. Too many Americans are unable to read above a sixth-grade level, and even more choose not to read. Yet children who are exposed to reading at an early age in the home are likely to become motivated readers (Figure 9.11). Because children now spend fewer waking hours at home, a great responsibility is placed on teachers in children's programs to provide role models for literacy. Children should have the opportunity to hear stories read every day. If there are too few staff members to sit down with a few children to read books, then reading should be structured into the day's activities at a time when everyone can listen together. This might be just before nap time or while the children are waiting for lunch.

There is more to reading than simply speaking the words on a page. For children, the page is a focal point for communication, a catalyst for dialogue. The most important part of the story is what is happening at that instant. When a child has a question or comment regarding the events or the picture, the teacher should stop and encourage conversation. If the teacher is reading and the children are listening but not interacting, the teacher should look for a point of interest or curiosity and ask open-ended questions of the children.

**Figure 9.12**    *At nap time, children are relaxed and comfortable on their mats—a good time for reading.*

Whether the teacher finishes reading the story has little to do with the way children experience and enjoy a story, and at preschool level the main reason for reading is pure enjoyment. Motivation for reading comes naturally when children see reading as fun for both the reader and the listener.

When you are reading to a group, it is important that you sit so the children can see the pictures to discuss them; seeing the pictures keeps your listeners focused. Children should be seated comfortably in positions appropriate to their age. My favorite time to read is at nap time when the entire group is relaxed and comfortable, each child on his own sleeping mat (Figure 9.12). I place the mats close together during story time so everyone can see, then separate them for sleeping. Children are limited to staying on their own mats, each child with his or her blanket and a nap toy (I ask that nap toys listen quietly). Nap-time stories impart a sense of intimacy and sweetness between the reader and the listeners.

Although children are encouraged to interact with the teacher as she reads, the focus of the interaction should be the story. If the story is about a cat, almost everyone will want to talk about his or her cat. If possible, everyone should have a turn, but if the stories stray too much the other children will become bored and restless. If this happens, the teacher might say, "I wish we could hear more about your kitty, but kids are ready to hear more of the story. Choose one more thing to tell us, then I'll read." Children are will-ing to finish if they can say just one more thing.

If children begin unrelated conversations with each other or if conflicts arise, the teacher can put the book down and tell the children, "It's hard for me to read when kids are talking (or fighting) with each other. I'll wait until you're finished." She can also say, "Other kids can't hear the story when some kids are talking to each other." To bring the focus back to the book, she can ask, "Would you like to say something about the book we're reading?" If a child continues to disrupt the story, the teacher can say in a neutral tone of voice, "If you're not interested in the story, it's OK. You can lie down and rest, or I could move you to another area so kids can hear." If many children seem restless, it might be because the story is boring or inappropriate for their age. In this case, it is usually best to stop the story and find another book.

What kinds of stories are appropriate for preschool children? Books should be chosen carefully, and with the availability of public libraries the choice is abundant. If your library allows teachers to borrow a dozen or so at a time, you can make a trip to the library every few weeks and keep the classroom well supplied. It pays to screen books before checking them out. Children's books can be deceptive, and you may decide to improvise parts of a story or completely eliminate what looked like a promising book.

Although the selection of books depends on the ages of the children, there are some general guidelines for choosing storybooks:

1.  The stories and pictures should be about people, animals, characters, or events that enhance or extend the child's own expe-riences so the children can relate to the story in a personal way.

2.  Something in the story should challenge children to broaden their horizons, think creatively or critically, or try something new. The level of understanding should be a bit higher than that of the average child in the group. If it is either too high or too low, the children become bored.

3.  The story should use correct grammar and complete sentences and model proper language usage. Dialects might be confusing to young children who are still learning their own language; how-ever, if a dialect is used for only part of the story and can be easily explained, the child's interest may still be held.

4.  Illustrations should be appealing and reflect the story. When you read to a group, the pictures in the book should be large enough for everyone to see.

5.  Currently there is an enormous trend in children's books to deal with issues such as divorce, step-families, ecology, sexual orienta-tion, adoption, race relations, pregnancy, sibling rivalry, feminism,

death—in other words, all the problems adults have created for children. A well-written book on a specific issue might prove very helpful when read by parents to their own children and used as a way to communicate. Many of these books, however, are poorly written and are filled with moralizing and preaching and lack any real story. The primary goal is to make a point, and little imagination or creativity is used. Select these books cautiously. Children who do not relate to these issues often feel anxious and uncomfortable when confronted by stories of divorce, bigotry, and death before they are ready.

6.  Similar caution should be used in choosing books that are written to promote television or movie characters. The program or film may be of good quality, but it is usually because of the animation or the personalities acted out on the screen. Books that use illustrations taken from television or movies may look like the original, but the text is usually rewritten and becomes flat and lifeless in the transition. For your young listeners, such books are a disappointing introduction to literature.

7.  Fairy tales have been criticized in recent years, mainly because of their inherent sexism and outdated values. Children, however, love these stories because of the richness of their symbolism, fantasy, and depiction of strong emotions such as hate, jealousy, love, courage, wisdom, joy, fear, and death. Fairy tales have endured for a reason: The emotions they present are universal and are certainly experienced by young children. Recently, many watered-down versions of fairy tales have appeared; they eliminate all strong emotions, thereby rendering the story useless. One possible solution to this dilemma is to save fairy tales until the children you read to are about age five; then, with a little commentary (not too preachy) from you, a child might still have the benefit of the wonder and glory of these stories.

8.  If a story has a "winner," make sure that at least sometimes the winner is the nonconformist who does things her own way. Many stories are based on a character who tries to be different only to be proven "wrong" and decides to reform and conform. Creativity, ideas, and differences should be applauded, not repressed.

9.  Be aware of stereotypes, especially in older books. You can change "fireman" to "firefighter" and point out that some doctors and dentists are women without belaboring the point or disrupting the story. If a book is too blatant in its use of stereotypes, discard it.

10.  Look for humor in a story. Nothing is more delightful than children who are laughing at a story. Their laughter shows that they are involved and understand what is happening and, above all, are having fun.

## Introducing Cooperation

Cooperation is something adults always want from children. Every teacher of young children would appreciate the cooperation of the group during routines, transitions, and activity times and might even wish they would learn in a cooperative way. Most books and television programs aimed at young children promote cooperation in some form. Yet the same program that promotes cooperation might offer a commercial that uses the phrase "be the first to buy a . . ." Can cooperation and competition coexist in a child-centered, problem-solving, open-ended program?

As we begin to study the development of boys, we learn that some stereotypes have validity and that many preconceptions do not. Competitiveness, for example, has acquired a negative connotation in recent years. Many educators, myself included, have attempted to eliminate competition from all phases of early childhood education. I began to change my views after several experiences with "cooperative musical chairs." Most of the girls were satisfied with the idea of trying to help everyone find a place to sit, but the boys were bewildered; they stood and cried because the concept was so foreign to them. I have tried it with different groups of children but have never succeeded in convincing the boys that there would be no winner! If the boys had not been so disoriented by the whole experience, it would have been comical.

In *The Wonder of Boys*, Gurian writes, "Boys need to compete and perform well to feel worthy. . . . Competition, for boys, is a form of nurturing behavior." Gurian adds that "nurtured competition is crucial to male development," and he cites studies that show the benefits of organized sports for boys.[3] Organized competition for school-age boys is one way to teach them how to deal with their natural aggressiveness. Toddler- and preschool-age boys, however, are not psychologically mature enough for such activities. Their self-esteem may still be too fragile to tolerate losing. As they grow older, boys in particular will seek out ways to compete, but, while they are still so young, boys and girls alike need to learn how to work together and cooperate (Figure 9.13).

How can teachers promote cooperation? Many ways are found in Chapter 7, "Affirmations," which offers guidelines for affirmations, improper uses of affirmations, and a section of examples. Rather than repeat them here, I suggest that you reread that section from the perspective of curriculum as well as behavior. The building of self-esteem is a primary factor in children's learning and contributes positively to children's willingness to cooperate.

In addition to the strategies mentioned in Chapter 7, there are more formal ways to build cooperation. During group times that are teacher initiated, look for activities that draw the entire group into cooperative endeavors. These can be as simple as working on a block-building project, creating a mural, putting on a puppet show, or assembling a floor puzzle.

**Figure 9.13**    *Boys and girls alike need to learn how to work together and cooperate.*

Children find cooperative efforts rewarding and take pride in one another's contributions.

## Play

Play is the child's own style of learning in a free, expressive, and safe way. The act of playing contains every element children need for the pursuit of knowledge and skill. The development of intelligence is enhanced as the child incorporates the outside world into his internal system of thought. During play, children use their senses, explore their environment, concentrate, solve problems, symbolize, improve vocabulary, and learn to be flexible. Play expands children's creativity and imagination.

Play also advances social development. Especially during "pretending," a child experiments with many roles and takes on behavior appropriate to these roles. There is little risk of failure or ridicule in these social situations. Children learn to cooperate, negotiate, share, take turns, and wait for a desired outcome. Play also permits the child to work out emotional problems in a safe, nonthreatening way.

During play, children express their fears and anxieties and seek ways to cope with them. This release helps them keep aggressive feelings under control and find acceptable ways to deal with them. Fantasy play is an extremely positive way for a child to develop a healthy emotional life. In fact, the absence of fantasy play in a preschool child might indicate the presence of a psychological disorder. Finally, play challenges the child's body. Children develop eye-hand coordination and both large and small motor skills through climbing, jumping, running, using manipulative toys, and working with creative materials.

At different ages and stages of development, children play in different ways. For an infant, play usually means an interaction with an adult, and typically the adult initiates the play. In fact, it may appear that it is the adult who is playing and that the goal is to elicit a response from the baby. The adult's reward is a smile, laugh, or gurgle so the adult uses facial expressions, voice, and movements that appeal to infants. The adult might sing, bounce, or otherwise amuse the baby in a repetitive way. As long as the adult is sensitive to the baby's rhythm and knows when to change games or stop, the infant will come to expect the repetition and the outcome of the game. She will show anticipation through her own facial expressions, vocalizations, and body movements.

As the infant develops, his play includes toys that he can grasp and put in his mouth. As a young toddler, he shows interest in other children, but play still revolves around adults and toys. Toddlers play side by side in parallel play, but they tend to see each other as objects to grab, crawl over, push down, and sometimes bite. They understand very little about cause and effect in their interpersonal relationships. For the young toddler, play involves getting a desired object and using it until he is bored, then repeating the process.

From older toddlerhood through the preschool years, play becomes increasingly a series of social interactions among peers (Figure 9.14). Adults are important in children's play primarily to provide an enriched environment and keep it evolving, to supervise for safety purposes, and to facilitate when there are problems between children. Although conflicts over toys arise at any age, after about thirty months children begin to see each other as people with needs. They can verbalize more effectively, so they can participate more cooperatively and negotiate to solve problems. Play offers endless situations for problem solving and open-ended learning.

## Creativity

"Creativity" is a word that defies definition in any concrete way. The dictionary uses the phrase "originality of thought and expression" as well as the words "productive or generative." The implication is that creativity is embedded in the internal, invisible processes of the mind and spirit and is also the external result of hands-on application. Unlike learning, which is the pursuit of knowledge or skill, creativity connotes an inner urge or passion that transforms original ideas into recognizable materials. Creativity is the innermost kernel of a child-centered learning program. It is within the very

**Figure 9.14**    *For older toddlers and preschoolers, play is a series of social interactions among peers.*

pebble that we throw into the pond, the pebble that causes the ripples. It is the "joie de vivre" that is the birthright of every child.

## Creativity Killers

Creativity is fragile and vulnerable to the layers of repression that society (frequently through children's programs) uses to hide and smother it. In studies on creativity, Teresa Amabile and her colleagues at Brandeis University identified the following "creativity killers":

1. Surveillance
2. Evaluation
3. Competition
4. Rewards[4]

How do "creativity killers" apply to children in early childhood programs? Following are some interpretations.

*Surveillance*    Supervising a child or group of children in a way that makes them feel guarded, inhibits their thought and behavior, or makes them self-conscious and embarrassed is a sure way to kill creativity. Supervision should always be nonintrusive unless a limit is being exceeded. Even then, unless there is a safety issue, teachers should always be aware of the power they represent and use it sensitively and wisely.

*Evaluation*   Commenting on the value or worth of a child's creation can kill creativity. This can be as subtle as asking "What is it?" or trying to guess what it is by assigning it a name. When we press a child to name a creation, we miss the point. Remember, the "process" is what counts. If a child feels compelled to give her creation a name when for her it was the process that mattered, she begins to feel that the process has little value unless it becomes a product.

*Competition*   Teachers should never compare children's work in a way that communicates a judgment or criticism or sets up a rivalry. Even if the child asks, "Do you like my picture better than Trudy's?" the teacher can answer, "I like the green swirls in yours, and I like Trudy's red stripes." Teachers should always be aware of children's attempts to draw them into an existing rivalry and should make every effort to remain neutral.

*Rewards*   It is important that teachers develop their skills in how to help children feel proud of their own creations and accomplishments. Material rewards such as stickers, food, or privileges have no place in the creative process. By building children's self-esteem, we give them the tools they need to find their own internal rewards, rewards that have real meaning for them and that they can carry with them for life. Most children want recognition for what they create, but material rewards only encourage them to produce rather than enhance the process. Rewards take the focus off experience, experimentation, and exploration and put it on mass production.

## Keeping Creativity Alive

If creativity can be killed, how can teachers keep it alive? Assuming that the environment is enriched and appropriate for each developmental level, and assuming that the teacher is not using "creativity killers," here are some ways teachers can promote and support creativity.

*Challenging Children*   Even the most enriched environment grows stale once children feel they have tried and mastered its contents. Although their mastery may be only for their particular stage of development, the children's perception is that they can progress no further with existing materials. The expanding environment is discussed in this chapter; in relating the environment to creativity, it is important to realize that creativity is at least partly stimulated by novelty, change of focus, and variation of ideas.

**Figure 9.15** *A growth of creativity depends on the reaching out of the mind.*

The growth and viability of creativity depends on the reaching out of the mind, as a flower reaches for sun and water (Figure 9.15). Although children find comfort and satisfaction in repeating familiar operations with familiar materials every day, children grow when something is added or changed. They experience a sense of excitement and anticipation, a burst of energy, a letting go of the old and an embracing of the new. They may feel some frustration and even pain in the process of letting go; by definition, challenge is not easy, but neither is growth. To make challenge appropriate, teachers must understand where the child is heading developmentally. Challenge should take the child one step higher than where he is presently. A challenge that is too great can frustrate him and dampen his enthusiasm. Challenge should always lift the child up to the next step, seductively, irresistibly, and irrevocably.

*Time and Space*   Creativity knows no boundaries of time and space. A program that is organized to meet adult needs or structured to promote adult concepts of learning may limit time and space in ways that are unrealistic for young children, thereby restricting their creativity. Children should be given as much time as possible to complete any activity to their own satisfaction and should have as much space as allowable in which to work on projects. When routines and transitions are necessary, there should be a notification such as "In five minutes it will be time to clean up for lunch." Consideration should be given to the child who is in the midst of creating, even if it is only allowing her to finish the project later in the day. Space may be extended by using alternatives such as putting newspaper on the floor and working there, providing an easel outdoors, letting children draw with chalk on a fence or concrete slab, or setting up an art table on the playground.

*Making Creative Messes*    Every teacher has a personal set of values, which are probably similar to those of the population in general. Cleanliness is a value shared by most people, and for many it relates to finances; some parents cannot afford to replace stained clothing. For some, it is a moral principle, like "cleanliness is next to godliness." For yet others, it is a matter of keeping up appearances so no one can criticize the parent. These values are handed down to children at an early age, and the children might fear getting messy without understanding why.

If creativity is to flourish in a children's program, it is the teacher's role to overcome biases against messiness and set the attitude for the classroom. Children use their senses to learn, and, when they play with sand, water, paint, glue, pudding, shaving cream, or markers, there is always the possibility and sometimes even the goal of getting messy. Scolding or otherwise inhibiting messiness is one way to kill a child's creativity, but it is also important to minimize conflicts with parents by demonstrating sensitivity for their concerns. Here are a few ways to lessen the mess:

1. Remove children's clothing during messy activities, leaving only the diaper or underwear (Figure 9.16).
2. Provide aprons for activities when some coverage will help.
3. Mix liquid or powdered tempera paint with liquid detergent.
4. Keep newspapers or a plastic cover handy for tables and floors (Figure 9.17).
5. Confine messy activities to appropriate areas.
6. Teach children to help clean up messes. Keep a pan of water nearby for washing hands and sponging off tables.
7. Notice and comment on the fun kids are having instead of talking about the mess they are making.

*Responding to Creativity*    The teacher's response to the creative efforts of children is of the greatest importance in encouraging the young creators to continue. An attitude of appreciation, wonder, and respect inspires children. There are certain skills teachers can learn for responding appropriately to children's creativity.

When you comment on a child's efforts, be specific. Saying "That's nice" or "That's beautiful" is easy, but it is frequently insincere. "How wonderful!" or "I really like that" may sometimes express the teacher's real feelings, but *all* comments about children's work should be sincere. This goal is

**Figure 9.16**    *Remove children's clothing during messy activities.*

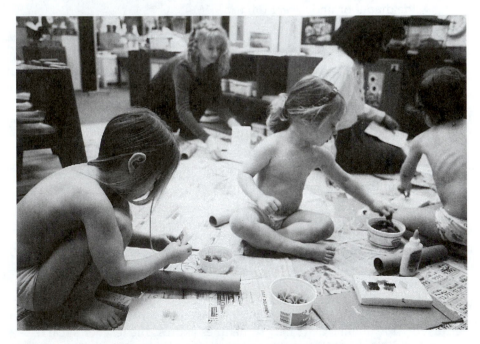

**Figure 9.17**    *Keep newspapers or a plastic cover handy for tables and floors.*

easier to achieve if teachers' comments are confined to what they see, implying no value judgment and addressing what is specific about the work. Following are some examples:

"I notice there are some red dots in this corner of your painting."

"That's a very tall block structure!"

"What fancy gold slippers you're wearing."

"You have a lot of blue glitter stuck to your glue."

"Look at you, pounding that playdough!"

"You've filled the container all the way up."

As previously mentioned, when children are pressed and asked to name something they create, they may give it an identity just to satisfy the adult. Many creations are born of pure immersion in process, and the child has no finished product in mind. Naming a creation to please an adult might compromise and diminish the child's work. There are, however, ways to talk to children about their creations that can help them expand their creative thinking. These are open-ended questions that elicit more than a yes or no answer from the child. Here are a few such questions:

"Would you like to tell me about your block structure? What can you tell me about it?"

"What would happen if you mixed those two colors?"

"How did you figure that out?"

"Would you like me to write down something you tell me about your painting?"

"Where are you going in those gold slippers?"

"Can you show me how you got all that water into the container?"

"What are some other things you can do with playdough?"

"What do you think makes the glitter so shiny?"

An additional way to respond to a child's creativity is to write her name on her work, using upper- and lowercase letters. This is a simple act, yet one that is often overlooked by a busy teacher. Having their name on their work gives children a sense of pride and ownership and allows others to comment on their work as well. I once visited a program where none of the work was named. The teacher explained that the parents already had so much art work from the children that they didn't want any more to take

**Figure 9.18**   *An easel is a symbol of a teacher's dedication to the creative process.*

home. This made me extremely sad, and my feeling was and is that parents are capable of dealing with that problem!

*The Easel Experience*   No other piece of equipment can offer children the magical experience of an easel. At the easel, a child discovers the freedom of self-expression; the joy of making an empty page come alive with color; the feeling and movement of a long, tapered brush in the hand; the awakening of imagination; and the firing of creativity. Where else is process more authentic and meaningful, more in tune with the needs, desires, and curiosity of a child, than standing at an easel? When is a child more fully absorbed in learning than when he applies paint to paper? The easel is more than a basic piece of preschool equipment; it is a symbol of a teacher's dedication and commitment to the creative process. Whenever I visit a children's program, the first thing I look for is an easel that is in plain sight, filled with paint, and ready to use. It tells me that here is a teacher who is willing to go the extra mile to provide a matchless experience (Figure 9.18).

Any walking child can use an easel. Low, toddler-sized easels can be either purchased or constructed from a piece of plywood and affixed to the wall. With toddlers, begin with one or two colors of paint and add more colors as they learn how to use the easel. Supervise diligently, and teach children how to use the easel responsibly; they will learn quickly. When you first introduce an easel, expect a rush; that will ease off in time. It helps to introduce another exciting activity at the same time so the children's attention will be divided.

All paints that are made for children are now nontoxic and relatively washable. To save money, use powdered paints and ask for donations of computer paper that has been used on one side. To save time, never clean your easel—it will just get painted over again! When enough paint hardens, it falls off or can be knocked off into a trash can. Instead of buying pots with lids, use sour cream containers and cut a hole in each lid; when you change colors, just throw away the old containers without washing them. Cut a simple apron from plastic-covered fabric to protect children's clothing. Then stand back and watch creativity blossom!

***Crafts Projects***   While the easel is a necessity, the same is not true of crafts projects, notably, projects that are prepared and initiated by the teacher. Every child can experience the process of art; all it takes is a supply of the simplest, most basic materials and the opportunity to experiment freely with those materials. Provide any child with crayons, markers, paper, easel, paints, glue, and "stuff" to stick to the glue, and you have art. There are books filled with art projects for preschoolers, but they invariably require a great deal of preparation by the teacher. The teacher may be asked to cut out pieces to glue, make photocopies, draw models, direct the child to assemble it in certain ways, and even assist the child in the actual assembling. By the time the child finishes what the teacher has prepared or colors inside the lines, we must ask ourselves what value this was to the child.

How many art projects are made primarily for the sake of adults, both teachers and parents? Teachers often plan such projects because they don't trust the *process* of art and are comfortable only when there is a *product* to send home. As in other areas of early childhood education, we have a responsibility to educate parents as well as children. If we demonstrate appreciation for the process that is art and respect for the child's creative expression, parents will soon do the same. By becoming a role model, a teacher can reach numerous parents and show them how to authentically support their child's creativity.

***Encouraging Children to Do Their Own Creating***   Children sometimes ask adults to make objects for them with playdough or to draw representative pictures or build a certain block structure. Young children, especially under age four, are seldom capable of making a representative creation such as an object that looks realistic. It is tempting to the adult to make things for children; however, doing so can be counterproductive. Children might become dependent on having adults perform for them and might not try to make the structure or draw the picture themselves. Adults can make things so much more realistically that a child may feel it's useless to try or might believe that the adult version is always better. Rather than inspire, the adult might discourage. A good response to a child's request is "I let kids do their own work."

## Diversity in the Curriculum

In recent years, greater emphasis has been placed on sensitivity to cultural diversity in the education of young children. This emphasis is valid because the self-esteem of children can suffer if they are made to feel uncomfortable, inferior, or excluded simply because they are different from most of the children in their center. All children can be enriched by exposure to the variety that exists in our world. This variety encompasses all races; both sexes in nontraditional roles; modern, realistic versions of the family; and people of all ages and handicaps. If a program's population of children and teachers is not very representative of this variety, the staff might consider ways to introduce some diversity into the children's environment.

The most desirable approach is to help children see diversity as it appears naturally in modern society—among workers, family members, community helpers, and others. There are different opinions about representing races and cultures in the dress and customs of their country of origin. Some call this the "tourist approach," arguing that presenting people in "native" dress makes them seem less relevant to children and their everyday lives. However, we live in a shrinking global community, and it is significant for children to know that people in other countries and cultures might dress and live in ways that are different from what the children know and are accustomed to.

Representing diversity is more complex than it seems and requires thought and planning. What is the goal of introducing diversity? Who will be represented and in what ways? Will religious or cultural holidays be celebrated, and, if so, which ones? What are the available positive resources? Who might be offended by a certain object or event? The issue is filled with political implications, and much depends on the population of the program and the surrounding community. The risk is politicizing children rather than sensitizing them, but if making children aware of their diverse world is approached with goodwill, respect, and high standards, the benefits can be deep and long lasting. Here are some standards to consider.

1. *Quality.* Any item that is used to heighten children's awareness of cultural diversity should meet the same standards of quality used for other items in the curriculum. For example, a book about interracial parents should be evaluated by the criteria presented earlier in the section on reading to children. If a book is not of high quality, no matter what the topic, it should be rejected and another book sought.

2. *Relevance.* Can children understand, identify with, and relate to this item? For example, a poster declaring peace for all humankind should depict people, preferably children, rather than an abstract picture of the globe.

3. *Durability.* A fragile doll in a festive costume is interesting, but if children are constantly required to be careful of it, they soon lose interest. Dolls that are durable are now available as anatomically correct males and females and as representatives of various races. The costume is less important than the doll's usability.

4. *Presentation.* A puppet show about a child in a wheelchair is inappropriate if the depicted disability makes children feel anxious, guilty, or fearful. Children worry that somehow they could have the same disability or believe that they could cause it to happen to others. Puppet shows, plays, stories, demonstrations, and other presentations made to children should always be positive and enriching rather than anxiety-producing.

Here are some items to consider including in a curriculum to represent diversity.

1. Dolls, both baby and adult, male and female, of various races

2. Books in which diversity is represented by the primary character and not always by people in the background with stories that appeal to all children

3. Posters of diverse people, especially children, performing real-life everyday tasks

4. Games, matching and pairing cards, and puzzles that depict all races and genders

5. Accessories such as little "people" or wooden figures, which now come depicting individuals of various ages and races

When you teach about differences in people, keep the topic general enough that all children are included and none is singled out. It is important to acknowledge the diversity in your own group and integrate some of these distinctions into the curriculum when relevant. Answer questions as honestly as possible without causing anyone embarrassment. Every child wants to belong to the group and feel special at the same time. Ask open-ended questions such as "Why do *you* think some people have darker skin?" or "How many of *you* have Moms and Dads that live in different houses?"

Most important, when you are incorporating diversity into the curriculum, remember that young children seldom take note of differences in people other than in a casual, curious way. They are first of all children before they are representatives of any other group. Modeling respect for all children is the most effective method for teaching children to respect all people.

## *The Intergenerational Curriculum*

Joan Whitley describes the adjustments or additions needed to make a curriculum meet intergenerational needs.

> One goal of an intergenerational curriculum is helping children and adults unlearn our society's stereotypes concerning older adults, such as comparing old women to witches. Words that are often used to describe the elderly include "doddering," "ugly," "scary," "smelly," "absent-minded," "forgetful," and "silly." Such stereotypes can be addressed in several ways: reading books that depict older adults as real, individual people; including grandparent dolls; providing access to equipment such as wheelchairs, walkers, and canes; and displaying photos showing children with their elderly friends. Teachers should talk to children about their experiences at the nursing center and help them think critically when they notice something untrue or unfair.
>
> Children may see older adults acting in unfamiliar ways. A confused elder may refer to a child as Tomas, thinking of her younger brother. An elderly woman may cry and want help until a group of children approaches and talks with her. At that point, her demeanor may change, and she may become very outgoing and want to shake hands and talk to the children. Teachers should be sensitive to the children's reactions and use active listening to help the children deal with their feelings. They can talk about memory loss as a condition that some older people experience and even plan some activities around memory. Children also need to know that such conditions are not "catching."
>
> Teachers and the nursing-center staff will need to plan some activities together to make sure the activities fit the needs of both groups. For infants and toddlers, it is common to do friendly visiting. This is akin to going for a walk in your own neighborhood and visiting close neighbors (Figure 9.19). You can take something to share or to show, but the children's own natural curiosity and interest in people and things will bridge the generations nicely. Rhythm instruments, scarves to dance with, and soft squishy balls for tossing are good toys to take along or to store in the areas you visit.
>
> Older toddlers and preschoolers may enjoy more structured activities, such as cooking, art, music, games, and exercises; these will encourage interaction between the groups. Some programs establish a ritual that occurs every time they meet. It may be shaking hands, exchanging a little greeting, or singing a song to begin or end their time together. After the two groups become well acquainted, the teacher might have a child or an elder choose a partner for a particular activity. The activity could be playing a game or making banana bread; the idea is for the child and the elder in the pair to help each other. One might stir while the other holds the bowl, or they might be partners in a game of horse racing in which one throws the dice and the other counts the spaces and moves the horse.
>
> Children can include their elderly friends in their plans for a picnic. Perhaps only one friend can attend, but that's enough. It isn't always necessary to

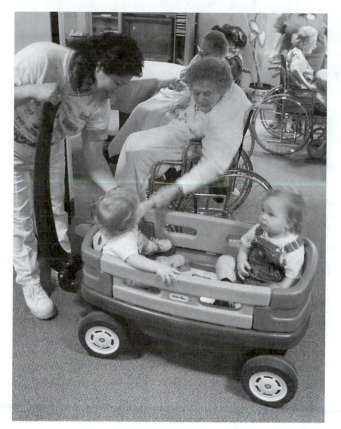

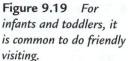

**Figure 9.19** *For infants and toddlers, it is common to do friendly visiting.*

have a big number of elders; a great experience can come out of one adult who becomes the special friend for a group of children. One friend can teach a whole group of children about the value that older adults can have in their lives. For example, an older adult with a friendly and safe dog can teach a group of children about dog safety.

More often than not, older adults will enjoy watching children play, create art, build with blocks, cut playdough, or perform any of the typical activities in an early childhood classroom. They may love listening to stories with children and listening to children sing and do finger plays. Some will volunteer to tell or read stories to the children. Their true joy, however, is in simply watching the children play and interact (Figure 9.20).

## Group Times

When children and teachers gather together as a group, the time spent can be used for building children's self-esteem, sharing discoveries, overcoming a child's shyness, helping the children develop skills, and having fun. Whether it is called circle time, activity time, or group time, this period is

**Figure 9.20**    *Older adults enjoy watching children "do whatever they do."*

typically set aside for a teacher-initiated activity. The type and length of the activity depend on the age of the children, the size of the group, the children's attention span, and other variables. The wise teacher plans this time carefully, but with a high degree of flexibility.

Children under age two rarely function as a group, but the teacher can plan a focus for the day, a special activity that is available throughout the day as children show interest. For infants, it might be making water play available, giving every baby who wants one a turn in the water. For toddlers, it might be finger painting with shaving cream, with only three or four children finger painting at a time. Toddlers tolerate small groups when there is an appealing focus. By about thirty months of age, children are able to sit in a circle or work at a table in a group of eight to ten if they are not required to wait long for a turn (also see "Gender and Learning").

Although a group time that is unplanned and spontaneous can be fun and successful, you will generally be more effective if you have a plan, even if you decide occasionally not to use it. Without a plan, there might be a loss of continuity, undue repetition, long waits, forgotten materials, or disorganization. For example, in a cooking activity, without careful planning there might be missing ingredients or utensils, too much waiting for each child to have a turn, too much crowding around a skillet, and even a resulting accident.

Adequate planning for group time helps the teacher decide what the goals are and what she hopes the children will gain from the experience.

She can also consider the individual children in the group and prepare for any foreseeable reactions. How will the shy children in the group relate to the activity? Will it last too long for the youngest in the group? Will it be challenging enough for the oldest? What about the child who cannot focus for more than a few minutes? Although it is not possible to provide alternatives for every child, effective planning helps the teacher be aware of needed flexibility.

At the beginning of this chapter, I noted that self-esteem is the most important factor in the learning process. Group times offer opportunities for raising children's self-esteem by focusing attention on and giving recognition to individual children and also by helping them develop skills that bring them satisfaction and self-respect. The child who joins the group in solving a problem, who sings with the group, or who contributes to a group mural feels a sense of achievement for herself as well as for the group. Because groups can accomplish some things that individuals cannot, children often develop an extra sense of excitement about what the group has achieved. Three- to five-year-olds especially express delight and pride in group projects.

Everything in this chapter applies to working with groups as well as with individuals. Group time offers an opportunity for raising children's self-esteem without embarrassing those who are shy. Songs that allow brief recognition of each child are ideal for this. Some examples are found in Chapter 7, "Affirmations." Participation in the song is voluntary, and the shy child who abstains the first time around should be given a second chance in case he changes his mind.

To facilitate the idea among children of working as a group and to help build their self-esteem, some special items can be kept in the area where the group normally assembles. A "self-esteem" wall might include a poster with photographs of all the children as they play in the classroom; photographs of each child celebrating his birthday with the group; a poster showing the birthdays as they occur during the year; a poster or other device for showing the height of the children and tracking their growth over the year; pictures of children taken with their families, relatives, and friends; and any other props that visually depict the children as individuals and as a group.

Group time is ideal for introducing new experiences, experimenting with materials and peer relationships, and exploring a process in depth. By expanding the environment in conjunction with the group activity, children will make their own discoveries, which they share with the group. As children learn from each other, they grow socially as well as intellectually. This is the ideal result and what we always hope for in group times.

Most group times, however, are less than ideal and often not at all what we hoped for. An inherent flaw in group time is that the teacher, who carefully plans, efficiently gathers materials, and clearly understands his or her goals, may forget temporarily that he or she is still working with the same individual children who sometimes engage in conflicts, who find some activities boring, and who are prone to tantrums when their demands are not immediately met. While envisioning the desired outcome of the group activity, the teacher may wish and imagine that everyone will cooperate, participate, learn, and enjoy.

If the expectation of group time is too high and idealized, even the best teacher can become disappointed and frustrated and feel like a failure. For example, in the middle of circle time, while children are enthusiastically singing about who is here today, two children begin kicking each other, two others scream about whose turn is next, and then a child demands help with her clothing. The singing is disrupted; the children become restless and aggressive. Or during an art project, two children push to get the same chair, two others tug on a paint brush and spill the water, and another cries for her blanket. In both examples, the teacher's expectations are shattered, and group time disintegrates into chaos.

To help form realistic expectations for group time, teachers can plan some strategies and address certain issues ahead of time. Remember that there are no right or wrong answers and decisions depend on the variables in the classroom. Following are some questions to guide your thinking. The issues raised here apply only to children over thirty months of age.

1. Is group time mandatory for all children? Are they required to join the group even if they choose not to participate?

2. If children are required to join the group, how is this accomplished?

3. If children are not required to join, what is the alternative for those who choose not to join the group? Is there a teacher available to supervise those children?

4. Are the same choices available for group time as for play time? For example, do children decide where to sit, whether to negotiate for materials, or whether they are permitted to bring toys, blankets, and other belongings to the group activity?

5. If there are conflicts during group time, do we consider first the well-being of the group or that of the individual involved?

6. If the activity turns out to be boring, too difficult, or unworkable, how do teachers and children deal with this? What are the alternatives to the group activity?

7. If choices are more limited during group time than during playtime, how is this communicated to the children?

## Summing Up the Problem-Solving Curriculum

Curriculum that is problem-solving and child centered is based on the needs, desires, and curiosity of children in the class. The self-esteem of the child is of primary importance to his ability to learn; self-esteem is built on the foundations of acceptance and trust. The child with healthy self-esteem participates eagerly in the learning process through experience, experimentation, and exploration.

Major elements of the problem-solving curriculum include the child and all she brings to the program, an environment that constantly expands to meet the child's needs, and a teacher who relates personally to the child. Children learn in an open-ended way by thinking critically and creatively, solving problems, taking risks, and making mistakes. Reading to children motivates them to become enthusiastic readers.

Play is the child's learning style and provides opportunities for social, emotional, and physical as well as cognitive development. Children work out problems during imaginative play and rehearse future roles. Creativity is sometimes a fragile characteristic that requires nurturing and challenge if it is to flourish. The environment promotes creativity in children by providing time and space and by allowing for creative messes. The teacher nurtures and supports creativity by his or her responses to the child's efforts.

Cultural diversity in the curriculum adds to a child's self-esteem and expands the child's world. Explorations of cultural diversity should meet the same high standards as all other elements of the curriculum. Bringing elders and children together is a natural way to topple intergenerational barriers and provide extra nurturing for both groups. Working with children in a group is rewarding but challenging for the teacher. Careful planning is required, and expectations should be kept realistic.

## *Practice and Discussion*

1. Describe the difference between the child-centered curriculum and one that is teacher centered. Give several examples of each.

2. Using your own example (similar to the glue bottle example), demonstrate how the learning process can be observed as children grow from infancy to preschool age. Explain the differences in each stage.

3. Demonstrate the progression from experience to experimentation to exploration by using an object such as a seashell, a lump of playdough, a tub of water, or any object of your choice. Pick any age child.

4. What need of children, similar to nursing bottles, wearing clothing or not, and bringing toys from home, might be unmet by children's programs? Pick an unmet need and devise a plan for meeting that need. Write a brief policy statement for parents and teachers.

5. In your own program or one you visit, list ten ways in which the present environment could be expanded.

6. Spend at least two hours observing a teacher you admire without telling her what you're looking for. Does she seem child centered? How does

she organize routines and transitions? How does she prioritize? How does she interact with children in general? Does she interact differently with boys than with girls? Does she teach in an open-ended way? What can you learn from her? What could she learn from you?

7. Pick a topic appropriate for three- to five-year-olds and make a list of at least five open-ended questions a teacher could ask about the topic.

8. In your college classroom, role-play one or several of the following: (1) A toddler asks the teacher to draw a picture for him. (2) The teacher shows her preschoolers an item such as a funnel, a nail file, a teapot, or a wrench and asks them what they can do with it. (3) A toddler insists on working a puzzle that is too hard for him. (4) Read a book to the class. How do you get them involved in the story? (5) Introduce a game to preschoolers. Encourage cooperation instead of competition.

9. Discuss reasons why many parents view play as time wasted or as non-productive, frivolous activity. How do you as a teacher respond to these concerns?

10. Observe a classroom, looking for "creativity killers"; report back to your college class. If this is not possible, discuss any "creativity killers" in your own childhood and how your own creativity was adversely affected.

11. In your own program or one you visit, list ten ways in which acknowledgment of cultural diversity could be improved or better expressed. If you have had personal experience with the absence of cultural diversity in a children's program, share with your classmates the impact this made on your life.

12. What are the pros and cons of group activities initiated by the teacher? How do you, as a teacher, feel about group times in general?

## Notes

1. Alison Gopnik, Andrew N. Meltzoff, and Patricia K. Kuhl, *The Scientist in the Crib* (New York: William Morrow & Co., 1999), Chapters 5 and 6.

2. William Pollack, *Real Boys* (New York: Henry Holt & Co., 1998), Chapter 10.

3. Michael Gurian, *The Wonder of Boys* (New York: Tarcher/Putnam, 1996), pp. 29–30.

4. The categories "surveillance," "evaluation," "competition," and "rewards" are derived from studies by Teresa Amabile and her colleagues at Brandeis University. These studies include T. M. Amabile, "Children's Artistic Creativity: Detrimental Effects of Competition in a Field Setting," *Personality and Social Psychology Bulletin* 8 (1982): 573–78; T. M. Amabile and J. Gitomer, "Children's Artistic Creativity: Effects of Choice in Task Materials," *Personality and Social Psychology Bulletin* 10 (1984): 209–15; B. A. Hennessey, T. M. Amabile, and M. Martinage,

"Immunizing Children against the Negative Effects of Reward," *Contemporary Educational Psychology* 14 (1989): 212–27; T. M. Amabile, P. Goldfarb, and S. C. Brackfield, "Social Influences on Creativity: Evaluation, Coaction, and Surveillance," *Creativity Research Journal* 3 (1990): 6–21.

## Recommended Reading

Amabile, Teresa M. *Growing Up Creative.* Creative Education Foundation, 1992.

Bean, Reynold. *How to Develop Your Children's Creativity.* Los Angeles: Price, Stern, Sloan, 1992.

Dodge, Diane Trister, and Laura J. Colker. *The Creative Curriculum.* Washington, DC: Teaching Strategies, 1992.

Faber, Adele, and Elaine Mazlish. *How to Talk So Kids Will Learn: At Home and in School.* New York: Rawson Associates, 1995.

Frost, Joe L. *Play and Playscapes.* Albany, NY: Delmar, 1992.

Goleman, Daniel. *Emotional Intelligence.* New York: Bantam Books, 1997.

Gopnik, Alison, Andrew N. Meltzoff, and Patricia K. Kuhl. *The Scientist in the Crib.* New York: William Morrow and Company, 1999.

Graham, Terry Lynne. *Teaching Terrific Twos and Other Toddlers.* Atlanta, GA: Humanics Learning, 1992.

Gurian, Michael. *The Wonder of Boys.* Tarcher/Putnam, 1997.

Pollack, William. *Real Boys.* New York: Henry Holt and Company, 1998.

Singer, Dorothy G., and Tracey Revenson. *A Piaget Primer: How a Child Thinks.* International Universities Press, 1998.

Sobel, Jeffrey. *Everybody Wins.* New York: Walker, 1983.

Sparks, Louise Derman. *Anti-Bias Curriculum: Tools for Empowering Young Children.* Washington, DC: National Association for the Education of Young Children, 1990.

Sprung, Barbara. *What Will Happen If: Young Children and the Scientific Method.* Mt. Rainier, MD: Educational Equity Concepts, 1985.

# 10

# *Training Teachers for Problem Solving*

P roblem solving is not only a way of interacting with children or a method of teaching. New teachers report that they begin to use active listening with their boyfriends, girlfriends, husbands, or wives and find themselves sending I-messages to their friends and roommates. If they have children of their own, they begin to facilitate when there are conflicts. Sometimes they are met by incredulous stares, but at least they are internalizing the problem-solving philosophy and incorporating it into their lives. It is similar to learning a foreign language. At some point, you begin to think in that language. When that happens, it is yours forever. Teachers who enthusiastically embrace and believe in problem solving will see its value and application throughout their life.

## Applying the Philosophy

In a children's center, problem solving requires working as a team. The same principles used with the children apply to the staff. Depending on the center's organization of staff, the director, coordinator, or head teacher may sometimes be called on to facilitate a conflict between teachers or send I-messages to assistants. It is also likely that the director will practice active listening when individual teachers ask for advice, and teachers will use their active listening skills on one another. The support and concern found in a team of problem-solving teachers should permeate the center and not be reserved for children.

Problem solving is not likely to be the philosophy in which teachers were reared by their parents; therefore, it is not usually their typical way of responding to children. Without training, most adults respond to children the way their parents responded to them. The teacher whose upbringing was positive and respectful may adapt to problem solving more easily than one who was reared with harsh discipline. Overcoming the messages of childhood is difficult. It may require the daily support of a group of like-minded individuals. A single teacher, such as a home day-care provider, could learn and grow in the problem-solving philosophy without such support, but it would not be easy. It would require great dedication and self-monitoring. Such a provider could benefit greatly from starting or joining a group of home day-care providers who are also committed to problem solving.

This chapter is directed primarily to the teacher or future director who will be involved in the process of training teachers. The new teacher may be in this position sooner than expected. As the demand for quality child care accelerates, so will the demand for quality teachers. Those with education may be put in positions of responsibility while they themselves are still testing their skills. This chapter should be a resource for the teacher who is called on to train others. I begin with some thoughts on leadership and teamwork.

## The Leader's Role

Any discussion of quality and training in a children's program must begin with leadership. What is good leadership? When it exists, you don't necessarily notice it because the program is progressing as it should. When leadership is missing, however, everyone feels stress and confusion. When leadership is lacking, the void is usually filled with gossip, back-stabbing, complaining, turf wars, and weariness. Not only the teachers but especially the children are the losers.

There is no substitute for experience when it comes to learning how to be a leader. Unfortunately, many of us learn the *negative* lessons of leadership by working as new teachers in a disorganized, poorly run program. There is a feeling of having been thrown in the ocean without a life jacket.

The program may be one in which every teacher does something different and there is no core philosophy, no one to turn to with problems, and no one to facilitate disagreements between teachers and assistants. If you are in a position of leadership, the following list of questions, which is far from complete, may help you identify your major strengths and weaknesses and set goals for becoming a strong leader:

> Do I always consider the needs of the children and put them first?
>
> Do I believe wholeheartedly in the purpose, philosophy, and goals of my program yet remain open to new ideas?
>
> Am I skilled enough to work with any of my teachers in any classroom?
>
> Do I understand the program from the bottom up, and do I know what each staff member goes through every day?
>
> Do I know every child by name and something about each child's family life? Do the children know me as a friend?
>
> Do I have a written set of child-staff-parent policies and uphold them consistently?
>
> Am I also flexible enough to make an exception when necessary?
>
> Do I avoid making assumptions, communicating clearly and directly instead?
>
> Do I meet regularly with my staff and listen to *their* problems?
>
> Do I adequately prepare staff, parents, and children for all major changes?
>
> Am I impartial, fair, and compassionate with all my staff members?
>
> Do I help teachers and assistants negotiate when there are conflicts?
>
> Do I inspire teamwork, not rivalry?
>
> Do I dismiss workers who fail to comply with our philosophy and policies after training, giving them a fair chance and the required notification?
>
> Do I remember to personally encourage each worker's efforts?
>
> Do I treat children, staff, and parents with dignity and respect?
>
> Do I go to bat for my staff for pay raises and benefits?
>
> Do I make decisions based on my program's highest standards?

## The Teammate's Role

In order to lead, one must have followers. The role of most teachers and assistants is to follow the philosophy, policies, and leadership of the program. Many workers in children's programs are just passing through; they are college students, aspiring entertainers, artists, people who lack experience in any other kind of work, and people who are between "real" jobs. In an ideal world, everyone who works with children would be a highly educated, experienced, and dedicated professional, but even those who are not professional teachers have much to give in the way of love, warmth, energy, and enthusiasm. Working with children demands more than most other jobs, and certain standards must be met. Following is a list of questions for followers and teammates in children's programs:

Do I always put the needs of children first and bring those needs to the attention of my leaders?

Do I work in this program because I believe in its purpose, philosophy, and goals?

Do I respect and admire the leaders of my program?

Am I open-minded and willing to learn from my leaders and other teammates?

Am I considerate of the other team members on our staff?

Do I have integrity? Do my outward actions match my inner beliefs?

Do I take initiative when a job or task needs to be done and just do it?

Do I arrive at work and return from breaks on time?

Do I abstain from gossip, hearsay, and criticism behind other people's backs?

Do I have high standards and work only where those standards are practiced?

Am I flexible enough to change plans quickly when necessary?

Do I refrain from criticizing my leaders in front of parents but have enough courage to give my leaders honest feedback?

Am I professional at all times? Do I conduct myself in the same manner whether or not someone else is watching?

Am I the kind of person I would like to have working for me if I were the leader?

Do I give my best self to my job at all times?

## On-the-Job Training

It would be wonderful if every teacher could be thoroughly trained before setting foot in a classroom. That is, indeed, one of the purposes of this book and of the class the reader is probably taking. But the need for child care workers far exceeds the numbers of those who are trained, especially in problem solving. The time will come when a teacher is needed and the main qualifications of the applicants will be that they like children and need a job. Upon being hired, this person may have to begin working immediately, and most training will, of necessity, occur on the job. Another scenario arises when a substitute teacher is needed. The substitute may be highly qualified or be only a "live body." Either way, he or she will probably need additional training in problem solving.

Two types of training are most effective in these situations: on-the-job training and the individual conference. Both are necessary and should be started as soon as possible. Both require assertiveness, strength, and tact on the part of the trainer. On-the-job training includes modeling (setting an example), giving directions, and correcting mistakes. All should be done in the spirit of problem solving and should use problem-solving techniques.

If the budget and other considerations allow, the new teacher should have at least a week in which to observe before beginning on the job. Primarily, the new teacher should be assigned to observe the best teacher available and the children with whom the new teacher will eventually work. It is also important to let the trainee know that other teachers may be functioning at a variety of skill levels. Some of what is observed may not be carried out perfectly. Yet mistakes are part of the learning process for teachers as well as children, and good teachers learn to listen to, monitor, and correct themselves. Just as trust is an essential ingredient in problem solving with children, it is also essential for adults; every teacher who is worth hiring is worth trusting.

Whether the trainee can spend a week or more or only a day or two observing, it is important that she understand what is being observed. Reading a brief summary of the philosophy before beginning to observe give her a head start. The training teacher should explain briefly what is happening and how the problem-solving philosophy is being applied. The trainee may want to carry a notepad and jot down any questions to ask at a later conference. It would be too distracting to the teacher and the children to carry on question-and-answer sessions while the trainee is observing the teacher.

One of the most important of the trainee's tasks is to learn the names and identities of the children who will be in the group. Problem solving depends heavily on relationships; the teacher works hard at knowing the children well. This is one way to build trust and also a way to know each child's capabilities and limitations. All this information is needed for effective problem solving. It is therefore not a waste of time or money for a trainee to simply make friends with the children. This is, of course, a two-way street. The children will be observing and evaluating the trainee as well and will decide whether the new teacher is acceptable to them.

As soon as the teacher and the trainee feel ready, which may even be during the first day, the trainee may begin trying a hand at active listening, negotiating, setting limits, and other facets of problem solving. As long as the trainee is well intentioned and kind, there is nothing to fear. If children like the trainee, they will not be critical. There is always time to say "Let me think of another way to say that." The children are not even aware of the philosophy; their focus is on the teacher and how they are treated.

If the program is built on the child-centered classroom approach, the new trainee will be only one of several teachers with whom the children will interact during their day. Because the trainee will not be isolated with a group, any mistakes she might make will not be so noticeable to the children. Other teachers, however, will be likely to notice and, in the spirit of problem solving and teamwork, should feel free to provide her with needed information. If they feel reticent about giving information, they should at least mention any noticeable mistakes to the teacher who is doing the training in order to help the trainee make corrections. Because the trainee is probably nervous and apprehensive, all information should be given with care and tact and with complete absence of criticism.

If the new trainee will be isolated in a classroom with the same group of children every day, a somewhat different direction is needed. Aside from learning to apply the problem-solving philosophy, she will have organizational tasks to learn. A major consideration is the transition for the children. They will be required to transfer their affection and trust from one teacher to another. For some children, such a disruption of their attachment to one teacher can be upsetting, at least temporarily, and supplies another argument in favor of the child-centered classroom, where children may develop close relationships with several teachers at a time. The trainee for the self-contained class will need special guidance in dealing with the sense of loss felt by some of the students and the resentment and testing of limits she may consequently encounter.

## Individual Conferences

In conjunction with on-the-job training, the new teacher needs time with the trainer to go over the philosophy point by point. Using this book or materials condensed or excerpted from this book in the form of a booklet or series of handouts, the trainee should have the time to skim the high points before on-the-job training begins. While on the job, the trainee can refer to the training materials for more detail; after the period of classroom training, he or she will certainly have questions as to why things are done the way they are. The new teacher is also likely to ask how to apply specific principles to specific children encountered during the training period.

The length of a training conference and the level of detail are individual decisions. Too much too soon may confuse and overwhelm the new teacher. No matter how much he or she appears to absorb at one sitting, a new teacher will forget how to apply a good portion of it when the time comes. It may be best during the first few weeks to hold shorter and more frequent conferences so the trainee can sort out and digest more and more detail. This also allows the trainee time to ask questions while they are still relevant and fresh. These conferences also serve the purpose of developing a rapport between the new teacher and the trainer and give the trainer insight into the new teacher and the progress he or she is making.

## Training Experienced Teachers

We are almost at the end of the book, and in this section I would like to share something with those of you who have come this far. I hope that you have developed more than just a passing interest in the child-centered, problem-solving philosophy I have described. With that in mind, I want to reveal to you what I believe could be the most challenging circumstance in which you would find yourself using this philosophy.

It is possible that you may be called on to supervise, teach, or train teachers and assistants who are already working in a program and are using either their own individual approach or a different approach espoused by the center. Some of these people may have as much education and perhaps even more experience than you, yet you may have been selected for such a position because of your problem-solving approach to working with children. Your position might be that of director, program supervisor, staff trainer, head teacher, or something similar. Because you did not hire all the teachers you must train, you cannot know in advance how they will respond to you and to a new philosophy. The staff may include some teachers who are eager and willing to learn, some who are indifferent, and some who are strongly (and vocally) opposed to any change. The teachers who were already working at the center may be either receptive, resentful, or somewhere in between. You will need some strategies to help you succeed in such a situation. Following are my suggestions:

1.  Never make assumptions about what people think or believe. Begin your job by listening, learning about the existing program, accepting people as they are, and observing them work without communicating criticism or judgment. Plan to give yourself a period of time, whether a few weeks or months, to get to know the staff. You may need to share this plan with the person who hired you or the board of directors to let them know that you are aware of problems but want to gain the trust of your staff before instituting radical change.

2.  Become acquainted with the children and the parents in the program and build relationships. Mention casually and informally the changes you plan to make. Begin using the problem-solving approach when you are with the children to act as a role model for

the teachers to observe. You may feel nervous and insecure about being observed, but keep in mind that you are there not to "perform" but to teach. If you make a "mistake," use the opportunity to talk about another way you could have tried. Your successes may inspire other teachers to try, too.

3. Hold a formal parent-teacher meeting for the purpose of introducing the new program and philosophy to everyone involved. Be well prepared to answer questions from even your worst critics. There will probably be some questions that are meant to confront your beliefs and cast doubt on the philosophy. Remember that not every problem requires an instant solution. Problem solving is an approach that is purposely flexible, but the major principle is always that children are treated with respect and accepted for who they are. It is usually better to say "I'm not sure but I'll think about it and let you know" rather than grasp at any answer that sounds good. A good way to introduce the problem-solving philosophy is by using posters, such as those in the appendix of this book, to focus attention on the most important points. Be enthusiastic and animated; problem solving should never be dull or boring.

4. When you begin training teachers, explain your overall goals for the program as clearly and directly as you can. Then divide your goals into small steps. These steps should be arranged sequentially and kept simple so that teachers feel they can easily succeed at each step. You may want to follow the sequence of the chapters in this book, beginning with an overview and advancing to the environment. Involve the teachers in each area in determining what changes are needed to make the environment supportive of the problem-solving approach. Be firm about any changes you believe are absolutely critical to the program and be flexible about non-essentials. You will find that eventually, as they become more accepting, the teachers will ask for even more changes than you recommended to accommodate the philosophy. After emphasizing the environment, concentrate on supervision, then active listening, and so on. Apply what you have learned about the staff to the methods you employ for training them. The better your teaching methods match the staff's learning style, the easier the transition will be for everyone.

5. Throughout this process, it is critical that you remain focused on your ultimate goal: to teach and apply the problem-solving philosophy to every staff member and to transform the program. Keep your attitude positive and, when needed, enlist moral support from any supporters. If your job is to be the leader, you must be a leader with high ideals and standards, but one who can lead with

compassion and empathy. Your guidance should be firm and gentle at the same time. Changes do not have to happen instantly or perfectly, but have faith that they will happen in time.

6. As you progress through the steps of getting acquainted, making gradual changes, and actually training teachers, it is possible that someone (or even more than one) will remain a dissenter and either try to undermine the process or blatantly refuse to participate. At that point, there are a few options open to you, depending on your position in the program. You may be able to spend extra time with that individual, discussing her problems and concerns and asking for her cooperation. You may assign her this book to read, then hold discussion sessions with her. Or you may be able to give her some long periods of time to observe other, more committed teachers. Perhaps she could temporarily, or even permanently, trade jobs with another teacher or assistant so she can work with someone who enjoys using problem solving.

The last resort is, of course, to terminate this employee. Some teachers may simply decide to leave because they hold such strong opposition to the philosophy or some aspect of the program you may have introduced. It is natural that you would feel responsible or even guilty about this separation; however, it is best for the program and especially for the children that all teachers be committed to the philosophy, work as a team, and strive to become the best possible teachers of problem solving. It is always upsetting to lose an employee, but it is realistic to expect that some teachers are not suited to and will refuse to work in a problem-solving approach. Be gracious, wish that teacher well, and search for someone who will be delighted to work in your program.

## *Staff Meetings*

The very words "staff meeting" conjure up images of boredom and tedium for many people. These are not attractive images. A staff meeting often consists of a supervisor lecturing and criticizing those who are under her and giving out information that is unwanted and impractical to use. Some staff meetings are reduced to gab fests and gossip sessions with little direction and even less accomplishment. The ideal staff meeting should have direction and focus and bring relevant and useful information to the staff. It should also provide a relaxed and sociable atmosphere in which business matters are interspersed with laughing and talking. After all, whether the staff meeting is held during working hours or after work, the goal is for everyone to gather willingly and eagerly with the expectation that what they learn from the meeting will make their daily jobs more rewarding. To make the staff meeting that appealing, some planning is in order.

The staff meeting should be a mandatory part of every staff member's job description. Without the support of the group and the upgrading of everyone's skills, those skills may begin to erode or risk being lost. Whether the staff meeting is weekly or monthly, all staff members should be expected to attend and should be paid for their time. One strategy for assuring attendance is to mark staff meetings for the entire year on a centrally located calendar. Then, several days before the meeting, post a notice to remind everyone of the date and time. On the notice, write the name of every staff member and ask each one to initial or otherwise indicate that he or she has read the notice. Depending on the size of the staff, it may be possible to change the date and time if someone cannot come. If staff meetings are weekly, this may not be practical. If they are monthly, it may, indeed, be easy to change the date.

Who should plan the staff meeting depends on the size of the staff, the involvement of the owner and director (who may be the same person), and the number of other qualified teachers. Teachers in various departments, such as infants, may need a portion of time to meet among themselves before or after the general meeting. The head of their department would probably plan that part of the meeting. Responsibility for planning may be assumed by the directors or department supervisors, or different parts of the meeting could be planned by various teachers. As long as the meeting is carried out effectively and all staff members have a chance to air their concerns, the meeting should be a success.

There are no hard-and-fast rules about what should actually take place at a staff meeting, and much depends on the length of the meeting. When the meeting occurs right after closing time, the staff might appreciate a meal of some sort. If the center itself can afford to send out for pizza, Chinese or Mexican food, hamburgers, or fish and chips (all relatively inexpensive) or if the staff takes up a collection to do so, a meal together gives the staff time to wind down, socialize, and solve their hunger problems. If the staff members prefer to provide their own food or have had time to eat at home, there can still be a brief time for socializing. Many teachers hardly see each other during work time, and, if they do, there is little time for conversation.

Another way to get the meeting off to a good start is to break the ice with a game or activity, which should be brief and fun to do, something that involves everyone. Some ideas for games and activities are given in the next section. After these preliminaries, there may be items of business to discuss, such as an upcoming event, a new piece of equipment, fire and safety information, children who are entering or leaving the program, jobs that need doing, or organizational tasks to be done. These topics should be of general enough interest to be brought up briefly at the meeting. After such business comes the heart and substance of the meeting, which is working to improve the skills teachers need in the problem-solving philosophy. There are many ways to accomplish this. One teacher may be particularly proficient in some aspect of problem solving and lead a discussion on that topic. Visual aids may be used or written handouts provided to support the subject being discussed. Another teacher may prefer to demonstrate a point, engaging the help of other teachers. Sometimes role playing may be the most effective tool. I discuss this more fully in "Role Playing" later in this chapter.

At every meeting, there should be an opportunity for problems pertaining to specific children to be brought up and discussed by the group. A teacher may feel stuck and think that no one else is having this problem or may be unable to figure out the best approach. In a situation like this, group input is very helpful and supportive and relieves the teacher's feeling of isolation. Problems with children tend to repeat themselves, and, often, more experienced teachers have dealt with similar problems and can offer suggestions. Another problem area may be interacting with parents. Sometimes a teacher needs discussion and support for dealing with certain parents. Staff meetings present such an opportunity for discussion. As mentioned, written material for teachers to keep and use for reference is important to any program. I discuss the use of materials in "Materials for Training" later in this chapter. First, the staff meeting begins with laughter.

## Ice-Breaking Games and Activities

A game that breaks the ice at a staff meeting should fit the spirit of the problem-solving philosophy. Everyone wins; no one loses; there is a spirit of cooperation rather than competition. The idea is to have fun but at no one's expense. The game should be playful and support trust and respect at the same time. Fortunately, there are now many books available that are filled with such games for both children and adults. Some of these books are listed at the end of this chapter.

One favorite game that requires no book is "Follow the Leader." Whoever is chosen to be the leader leads the group on a child's-eye tour of the center. The tour may include crawling across floors or running across the slide. (It is assumed that everyone will be dressed in casual work attire.) The more childlike and adventurous the leader, the more fun everyone will have. A less active but nevertheless hilarious game is "Barnyard." Various versions are found in books. One version involves writing down the names of farm animals such as cows, pigs, chickens, horses, goats, and others that make distinct sounds. There should be at least three or four of each animal. Teachers then draw the animals' names. With eyes closed (no cheating), everyone gets down on the floor and makes the sound of his or her animal. From hearing sounds, the "animals" try to find their own kind and get close to them. The game ends when everyone has found the right group.

Another ice-breaking game that encourages cooperation is "Cooperative Musical Chairs." It begins like ordinary musical chairs, but as the chairs are removed the players help each other find places to sit. There may be two or three sitting on one another's lap, or some players may make themselves into chairs on the floor and invite others to sit on them. By the time the last chair is removed, everyone is on the floor, reduced to laughter. A similar game is "Musical Hoops." Hula hoops are laid on the floor; everyone dances or skips around them until the music stops; then everyone jumps into a hoop. As the hoops are removed, more and more players must squeeze into fewer hoops and finally only one hoop.

One last example of a game for breaking the ice is "Washing Machine." Each player decides to be an item of clothing in the washing machine. The leader then calls out parts of the washing cycle (such as wash, soak, spin, and rinse), and the clothing responds accordingly. Players can also go through the dryer together. Many of these games can be found through word of mouth and in books; it is fun for the leader to explore the possibilities. They are guaranteed to get the staff meeting off to a good start.

There are also activities, such as those one would do with children, that promote goodwill and social interactions among the teachers. Some of these may be seasonal, such as making valentines. Teachers secretly draw each other's names and use materials such as red, white, and pink construction paper, stickers, ribbons, and glitter to make a valentine for the person whose name they drew. Lots of humorous interactions take place during the activity time, and everyone receives a reward when the valentines are distributed.

Another seasonal activity may happen at an October staff meeting. Each teacher is given a small pumpkin (pick various shapes) and the kind of marking pens that will write on a pumpkin. The teachers secretly choose one of the children in the center and try to make their pumpkin look like that child. Then they take turns describing some of their child's characteristics, and everyone tries to guess which child it is. The teachers may keep their pumpkins or leave them as decorations for the center. The children need not know that the pumpkins were supposed to represent any of them, although, if they are told, they will love the idea.

A similar activity can be done with eggs in the springtime, or teachers may use live flowers to make May baskets. The December staff meeting might be a potluck dinner with families invited and little or no business included. This is another way to bring a team spirit to the staff. Depending on religious or cultural considerations, December may be a good month for starting and continuing a tradition. One such tradition is to buy an assortment of holiday tree ornaments, preferably the funny, whimsical kind, hang them on a branch of some sort, and invite each staff member to claim one. The ornaments need not be expensive, but the tradition is one that many staff members look forward to in December.

Teachers who know that their staff meetings will start with play and humor usually look forward to staff meetings with at least some degree of anticipation. However, there are shy people in the early childhood field as in any profession, so it is important to be sensitive when planning icebreakers. No one should feel singled out or intimidated; indeed, the goal is just the opposite. An icebreaker should help all the participants relax, feel included in the group, and sense that they are trusted and respected.

## Role Playing

After the icebreaker and items of business are concluded, it is time for training teachers, improving skills, and applying the problem-solving philosophy. One of the most effective ways to learn and improve skills is through role playing. Role playing works especially well with the problem-solving philosophy because it enables those participants who take on the roles of children to actually feel the way children would feel and to contribute their own ideas for solving problems. No lecture or discussion, however well presented, can convey those same feelings. Actually "becoming" a small child for a few minutes can change one's perspective of the world. When facing a conflict with another "child" or when challenging limits set by a larger, more powerful "teacher," there is an empathy for the child's position that stays with the teacher when he or she is relating to real children.

Role playing is the act of pretending to be someone else. For the purpose of teaching young children, the staff members pretend to be infants, toddlers, or preschoolers; they also pretend to be teachers. Each role-play consists of setting a scene that visually portrays a problem that is occurring among certain children in the program. The scene may be set in various ways. It may be planned ahead of time by whoever plans the staff meeting. In that case, the basic elements of the scene may be written on an index card, which will be given to one of the teachers at the meeting. While planning the staff meeting, the planners consider any problem they have observed since the last staff meeting and convert it into a role-play. Before their planning session, the planners should also ask teachers to contribute their own ideas for role-plays based on their own problem areas. The role-plays may be written in a variety of formats, such as these:

> Two young, preverbal toddlers want the same toy.
> Needed: One teacher, two toddlers.

> You are eight months old and interested in younger babies. You love to pinch and poke at their eyes.
> Choose someone to be the baby you pick on.
> Choose someone to be the teacher.

> Jarret is six months old. He is very sleepy but won't fall asleep. He just cries and cries.
> Needed: Jarret and his teacher.

> One preschooler knocks down a smaller child and runs away. The teacher deals with this.
> You may be the teacher or either child or another teacher who is in the yard. Please choose three others.

Most role-plays and the discussion that follows them take between ten and fifteen minutes to complete, so there may be time for only three or four at a meeting. It is desirable, but not always possible, to include every teacher in at least one of the role-plays. There are various ways to decide who will participate in the role playing. In some groups, simply asking for volunteers brings enough participants, although they may be the same volunteers every time. In other groups, people may be shy or inhibited, and the leader may have to assign roles or assign a card to one teacher and allow her to choose her fellow role players. People who are shy may resist taking part. It is best not to make an issue of it. Perhaps they'll agree to play an infant or a preverbal toddler later. Some people love playing children who are behaving inappropriately. They seem to identify with the aggressor. Fewer are willing to take on the teacher role in front of their peers. The leader can only do her best to help everyone feel relaxed and comfortable about playing any role.

There is another way to approach role playing. That is to allow it to occur spontaneously during discussion at the staff meeting. A problem or a certain child's behavior may be the topic of discussion, and the problem may lend itself to role playing. An alert leader recognizes the opportunity and invites the staff to role-play the problem. This method may seem less threatening to some people than a preplanned session of role playing, but it is a rather unpredictable way to tackle problems. A combination of both preplanned and spontaneous role playing may be effective. In order to give the reader a clear idea of how role playing works, an example of a staff of twelve teachers using role playing as a learning tool follows.

The teachers are sitting around the room in an informal circle on the floor. Some are leaning on pillows or against the wall, or they may be sitting in child-sized chairs. The director, head teacher, supervisor, or whoever is leading the role playing passes out an index card to every third teacher, going around the room. On each card is written a scene depicting a problem and the players needed to role-play it. The leader chooses one of the card holders to begin the session. The card holder, Joan, has a card that says: "Three two-year-olds are playing with the train set. Two of them start taking the parts away from the third one, who only cries and refuses to talk. Needed are three children and one teacher."

Joan decides that she will play one of the aggressors and chooses from the group two other people to play the remaining children and one other person to play the teacher. She chooses among the people who are not holding the remaining cards. This helps get everyone involved in the role-play. If the players who are chosen prefer to trade roles with each other, this is acceptable. The more comfortable all are with their roles, the better they will play them.

The players move to the center of the room, and Joan describes the scenario to players and spectators. If the scene fits certain children, Joan assigns their names to the players. Naming the children helps the players identify with the children whose parts they are playing. If props are used, such as the train set, they are also put in the middle of the room. The three "children" sit on the floor and play with the train set. The "teacher" positions herself appropriately. The adults taking the part of children use the names Jonny, Robert, and Kelly. The teacher, Debbie, keeps her own name. The children are on the floor playing with the train set. Suddenly, Kelly grabs a small train away from Robert. Jonny follows her lead and grabs the piece of train track from in front of Robert. Robert begins to cry. (As Robert cries loudly, there are chuckles from the spectators. The players try to ignore the chuckles and proceed.) Kelly and Jonny, playing two-year-olds, say "I want it" and "My train." As Robert cries, the two other children seem oblivious to him and continue to play with the train set. The teacher, Debbie, approaches, kneels down, and puts her arm around Robert, making eye contact. She says, "It sounds like you're upset. Do you want to talk to someone?" Robert continues to cry without stopping to talk.

During the role-play, it is important for both the players and the spectators to take their parts seriously. The players should come away with an idea of how it feels to be a child in that position. How did it feel to be Kelly and Jonny, powerful enough to take another child's toy and reduce him to tears? How did it feel to Robert, outnumbered by uncaring children who he thought were his friends? Could the presence of the teacher give Robert some self-confidence? Could he overcome his self-pity and call on his inner resources? In a well-enacted role-play, teachers should develop their sense of empathy toward the children they play. The person who plays the teacher should also learn and grow from the experience. She is the one who must function in her real-life role in front of her peers. As they observe her, the spectators recognize their own similar strengths and weaknesses. Figure 10.1 shows teachers role playing.

Leadership is important in role playing. Without strong leadership, the entire experience may be reduced to silliness. Teachers should be asked ahead of time to act their parts as realistically as possible, and spectators should be asked to observe thoughtfully and respectfully. For some people, role playing is embarrassing, and they are easily distracted by the audience's reactions. It is the leader's job to offer encouragement to the players and perhaps even set some limits if the spectators forget their role as observers.

As the one who plays the teacher in the role-play carries out the assigned role, there may be the feeling that the child players are not responding as expected. If the "teacher" feels stuck and forgets the alternatives, it may be a good idea to stop and ask the audience for help. This is a perfectly legitimate move, and, if the spectators have been observing thoughtfully, one of them will probably have some good advice to offer. That person may even enter the role-play and act out the suggested idea. The goal is always to help the children solve their problem, and there should be no feeling of competition or superiority among the teachers. Good ideas are helpful to everyone and are meant to be shared.

**Figure 10.1**    *Role playing is an excellent training tool for teachers. During role playing, teachers can learn how it feels to be children with a problem to be solved.*

The role-play is usually over when the players feel that there has been a resolution or they have reached a stalemate. As in real life, problems are not always solved neatly, according to adult standards. In this example, the teacher was able to give Robert enough support that he could stop crying long enough to express himself verbally. When he could say "Mine" to the other children and let them know that he still wanted his part of the train set, the teacher used active listening and negotiating. The three children returned to playing cooperatively with the train set, and the problem was solved.

The period of time after the role-play is as important as the role-play itself because it is a time when the leader asks the players to express to the group how it felt to them to be the children they were playing. What, if any, insight was gained by the experience? How did they feel about the teacher's interactions and the way the problem was handled? Did the teacher get down to the children's level and make eye contact? How did her arm feel around Robert? Did her voice sound neutral and respectful? Did the players feel satisfied with the solution, or were feelings left unexpressed? What about the teacher? Did she feel that the players responded as real children would? Did they take their roles seriously? This is also a time for the spectators to offer positive reinforcement or constructive advice to the teacher. The more involved everyone becomes, the more benefit will be derived from the role-playing experience. The leader may also have remarks to make, but again, this should not become an exercise in competition or criticism. Everyone should come out of the experience feeling enriched and enlightened.

Almost any kind of problem or situation can be used for role playing, depending on the number of staff members. If there are fewer than four teachers, some situations may be difficult to play. But it is possible for even two teachers to do some role playing of certain problems. Following are a number of examples of role-playing scenes.

A toddler bites another child. Needed are one teacher and two children.

A three-year-old is working on a hard puzzle. He works on it for a short time, then leaves. When the teacher brings him back, he keeps leaving. Needed are one teacher and one child.

A fourteen-month-old child goes from toy to toy, dumping them on the floor. Needed are one teacher and one child.

An older infant is constantly taking toys away from younger babies. Needed are one older infant, one younger infant, and one teacher.

Two preschoolers are on the climbing structure. They begin to push each other. Needed are two children and one teacher.

A toddler is throwing blocks at other children. Needed are three or four children and one teacher.

A three-year-old tries to take a riding toy away from a less verbal two-year-old. Needed are two children and one teacher.

A child of any age asks the teacher to come look at the picture she painted. Needed are one child and one teacher.

Several toddlers are in a room waiting for lunch. They are bored and hungry. Needed are several toddlers and one teacher.

A child's mother leaves, and the child is crying. Needed are one child, one mother, and one teacher.

A teacher is reading a story to a group of preschoolers, and one child keeps standing up, talking, and interrupting. Needed are several children and one teacher.

An older infant or younger toddler is getting his diaper changed. He begins to explore his genitals. Needed are one child and one teacher.

An eighteen-month-old wants to go down the slide but is afraid. She tries to get the teacher to hold her as she climbs the ladder and goes down the slide. Needed are one child and one teacher.

A preschooler comes to tell the teacher that something was done to her by another child. Needed are two children and one teacher.

A twenty-two-month-old loves to paint on everything, including other children's work. The others get upset at this. Needed are two or three children and one teacher.

The teacher is watching a group of toddlers when a parent arrives and engages her in a long conversation. Needed are five or six toddlers, one parent, and one teacher.

A two-year-old tries to take a toy away from another, equally matched two year old. Needed are two children and one teacher.

Three older preschoolers want to have a tea party but want to exclude a younger preschooler. Needed are four children and one teacher.

A three-year-old is teasing younger children. He gets his friends to join him. Needed are four or five children and one teacher.

## Discussing Problems

Although role playing is perhaps the most effective training tool, it is not always the most appropriate. Teachers also tire of it if it's used too often. Sometimes what is needed is a way of sharing information, frustrations, and creative ideas. This can be accomplished through discussion. There are two main varieties of discussion. One is more formal: A leader may use a poster, a chart, written handouts, or other visual aids to focus the group on a particular point of philosophy or a problem area. This type of lecture discussion may become boring unless the leader can successfully hold the group's interest and engage them in the discussion.

The second type of discussion is open-ended and informal. The leader might ask, "Does anyone have a problem or a particular child she wants to discuss?" This usually leads to a free-flowing expression of ideas that are shared by teachers. Some teachers may have dealt successfully with the problem; others may share the same problem. During this type of discussion, it is important that the leader keep the group on the subject and direct them toward solutions. Otherwise, such discussions may deteriorate into gabbing or complaining sessions. If a certain child is being discussed, it is also important that the discussion be balanced and bring out his positive side as well as problem areas. Any reasons for the child's behavior, such as his home situation, that are known to the directors and are not too confidential to reveal should be explained to the teachers. This helps them view the child with greater empathy and perhaps greater determination to relate positively to him. During discussion sessions, it is important to refer to the problem-solving philosophy and try to discuss problems from the child's point of view and with the child's perception in mind. The goal, as always, is to involve the child in the solution.

There is probably no need for further discussion on how to talk through or role-play problems. In "Materials for Training," I present ideas for conducting planned, formal discussions. There are also many other activities that can be incorporated into staff meetings. Some are found in the section "Retreats."

## Intergenerational Teacher Training

On the subject of training staff for intergenerational programs, we hear from another expert in the field, Vicki Rosebrook, director of intergenerational studies at the University of Findlay, Ohio.

> The Lifelong Educational Center is a new and innovative program at the University of Findlay. Children are combined with residents at Winebrenner Village, a living center for senior adults. When we combined the children and elderly residents, we combined the staffs at the child care center and the long-term care facility as well. Each of these facilities had its own style of teaching, terminology, and ideas relating to client care; this created many problems. Key terms had different meanings for each group, so discussing and solving problems presented a challenge. We had to get everyone "on the same page" so that training would benefit both groups. We realized that the staffs of the two facilities must be cross-trained so they would be united in a common goal. Our objective was to model a supportive, collaborative practice that would provide exemplary intergenerational care.
>
> There were many "unknowns" and no guidelines for educating two such different groups, but we were excited by these challenges. We had many years of combined professional experiences, supportive administrations, and enthusiastic staff members who would bring our dream to fruition. We had a proverbial blank canvas on which to create something extraordinary from many fragmented pieces.
>
> We began by establishing common terminologies to help communication flow more easily. We discovered that many terms held similar meanings but were perceived differently by the geriatric and early childhood staffs. We listened carefully to what people were really saying, and by structuring our plan of action around the sentiments expressed we were able to help both groups discover that they had much in common. The similar experiences in each of these unique professions are now helping bridge the gaps that had first divided them. In the end, we succeeded in developing an effective and responsive line of communication. Happily, both children and residents are now reaping the benefits (Figure 10.2).

## Managing Stress

As in every occupation, there are certain stresses connected with caring for children. It is important that teachers be aware of stress and its causes and symptoms. If they are not, they may suffer from it without realizing the source of their discomfort. Because teachers are responsible for the safety

**Figure 10.2**    *Cross training assures that the residential care staff (background) and the child care staff (foreground) are "on the same page."*

and well-being of children, they may feel guilty and inadequate when their performance on the job does not meet their own standards. We all have days when we go home feeling we have failed in some way to be the "perfect" teacher. We blame ourselves or perhaps blame the children. Feelings of inadequacy send our self-esteem plummeting, even if only temporarily.

Rather than trying to blame ourselves or the children, we should examine the underlying causes of our stress and attempt to counteract them. The same goal of helping children understand and express their primary feelings applies to teachers when they are trying to deal with their feelings of stress. The staff meeting provides a perfect setting for discussing stress, gaining group support, and finding solutions. Of course, we all carry stresses from home to the workplace, and, if there is enough trust and rapport among teachers, it may be appropriate to express those personal feelings in the group. More appropriate is dealing with the stresses that may emanate from the workplace itself.

Some common stresses for teachers are trying to care for too many children within too small an area; a high level of noise and crying; friction between teachers who work together; gossiping on the job; unpleasant encounters with parents; lack of appreciation and support from some parents, supervisors, or both; and inadequate training for their job. Often overlooked is the very nature of caring for children. In many professions, there is a general feeling of recognition from the client himself if he has been well served. Sometimes it takes the form of financial reward. In a children's program, however, the real client is the child, and, although young children generously return love and affection, they seldom say "You did a great job watching me today" or "Thank you for your hard work on my behalf." Teachers rarely receive such verbal reinforcement from children in their care. They must be satisfied with the feeling that they have nurtured their children in some way throughout the day and have returned the children intact to their parents. Of course, hugs, smiles, and shared giggles are in themselves enormous rewards.

There are many ways to reduce stress on the job, but mainly what is required is teamwork and cooperation among supervisors and staff alike. The problem-solving philosophy works with adults as well as children and should be the basis for solving problems that result in stress. When there is a problem between teachers, for example, a neutral teacher or director can serve as a facilitator to enable the teachers to talk it out. Active listening, negotiation, and positive reinforcement should be part of the process of working out problems among the staff.

There are many books and courses on managing and reducing stress in the workplace, and it may benefit the staff to investigate the value of these courses for use at staff meetings. But perhaps the most powerful stress reducer is the teacher's own sense of humor. Laughter is a potent antidote to stress and especially helps to put things into perspective. We are, after all, involved in a joyful profession and lucky enough to be sharing the daily unfolding of wisdom and delight through the eyes of children. My own amazement never ceases when it comes to learning about myself, humanity, and the world from a child's point of view. It is what keeps us coming back for more.

## Room or Section Meetings

In addition to the general staff meeting, a brief, weekly meeting of the teachers in each room or section is invaluable (Figure 10.3). If the program is fortunate enough to have a separate program supervisor or assistant director, or an on-site trainer, one of her priorities should be to spend at least several hours in each room or section in the center every week. During that time, she should work with and alongside the teachers in that section as one of them in order to better understand their needs and problems. She can also observe their interactions with the children and with one another, evaluate the organization of the room, and notice any flaws in the system. It is also a good time to take note of the condition and accessibility of the toys and materials and know when new items are needed. It may help to carry a notepad so she can jot down what she wants to remember.

**Figure 10.3**  *Teachers need a weekly planning session.*

On the same day she spends time in this particular room, the supervisor should lead a meeting of just the teachers in that area. The meeting may last only thirty minutes and be held during the children's nap time. This may require rearranging some teachers' lunch breaks, but it is worth the effort. Everyone, including the supervisor, should be able to bring up problems and concerns and deal with them before they become bigger. Addressing issues as they arise reduces stress and keeps the section running smoothly. If possible, the same group of teachers should have some planning time together, with or without a supervisor. This might be achieved by lengthening the weekly meeting and dividing it into business and planning or by arranging for a second short meeting every week during which the teachers can plan circle times, group activities, changes in the environment, field trips, and other aspects of the program. The benefits of giving teachers time to work together as a team are enormous.

## Individual Planning Times

In addition to meeting as a group, every teacher needs time to gather materials for a group activity, work on record keeping, call to enlist parents for a field trip, learn a new song for circle time, and take care of other tasks. A head teacher at least should be allowed a half-hour or more several times a week when someone else can take her place in the classroom. Having a relief system is another stress reducer; a major complaint among teachers is the lack of off-floor planning time.

## Learning to Talk to Parents

Parents of every child in every center have some concern, some anxiety, some feeling of guilt, or some unasked question. This statement does not come from a researched study on parents; it is simply an observation made during years of experience. No matter how excellent the care that is given, parents worry about something. In effect, it is their job to be concerned for the well-being and safety of their child. There is also a basic conflict. Parents want their child to like and become attached to their teacher, but parents also want to be the primary people in their child's life. They want and have a right to feel that their child loves them first and best and that no one will come between their child and themselves. Therefore, any teacher who cares for children must also learn to care for parents. Too often parents are perceived as the enemy: They do not know how to rear their children properly; the parents are either too strict or they "spoil" their children. There are teachers who believe that there is only one right way to rear a child, and they ridicule parents who have different ideas. This self-righteous attitude and insensitivity are felt by the parents and only make them more concerned, anxious, and guilt ridden.

A big part of any teacher's job is to earn the trust of parents as well as children. When young parents bring their first tiny infant to a stranger for care, they are facing one of the most difficult moments of their lives: turning over a big part of their baby's life to someone else. Many of them cry when leaving their child for the first time and may become depressed. Even if working outside the home is an absolute necessity, the parent has a feeling of guilt. "Why am I not taking care of my own baby? What kind of parent am I, leaving him this way?" they ask themselves. Even if the child is a toddler or preschooler, parents sometimes feel as if they are abandoning her.

Although it is usually the director or head teacher who has the most contact with parents, every teacher should be able to communicate clearly and sensitively with them. Even an assistant, a cook, or a janitor can smile and make parents feel welcome. The training in active listening that the staff receives should certainly be applied to parents and could be the basis for role playing as well. Parents should be encouraged to express their feelings and even criticism. When staff members are open to the parents' feelings and criticism, the program can only benefit.

It is my opinion and policy that new parents deserve to be pampered and spoiled. The infant staff should be willing to spend time talking with them; should always have positive things to say about their baby; should be sure the baby's diaper bag, bottles, and clothes are organized and ready for the parents at the end of the day; and should generally cater to them as much as possible. Usually, the head infant teacher does most of the conversing, but she cannot be there from opening to closing, so other infant teachers should also make parents feel as comfortable as possible. There are, of course, times when caring for the infants themselves is too intense and time-consuming to allow teachers to stop and talk, but even when teachers are busy, parents should be treated with respect and sensitivity. Most parents are themselves sensitive to the need for caring first and foremost for the babies. The care and attention new parents need is another reason for keeping a high ratio of teachers to infants.

When infants become toddlers, the required ratio of teachers to children changes, giving teachers less time to attend to the needs of parents. If the program is a child-centered classroom, there will probably be a director or coordinator available to spend time responding to parents' questions and concerns and to help find missing items. There may, in fact, be a program policy regarding whether teachers are expected to discuss problems with parents or how long teachers should spend talking to parents. A good rule of thumb is that, if the conversation draws the teacher's attention from the children she is watching, the teacher says something like "I wish I could spend more time with you, but my group really needs my attention. Do you have a minute to talk this over with our director?" Parents are almost always understanding and even appreciate the attention shown to the children. If this system does not work in your program, the teacher is probably expected to take time from her group to respond to parental concerns. The teacher in this position needs to learn to walk a tightrope, knowing how much time is appropriate to give the parents without taking the teacher's attention from the group. She should avoid any lengthy discussions by asking the parents if they can talk about the problem later on the phone or if they wish to set up a conference to explore the problem more fully.

Parents of toddlers have the same feelings as parents of infants. In addition, their child's behavior often increases their guilty feelings. Many toddlers cry and cling to parents when they leave, although moments after the parents depart the child is playing happily with her friends. The child is letting her parents know that she protests being separated from them and that she will miss them. Mom and dad, however, feel like criminals.

When parents come to pick up their child after work, they should never be met with a negative report of their child's behavior that day. Even if it is absolutely necessary that the behavior be discussed, it can wait until parent and child have had a chance to greet each other joyfully at the day's end. After all, the parent has been working all day, is tired, and wants to get home to eat dinner and relax with his family. The last thing he wants to hear immediately on arriving at day care is that Billy has been a terror all day and has driven the teacher crazy or that Jane has bitten several children throughout the day. Billy, Jane, and their parents deserve some time to simply be glad and relieved that they made it through the day.

If there is a problem that requires discussion, the director or teacher should first decide whether it can best be handled in the child's presence or a more private phone call or appointment would be better. Although it is easy and tempting to discuss the problem immediately, while the child is still present, it is important that the discussion be handled discreetly so that other parents do not overhear and so that adults never talk over the heads of children. If the child is within hearing distance, he should not be discussed as if he were not there or did not understand. This is a very common act of rudeness that adults commit against children, and it is often hard for teachers to avoid. Parents themselves are usually the culprits. Even when they are holding the child in their arms, they talk about her in the third person.

There are some subtle yet effective ways for the teacher to avoid becoming involved in such a situation. When the teacher must bring up a problem, she can begin by using phrases that are neutral rather than blaming. For example, instead of saying that Billy's behavior was awful, the phrase "Billy had a hard day today" indicates that there were problems but does not indicate that Billy purposely created the problems. If Billy is hearing this conversation, he should be directly included in it.

Here is an example. After Billy, age three, and his father have greeted each other, the teacher feels that she must bring up a problem that arose during the day.

TEACHER
TO PARENT:    Billy had a hard day today. He may want to tell you about it.

*The teacher gives Billy a chance to respond before proceeding.*

TEACHER
TO BILLY:    I'm feeling that you were angry today, Billy, and that may be why you kicked several of your friends. You did have some nice times playing, too, but the kicking really hurt.

TEACHER
TO BILLY
AND PARENT:    I hope you get a chance to talk about it. If I can help, let me know.

What about Jane and her biting? Because most biters are under age two, here is an example with a younger, less verbal child. After they greet each other, Jane's mother picks her up to leave.

TEACHER TO
PARENT:    It seemed that whenever Jane couldn't find the right words to say, she became frustrated and bit someone. I was wondering if she has been biting at home, too.

TEACHER TO

JANE:    Do you remember that we talked about biting? Biting hurts kids.

*The teacher waits a few seconds to see if Jane responds.*

PARENT:    Jane has bitten me several times, but I don't know what to do about it. I'm really sorry she's been biting kids.

TEACHER TO

JANE:    Maybe it would help if I tell your mom what we do when kids bite here at day care. Do you remember what we say? We say, "Biting hurts! It's not OK to bite other kids." And we move you away from other kids until you've finished biting.

PARENT:    Maybe that's what I should do when Jane bites me. I guess it's worth a try.

TEACHER TO

PARENT:    When toddlers bite, it's usually because they can't express themselves well verbally.

TEACHER TO

CHILD:    Jane, when you can say more words, you won't feel so much like biting. But for now we can't let you hurt other kids.

Even when the child concerned is a tiny infant who seems to be unaware of what is being said, the parent and teacher can still include him in the discussion by using his name, making eye contact with him, and speaking directly to him (Figure 10.4).

TEACHER TO

PARENT:    Danny has been unusually fussy today but didn't have any signs of illness.

TEACHER TO

DANNY:    This was a rough day today, wasn't it? I hope tomorrow is a better day.

PARENT:    Oh, yes. Danny's grandparents came to visit last night and wanted to play with him. They kept him up much later than usual. Then I had to wake him up early, so he probably didn't get enough sleep.

TEACHER TO

DANNY:    Sounds like you had a big night last night. Try to get lots of sleep tonight so we can have more fun tomorrow.

Talking to parents about various subjects and under various conditions lends itself to role playing at staff meetings. A program's reputation and the

**Figure 10.4**    *The teacher should always include the child in parent-teacher conversations.*

word-of-mouth referrals given by parents will depend on parents' feeling that they, as well as their children, are treated with respect and sensitivity. Teachers who are short with parents or take a self-righteous attitude are no asset to a program. No matter how good they are with children, they need to work on their social skills with parents.

## The Daily Report

An extremely effective way to communicate with parents is through writing a daily report on every child. This can be accomplished by having each teacher take notes on all the children throughout the morning. Usually, all that is needed is a word or two to describe what the child is doing. If he is playing with another child, jot down that child's name, too. An example of a note on two children playing in the sandbox is "Jack and Jane, sandbox." Note taking is facilitated by having all the children's names on a sheet of paper, leaving a space under each name so the teacher can write in that space. These pages can be made up in advance and photocopied so they are ready every morning. During nap time, the notes should be shared and divided up among the teachers who then write the reports.

In the report, the notes should be transformed into complete sentences, telling a story about the child's morning. The focus should be on that particular child, his activities, and the children with whom he played. Reports should be kept positive; problems and conflicts can be described nonjudgmentally, but save any major problems for a face-to-face conversation or conference with the parents. Parents enjoy reading quotes in their child's own words, especially when they are humorous. Be sure to use correct punctuation, grammar, spelling, and action words, rather than repeating "He did this, then he did that." Two helpful items are a dictionary and an ink eradicator.

The reports should be placed in an easily accessible spot, perhaps taped to the door where parents will see them when they leave. Once parents get into the habit of reading their child's daily report, they look forward to seeing it every day. I know of parents who make scrapbooks out of them, make copies to send to grandparents, and read them out loud at Friday dinner. The reports should remain in the center until the last day of that child's week, then be sent home for parents to keep. Figures 10.5, 10.6, and 10.7 show sample reports that were actually written for three children: an infant, a toddler, and a preschooler. Each report has a slightly different format to fit the needs of the particular age group.

## Retreats

One of the best ways to provide staff training is through a retreat. The retreat not only allows for training; it also gives teachers time to get to know one another in a relaxed atmosphere away from work. Although it is possible to have a one-day retreat and also possible, if finances allow, to have a retreat that lasts for several days, an overnight retreat that includes most of the day before and most of the day after also works well. This section focuses on the overnight retreat, but individual programs can easily shorten or lengthen the time spent. Retreats may be held once a year or more often if they are desired and can be afforded.

There are many approaches to retreats, and I have been involved in several. The viability of each approach depends on many factors. How large is the staff? Are staff members mostly younger or more mature? Are there both men and women? Who is financially responsible for the cost of the retreat? Are teachers paid for their time? Do they pay any of their retreat expenses? What kinds of accommodations are available and affordable in the area? How long will it take to get to them? Will the retreat be planned and carried out by a committee, or will everyone be expected to contribute? How much work, such as cooking and cleaning, should the staff be required to do? These and other questions should be answered when you are trying to determine a program's approach to retreats.

When I worked at the Isabel Patterson Child Development Center at California State University at Long Beach, almost all the teachers were themselves students in their early twenties. They were active, energetic, and had few or no family responsibilities; many knew each other outside of work. Because there was a turnover of staff at semester breaks, retreats were held

# Green Tree Child Care

Name: Caitlin

Week of: 7/25-29

| Day | MEALS | Accidents or Illness / Medicine / Diapers / Nap | ✗ | ACTIVITIES AND PLAYMATES |
|---|---|---|---|---|
| Monday | 8:10 Breakfast 7oz<br>9:30 lunch<br>11:10 lunch<br>3:00 6 oz<br>3:30 snack | Accidents or Illness:<br>Medicine:<br>Diapers: ////<br>Nap: 11:30 - 12:55 | x | Caitlin had been very busy today. She crawled everywhere. She stood up by cabinets, manipulated toys, and played with sand. She also rocked the tent by herself. She enjoyed a lunch of noodles, fruit and milk. She's been happy all day. |
| Tuesday | 8:15 Breakfast<br>10:00 4 oz<br>11:10 lunch<br>1:00 5oz<br>3:15 snack<br>4:50 4oz | Accidents or Illness:<br>Medicine:<br>Diapers: ///<br>Nap: 10:25 - 11:10 | x | Caitlin loved the walk to Westlake Park. She smiled, waved and was so cheerful on the way. She got fresh air and sunshine. Back from the walk, she took a good nap. She played with friends, Mark, Matthew and William. |
| Wednesday | 8:20 Breakfast<br>9:30 2 oz<br>11:00 lunch<br>1:45 5oz<br>4:10 snack | Accidents or Illness:<br>Medicine:<br>Diapers: ++++<br>Nap: 11:20 - 12:15<br>3:22 - 4:00 | x | Caitlin had lots of things to do today. She played on the porch pushing a truck, rolling a ball and crawling around. She rode on the rocking chair. She enjoyed rocking it. She visited the sand bucket to play with sand, too. |
| Thursday | 8:30 Breakfast<br>11:30 lunch<br>11:45 4 oz<br>2:45 snack | Accidents or Illness:<br>Medicine:<br>Diapers: ###<br>Nap: 11:45 - 12:45<br>4:20-5:25 | x | Caitlin had been very active pushing toys, standing by the cabinets. She visited the Toddler class. She loved being there playing with new toys and bigger kids as well. She came back happy and tired, so she ate and slept good. |
| Friday | 8:15 Breakfast<br>11:30 lunch<br>2:00 6 oz<br>3:00 snack<br>4:30 6 oz | Accidents or Illness:<br>Medicine:<br>Diapers: ////<br>Nap: 11:40 - 12:10 | x | Caitlin spent time in the Toddler class today. She also tried to balance herself (stands up not holding onto anything). She was so proud doing this. She looked happy with sparkling eyes. She waved bye-bye to her Dad this morning. |

**Figure 10.5** *Sample report for an infant, written by Corazon Golla.*

# Green Tree Child Care

Week of: 7/11 – 7/15

Name: John

| Day | MEALS | Accidents or Illness |
|-----|-------|----------------------|
| **Monday** | Breakfast — Normal ✓ / Small / None — Lunch — Normal ✓ / Small / None<br>BM's ✓<br>Nap: ✓<br>Medicine: | ACTIVITIES AND PLAYMATES John threw the yellow ball outside. Save time. He also did some water painting outside, rode the motorcycle, climbed on the climber, and sat on the cabin to read a book. He got interested in working on puzzles. In the afternoon → |
| **Tuesday** | Breakfast — Normal ✓ / Small / None — Lunch — Normal ✓ / Small / None<br>BM's ✓<br>Nap: ✗<br>Medicine: | ACTIVITIES AND PLAYMATES John had a really good day. He played in the water table — he tried to drink the water, but before he could the water went out of a hole. He was surprised! He also enjoyed water coloring and bubble painting. John also liked doing an airplane puzzle. → |
| **Wednesday** | Breakfast — Normal / Small / None ✗ — Lunch — Normal / Small / None ✗<br>BM's 3:30<br>Nap: ✗<br>Medicine: | ACTIVITIES AND PLAYMATES John was a bit fussy today as a result of his shots, but he had a pretty good day. He enjoyed playing with the wooden blocks with Cooper & Brandon. He also played with the plastic animals, arranging them on the floor. Outside John enjoyed throwing one of the balls → |
| **Thursday** | Breakfast — Normal / Small / None ✗ — Lunch — Normal / Small / None ✗<br>BM's ✓<br>Nap: ✗<br>Medicine: | ACTIVITIES AND PLAYMATES John had an active day today. He spent a lot of time on the silver climber outside. He also drove the pink car and one of the tricycles. While inside John enjoyed playing in the sensory tables, especially the corn meal, which he tried to sweep off the floor with a broom → |
| **Friday** | Breakfast — Normal / Small / None ✗ — Lunch — Normal / Small / None ✗<br>BM's 11:30<br>Nap: ✗<br>Medicine: | ACTIVITIES AND PLAYMATES John had a great day! He especially enjoyed painting and did several pictures. He also did a lot of climbing on the silver climber outside — he seems to like climbing! John chased after bubbles and even tried to blow them himself. John also spent some time with Alexander → |

**Figure 10.6** *Sample report for a toddler, written by Megan Stout.*

## Green Tree Preschool

Name: **William**  
Week of: **1-11-95**

| Day | Meals/Care | | Domains | Comments |
|---|---|---|---|---|
| **Monday** | Breakfast ∅<br>Lunch ✓<br>Nap ✓ | Medication<br><br>Miscellaneous<br>William started using the potty today! | cognitive water table and funnels<br>physical red scooter, trikes<br>creative-sensory sandbox with Tait<br>music circle songs in Room A<br>language stories<br>imaginative dress-up clothes | Comments: Dressed in cowboy boots and work-goggles, William told the teacher, "Look, I'm dressed up in high heels and glasses." Later, William and Joe worked together to complete a challenging wooden puzzle. |
| **Tuesday** | Breakfast ✓<br>Lunch ✓<br>Nap ✓ | Medication<br><br>Miscellaneous<br>William continues using the potty. | cognitive live reptile program – library<br>physical jumping from the tires<br>creative-sensory let a stick-insect explore his forearm<br>music cassette tapes<br>language discussion of reptiles<br>imaginative built a unit block boat with Jenny | Comments: William and Joe negotiated for use of the lacing cards, eventually agreeing to share them. William showed me his lacework and said, "Look what I can do because I'm so clever." |
| **Wednesday** | Breakfast ✓<br>Lunch ✓<br>Nap ✓ | Medication<br><br>Miscellaneous | cognitive experimenting with the seesaw ↗<br>physical giving wagon rides<br>creative-sensory making "GAK"<br>music music and movement at circle<br>language looking at books with Jenny<br>imaginative chalk drawings on playground | Comments: William gave and received wagon rides on the playground. He also figured out a way to stretch out belly-down on the seesaw and rock it all by himself. |
| **Thursday** | Breakfast ✓<br>Lunch ✓<br>Nap ✓ | Medication<br><br>Miscellaneous | cognitive building peg structures with Meredith<br>physical playing catch with Geena and Chris<br>creative-sensory making "crazy hats"<br>music William sang exuberantly at circle<br>language stories<br>imaginative pretended to be a fierce lion | Comments: William and Tait each poured a cup of water into the sandbox. They squished the sand with their feet, and William said, "This is a world of mud." |
| **Friday** | Breakfast ∅<br>Lunch ✓<br>Nap no | Medication<br><br>Miscellaneous | cognitive magnet board<br>physical climber and slide<br>creative-sensory glue and glitter project<br>music dancing to music<br>language "reading" a book to Jenny<br>imaginative "Simba" game with Miranda | Comments: William and Geena traded tools back and forth at the seed table. William focused on the eggbeaters for quite a while, and watched closely as their movement caused the seeds to fly in all directions. |

**Figure 10.7** *Sample report for a preschooler, written by Jeannine Prince.*

in spring and fall. On Friday afternoon, the head teachers left for the retreat site, and the rest of the staff followed after the center closed. Friday evening consisted mainly of a meal cooked by a selected committee and kitchen cleanup by another committee. Then everyone staked out a bed, if available, or a place to unroll a sleeping bag. The sites chosen were usually large, rustic cabins in the mountains, part of some sort of children's camp or church camp. Everyone had some job to do each day, and there were ample periods of free time for exploring, recreating, and socializing. As an older student, I sometimes felt out of place but always managed to find another returning student with whom to spend free time.

The student retreats were included in the yearly budget supplemented by the university and were relatively inexpensive. As co-owner of a private child care program supported only by parent fees, I took a different approach. With a lower turnover of teachers and a smaller budget, we made do with one yearly retreat for two days and one night. Another factor was the makeup of this staff, which consisted only partly of college-age people; most were women with families, and they would have found it difficult to leave home for two nights. They would also have been uncomfortable sleeping on the floor in a rustic cabin. Because all teachers were expected to attend the retreat, we decided that they would be treated to the best accommodations we could afford.

Ways to finance the retreat were discussed by the original staff and were discussed again by subsequent staffs. We decided that the center would pay all expenses and the staff would, in essence, volunteer their time. The first few years, committees prepared all meals at the retreat. Then the teachers decided they wanted to eat their big meal, Saturday dinner, at a nice restaurant. By consensus, Saturday dinner was then eaten out, with each teacher paying a percentage toward her meal and the center paying the rest. All other expenses were paid by the center. Accommodations varied from a beachfront chalet on a nearby island to a mountain hotel next to a river. There were always enough beds, although sometimes beds were shared; several people preferred to bring sleeping bags and sleep in front of a fireplace. The bathrooms were always clean and plentiful, and in one private beach home (the all-time favorite place) there was also a hot tub.

This approach puts participants' comfort first. It would be counterproductive to require mature people to attend a weekend retreat where they would be uncomfortable and have to work. Another option, however, is to pay the teachers for their time at the retreat and ask them, in return, to pay a share of all expenses, including accommodations and food. Whatever approach is agreed on, the main ingredient of a successful retreat is teamwork. Teachers must feel that they will benefit from the experience and look forward to a pleasant time with the group. This can happen only when past retreats have been successful and when the word is passed along from previous participants to new teachers. Assuming that the director and other supervisors will inspect possible retreat sites and the surrounding area, much of the responsibility for the success of the retreat is theirs.

An effective retreat will alternate structured learning activities with free, social time. Learning activities should focus on the problem-solving philosophy along with the educational component of the program. Activities can be longer and more comprehensive than time allows at a staff meeting, but they can be of the same type. It is also beneficial to have a relaxation or stress-reducing activity at the beginning, along with an activity that will serve as an icebreaker. At least one activity should be done outdoors, depending on the environment.

When the teachers are involved with the planning, they get greater enjoyment and benefit from the retreat. Beginning at least two months before the retreat, the group should make the decisions. They may be given a choice of accommodations and where to eat Saturday dinner if they are eating out. Committees should be formed for planning activities. This may be done in several ways, depending on circumstances. The leaders pick a number of categories that can be converted relatively easily into activities in which all group members can be included. They should be activities that can be acted out in verbal, visual, or physical ways and, of course, that teach the participants something they can use in their work with children. After choosing the categories, the leaders should try to group teachers who have already attended a retreat with new teachers who have not. Depending on group size, two or three people may be responsible for each category. Sometimes it works well to allow the experienced teacher to draw the names of new teachers. Then one person from each pair or threesome may draw the category they will represent. After that, ample time should be allotted at staff meetings for planning activities. All activities should be subject to leadership approval, and a list of materials needed should be given to whoever will be doing the shopping.

The leaders themselves may also plan some of the activities, as well as advising and providing resources for the teachers. Books such as those included in "Recommended Reading" may provide ideas for activities. The samples in this section may inspire other ideas. The leaders need to carefully coordinate the activities the teachers plan so that certain of them fit particular time slots and the amount of time allotted to each activity is adequate. Activities that require physical involvement should be alternated with those that are more passive, and enough time should be given each committee to organize and set up its activity. A checklist of all possible items and materials needed should be made, and everything should be packed and ready to take by departure time. Someone may need to be in charge of carpooling; all cars used should be in good working condition and insured.

Someone should also be in charge of buying food to take. Food seems to be very important at retreats, and snacks are especially enjoyed. Because the first meal eaten together may be Saturday lunch, it saves time if participants bring their own sack lunch to eat on arrival. Saturday dinner may be eaten out, or you might appoint committees to plan it, cook it, and clean up after it. Between lunch and dinner, there should be at least one break with snacks provided. Sunday breakfast should be simple, filling, and easily prepared. An ambitious committee could cook, but the preparation time is deducted from learning activities. Foods such as bagels and cream cheese, granola, and fruit, which require little or no preparation, are usually satisfactory. The last meal, Sunday lunch, might be sandwiches, with everyone making his or her own.

Some activities will evolve into traditions. The retreat presented here is a composite of actual ones conducted by the Discovery Center over a ten-year period. I have annotated the schedule to provide a description of some of the activities. Along with plenty of snacks, a camera and film are necessities. They keep memories alive.

## Outside Educational Resources

Those who elect to work with young children choose a profession in which there is never an end to learning. The greatest teachers are the children themselves. The adult who observes young children is in awe of the constant change that occurs with children and the brand-new perspective of the world he or she can gain by seeing it through the eyes of a child. Teachers are actually observing a laboratory of human behavior and learning more about themselves and the human race than they ever expected.

The reader of this book is probably in the process of studying children from many perspectives. The goal may be to become a professional in child care and preschool. Once this goal has been attained, the educational process is not finished. While learning from the children, the early childhood professional may seek out other sources for learning about more specific topics in the child care field. The local community college or university may offer classes on subjects such as recognizing child abuse, using rhythm instruments, choosing children's literature, child safety, and science for preschoolers. Organizations such as the National Association for the Education of Young Children (NAEYC) also hold workshops and seminars in many locations. By attending local meetings, the professional will learn more about children's issues as well.

Whenever they are financially able, program directors should seek out ways to help teachers improve their knowledge of child development and other children's issues. Some resources are free or relatively inexpensive. If only one or two teachers can be subsidized to attend a conference on children, they may be asked to report back to the group at a staff meeting. This is a way to share new information with other teachers. Regardless of whether the knowledge they have gained is compatible with the problem-solving philosophy, discussion at the staff meeting should emphasize how the new information might be applied in a problem-solving program. The discussion

## A Sample Retreat

## SCHEDULE

DATE:   A Saturday in April

PLACE:   Mutiny Bay Resort, Whidbey Island

| 9:00 A.M. | Meet at center | Bring sack lunches. Orientation. Car pool from center. |
|---|---|---|
| 9:30 | Catch ferry | |
| 10:15 | Arrive at Mutiny Bay | Check in. Unpack cars. Choose beds. Explore area. |
| 12:00 | Eat lunches | |
| 12:30 P.M. | Relaxation exercises | (Soft music is played. Everyone lies on the floor. A leader asks us to visualize ourselves in a quiet, beautiful place. The leader gives directions for taking deep breaths and relaxing each muscle.) |
| 1:00–2:30 | Outlines | (Choose partners. One person lies down on a long piece of butcher paper and her partner draws an outline around her. Then they switch. Each person writes her feelings about parts of her body [e.g., in her head, she writes her most important thoughts; in her heart, she writes her most important feelings; on one foot, she writes where she has been; on the other foot, she writes where she is going; on one hand, she writes her proudest achievement; on the other hand, she writes what she hopes to achieve, etc.]. When finished, outlines are hung on the walls and shared.) |
| 2:30 | Snacks available | |
| 3:00–6:00 | Role playing | (The same procedure used for staff meetings but more time for more topics covering all phases of problem solving. There is greater involvement by everyone and more time to evaluate the role-plays.) |
| 6:00–8:00 | Dinner | (Dinner at a nearby restaurant.) |

Free time until bed

## SUNDAY

| | | |
|---|---|---|
| 7:00 A.M. | Breakfast | |
| 8:00 | Silent walk | (There is no talking at all as participants walk along the beach. They communicate like nonverbal infants and toddlers by using facial expression, hand signals, and other body language. The object is to share whatever is seen or found with others.) |
| 9:00 | Trust walk | (When a destination is reached, teachers pair off. One leads his partner on a blindfolded walk on the beach. Then they switch. The object is to inspire trust, not to trick or frighten one's partner!) |
| 9:30 | Return, snack, write a poem | (Each participant receives a form to use if needed. The form is titled "A Walk on the Beach" and looks like this: |

I see _____

I hear _____

I touch _____

I feel _____

I see _____

I taste _____

I experience _____

Teachers fill in the blanks, or each writes her own poem describing the beach walk; then the teachers share their poems with one another.)

| | | |
|---|---|---|
| 10:30–12:30 | Piaget | (Curriculum based on the teachings of Piaget. Part lecture, part demonstration—everyone has brought an activity to share, including infant teachers.) |
| 12:30 P.M. | Lunch | (Prepare lunch, eat, and clean up. Pack to leave.) |

| | | |
|---|---|---|
| 1:30 | Strokes | (Everyone has a stiff piece of paper taped to his back. Each participant is given a marking pen. Teachers write only positive things about one another on the paper taped to each one's back. They cannot see who is writing. The result is a warm, fuzzy souvenir to take home.) |
| Before leaving | Marshmallow fight | (A large section of ground is marked off and everyone is given a handful of soft, fluffy marshmallows to throw at each other, staying within the boundary lines. This becomes hilarious and is finished only when everyone is exhausted and ready to leave.) |
| | Pile in cars and leave | |

itself is beneficial because it encourages teachers to refocus on the philosophy, question and evaluate their daily interactions, and recognize ways to improve their skills.

The purpose of this book is to provide a wealth of material with which to train those who aspire to be teachers and caregivers of young children. The focus of that training is problem solving as described within these ten chapters. Those who are using this book in a classroom where there is ample discussion and opportunity for role playing and feedback from fellow students and teachers should gain a great deal of information and skill. After completing this book in a classroom, the volume will serve well as a reference when problems arise, as a refresher course if skills begin to lag, and as a source for developing posters, handouts, and other more condensed materials. Such posters and handouts may have a variety of uses.

An attractively made poster on the subject of acceptance, for instance, may remind both teachers and parents of the importance of accepting children as they are. Posters placed on classroom walls may briefly focus attention on active listening, negotiation, setting limits, supervision, and giving affirmations. At one staff meeting, teachers were each given a piece of brightly colored poster board and marking pens and asked to be as creative as they wanted and make posters featuring phrases of affirmation. The posters they made were so appealing that some of them have remained on the walls for years as a daily reminder for others as well as the teachers who made them.

In order for a poster to have maximum effect, it should be taken down from the wall from time to time and used as a focal point at a staff meeting. If there are new teachers, they may not fully understand the meaning of the poster without a formal discussion. This may sound dull, but it need not be. A well-made poster should provoke thoughts and ideas and promote lively discussion. The discussion leader also determines whether it becomes interesting or boring. In order for posters to remain current and attract attention, they should be rotated fairly often. Posters serve another purpose: Parents who frequent the center may also stop for a second or two to read a bit more of the philosophy that is influencing their child's life.

Handouts (copies of written or typed materials on a given subject) are also useful for discussion. Within the chapters of this book are numerous sections that may easily be condensed and highlighted to make a variety of handouts to discuss at staff meetings. If a particular problem needs solving, a handout might be quickly excerpted from the section of this book that applies to the problem. An effective handout is simple and succinct and covers only one topic or a group of topics that naturally fit together. Handouts used for training should be written from the teacher's perspective, but it is also a great help to parents to provide handouts written from their perspective. To fill this need, I published The Problem Solver, a collection of articles based on the problem-solving approach.[1]

Many other books also provide materials for staff training, including some by Thomas Gordon, Haim Ginott, John Gottman, Stanley Greenspan, Mary Sheedy Kurcinka, Daniel Goleman, William Pollack, and Michael Gurian. Jean Piaget, the great master of research on intellectual development, is best understood by reading his interpreters, such as Mary Ann Pulaski. Although these authors and many others in the field of childhood behavior and development may not directly promote the exact philosophy found in this book, their approaches are neither opposed nor contradictory. Many of their ideas have been incorporated into problem solving to make it the eclectic philosophy presented in this book. A series of posters in the appendix of this book highlight the problem-solving philosophy. Feel free to use them in your classrooms.

## Summing Up Training Teachers

This final chapter has covered the many ways in which teachers may be trained to work within the problem-solving philosophy. On-the-job training is the most intense option and requires working closely with a more experienced teacher as he or she models and interprets problem solving. From time to time, the new teacher and the experienced teacher will benefit from a conference in which the experienced teacher can give specific guidance and help the new teacher work on problem areas. Strategies are also given for training experienced teachers.

Staff meetings are necessary in order to promote teamwork and upgrade teachers' skills. The staff meeting need not be dull or tedious and, by beginning with an ice-breaking game, may even be fun. A primary teaching tool for staff meetings is role playing, during which teachers take on the role of children as well as teachers and act out various problems. Open discussions of problems and sharing of feelings also help teachers solve problems by sharing their ideas and successes. This is also a good way to get to know fellow workers better. During role playing and discussion, teachers become more sensitive to the feelings of children and to each other.

Other on-site training possibilities include room or section meetings, group planning times, and off-floor planning times for individual teachers. During these times, teachers can deal with current problems, organize their areas, plan and gather materials for activities, and update records.

It is important that teachers learn to communicate effectively with parents, either in brief conversations that include the child or in written daily reports that describe the child's day. Sample reports are shown along with other materials appropriate for use as posters.

In addition to regular staff meetings, a periodic retreat is recommended. Ideas from retreats were presented in this chapter, along with a sample retreat. It was also suggested that teachers be sent and subsidized, when possible, to attend college courses on topics related to child care as well as workshops and seminars held by organizations such as the National Association for the Education of Young Children. Professional child care teachers never stop learning. They learn every day from their children. This informal learning should motivate them to seek further knowledge and information in order to understand children as fully as possible. Teachers will consequently enjoy their work more and bring more to the children in their care. Nothing can be more important.

## Practice and Discussion _____

1. Pretend you are applying for a job as a teacher in a child care center. In your cover letter, describe your philosophy for working with young children. When you have finished, compare it with the paper you may have written following Chapter 1. Has your philosophy changed during the reading of this book?

2. While you were reading this book, what conflicting ideas did you discover between your own upbringing and the problem-solving philoso-

phy? Which of your old ideas have changed? Which have remained the same? How would you be different had you been reared with problem solving?

3. Using the lists for leaders and teammates, decide which role is best for you and why. Are you surprised by your decision?

4. Name the two primary ways to train new teachers.

5. Plan a staff meeting for a group of day-care or preschool teachers. Include elements discussed in this chapter and give examples of each element. Also add some of your own elements.

6. In your college class, role-play talking to a parent and child together. Pick any topic that might be a problem.

7. Choose one of the major terms in the problem-solving philosophy and write a training handout on that topic. Include examples from which new teachers can learn.

8. Plan at least one day of an overnight retreat. Describe the environment in which your group will be staying and write up a general schedule of activities.

9. Evaluate your own ability to work as part of a team. Do you have any personality characteristics that might need improvement in order for you to work harmoniously with other people?

10. What is your overall feeling about the problem-solving philosophy? Do you feel comfortable about using it? Do you feel that it is right for you? Where will you go from here?

---

## Note

1. For a free sample of The Problem Solver, call 800-989-7643.

## Recommended Reading

Benson, Herbert. *The Wellness Book.* New York: Simon and Schuster, 1993.

Fox, William M. *Effective Group Problem Solving.* San Francisco: Jossey-Bass, 1987.

Hendricks, Gay, and Kathlyn Hendricks. *At the Speed of Life.* New York: Bantam, 1993.

Luvmour, Sambhava, and Josette Luvmour (ed.) *Everyone Wins! Cooperative Games and Activities.* Gabriola Island, BC, Canada. New Society Publishing, 1990.

MacGregor, Cynthia. *Everybody Wins! 150 Non-Competitive Games for Kids.* Holbrook, MA: Adams Media, 1998.

Orlick, Terry. *The Cooperative Sports and Games Book.* New York: Random House, 1978.

Orlick, Terry. *The Second Cooperative Sports and Games Book.* New York: Random House, 1982.

Quinlivan-Hall, David. *In Search of Solutions: Sixty Ways to Guide Your Problem-Solving Group.* San Diego: Pfeiffer, 1993.

Sutcliffe, Jenny. *The Complete Book of Relaxation Techniques.* Allentown, PA: People's Medical Society, 1994.

Tagliere, Daniel A. *How to Meet, Think, and Work to Consensus.* San Diego: Pfeiffer, 1993.

# *Appendix*

## PROBLEM-SOLVING POSTERS

**Feelings Poster**

# The Problem-Solving Environment

## The child-centered classroom offers

Freedom with safety

Organized learning centers

Experience, experimentation, exploration

Choices and decision making

Responsibility

Risk taking

Play of every kind

## The environment provides

Open spaces for active play

Soft, quiet spaces

Sociable spaces

Private spaces

Low, accessible shelves

Bright colors

## The teacher's role in the environment is to

Supervise: interact, facilitate, role model

Modify: childproof, simplify, restrict

Enrich

Impoverish

## The Environment Lets "Kids Do What Kids Do"

# Supervision

## The teacher supervises by

Staying with the children at all times

Positioning to see all the children at the same time

Circulating, like a host at a party

Concentrating on the children

Keeping personal adult conversations at a minimum

Staying close to allow children's risk taking

Setting limits when needed

Giving affirmations

## The program is structured by

Designating a coordinator to
    Change diapers, fill bottles, prepare for meals,
    control traffic, care for sick or injured children

Maintaining an age-appropriate ratio

Using "family style" mixture of ages

## Children take responsibility by

Putting away toys and belongings after use

Dressing and undressing when capable

Listening to other children when there's a conflict

Cooperating during routines and transitions

**Routines and transitions should be supervised, organized, described, explained, kept consistent. Give children time; teachers should react quickly.**

# Active Listening

## When the child "owns" the problem

**Nonverbal**—Smiling, touching, holding, rocking, patting
**Verbal**—Decode feelings and give them names such as "frustrated," "upset," "excited," "scared," "happy," "disappointed." The child's reaction tells you if your interpretation is correct.

## Active listening communicates acceptance and trust, builds self-esteem, opens dialogue, enhances growth

## Steps to Active Listening

1. Teacher is open, approachable, and accessible; respects and shares feelings.
2. Teacher plays the "guessing game" with preverbal infants and toddlers.
3. Feelings are accepted and respected, never discounted or distracted.
4. Teacher reflects feelings: "It sounds like . . ." "I hear you saying . . ."
5. Names are given to feelings: "How upsetting," "That must be frustrating."
6. Teacher's voice is neutral, but warm, accepting, and empathetic.
7. Teacher communicates trust and confidence in child to deal with feelings.
8. Teacher is authentic, accepts his or her own feelings as "normal."

# Negotiation
## When the relationship "owns" the problem

No one wins or loses; solution is acceptable to all concerned.

All concerned have equal input; all ideas are considered equally.

Children decide on solution, stick to it, or renegotiate.

## Remember the process and allow lots of time.

## Steps of Negotiation

**Use active listening when appropriate; then**

1. Help children identify the problem, focus on the problem.
2. Encourage children to contribute ideas, talk to each other.
3. Restate all ideas in a positive, understandable way.
4. Help children decide on the idea they like best, or think of others.
5. Help children figure out how to put their solution into action.
6. Reinforce the process when they have solved the problem.

**Avoid forced sharing, forced taking turns, forced saying "I'm sorry," asking "Who had it first?" or blaming. Encourage using words, talking to each other.**

# Guidelines for Setting Limits

## Limits are set to

1. Assure the safety of each child and adult
2. Prohibit the destruction of nondisposable materials
3. Assure individual acceptance of responsibility for one's actions
4. Assure equal and respectful treatment of all people

## Limits are also needed during routines and transitions.

## Limits versus Rules

| Limits | Rules |
|---|---|
| Based on values | Based on authority |
| Power is shared | Adults control all power |
| Expect cooperation | Require punishment |
| Flexible, may be negotiable | Rigid, may be broken |
| Encourage logical thinking | Restrict logical thinking |
| Circumstances count | Circumstances don't count |
| Bring respect | Bring resentment |
| Foster independence | Foster dependence |
| Promote decision making | Inhibit decision making |
| Seek alternatives | Alternatives are restricted |

## Limits allow teachers and children to use their judgment, remain authentic, and build relationships.

# Setting Limits
## When the adult "owns" the problem

### Use a neutral, respectful, nonjudgmental tone of voice.

**I-Message** (Most ideal.) "It scares me to see you climbing on the bookcase because you might fall and get hurt." (Lift child down as you speak if it's dangerous.)

**Giving Information** (Wait for the child to react.) "I see that a book is on the floor." (Wait, then) "The book goes on the shelf."

**Natural or Logical Consequences** (An outgrowth of the child's behavior.) "If you wait too long to get ready, you might miss outdoor playtime."

**Contingencies** (A second action depends on a first action.) "When the blocks are picked up, you'll be ready to work on a puzzle."

**Giving Choices** (Both choices must be acceptable.) "You can walk to get your diaper changed or I can carry you. It's up to you."

**Removing and Sitting Apart** (A last resort only.) Not "time out." Remove the child from the situation. "You can decide when you're ready to play without hurting kids."

### During routines and transitions, use phrases such as "It's time to," "It's important to," "I need you to."

# Setting Limits During Routines and Transitions
## Examples of what to say

**Its Time To:** wash hands, go outside, get ready to eat, rest quietly.

**It's Important To:** use soap to remove germs, brush teeth to remove food, ask someone to trade areas, stay where a teacher can see you.

**I Need You To:** look at books while I clean up, wait for me before you go outside (or inside), help me get the room ready (for lunch, naps, circle time).

**When Kids:** play during meals, food might get spilled . . . . make noise during stories, I can't read; I'll wait until it's quiet. . . . finish going potty, they sit on their mats for our nap story.

**I Can't Give You a Choice Now, But I Will Explain:**

We all go outside after breakfast (so someone can clean the room).

Kids all come to group time (but you don't have to participate).

Kids sit on their bottoms during meals (so they don't fall off their chairs).

When diapers are wet or poopy, they get changed (so your bottom won't hurt).

Kids stay on their mats at nap time (so everyone can rest).

# Authenticity or Consistency

## Problem Solving Should Be Used Consistently but

Every Adult Can Be an Authentic Individual
With a Personality, Style, Preferences, Feelings, and Tolerance Level

| authenticity teaches ⟷ | consistency teaches |
|---|---|
| adults are individuals | adults are all the same |
| adults sometimes exceed limits | adults are always obedient |
| adults make mistakes, too | adults are always right |
| adults are willing to share power | adults have all the power |
| ideas are more important than limits | limits are more important than ideas |
| adults can be trusted to make judgments | adults can only enforce limits |

## Consistency Is Important During Routines and Transitions

**Routines:** washing, eating, diaper changing, napping, brushing teeth, dressing, group times.

**Transitions:** moving from play to structure, indoors to outdoors, room to room, to and from meals, for naps and other routines.

# Affirmations
## Raise self-esteem,
## help children feel important.

**Positive I-Messages**  (State your feelings, what is happening, why you feel that way.) "I appreciate your help. We're getting finished so quickly."

**Reinforcement**  (Comes after the behavior.) "Good work. You got them all put away."

**Noticing**  (Acknowledge the child's existence.) "You're looking happy today."

**Strokes**  (Rituals that give recognition.) "Hi, it's nice to see you."

**Narration**  (Put into words what is happening that is noteworthy.) "I see Billy working hard on a puzzle."

# Affirmations
## in the Environment include

Photos of kids, posters, outlines, birthday parties, growth charts, children's artwork and narrations, books, songs, finger plays

### Be specific.

### Avoid value judgments, use body language.

### Be sincere, be authentic,
### comment on the behavior—not the person.

# Problem-Solving Curriculum

## Acceptance and Trust Build Self-Esteem

Curriculum should address the needs, desires, and curiosity of the children. Infants need bonding, toddlers need independence, preschoolers need responsibility, but all children need acceptance, approval, validation, and trust.

## The Learning Process

**Experience:** to encounter something and gain knowledge from the encounter

**Experimentation:** to initiate, make things happen, try out and test ideas

**Exploration:** to investigate, probe, inquire, search out, pursue

## The Child: Every child has a personality comprising temperament, inherited characteristics, physical traits, and learned behavior. Personality influences the way children learn. Problem-solving curriculum puts the child first.

## The Expanding Environment: Rotate, rearrange, accessorize, extend, and add materials; take field trips.

## The Problem-Solving Teacher: Accepts children, trusts in the learning process, respects children's rights, enjoys children and learns from them, forms close relationships, communicates his or her feelings, takes time to listen, and is interested, creative, flexible, and organized. Being organized is an often overlooked quality of a problem-solving teacher.

# Open-Ended Learning

## Child, Teacher, and Environment interact to solve problems and help children think creatively and critically.

Ask open-ended questions.

Encourage children to "try it yourself."

Present problems to solve.

Support risk taking and mistakes.

Read stories.

Introduce cooperation and eliminate competition.

**Play:** a child's natural way to learn freely, expressively, and safely and develop socially.

**Creativity:** grows through challenge, time, space, and freedom to make messes; is "killed" by surveillance, evaluation, competition, and rewards.

**Diversity:** The environment should represent the children in the group. Standards include quality, relevance, durability, and appropriate presentation.

**Group times:** should be used to raise children's self-esteem through circle songs, stories, and games that focus on individuals without causing embarrassment.

Very creative

What fun!

Super

Great Idea

I appreciate your help

Fantastic!

Looks like you really worked hard on this

How delightful!

Wow!

What a nice smile!

Marvelous

How Impressive

Terrific!

Keep up the good work

GOOD FOR YOU!

Excellent

Now you've figured it out

Glad to see you

I like the way you're cooperating

Sharp!

**The Freedom Balloon**

# Index